The Naval Academy

Illustrated History of the United States Navy

The Naval Academy
Illustrated History of the

United States Navy

E. B. Potter

Professor of Naval History, United States Naval Academy

GALAHAD BOOKS · NEW YORK CITY

The assertions and opinions expressed herein are those of the author and are not to be construed as official or as necessarily reflecting the views of the Department of the Navy.

Maps by Donald T. Pitcher

Copyright © 1971 by E. B. Potter

Library of Congress Catalog Card Number: 73-92821
ISBN 0-88365-196-3

Published by arrangement with T. Y. Crowell Company

Printed in the United States of America

Designed by Abigail Moseley

Preface

Here in compact form is the story of United States naval operations in war and peace. The book is also a portrait gallery in words and pictures of the Navy's past leaders. It is a story of exceptional men and their achievements, particularly in the stress of battle. While it does not pretend to be a treatise on national policy or the art of war, brief explanations of political, strategic, and tactical decisions are included. Because my aim has been to arouse interest and to inform, rather than to instruct or to reveal, I saw no point in providing footnotes or bibliography. I drew my facts from dependable sources, however, and I believe that my narrative is accurate.

Despite the book's imposing title, used by permission of Vice Admiral James F. Calvert, Jr., USN, Superintendent of the United States Naval Academy, this is in no sense an official history. The opinions expressed are my own. Nothing has been included or excluded with the sanction of the Naval Academy or the Department of the Navy.

Over the years I have been impressed with the fact that few books on naval history provide adequate aids to enable the reader to visualize battles and campaigns. Hence when I began to write naval history textbooks, I provided plenty of maps and diagrams. In the present volume I have, by grace of the publisher, been able to include also a liberal provision of pictures. The story is told as much by the pictures, maps, and diagrams as by the text.

In the pictures reproduced from paintings there unfortunately happen to be a few errors —the wrong number of stars in the American flag, small inaccuracies in ship construction. Such flaws, I suppose, are inevitable, for the artists were neither historians nor shipwrights. I have simply used the most authentic pictures I could find, choosing accuracy over art.

I wish to thank the staffs of the following offices and institutions for helping me to locate the pictures I needed: the National Archives, the Library of Congress, the United States Naval Academy Museum, the United States Naval Institute, the Navy Department's Magazine and Book Branch (especially the blithe assistant head, Miss Anna Urband), the Division of Naval History (particularly the former Director of Naval History, Rear Admiral E. M. Eller USN, Ret.; Commander D. V. Hickey USN; Messrs. Charles Haberlein and Charles T. Weaver; and Lieutenants (jg.) William F. Rope and G. M. Quigley, both USNR), and the photographic centers of the U.S. Army, the U.S. Navy, the U.S. Marine Corps, the U.S. Coast Guard, and Time, Inc.

Between pages 188 and 208 of this book are a few paragraphs which I formerly wrote for *Triumph in the Pacific,* published by Prentice-Hall, Inc., in 1963 and now out of print.

These are reproduced with the permission of the publisher, who is also the copyright holder. I reused my old paragraphs in the interest of economy of effort and because I could not think of any better way to express myself.

I take this occasion to thank Admiral Calvert not only for his permission to use "The Naval Academy" in my title but also for granting me an extra leave period to catch up with my writing chores. Thanks are due also to my colleagues Mr. J. Roger Fredland, who read the complete typescript and made valuable suggestions, and Commander Frederic N. Howe, Jr. USN, Assistant Chairman of the Naval Academy's Weapons and Systems Engineering Department, who read and corrected the section titled "New Naval Weapons." I likewise acknowledge my debt to my other Naval Academy associates—my officer and civilian colleagues and my midshipman students whose ideas threshed out in class and in the coffee mess I have brazenly purloined. Any false or ridiculous ideas herein are, of course, strictly my own.

Above all, I want to thank my long-suffering wife for her patience, her advice, her typing, and her willingness to forgo vacations in order to get this job done.

E. B. Potter

History Department
United States Naval Academy

Contents

Illustrations

Maps and Diagrams

The Naval Academy

Illustrated History of the United States Navy

I

The American Revolution

"The port of Boston closed!"

The news resounded through the American colonies like a thunderclap.

Americans had long protested as illegal the new taxes imposed on them by the British Parliament. The Boston Tea Party, in which Bostonians disguised as Indians dumped £15,000 worth of taxable tea into Boston harbor, had at last brought Parliamentary retaliation. New Coercive Acts, among other disagreeable provisions, sealed off Boston from the sea. To enforce the Acts came 2,000 British regulars, backed by armed vessels of the Royal Navy.

The closing of America's busiest port struck a severe blow at the colonial economy. For Americans were seafarers, depending heavily for their livelihood on access to the Atlantic and its tributary waters, not only for fishing and foreign trade but also for communication within the colonies. Farmers of western Massachusetts customarily floated their produce down the Connecticut River and thence roundabout by sea to Boston. A traveler from New York to Philadelphia normally chose to sail by way of the Atlantic Ocean and the Delaware River, rather than struggle across New Jersey over the primitive roads of the day.

New Englanders now prepared for armed assertion of their rights. At Boston, British General Thomas Gage, learning of a large quantity of powder and arms collected at nearby Concord, on the night of April 18, 1775, sent out a column of 800 troops to seize it. These were met by colonial gunfire at Lexington, again at Concord, and on the retreat back to Boston, which the colonial Massachusetts militia promptly put under siege.

Boston and its water approaches were dominated by Dorchester Heights to the south and by Bunker and Breed's hills behind Charlestown to the north. Gage planned to occupy the northern heights. But the Americans got to Charlestown peninsula first and in great confusion began to throw up earthworks on both hills.

General Gage now turned to Major General Sir William Howe, who had recently arrived in Boston with reinforcements, and ordered him to remove this nuisance. Howe, having superiority in numbers and ample water transport, might have sealed off the Americans by seizing Charlestown Neck at their rear. Instead, with something like contempt, he ordered a frontal assault across the Charles River, thereby precipitating the Battle of Bunker Hill, the first major action of the Revolutionary War.

The steady Americans held their fire as the British soldiers, in perfect order and in full dress uniform, advanced on them. When the redcoats were 40 yards away, the entrenched colonials released a terrible volley that swept down the first British line like the slash of a giant scythe. The British retreated, but returned to the attack, reinforced and supported by naval gunfire. After three assaults they finally carried the position, while the Americans expended the last of their ammunition and fled. British losses amounted to more than 1,000 men; American losses were fewer than 500.

The Bunker Hill battle revealed that the colonials, amateur warriors, could give a good account of themselves even when opposed by superior numbers of trained infantry. Among Americans it crystallized confidence and a will to win, but it also bred a false notion that patriotic ardor could outbalance discipline. Among the British officers the battle erased in some measure their scorn of the armed "peasants." General Howe was sufficiently impressed to avoid ever afterward frontal assaults on entrenched Americans.

The Continental Congress, meeting in Philadelphia, now appointed one of its number, George Washington of Virginia, to command the American army. On his arrival in the Boston area in July 1775, Washington found the besieging Americans ill clothed, ill fed, ill housed, and lacking sufficient ammunition to return the British fire. The besieged Britons, on the contrary, appeared well provided for in every respect. Although tightly sealed by land within the Boston and Charlestown peninsulas, they had free access to the sea. Ships arrived regularly, bringing them provisions, clothing, munitions, and every other necessity. It was perhaps at this time that Washington conceived the objective of isolating his foe from the sea,

which was controlled by the British navy, and which was the main source of the British army's strength.

If Washington lacked a means of blockading the British in Boston, he found a means of participating in their abundance. He hired and armed merchant vessels and called on his army for volunteers with seagoing experience. To the volunteers he offered, in addition to their army pay, the lure of prize money from captured ships. He thus created what has been called "Washington's Navy."

The schooner *Hannah*, commanded by Captain Nicholas Broughton, was the first vessel commissioned by General Washington and may therefore be considered the first national American warship. Her only capture, before being chased aground by a British cruiser, was the ship *Unity*. It turned out, however, that the *Unity* was owned by a member of the Continental Congress and a noted patriot; she had been seized by a British man-of-war and the *Hannah* had recaptured her from a small prize crew

Boston and vicinity, 1775.

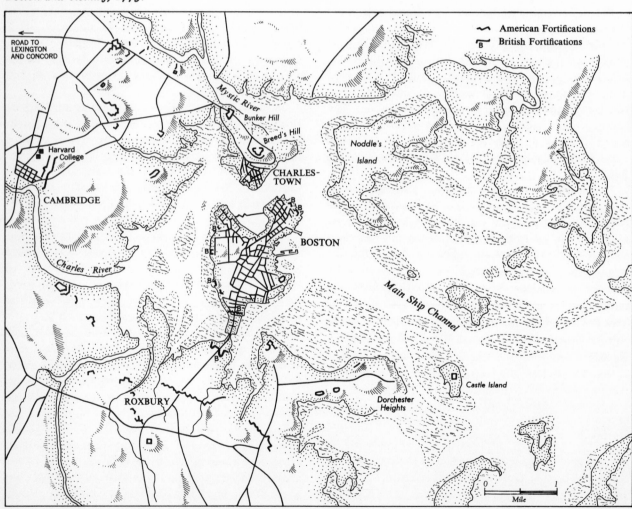

carrying her into Boston. When the *Hannah's* soldier-sailors learned that they were to receive no prize money, they broke into open mutiny, which was suppressed only by a detachment rushed to the scene by General Washington. In subsequent courts-martial 14 of the men were condemned to be whipped in public and drummed out of the army. Washington, however, remitted the whipping part of the sentence except in the case of the ringleader, Joseph Searle.

The most successful of the sea captains was John Manley of Marblehead, a former merchant skipper. Among Manley's numerous captures was the brig *Nancy*, which carried 2,000 muskets, 31 tons of musket shot, and a 13-inch brass mortar, together with 300 shells—munitions the Americans could not have produced for themselves in many months. In January 1776, Washington appointed Manley commodore of his little navy, in which, at one time or another, a total of eight vessels, all schooners, served.

The squadron's most valuable capture was the powder ship *Hope*, which was taken by the *Franklin* under James Mugford, and which carried, among other stores, 1,000 carbines and 1,500 barrels of gunpowder. In October 1777, the squadron took its last prize, the brig *Dolphin*, laden with rum and sugar. Despite some incompetence among the captains and the general unruliness of the crews, "Washington's Navy" seized 55 vessels, of which 38 reached port and were declared lawful prize. These captures, a severe loss to the British, proved a boon to the American army, which was usually short of everything.

It became evident that General Washington was unlikely to dislodge the British from Boston without heavy guns. There were 240 iron and brass cannon on Lake Champlain at Fort Ticonderoga, which militia under Ethan Allen and Benedict Arnold had captured from the British in May 1775. The following November Washington sent his chief of artillery, twenty-six-year-old Colonel Henry Knox, to Champlain to bring back some of the Ticonderoga ordnance. Knox selected 59 pieces, which had a combined weight of 60 tons. By dint of prodigious labor Knox's work crews hauled these guns to the Boston area, using log rollers, boats, and sleds drawn through the snow by horses and oxen.

The guns, to be effective, had to be emplaced on Dorchester Heights, the only high ground dominating Boston that was not in British hands. Fortifications were required to protect the guns and gunners from British fire. Since the frozen ground forbade quick throwing up of earthworks as was done at Bunker Hill, the Americans constructed forts of timbers, bales of hay, and baskets and barrels filled with earth. These they hauled to the heights during the night of March 4, 1776, under cover of a diversionary bombardment. By dawn the men, working in shifts, had assembled a large part of their fortifications; sharpshooters had concealed themselves along the shore to throw back water-borne troops; and the earth-filled barrels were available to be rolled downhill on an advancing enemy.

The astonished British found that they could not elevate their guns sufficiently to reach the new American redoubts. The British admiral notified General Howe, who had succeeded to the command of the occupation forces, that he could not maintain his fleet off Boston unless the Americans were dislodged. Howe had no choice but to attack the Americans or evacuate the city, and honor dictated attack. He prepared to storm Dorchester Heights by amphibious assault—exactly what Washington wanted, for he had no stomach for pounding Boston to rubble, crowded as it was with civilians as well as troops. Before the British boats could set out across Boston harbor, however, a severe and extended storm made amphibious operations impossible. When the winds at last subsided, the American fortifications were complete, the guns emplaced.

Short of surrender, Howe no longer had any alternative to evacuation. But would the Americans, secure behind Ticonderoga's guns, permit him to go? Playing his last trump, the British general threatened to destroy Boston unless he were allowed to depart in peace. Washington, in tacit consent, greatly moderated his fire.

On March 17 began the evacuation of 11,000 Englishmen and about 1,500 Loyalists, the latter preferring exile to taking their chances with the patriots. Ten days later they sailed away to Halifax, Nova Scotia.

THE CAMPAIGN INTO CANADA

To the thirteen United Colonies Canada was both a threat and an opportunity—a base from which a British army might drive south and a potential fourteenth colony where the Canadians, presumably smarting under British rule, would welcome the invading Continental Army and flock to the cause of freedom.

Since the obvious and oft-used invasion route in both directions was the Hudson-Champlain valley, Congress in the early summer of 1775 ordered Major General Philip Schuyler to assume command in the Lake Champlain area and to strengthen the American forces there for defensive and offensive operations. Schuyler set about repairing dilapidated Fort Ticonderoga, building up the garrisons there and at nearby Crown Point, and constructing gunboats for use on the lake.

Before the end of July, Schuyler had learned that there were no more than 700 British regulars in Canada and that these men were assembling and building a fort at St. Johns, on the Richelieu River not far from where it flowed out of the northern end of Lake Champlain. Soon afterward a scout reported war vessels, including a 12-gun schooner, being built at St. Johns. "Now, sir," said the scout, "is the time to carry Canada!"

Schuyler agreed, but he hesitated to give the order to advance, not feeling that his forces were sufficiently numerous or adequately supplied. In mid-August he departed for a conference at Albany, leaving in command Brigadier General Richard Montgomery. The latter was an Irishman of French descent who in 1759, as an officer in the British army, had participated in the capture of Fort Ticonderoga from the French; he had later settled in America and taken an American wife. In the absence of orders to the contrary, Montgomery, a man of action, prepared to move without further delay. On August 28 he embarked with 1,200 men and several artillery pieces and sailed north down the lake to the Richelieu River.

After an abortive attack from the south, Montgomery succeeded in running two gunboats past St. Johns at night and forcing the surrender of a small military post downstream. Here the Americans captured 88 prisoners and a sizable supply of provisions, arms, and powder. An even more important accomplishment was the isolation of St. Johns from Montreal and the rest of Canada.

The Americans next laid siege to St. Johns, early sinking the armed schooner with gunfire. After 55 days, its provisions nearly exhausted, the fort capitulated. The American soldiers were most gratified to acquire, among the great quantity of supplies captured here, warm clothing in which to face the oncoming Canadian winter.

During the siege and the subsequent march to Montreal, the Americans learned that, for the most part, the Canadians were not interested in fighting. The latter had no quarrel with the English, who had not interfered with their religious or other liberties. They were willing, however, to provide the Americans with food and other supplies, but only for payment in hard money, of which the Americans were in exceedingly short supply.

Upon the arrival of Montgomery's army before the crumbling walls of Montreal, the city fathers concluded that they had no recourse but to open their gates and submit to the invaders. However, Lieutenant General Sir Guy Carleton, Governor-General and commander of the British armed forces in Canada, managed to escape to Quebec, determined to fight another day.

Quebec was in fact Montgomery's main objective. The capture of this city by British forces under James Wolfe 16 years earlier had effectively wrested Canada from the French. Montgomery hoped similarly to take Canada from the British.

From Indian couriers Montgomery had learned that a small American force already confronted Quebec. This force was a contingent of picked men sent north from Boston by General Washington. A thousand strong and headed by firebrand Colonel Benedict Arnold, it had sailed on September 13 from Newburyport to the mouth of the Kennebec River, up which it advanced in boats.

Arnold's expeditionary force soon encountered a series of rapids and falls around which the 400-pound boats and 65 tons of provisions had to be carried or dragged. The boats, hurriedly built of green wood, began to leak. Provisions were lost or spoiled or were washed away by floods. One discouraged battalion turned back, carrying away a large part of the remaining food.

The rest of the force at length abandoned the river and struggled over the watershed through the wilderness of Maine and Canada. After the men had consumed the last of their provisions, they lived on roots and on roast dog—entrails, feet, and all. Some tried to eat shoes, leather breeches, and shot-pouches. One of the men wrote later, "No one can imagine, who has not experienced it, the sweetness of a roasted shot-pouch to the famished appetite."

On November 9, 600 emaciated scarecrows and the indomitable Arnold reached the right bank of the St. Lawrence River opposite Quebec. Scouring the countryside roundabout, the Amercans collected enough canoes and dugouts to cross the river by night. On November 14 they stood on the Plains of Abraham where in 1759 Wolfe had won Canada for Britain.

Carleton did not dash forth from his walled city to do battle; with fewer than 70 soldiers and about 300 marines and sailors, he was too weak to make a sortie. Arnold's men, for their part, had no artillery and were short of small arms and ammunition. Nevertheless, Arnold boldly sent forward, under a white flag, a party seeking a parley at which they would demand the surrender of the city. Carleton replied with round shot.

In early December, Montgomery joined Arnold with 500 men and assumed overall command of the American forces. Because many enlistments were due to run out at the end of the year, Montgomery knew that he must assault Quebec before the remainder of his army melted away. Carleton's situation, moreover, was improving as soldiers arrived from Newfoundland and citizens within the walls were drilled in the rudiments of artillery and small arms fire.

On the last night of 1775, during a howling blizzard, the Americans attacked. Surprise was essential, but the British were alert. Consequently, Montgomery was killed,

Arnold was shot in the leg, and nearly half of their men were killed or captured.

Despite this fearsome setback, the Americans, with minor reinforcements, resumed their siege. Had they been promptly and adequately reinforced, and had the big guns of Ticonderoga been sent to Canada instead of Boston, it is probable that the city would have fallen. For Quebec was isolated by the besiegers on one side and by the frozen St. Lawrence on the other. With the coming of spring, however, British warships escorting a large troop convoy from England pushed their way through the melting ice floes at the mouth of the river. On May 6, 1776, the first of the ships reached Quebec, whereupon the Americans hastily retired.

THE BRITISH COUNTEROFFENSIVE

In 1776 the British armies in America, heavily reinforced by British regulars and German mercenaries, shifted to the offensive both in the colonies and in Canada. It was widely predicted in London government and military circles that the rebellion would be suppressed before the end of the year.

Washington had never doubted that the British would return from Halifax, and he correctly estimated that Howe intended to base his army not on Boston, as before, but on more centrally located New York. Thither, therefore, he led his army, which began throwing up earthworks and erecting fortifications. Because Brooklyn Heights dominated New York, Washington divided his army between Manhattan Island and Long Island.

At the end of June, Howe and his 6,000 Boston veterans arrived in convoy and several days later landed on Staten Island. In the next weeks more troops arrived, some from England, some from an abortive diversionary attack on Charleston, South Carolina. By mid-August Howe had 32,000 professional soldiers in his Staten Island camp. Congress, which on July 4 had adopted the Declaration of Independence, strove to match or exceed this number of men, but most of the reinforcements sent to General Washington were short-term, ill-trained militia.

The British display of force having failed to awe the Americans into submission, General Howe prepared to

Campaigns of 1775 and 1776.

attack. Like Washington, he saw the necessity of controlling Brooklyn Heights, and so, beginning on August 22, he transferred the bulk of his army across the Narrows to Long Island. The Americans, entrenched behind fortifications on high ground, braced themselves for an immediate assault, but Howe had digested the lesson of Bunker Hill. Instead of launching a frontal attack, the British general probed for weak spots. Then, after midnight on August 27, he sent two columns against the American front and led a third around the American left flank.

Overpowered, outmaneuvered, and partly surrounded, most of the American army retreated in disorder to prepared positions on Brooklyn Heights, leaving 1,000 prisoners in enemy hands. As the British began obvious preparations for siege, Washington turned for help to Colonel John Glover's regiment of Massachusetts fishermen. These men collected every vessel, from rowboat to sloop, in the New York area, and after dark on the 29th began ferrying the American troops and their supplies across to Manhattan. When the fog lifted the next morning, the bewildered British found the American positions completely empty.

On September 15 Howe crossed to Manhattan, whereupon Washington began a retreat to the north. Entrenching his forces always on high ground with their flanks carefully secured, he refused all challenges to battle, and Howe refrained from frontal assault. At the end of October, the American army, reduced by illness, captures, and desertions to half of its original strength, was entrenched at White Plains, north of New York.

On the grand strategic scale, Howe's northward advance from New York was only one arm of a giant pincer intended to cut off New England from the rest of the American colonies and to squeeze Washington's army in a vise. The other arm was to drive down from Canada.

The Americans retreating from Quebec, in the face of 8,000 reinforcements from England, were soon beset by an epidemic of smallpox. Their retreat became a rout. By July 1776, a mere remnant of the expeditionary force that had invaded Canada was back at Fort Ticonderoga. Sir Guy Carleton, advancing with overwhelming strength, was at St. Johns. His army was the other arm of the pincer.

In order to advance southward, Carleton would have to control Lake Champlain, for there were no roads between St. Johns and Ticonderoga. Hence the British and the Americans began a shipbuilding race.

The Americans had the advantage of already having a few armed vessels on the lake. They began building more ships under the direction of Benedict Arnold, now a brigadier general, who had had extensive experience as shipowner and shipmaster. By September Arnold had on the lake a sloop, three schooners, three 70-foot galleys, and nine 56-foot gondolas. These vessels were manned chiefly by volunteers from the army who were inexperienced in shiphandling.

The British won the race in firepower but not in time. St. Johns had the advantage of being near the St. Lawrence, where there were shipyards and where the fleet that had brought Carleton's reinforcements was still moored. Vessels could be brought up the Richelieu River, but to reach Lake Champlain they had to be carried past a stretch of rapids. Attempts to haul the larger vessels overland on rollers bogged down in unseasonal rains, so that all these ships had to be taken apart and reassembled. As a result, the British lake squadron was unprepared to sail before October. It was a formidable force, however, able to throw a weight of metal of more than 1,000 pounds to Arnold's 605. Its crews, commanded by the Royal Navy's Captain Thomas Pringle, were drawn mainly from the British fleet. When Pringle's squadron set sail, Carleton himself was aboard the flagship in order to have a ringside seat at the anticipated defeat of Arnold.

THE BATTLE OF VALCOUR ISLAND

Arnold, warned of the British approach, concealed his vessels between Valcour Island and the west shore of Lake Champlain. On the morning of October 11, Pringle's squadron, sailing before a northerly wind, passed the island on the opposite side without sighting Arnold's force. Before a shot was fired, in what is known generally as the Battle of Valcour Island, the Americans took their first loss—the schooner *Royal Savage*, which Arnold had sent forward briefly to attract the enemy's attention. The schooner, returning to the line, ran hard aground on the island's southern point and was later set afire by the British.

As Arnold had foreseen, the British formation was broken by the necessity of beating into the wind in order to engage. Of the five large vessels, each with different sailing characteristics, only the schooner *Carleton*, accompanied by 20 small gunboats under oars, was able to work her way without delay to within close range of the American line. Here she was battered so severely that Pringle at length ordered a pair of longboats to tow her back to safety.

At 4 P.M. the sloop *Inflexible*, armed with eighteen 12-pounder guns, reached effective range and gave the American line a severe drubbing, leaving the gondola

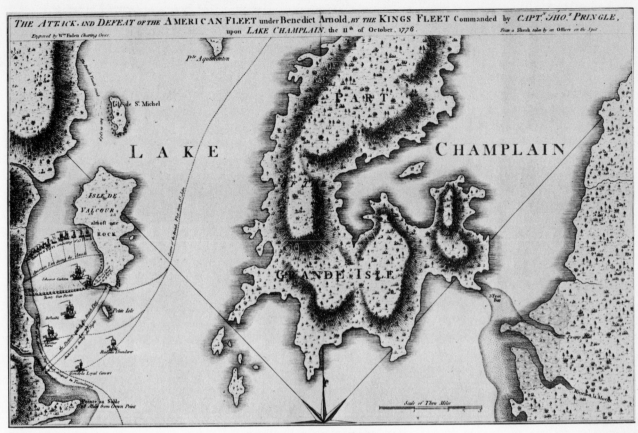

THE ATTACK AND DEFEAT OF THE AMERICAN FLEET under Benedict Arnold, BY THE KINGS FLEET Commanded by CAPT.ⁿ THO.ˢ PRINGLE, upon LAKE CHAMPLAIN, the 11ᵗʰ of October, 1776.

The Battle of Valcour Island, from a contemporary British broadside.

Philadelphia in a sinking condition. Pringle, in the schooner *Lady Maria,* which had not been able to close the enemy, now recalled all his vessels. That night, confident that between the north wind and his squadron he had the Americans trapped for leisurely execution the next morning, he stretched his line of ships from the island nearly to Lake Champlain's west shore. The Americans, however, slipped past the British left under cover of darkness and fog.

At dawn Pringle was dumbfounded, and Carleton furious, to find the Americans gone. After fruitless searches in the area, the British squadron at length headed south. On October 13 the leading British ships caught up with the heavily damaged galley *Washington* and forced her to surrender. To avoid capture, Arnold ran his flagship, the galley *Congress,* and four gondolas ashore. Here he set them afire and escaped with his men into the forest.

The British had won a tactical victory, but it had come too late. If Carleton now undertook an advance into New York, his supplies would soon be cut off by ice on Lake Champlain. He reluctantly canceled opera-

tions for that year and withdrew with his forces to winter quarters in Canada.

At the other end of the Hudson-Champlain valley, General Howe no longer had any immediate reason for pushing Washington northward. In mid-November he retired into winter quarters at New York, sending the main part of his army, led by Major General the Earl Charles Cornwallis, across the Hudson River toward Philadelphia, the rebel capital. Washington's army, reduced to 3,400 and still dwindling, could do no more than delay Cornwallis and then escape across the Delaware River into Pennsylvania, while Congress fled Philadelphia.

The night after Christmas, Washington in desperation recrossed the Delaware because the enlistments of his militia were due to end. At dawn he attacked British-occupied Trenton, capturing nearly a thousand of Cornwallis' mercenaries. Further American raids impelled the British to abandon most of New Jersey. Washington retired into winter quarters at Morristown in the Jersey highlands, for from here he could threaten any renewed British move up the Hudson or toward Philadelphia.

SARATOGA AND
THE FRENCH ALLIANCE

In the spring of 1777 the British prepared to resume their offensives. They would now meet more numerous, better-armed American forces, for Washington's Trenton victory had galvanized American patriotism; in addition, the colonies were beginning to receive substantial quantities of munitions from France, who, resentful at having lost her overseas empire to Britain in the Seven Years' War, was not displeased to see her old enemy lose ground.

The British plan, as understood in London, was the same as that of the previous year, with two differences: Lieutenant General John Burgoyne would now command the expedition driving down from Canada, and a new expedition, led by Brigadier General Barry St. Leger, would advance from the west via the Mohawk Valley. The armies under Burgoyne and St. Leger and Howe's army from New York would come together in a grand reunion at Albany.

Toward the end of June, Burgoyne's army of nearly 8,000 headed south from St. Johns via Lake Champlain. It easily ousted the Americans from undergunned, undermanned Fort Ticonderoga by the simple expedient of hoisting artillery to the top of a nearby hill that dominated the fort. When Burgoyne left the lake and headed for the Hudson Valley, he soon ran into trouble. American troops felled trees and destroyed bridges before and behind him and disrupted his 600-wagon supply train by sniping. Farmers along his line of march burned their crops and withdrew their cattle. When Burgoyne sent a column of 800 troops to seize desperately needed supplies at Bennington, the men were all killed or captured by New England militia.

The whole British plan began to fall apart. St. Leger's army was halted by the determined resistance of local patriots at Fort Stanwix, and when exaggerated reports of an approaching relief force under General Arnold caused his Indians to flee in panic, St. Leger and his whites were obliged to retire to Oswego.

General Howe, left with a large measure of initiative, decided that he could best cooperate with Burgoyne and sooner put down the rebellion, not by advancing up the Hudson but by destroying Washington's army. He concluded that the best way to draw Washington out of his highland fastness was to seize Philadelphia. Anxious to avoid another Trenton, Howe embarked the main part of his army on ships and went by sea, approaching the colonial capital by way of Chesapeake Bay rather

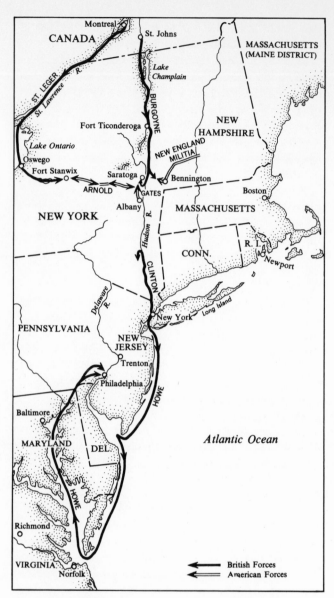

Operations of 1777.

than the Delaware River, which was lined with rebel forts. He thrust aside Washington's army at the Battle of Brandywine and occupied Philadelphia in late September.

In the upper Hudson Valley, Burgoyne was encountering steadily increasing resistance. Two clashes with American forces under Major General Horatio Gates cost him 1,200 men. Finally, at Saratoga, his remaining 4,700 troops were surrounded by 9,000 of Gates' Americans. On October 17, Burgoyne formally surrendered. The news of Burgoyne's defeat electrified Europe and encouraged Britain's potential enemies to act. France, fearful that the British might now offer concessions that would bring the war to an end, signed treaties of commerce and alliance with the Americans.

There is a clear connection between Arnold's shipbuilding on Lake Champlain and American independence, for the delay of a year in the British invasion from Canada set the stage for the American victory at Saratoga. The evidence that the rebels had a chance of winning brought France and, later, Spain into the war against England and made an ultimate American victory possible.

Britain now completely revised her strategy. Her paramount objective became the saving of England and the empire, rather than quelling the rebellion in America. General Sir Henry Clinton, who had relieved Howe, was ordered to evacuate Philadelphia and to concentrate his forces at New York and Newport. General Washington moved back to White Plains.

On July 11, 1778, a French fleet, which included 12 ships of the line under Admiral the Comte d'Estaing, stood off Sandy Hook. Inside New York Bay was a British fleet of nine ships. Washington had high hopes for a French naval victory that would isolate Clinton's troops from the sea, enabling the Americans to bring all of their forces against an army that could not be supplied, reinforced, or evacuated. This was not to be, for d'Estaing's deep-draft ships could not be brought over the bar. After 11 days the French fleet sailed away. Washington's plan for coordinating land and sea power against the British was not realized until three years later.

THE PRIVATEERS

No American maritime operation during the Revolution accomplished more than privateering, which was the government-authorized use of privately owned and armed vessels to prey on enemy shipping. A vessel captured by a privateer was brought to a friendly port. If the capture was declared legal by a prize court, vessel and cargo were generally sold and the proceeds were divided among owners, officers, and crew.

Americans had developed skill in privateering when, as British subjects in the Seven Years' War, they had preyed on French and Spanish merchantmen. They had a vessel well adapted to the work—the swift, maneuverable schooner, an American specialty.

Early in the Revolution the states, and then Congress, began to issue letters of marque which authorized privateering. Because of the wartime eclipse of American fisheries and shipping, large numbers of vessels and seamen were unemployed and available for this ac-

tivity. The prospects for quick money and the lax discipline in privateers appealed mightily to the acquisitive, individualistic Yankee. Landsmen as well as seafarers flocked to enroll. Members of the gentry and professional men enlisted, usually as "gentlemen sailors" having no duties but combat. So popular was privateering that some New England towns were virtually stripped of adult males, and vessels of the regular Navy were often unable to sail for want of crews.

The success of the privateers was a direct result of their numbers, which in the course of the Revolution exceeded 2,000. The capture of merchantmen and their cargoes seriously impeded British military operations in America and went far to provide for the needs of the rebel forces. Americans could boast that they were conducting the war largely at British expense. When in 1778 Boston lacked the means to provision d'Estaing's 12 ships of the line, they were enabled to sail through the timely arrival of privateers bringing in prize vessels laden with supplies intended for Clinton's army.

Early in the war the favorite hunting grounds for American privateers were off Halifax, in the Gulf of St. Lawrence, and in the West Indies, where their depredations reduced the British colonies to near starvation. Then and later, however, individual cruisers ventured wherever British shipping was to be found, even into European waters.

Although swift, heavily armed British merchantmen continued to sail alone, severe losses early impelled England to herd most of her transports and commercial vessels into convoy. The use of convoy, while it saved ships, cost time and hence did little to relieve British problems of supply and reinforcement. Assembling the convoy, which sometimes included hundreds of vessels, usually took several weeks; and when it was at sea, the whole formation was held down to the speed of the slowest vessel. Moreover, the convoys had to be escorted by warships, which might otherwise have been occupied in harrying American ships or directly supporting British land operations.

Because of the slow assembling of vessels in port, the sailing of a convoy usually became known to American privateersmen, who fell in behind on the chance of picking off stragglers. Sometimes a swift American cruiser deliberately exposed herself in order to lure the escorts into a chase while other privateers closed in to capture some of the temporarily unprotected merchantmen.

As captures of British vessels mounted—229 in 1776, 331 in 1777—Britons began to feel the pinch at home as well as in America. Business houses depending on overseas trade were ruined; prices for sugar, tobacco, and other imported products rose steadily; maritime insurance rates became so high that many British firms resorted to shipping their goods in foreign bottoms. Even in British home waters, coastal vessels sometimes moved in convoy for protection from the ubiquitous American cruisers.

While the fortune-hunting privateers tended to pounce only on unarmed vessels or on vessels more lightly armed than themselves, there were numerous exceptions, some resulting in fierce and bloody battles. These battles have received little attention in histories, partly because of poor record keeping and partly because of the dubious reputation of private warfare, in which the attacker fought for pelf rather than patriotism or glory.

Early in the war, when ordnance was hard to come by in America, the privateers were usually small and lightly armed. Some ventured to sea with only small arms, hoping by luck or surprise attack to capture a vessel armed with guns they could use. Others slipped through the British blockade with cargoes of tobacco or other merchandise which they sold abroad, using the proceeds to buy armament. Later, when munitions from overseas were relatively plentiful, Americans took to sea large, heavily armed privateers built expressly for preying on commerce. The most successful of these was the *Marlborough*, from Massachusetts; it took 28 prizes, including a slaver carrying 300 Negroes.

On making a capture, the captain of a privateer usually ordered the defeated crew to be brought aboard his cruiser as prisoners, and put a prize crew from his own ship's company aboard the captured vessel to take her into port. After a series of captures, the number of prisoners aboard a privateer might considerably exceed that of the depleted crew. On several occasions the prisoners rose against their captors and seized the vessel.

Although privateering seems mere legalized piracy by today's standards, it carried no stigma during the Revolution nor for a long time thereafter. Many officers, including such prominent men as John Manley, Joshua Barney, and John Barry, served impartially in regular naval vessels and in privateers, as opportunities arose. Successful privateersmen were likely to be offered commissions in the Navy, and as naval officers some of these men later achieved enduring fame; among them were Thomas Truxtun, David Porter, and the Stephen Decaturs, junior and senior.

THE CONTINENTAL NAVY

A proposal to establish a Continental Navy, placed before Congress by the Rhode Island delegation in Oc-

tober 1775, at first met with considerable opposition. Its opponents pointed out that the operations of General Washington's army, then besieging Boston, could be construed as defensive; but a navy, by its nature a weapon of offense, would prove a bar to conciliation with the Crown. Moreover, it was argued, how could any fleet the Americans could produce be able to challenge the overwhelming might of the Royal Navy?

Proponents of the measure pointed out the need of warships to defend American coasts and coastwise shipping, frequently attacked by British vessels, and to keep open commercial and diplomatic communications with foreign powers. The example of Washington's little navy and its useful capture of munitions and other supplies provided another powerful argument.

On October 30, 1775, Congress established the Continental Navy by appointing a Naval Committee of seven and authorizing the purchase and arming of vessels "for the protection and defense of the United Colonies." On November 10 it established a marine corps of two battalions. On November 25, its resolution hardened by the ruthless burning of the town of Falmouth (now Portland, Maine) by men from British warships, Congress specifically authorized capture of British naval and commercial vessels.

The first Continental squadron consisted originally of eight converted merchantmen: the ships *Alfred* and *Columbus*, armed with 30 and 28 guns respectively; the brigs *Andrew Doria* and *Cabot*, with 16 and 14 guns; the sloops *Providence* and *Hornet*, with 12 and 10; and the schooners *Wasp* and *Fly*, with 8 and 6. The Naval Committee appointed Esek Hopkins of Rhode Island to command the squadron, giving him the impressive title of Commander in Chief. Hopkins, aged fifty-seven, was a master mariner of long experience who had commanded privateers in the Seven Years' War. For this reason he was a logical choice, but an added reason for his selection was that he was the brother of a leading member of the Naval Committee. Of the other officers selected, only Captain Nicholas Biddle of the *Andrew Doria*, a former midshipman of the Royal Navy, had had any naval experience whatever. The crews were for the most part composed of undisciplined seamen from the extinct merchant marine.

In mid-February 1776, Hopkins sailed with his squadron under orders to attack British and Loyalist armed vessels in Chesapeake Bay and to clear the enemy from the coasts of the Carolinas and Rhode Island. Taking advantage of a discretionary clause in the orders, he ignored them and shaped course for the island of New Providence in the Bahamas, where guns and gunpowder were known to be stored.

The Continental Navy ships Alfred *and* Providence *capture a British supply vessel.*

Arriving off New Providence, Hopkins made the mistake of sailing his squadron within sight of the town of Nassau before putting a landing party ashore. The governor, thus forewarned, was able to send away 150 casks of gunpowder in a sloop. The landing party seized the two forts flanking the town without opposition, thereby capturing 88 cannon, 15 mortars, and considerable shot, shell, and gun carriages; they seized only 24 casks of powder.

Off Long Island Sound on the return trip, the squadron captured two small British men-of-war. In the same area, however, in the early hours of April 6, the Americans demonstrated their lack of training for coordinated fleet action. The *Cabot* identified a vessel approaching in the moonlight as British, and opened fire. There ensued a confused hour-and-a-half melee, followed by a chase in which the stranger escaped. She turned out to be the 20-gun *Glasgow;* though badly battered, she had suffered only 1 man killed and 3 wounded. American casualties were 10 killed and 14 wounded.

Commodore Hopkins took his squadron into the port of New London, later shifting it to Providence near the head of Narragansett Bay. By this time privateering was flourishing, and its greater rewards and presumably lesser perils lured seamen away from government vessels. As a result the squadron was never again able to sail as a unit, despite peremptory orders to go to sea and do something. The best Hopkins could do was to send out such individual vessels as he was able to man. These vessels simply preyed on British commerce like privateers—an activity that was popular with the crews, who nevertheless grumbled because Congress took a large share of the prize money.

The most successful of the cruiser captains was sharp-nosed, sharp-eyed little John Paul Jones. In August 1776 Jones took to sea the sloop *Providence* and soon captured a whaling brigantine. Near Bermuda he was chased all day by a frigate. By clever shiphandling he managed to escape, after which he made two more captures in the area and then headed north to the

British shipping lanes off Halifax. Here the *Providence* was chased by another frigate, which she easily outran, but Jones deliberately remained just beyond gun range to tempt his pursuer to waste ammunition, and tauntingly returned the frigate's ineffective fire with a musket shot. Jones then boldly entered two small Canadian ports, capturing the fishing fleets in both. The best of the captured vessels he sent away as prizes; the rest he destroyed, leaving two to convey the English fishermen back home. On October 8 the *Providence* returned safely to Narragansett Bay, having taken 16 vessels on a 49-day cruise. Of these vessels, 2 were recaptured by British ships and 8 reached port as prizes.

Within three weeks Jones was again at sea, this time in the ship *Alfred*. His most important capture on this cruise was the 350-ton armed transport *Mellish*, laden with winter uniforms and other supplies for General Carleton's army in Canada. Once more Jones eluded a pursuing frigate, decoying her away at night from several prizes that were sailing in company with the *Alfred*. He put into Boston on December 14 and later had the satisfaction of learning that the warm British uniforms from the *Mellish* had reached Washington's needy army before the Battle of Trenton.

Commodore Hopkins' career, marked by one inept move after another, was now going into swift decline. In a desperate effort to enlist seamen, Hopkins denounced privateering and even requested the Rhode Island government to embargo privateers until he could man his squadron. This request not only fell on deaf ears but earned the commodore the enmity of politicians, many of whom were heavy investors in the private warfare on British commerce. Complaints from these politicians and from a cabal of his own junior officers, who accused the commodore of tyranny and poor judgment, caused the Marine Committee (successor to the Naval Committee) to investigate formally Hopkins' disregard of his orders in leading the expedition against New Providence, his failure to capture the *Glasgow*, and his subsequent conduct.

In December 1776, while Hopkins' enemies were thus undermining him, he suddenly found his squadron blockaded by a powerful British fleet which had entered Narragansett Bay and landed an army of occupation at Newport, a situation brought about by the commodore's failure to maintain proper patrols. The American squadron, still at Providence, could only warp up the Providence River to safety.

The British frigate *Diamond*, advancing to the head of the bay to investigate, ran aground on a shoal; north-

Loss of the Randolph.

erly winds prevented the other British warships from coming to her aid. Hopkins then went downriver in the *Providence*, took position under the stranded frigate's stern, and banged away without inflicting much damage. When the commodore went ashore to confer with militiamen at an improvised coastal battery, his boat drifted away. Before he could get back to the *Providence*, the *Diamond* lightened ship and escaped. This absurd series of events gave Hopkins' enemies the ammunition they needed: the commander in chief was suspended from duty and subsequently dismissed from the service.

With the dead hand of Hopkins removed, most of the vessels of his squadron succeeded singly in running the British blockade, and some performed valuable service in the war on British shipping. These, together with other merchantmen converted into warships, convoyed or transported from West Indian entrepots munitions originating in Europe. None survived the war: all but two were captured or destroyed to prevent capture, and the two exceptions were a ship that sank at sea and a brig that ran aground and was wrecked trying to escape the blockade.

A similar fate awaited the Continental Navy's second squadron, 13 fine frigates authorized by Congress in late 1775 and built as warships from the keel up. Of these, most were captured or destroyed to prevent capture. The exception in this squadron was the *Randolph*, 32 guns. Under the command of Captain Biddle, she was challenged near Barbados in March 1778 by the 64-gun ship of the line *Yarmouth*. She replied with a broadside, and in a 15-minute battle the *Yarmouth* took far more damage than she inflicted. When, however, Biddle was wearing ship to get on the enemy's quarter, the *Randolph*'s magazine exploded, blasting her to fragments, many of which came raining down on the *Yarmouth*. Captain Biddle was not among the *Randolph*'s only four survivors, who were rescued from a piece of wreckage several days later.

Although ships of the Continental Navy ran up a proud score of captures, it was early evident that they could not appreciably affect the outcome of the war, or even survive. They were a small, improvised fleet with untrained officers confronting the most powerful, most experienced navy in the world. Remarkably enough, however, some of the most profitable cruises of Continental vessels were made in British home waters.

The first to operate off Britain was the 18-gun Continental ship *Reprisal*, commanded by Captain Lambert Wickes. In November 1776, the *Reprisal* reached St.-Nazaire, France, bringing Benjamin Franklin to act as chief American commissioner in Paris; the ship was accompanied by two prizes, which had been captured

en route. Protests by Lord Stormont, the British ambassador, concerning the use of a French port to shelter prizes elicited only polite evasions from the French.

Early in 1777 Wickes boldly sailed the *Reprisal* into the English Channel, where he captured five prizes, including the king's Falmouth–Lisbon mail packet. When the packet, armed with 16 guns, put up resistance, the *Reprisal*'s crew quieted her with a few broadsides and then took her by boarding. While Lord Stormont was again protesting, Wickes sold his prizes at bargain rates to delighted French merchants, who disguised their purchases with fresh paint and new figureheads.

The following May Captain Wickes took out from St.-Nazaire a small squadron consisting of his *Reprisal*; the 16-gun Continental brig *Lexington*, recently arrived from the United States; and the cutter *Dolphin*, 10, a former British vessel secretly purchased by American agents in a cloak-and-dagger transaction at Dover. In a clockwise circuit around Ireland, the swift little cruisers captured 18 prizes. While approaching the French coast on the return voyage, they were chased by the 74-gun ship of the line *Burford*. Wickes, ordering his cruisers to scatter, fled east in the *Reprisal* with the *Burford* in hot pursuit. He escaped only by heaving his guns overboard and sawing through some of his ship's beams to give the vessel more spring and thereby decrease her resistance to the water.

In England Wickes' remarkable cruise caused widespread alarm, sending maritime insurance rates soaring and utterly snarling maritime traffic. The French government, unprepared for war and unable any longer to placate the furious Lord Stormont, ordered the American raiders out of its ports. En route back to the United States, the *Lexington* was captured by a British cutter after a furious fight in which the Americans shot off all their ammunition. The homebound *Reprisal* foundered in a storm off Newfoundland, and Wickes went down with his ship. "This loss is extremely to be lamented," reported Dr. Franklin, "as he was a gallant officer and a very worthy man."

Another cruiser captain operating out of France in the spring of 1777 was Gustavus Conyngham, a young Philadelphia skipper whose ship had been seized by the Dutch for smuggling munitions out of Holland. Conyngham offered his services to the American commissioners, who provided him with a captain's commission and gave him command of the lugger *Surprise*, another British vessel purchased at Dover.

In a brief cruise in early May, Conyngham took two prizes, including a British mail packet, and brought them triumphantly into Dunkirk. This choice was a mistake, for in this busy port were many English merchants who

Captain Gustavus Conyngham.

The Surprise capturing the Harwich packet.

readily recognized and reported the presence of the packet. The French government, caught red-handed supporting depredations on British commerce, could not feign ignorance. They released the prizes and briefly jailed the "Dunkirk pirate," as the wrathful British ambassador called Conyngham.

The following July, Conyngham was at sea in another purchased vessel, the cutter *Revenge*, with orders not to return to France. He cruised in British waters, capturing or destroying numerous vessels. His prizes he sent to Spain, the West Indies, or the United States, wherever he thought the cargoes would bring the best price. From the English Channel he shifted to the Bay of Biscay, to the waters off Portugal, to the Canary Islands, across the Atlantic to the West Indies—at last arriving in Philadelphia in February 1779, having taken or destroyed more than 60 British vessels.

When Congress sold the *Revenge* at public auction, the ship's new owners sent her to sea again, this time as a privateer with Conyngham as captain. But the famous raider's legendary luck had now run out: the *Revenge* was captured off New York by a British frigate. Conyngham, sent to England in irons, was placed in infamous Mill Prison and treated with great severity. At length he escaped and made his way to Holland, where he was received with admiration aboard the flagship of John Paul Jones, who had recently won the Battle off Flamborough Head.

The depredations of Wickes and Conyngham had dealt British shipping a severe blow. More important, the raiders had brought Britain and France to the brink of war, which after all was their secret assignment. In the tense diplomatic atmosphere that followed their expulsion, American warships were for several months unwelcome in French ports.

JOHN PAUL JONES IN EUROPEAN WATERS

In December 1777 the Continental Navy's sloop-of-war *Ranger*, 18, under command of Captain John Paul Jones, arrived in France and dropped anchor in the Loire River. Neither her coming nor the arrival of her two prizes, taken en route from America, brought forth protests from the French government, for news of Burgoyne's surrender at Saratoga had suddenly changed official attitudes. The following February, shortly after the still-secret alliance had been signed between France and the United States, Jones had the satisfaction of exchanging gun salutes with the admiral of a powerful French squadron at anchor in Quiberon Bay.

John Paul Jones.

On April 10, 1778, Jones took the *Ranger* to sea for a cruise in British waters. His prospects were not encouraging, for his officers were not of his choosing and his seamen, mostly New England boys who had gone to sea admittedly in hopes of winning quick prize money, had become homesick and sullen. Both officers and men, moreover, considered their captain a foreigner.

Jones, the son of a gardener, had been born in Scotland and had gone to sea at the age of thirteen, embarking at the English port of Whitehaven, across Solway Firth from Kirkbean, his home and birthplace. Between the ages of twenty-one and twenty-six, Jones served as master of merchantmen trading mostly with the West Indies. He was in Virginia when hostilities broke out between England and the colonies. Promptly casting his lot with the rebels, he offered his sword and knowledge of shiphandling to his newly adopted country. On December 7, 1775, Jones was commissioned first lieutenant in the Continental Navy and served in that rank aboard Esek Hopkins' flagship *Alfred* in the New Providence expedition.

Because Jones had little political influence and no geographical roots in his new country, his advancement in the Navy was comparatively slow—at least in Jones' own impatient opinion; the Congressional list of October 1776 placed him 18th among 24 captains. Nevertheless, his brilliant cruises in the *Providence* and *Alfred* so impressed the Marine Committee that it marked him down for an important command. In July 1777 they ordered

Jones to fit out the recently launched *Ranger* and take her to France, presumably to emulate the achievements of his predecessors in European waters.

As has been stated, Jones reached France at the end of the year and the following April set out from Brest on his first raiding cruise in the *Ranger*. Entering the Irish Sea, he captured several vessels, but to the disgust of his men, avid for prize money, Jones sank all but one after removing the crews. He had no choice because his ship's company was so depleted by desertions that he could not spare men to take the prizes into port.

Learning that H.M. sloop-of-war *Drake*, 20 guns, was at Carrickfergus, Ireland, Jones entered the harbor at night for a surprise attack. When the ineptitude of his crew, compounded by drunkenness, cost him surprise, he abandoned the attempt, but filed the *Drake* away in his mind for future treatment.

Jones now headed east across the Irish Sea to carry

European cruises of John Paul Jones.

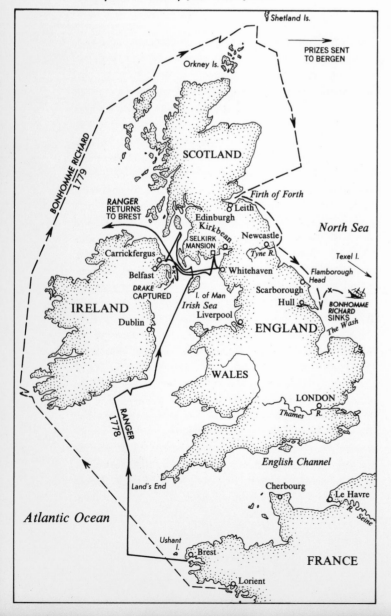

out his principal self-imposed mission—nothing less than a hit-and-run raid on harbor shipping. For this exploit he chose Whitehaven, simply because it was the port he knew best, the one into which he could most readily find his way by night. His purpose was to shock and humiliate the British, to draw their warships from offensive operations to coast defense, and, above all, to retaliate for the British policy of burning American coastal towns.

Off Whitehaven Captain Jones had to quell a mutiny by putting a loaded pistol to the leader's head. He was able nevertheless to engage 40 volunteers, who in darkness rowed in two boats into the harbor. Delayed by an ebbing tide, they did not reach shore until dawn. One boatload of men managed to enter an alehouse, where they drank themselves tipsy; they then rowed away. Jones led the other group in scaling the walls of the harbor batteries, tying up the sleeping guards, and spiking the guns.

Meanwhile one of the *Ranger's* sailors, an Irishman who had enlisted in America as a means of getting back home, had slipped away and was arousing the town, shouting and knocking on doors. By the time Jones was able to turn his attention to firing the 200 or more small vessels in the harbor, the waterfront was swarming with belligerent but confused citizens. He was able to remain long enough to set fire to one of the larger vessels and, with the aid of his men, to toss a barrel of tar on the flames. With his men he then rowed coolly back to the *Ranger*.

Captain Jones next sailed his sloop across Solway Firth and landed near the site of his boyhood home. His purpose here was to kidnap the Earl of Selkirk, whom he may have seen as a child and whom he naively supposed to be a great and influential lord. By holding the earl as hostage, he hoped to induce the British to release American seamen languishing in prison.

On learning from a gardener that the earl was not at home, Jones was about to return to his ship, but two of his officers insisted that after running so many risks they would not go away empty handed. Realizing that he must give way to some degree, Jones consented to their entering the Selkirk mansion and demanding the family silver of the countess, but he ordered them most particularly to molest no one and to refrain from pillaging the house. The officers, following these instructions, committed a most polite robbery and then returned the way they had come. Jones, forced thus by his undisciplined subordinates to act contrary to his instincts, was actually appalled at the thought of American officers stooping to pilfer silver. After the cruise he purchased the plate with his own money and at the end of the war sent it back to the Selkirks.

The Ranger *exchanges salutes with a French fleet in Quiberon Bay—the first recognition of the Stars and Stripes by a foreign government.*

Disregarding the obvious fact that all Britain would soon be aroused by his bold expeditions ashore, Jones headed back across the Irish Sea to settle his account with the *Drake*. The next morning, meeting the British sloop coming out of harbor, he came about and led the way into North Channel for more maneuvering room. Then, ordering the helm up, he swung the *Ranger* across the *Drake*'s bows and raked her with a broadside of grape shot. In the ensuing hour-long battle the American crew, inspired by their captain's example and by prospects of good prize money, fought like demons. Jones, using mostly grape and chain shot, aimed high at spars, sails, and rigging so as to prevent the *Drake*'s escape while preserving her hull. The *Drake*, in the traditional British manner, fired at the *Ranger*'s hull but achieved little damage to the American vessel's sturdy sides. When the *Drake*'s captain had been killed and his second-in-command mortally wounded, her master cried "Quarters!" and the gunfire ceased.

The *Ranger* took the helpless *Drake* in tow until she could be jury-rigged. Then, while alarm beacons lighted up the British coasts and British warships searched the Irish Sea, the *Ranger* and her prize headed around north and west of Ireland. On May 8 both sloops entered Brest, the *Drake* with her English colors inverted beneath the Stars and Stripes.

Jones at this time was thirty years old. Slight of frame, wiry, taut, he was the embodiment of ambition and determination. By sheer intelligence and applica-

tion he had educated himself to the degree in which he could express himself in speech and writing better than most officers of his day, and could move with ease and assurance in the highest social circles. A superb shiphandler and a dedicated professional officer, he was also fertile with ideas for improving the naval service; most of these ideas were eventually adopted by the U.S. Navy. He had an extraordinary ability to seize unforeseen advantages and to snatch victory out of defeat. In battle his force of will and example could convert a lubberly, half-hearted crew into a band of heroes.

Yet Jones made many enemies and never enjoyed the unqualified support of his subordinates. Extremely self-centered, he neither inspired complete loyalty nor attracted abiding friendships. To his superiors he continually addressed complaints and demands for recognition. Though he took good care of his men, it was not because of sympathetic consideration but because they were to him, like his ships and guns, the means of attaining his ends. A perfectionist, he was ever criticizing and nagging his subordinates or blasting them in fits of temper. He seldom praised or gave credit, and he thirsted for glory which he was loath to share.

After his cruise in the Irish Sea, Jones released the *Ranger*, which soon headed for America with her homesick crew. Then for nearly a year he waited in France for the suitable command promised by the American commissioners. Offered his choice of British prizes brought into port, he spurned them all. "I wish to have no connection with any ship that does not sail *fast*," he wrote, "for I intend *to go in harm's way*."

The ship that in desperation Jones at length accepted was a slow, half-rotten East Indiaman, which, to compliment his patron Dr. Franklin, he renamed *Bonhomme Richard*—the French name for "Poor Richard." Jones armed his ship with such new and second-hand guns as he could procure: six 9-pounders on quarterdeck and forecastle, twenty-eight 12-pounders as main battery on the covered gundeck, and six old 18-pounders, for which ports were pierced below the gundeck not far above the waterline. The ship's company was a polyglot mixture of a dozen nationalities, but the men were generally experienced and competent. Included were 79 Americans, many exchanged or escaped from British prisons. Among the escapees was the capable Richard Dale, whom Jones appointed first lieutenant. In addition to the crew, there were 137 French marines, who were seasoned fighters and excellent marksmen.

When the fine new American frigate *Alliance*, 36 guns, arrived in France, Dr. Franklin attached it to the *Bonhomme Richard*, forming the nucleus of a squadron to be commanded by Jones as commodore. Commanding the *Alliance* was Captain Pierre Landais, a former French naval officer who had gone to the United States and so ingratiated himself with certain congressmen that he had been commissioned a captain in the Continental Navy. Jealous, erratic, suspicious, Landais proved a source of tribulation to Jones.

To complete the squadron the French government assigned the frigate *Pallas*, 32 guns; the cutter *Cerf*, 18; and the brig *Vengeance*, 12. The French captains of these ships were given commissions in the Continental Navy and the squadron was empowered to sail under the American flag. On August 14, 1779, it put to sea from Lorient for a clockwise circuit of the British Isles.

It soon became apparent that none of Jones' captains took his authority very seriously. When Jones signaled the *Alliance* to cease chasing near a dangerous shore on the Irish west coast, Captain Landais came storming aboard the flagship and grossly insulted the commodore before other officers, stating that he would chase when and where he thought proper. Shortly afterward, all the ships except the *Vengeance* separated from the *Bonhomme Richard* without permission. The *Cerf* returned to France, but the *Pallas* and the *Alliance* rejoined from time to time at designated places of rendezvous. Off northern Scotland, Landais, in defiance of Jones' orders, sent two valuable prizes into Bergen, where the Norwegians promptly turned them over to the British consul.

Jones now conceived a daring plan for landing at defenseless Leith, the port of Edinburgh, and setting fire to the town as a reprisal for the continuing British practice of burning American seaports. In the absence of the *Alliance*, which was over the horizon as usual, Jones called the captains of the *Pallas* and the *Vengeance* to the *Bonhomme Richard* and laid his plan before them. During the all-night session the captains at first flatly refused to participate in so wild a venture, but when Jones suggested demanding a heavy ransom as an alternative to burning, they entered into the scheme with enthusiasm. On September 17 the three ships sailed boldly into the Firth of Forth, striking terror among the citizens of Leith and Edinburgh. Women, children, and old folk were hustled off into the countryside, while the young men, armed with muskets and pikes, assembled at the waterfront.

Jones' squadron, within cannon shot of Leith, was at the point of hoisting out boats for the landing when a sudden, severe offshore gale sprang up and blew the ships out of the firth into the North Sea. Having lost the advantage of surprise, Jones abandoned the project. When he proposed the alternative of raiding Newcastle-on-Tyne in order to cut off London's coal supply, the captains threatened to desert him for good if he attempted anything so rash.

Jones' ships, taking prizes, now moved southward off the English coast, often appearing within sight of land and causing widespread alarm. Militia beat to arms, ancient cannon were trundled out, and leading citizens dispatched indignant demands to the Admiralty for protection.

During the night of September 22 the *Richard*, the *Pallas*, the *Vengeance*, and the *Alliance* rejoined near Flamborough Head, a chalk-cliff promontory jutting out from the Yorkshire coast. The following afternoon lookouts in the squadron sighted numerous sails to the north. The commodore learned from a captured pilot that this fleet was a main objective of his cruise—a convoy from the Baltic Sea laden with naval stores. As Jones' ships, cracking on additional sail, gave chase, the convoy fled toward the protection of the guns of seaside Scarborough Castle, while its two escorting warships hastened to interpose themselves between the fleeing merchantmen and the American squadron.

Jones was informed by the captured pilot that the escorts were the 50-gun frigate *Serapis*, under Captain Richard Pearson, and the 20-gun sloop-of-war *Countess of Scarborough*. The commodore decided that, in order to attack the convoy, he must use his entire squadron to eliminate the escorts as quickly as possible. Because of the lightness of the southwest wind, the American ships made such slow headway that the sun had set when the opposing forces came within hailing distance. The Battle off Flamborough Head was about to begin.

It turned out to be not at all the sort of battle that Commodore Jones had in mind. Intending a fleet-type action, he signaled "Form line of battle," but his captains simply ignored the order, hauling their wind or sailing about at a safe distance. Eventually the *Pallas* attacked and captured the smaller *Countess of Scarborough*, but the *Bonhomme Richard* was left to fight the *Serapis* alone.

Unlike the *Richard*, the *Serapis* had a homogeneous crew. She was new, her bottom was copper-sheathed to prevent fouling and improve speed, and her main battery was of 18-pounders, opposing the *Richard*'s 12s. The *Bonhomme Richard*, however, had two advantages that, as events proved, more than made up for her shortcomings—the skill of her marksmen and the alert mind and unshakable determination of her commander.

When the moon rose at about 7 P.M., the two vessels were abeam within pistol shot. Captain Pearson hailed, whereupon Jones ordered the American ensign raised, and both ships fired broadsides. At the first salvo two of the *Richard*'s old 18-pounders shattered, knocking out the others of that caliber, blowing a huge hole in the deck above, and killing many gunners. The *Richard*'s weight of broadside was now reduced to 195 pounds, opposed to the *Serapis*' 300.

Jones, aware that he could not win a gunnery duel, ran up on the *Serapis*' starboard quarter in an attempt to board but, attaining too narrow a contact, sheered off (position 5 in diagram). Pearson next tried to place his ship across the *Richard*'s bow, out of reach of her broadsides, and sweep her decks with raking fire. The *Richard*, turning to avoid being raked, ran her bow into the *Serapis*' stern (position 6). The British captain, having demonstrated his frigate's superiority in fire-power and maneuverability, now confidently called out, "Has your ship struck?" To which Jones made the celebrated reply: "I have not yet begun to fight!"

Presently the two vessels were again abeam (7), the *Richard* taking heavy punishment. Jones' upwind position permitted him to take advantage of a sudden gust of wind and forge ahead in an attempt to cross Pearson's bow and rake. But the clumsy old East Indiaman fell short, so that the *Serapis* ran her jibboom into the *Richard*'s mizzen rigging (8). The ships then swung alongside each other bow to stern, and a fluke of the *Serapis*' spare anchor hooked the bulwarks of the *Richard*'s starboard quarter (10).

Instantly sizing up the situation, Jones called for grappling irons to bind the vessels inseparably together and himself seized a broken line from the *Serapis* and made

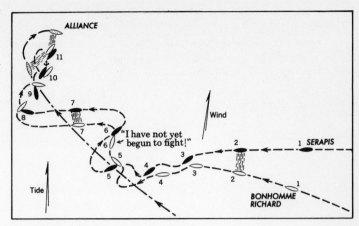

The Battle off Flamborough Head.

it fast to his mizzenmast. Attempts by the *Serapis*' crew to cast off the grapnels were frustrated by murderous small arms fire from the *Richard*'s sharpshooters. When Pearson ordered an anchor dropped, hoping thereby to pull the *Serapis* clear, the only result was that both vessels, still in close embrace, swung in a semicircle before wind and tide (11).

Because the gunports of the *Serapis*' starboard battery, hitherto unengaged, were jammed so tightly against the *Richard*'s hull that they could not be opened, the gunners fired a salvo through the lids. Thereafter, gunners in each of the ships extended their ramrods into the other to reload, and the heavy shot from the guns, which were almost muzzle to muzzle, holed and gutted both ships. Meanwhile Yorkshiremen, attracted by the thunder of the cannonade, lined the heights of Flamborough Head to watch the battle, illuminated now only by the flash of gunfire and by moonlight shining intermittently through the clouds.

The *Serapis*' 18-pounders soon shattered or dismounted all of the *Richard*'s 12-pound main battery, leaving Jones only three usable guns, 9-pounders on the quarterdeck. One of these guns Jones himself served, aiming at the *Serapis*' mainmast. In the midst of this desperate situation, help appeared suddenly on the way as the *Alliance* was seen approaching. But, to the amazement and consternation of Commodore Jones and his crew, the American frigate opened fire on the *Richard*, holing her at the waterline and killing several men. The *Alliance* then disappeared again into the darkness. Early in the battle, shot from the frigate had struck the *Bonhomme Richard*. Now it was clear to all observers that she had aimed at the flagship deliberately. Captain Landais's purpose, as he afterward confided to an intimate, was to sink the *Richard*, capture the *Serapis*, and emerge the victor.

Sharpshooting marines and seamen in the *Richard*'s tops had now cleared the *Serapis*' weather decks of men.

The Bonhomme Richard, *bow to stern behind the* Serapis *(left), is fired upon by the* Alliance.

Captain Pearson, on his quarterdeck, alone was spared —probably by Jones' orders. Other sharpshooters, concealed in the *Richard*'s shattered gun deck and firing through ports and shot holes, picked off so many British gunners that the boy powder-monkeys were soon bringing gunpowder cartridges from the magazine faster than they could be used. The boys simply threw the spares on the deck and went for more.

Far overhead, one of the *Richard*'s seamen crawled out on a yardarm that projected over the *Serapis*. Through an open hatch he dropped a grenade that landed among the spare cartridges. These went off with a searing flash, killing at least 20 gunners and fearfully burning others. "Many," reported Lieutenant Dale, "stood with only the collars of their shirts upon their bodies." Others, their clothing afire, leapt screaming through the ports into the sea.

Pearson, unnerved, was about to strike his colors, when Jones' chief gunner, discovering that the *Richard* was sinking, bawled, "Quarters, quarters, for God's sake!" From his quarterdeck Pearson hopefully called, "Sir, do you ask for a quarter?" to which Jones replied, "No, sir, I haven't yet thought of it, but I am determined to make *you* strike."

Rising water would soon have drowned the hundred or more prisoners in the *Richard*'s hold had not the master at arms at this point opened a hatch and let them out. Most of the prisoners he set to work manning the pumps, but one wily fellow slipped away, wriggled through a port into the *Serapis*, and advised Captain Pearson that if he would only hold out a little longer, Jones must surely strike or sink.

The last half hour of the battle was chiefly a contest of nerve between Jones and Pearson. The *Serapis*' remaining below-deck guns continued to fire, splintering the *Richard*'s hull and frame until only a few stanchions held up the weather decks. Fires broke out intermittently in both ships. Jones, with the *Richard* slowly settling beneath him, kept banging away with single-minded intensity at the *Serapis*' mainmast, and at last the mast began to crack and sway. It was then that Pearson's nerve broke. With his own hands he tore down the ensign, which had been nailed by his orders to the staff; shortly afterward the mast came crashing down. The battle had lasted for more than three hours. Aboard the *Richard*, 150 men were killed or wounded, and at least 100 were dead or dying in the *Serapis*.

Despite continuous pumping, the *Bonhomme Richard*

proved beyond salvage. The day after the battle Jones ordered the ship abandoned and transferred his commodore's flag to the *Serapis*. From the *Serapis'* deck the next morning he watched "with inexpressible grief" as the old East Indiaman went down, her colors still flying. Then, while British warships frantically searched in all the wrong places, Commodore Jones' squadron, accompanied by its prizes, sailed unmolested across the North Sea and anchored off Texel Island in Dutch waters.

Dr. Franklin now summoned Captain Landais to Paris to explain his conduct. Landais was eventually court-martialed and dismissed from the Continental Navy, not for his actions off Flamborough Head but for his subsequent erratic behavior, which demonstrated that he was at least partly insane.

For the purpose of simplifying diplomatic negotiations over the presence in neutral Dutch waters of warships of a belligerent power, all of Jones' squadron except the *Alliance* was placed under French colors. Jones, assuming command of the *Alliance*, put out to sea on December 27, eluded the British blockade, and slipped by night past a British fleet anchored in the Downs. After a commerce-raiding cruise in Spanish waters, he brought the *Alliance* back into Lorient.

Jones now found himself the toast of France. Louis XVI presented him with a gold-hilted sword and invested him with the Order of Merit and the title Chevalier. Part of the reason for Jones' almost ecstatic reception by French society was that his victory stood out conspicuously in contrast to the failure of the combined fleets of France and Spain. During his cruise these fleets had sailed forth in brave array to stage an invasion of England, but had retired ignominiously without landing a man or firing a shot.

On returning to the United States, Jones received the thanks of Congress and was given command of his adopted country's first ship of the line, the *America*, then building at Portsmouth, New Hampshire. Before the ship was completed, the British defeat at Yorktown brought the war in the United States virtually to a close. In a gesture of gratitude, Congress presented the *America* to France.

Jones, deprived of his wartime profession by the coming of peace, was at loose ends. He spent several years abroad negotiating for prize money due him and his officers and men. He served in one unhappy campaign against the Turks as a rear admiral in the Russian navy. At last in 1790 he settled in Paris, once the scene of his greatest acclaim, now a city torn by revolution. In the midst of the storm Jones lived quietly in genteel poverty, without intimate friends, generally neglected,

and in declining health. Dying in July 1792 at the age of forty-five, he was saved from a pauper's funeral by the charity of a minor French official.

In 1905 the body of the great captain was finally claimed by the United States. President Theodore Roosevelt sent four cruisers to bring it home, and these were escorted into Chesapeake Bay by seven battleships. Jones' remains lay in a temporary brick vault at Annapolis until 1913, when, Congress having at last appropriated the necessary funds, they were placed in a marble sarcophagus with appropriate surroundings in the crypt beneath the U.S. Naval Academy chapel.

THE PENOBSCOT EXPEDITION, 1779

While Commodore Jones was bringing credit to the United States in the *Bonhomme Richard*, the Continental Navy back in home waters was involved in a dismal fiasco. The affair began bravely as an expedition to destroy a fort which the British and Loyalists were building in Penobscot Bay, a deep indentation in the coast of Maine, then a part of Massachusetts. It was believed that the fort was the nucleus of a base for naval operations against New England ports.

The Continental vessels in the expedition were the frigate *Warren*, the brig *Diligence*, and the sloop *Providence*, Jones' first independent command. Also on the expedition were 1 New Hampshire and 3 Massachusetts state navy vessels, as well as 12 privateers temporarily taken into the Massachusetts navy. The landing force of 3,000 men was carried in 20 transports. This respectable array of force, mounting 324 guns, put out from Boston on July 19, 1779, with Commodore Dudley Saltonstall of the *Warren* in overall command.

On arriving in Penobscot Bay on July 25, Saltonstall's squadron exchanged generally ineffective fire for two hours with three British sloops-of-war having a total of 56 guns. On the 28th, the American troops, supported by warships, landed on steep-banked Bagaduce peninsula (modern Castine) and chased the defending forces into their unfinished fort, then a mere breastwork.

It was obvious to most of the American officers that so large an operation as theirs could not be kept secret, and in fact it was known to British Commodore Sir George Collier in New York two days after the expeditionary force left Boston. Speed was therefore essential, but, while the defenders at Bagaduce were busily strengthening their fort, the American leaders settled down to a protracted debate. Because the British sloops were able to support the fort with gunfire, General Solomon Lovell, who commanded the expeditionary troops, would not move until the American fleet had captured, destroyed, or chased the sloops away. Commodore Saltonstall, supported by the privateer captains, replied that he would not expose his ships to the fire of the fort while going in after the sloops; the troops would first have to storm the fort and silence the guns.

While the debate continued, the squadron remained idle. On August 13 Commodore Collier arrived with a ship of the line, five frigates, and a sloop-of-war, whereupon the American ships fled up the Penobscot River with the British in hot pursuit. Had the American squadron been better led and disciplined, it might have turned on the British vessels, stretched out in a long line by the chase, and defeated them piecemeal. But among the panicky Americans it was every ship for itself. The captains ran their vessels aground, set fire to those that British guns did not destroy, and escaped with most of their men through the forest. American casualties were 500 killed or captured. Commodore Saltonstall

Drawing by a British officer of the Continental Navy expedition to Penobscot Bay.

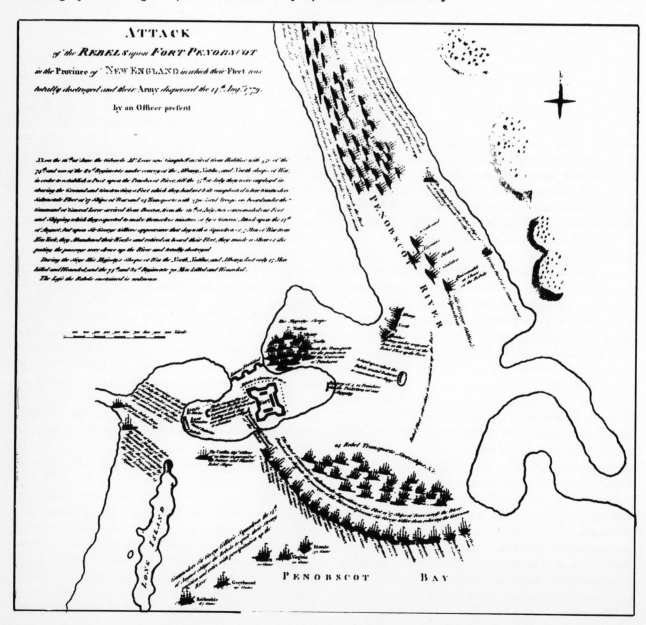

was later tried by court-martial and dismissed from the Navy.

THE YORKTOWN CAMPAIGN

Militarily the Revolution in America was a drawn-out stalemate in which only two campaigns, those of Saratoga and Yorktown, affected the outcome. The Saratoga campaign resulted from a British penetration into the United States from the north. The Yorktown campaign resulted from a British penetration from the south. Each ended with the defeat and capture of a British army, the defeats in each campaign being made possible by prior naval operations. Burgoyne's plan for the Saratoga campaign required the converging of distant British forces; this plan failed utterly. Washington's plan for the Yorktown campaign required the coming together of even more widely separated Franco-American forces. It succeeded with such precision—partly by chance—that it was the military wonder of the age.

In late 1779 General Clinton evacuated Newport in order to concentrate his forces at New York. A part of his New York army, thus enlarged, he took south by sea early the following year and laid siege to Charleston, South Carolina. Participating in the defense of Charleston were 10 ships, including 3 Continental frigates and the Continental sloop-of-war *Ranger.* Instead of contesting the entrance of the small British fleet through the narrow channel into Charleston harbor, the defending warships withdrew behind a boom and served as mere stationary gun platforms. When Charleston fell, they tamely surrendered. The *Ranger,* in which John Paul Jones had won fame and glory, became H.M.S. *Halifax.* Loss of a second squadron following hard upon the Penobscot disaster earned the Continental Navy general contempt.

In June 1780 Clinton, warned that General the Comte de Rochambeau had sailed from France for the United States with a division of troops, hastened back to New York with part of his army. He left 8,000 men, half of them Loyalist recruits, with Major General Cornwallis, his second-in-command. Rochambeau landed at Newport with 5,000 French soldiers on July 12.

From Charleston Lord Cornwallis set out to subdue the rebellion in the Carolinas. At Camden, South Carolina, he met an American army led by General Horatio Gates, victor at Saratoga. This time, however, Gates was so ignominiously defeated that he was hastily replaced by General Nathanael Greene. Detachments from the British southern army were wiped out at Kings Mountain and at Cowpens, but Cornwallis continued advancing northward and in March 1781 engaged Greene's army at Guilford Courthouse, North Carolina. Although the British at length routed the Americans, a quarter of Cornwallis' soldiers were killed or wounded. To restore his shattered army, Cornwallis marched into Virginia in order to take under his command a powerful British raiding force operating there. Greene moved south to reconquer the Carolinas with the aid of guerrilla troops.

In early August 1781, the main fighting forces in the American theater of war were located as follows: General Clinton was at New York with 17,000 troops; Rochambeau was at White Plains, having brought his 4,000 soldiers to join Washington's army of 6,000. Cornwallis was at Yorktown, Virginia, with 9,000 men; he was confronted by Major General the Marquis de Lafayette commanding 5,000 Americans, of whom about half were Virginia militia. At Newport was a French squadron of eight ships of the line under Commodore the Comte de Barras. At New York were five British ships of the line under Admiral Thomas Graves. In the West Indies was a French fleet of 28 ships of the line commanded by Admiral the Comte de Grasse, who had agreed to operate briefly on the U.S. coast; also in the West Indies was a 14-ship British fleet under Admiral Sir Samuel Hood. The movements and operations of these widely scattered forces constituted the Yorktown campaign.

To General Washington the most important units were the French fleets, which were powerful enough to isolate the British from the sea at either New York or Yorktown. He would have preferred to attack Clinton at New York but yielded to the preference of Rochambeau and de Grasse for a concentration against Cornwallis at Yorktown. Leaving behind 3,000 U.S. troops to garrison the Hudson forts, a Franco-American army of 7,000 men began crossing the river on August 20. After making a feint at Staten Island, they headed for Virginia. Clinton, who had captured a copy of Washington's original plan for an attack on New York, was deceived until too late.

Washington and Rochambeau, detained briefly in Philadelphia after their armies had marched through, proceeded for a time separately—Washington and his staff on horseback, Rochambeau by water in order to inspect the Delaware forts. As Rochambeau's boat came alongside the wharf at Chester, the French general was astonished to behold the usually sedate Washington wildly waving his hat in one hand, his handkerchief in the other. When Rochambeau stepped ashore, Washington flung his arms around him and announced

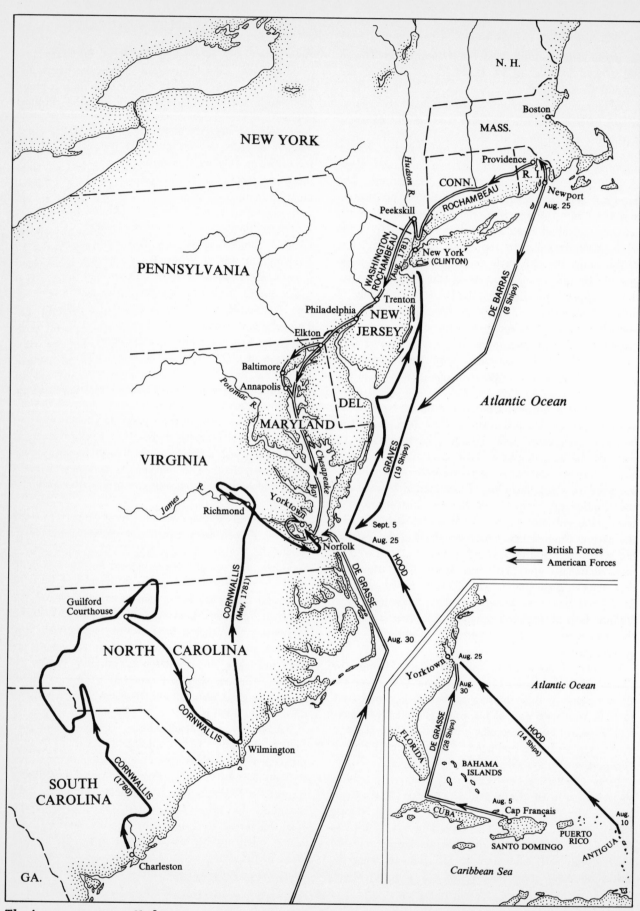

The forces converge on Yorktown.

the joyful news just received from Virginia: de Grasse had arrived in Chesapeake Bay with 28 ships of the line and 3,000 troops!

De Grasse, sailing from Santo Domingo on August 5, had taken a roundabout route west of the Bahamas to conceal his destination. Hood had sailed five days later from Antigua and, proceeding by the direct route, had reached the Virginia capes first. Finding the Chesapeake empty, he continued north, looked into Delaware Bay, and then proceeded to New York. Here Graves added his 5 available ships to Hood's 14 and, as senior, assumed the fleet command. He then shaped course for the Chesapeake. De Barras's 8 ships had left Newport several days before, escorting 18 transports loaded with siege guns, provisions, and military stores vitally needed in the Yorktown campaign.

De Grasse entered Chesapeake Bay on August 30, anchoring most of his ships just inside Cape Henry. On the morning of September 5, a frigate posted outside the bay signaled that sails had been sighted. It was the British fleet from New York. Although nearly 2,000 French seamen were ashore and four French ships were absent blockading the rivers, de Grasse prepared to sortie, since keeping his fleet in the bay would condemn the approaching de Barras to certain capture. The result was the curious Battle of the Virginia Capes.

The British, coming down before a northeast wind, altered course first to west and then, just outside the bay, to east in order to bring their column of ships alongside the emerging French formation for a formal line battle. Because the British van led down to engage, and because the French center and rear, beating out of the bay against the wind, were blown to leeward, the result was not two parallel lines of ships but a V, pointed seaward. Hence the opposing vans engaged furiously at close range, the centers at too great a distance, and the rears not at all.

In this situation both fleets were hampered by national traditions. The British, having the upwind position, could have closed all down the line, but not without breaking their line formation, which British tactical doctrine made inviolable. Many British naval officers were beginning to discard this old rule, but not Sir

Contemporary drawing of the Battle of the Virginia Capes.

Samuel Hood, who now commanded the British rear. A traditionalist, Hood kept his whole division on a straight line which extended through Graves' flagship at the center and as far as the leading British vessel. De Grasse might have taken advantage of the British rigidity by massing his whole fleet on the British van and center. But French doctrine was army-oriented, calling for defensive warfare at sea with minimum risk to ships. The result was a tactical draw, with the vans of both fleets severely mauled. Nevertheless the French had won a great strategic victory merely by insuring that de Barras would arrive safely and that Cornwallis would remain isolated at Yorktown.

The fleets maneuvered within sight of each other until September 9, when de Grasse, satisfied that de Barras had reached the Chesapeake, proceeded thither himself. Graves, opposed now by 36 ships, could only take his battered fleet back to New York, where he planned to refit, find more ships, and return with an army to reinforce Cornwallis. He was too late. On October 19, as Graves, with 23 ships and 6,000 troops, was putting out from New York a second time, Cornwallis surrendered his entire army to Washington's Franco-American forces besieging him at Yorktown.

Although fighting continued for more than a year in the Carolinas and Georgia, on the seas, and in India, Washington's victory over Cornwallis assured the independence of the United States. Lord North's Tory government in England was soon replaced by peace-minded Whigs, who promptly sent emissaries to Paris to negotiate peace terms with Dr. Franklin.

THE END OF THE CONTINENTAL NAVY

The Continental Navy, in which more than 50 ships had served, was reduced by 1781 to the frigates *Confederacy, Trumbull, Alliance,* and *Deane* and the sloop-of-war *Saratoga*. The Royal Navy in 1781 had nearly 400 ships in commission, including about 60 on the North American station. Before the end of the year the inefficient system of Congressional naval committees was abandoned, and Robert Morris, the Superintendent of Finance, administered what was left of the Continental Navy as a part-time job.

In March 1781 the *Confederacy,* the *Deane,* and the *Saratoga,* after a fruitless winter cruise in the West Indies, headed for home. As was usual when leaving the West Indian entrepots, they carried cargoes of military stores for the Continental Army. Of the three American vessels only the *Deane* made port. The *Saratoga* disappeared at sea; the *Confederacy,* so loaded with stores that the gunners could not work their guns, surrendered to a pair of British frigates.

The *Trumbull,* the last of the original 1775 frigates, spent most of the war in the Connecticut River, where she had been built, unable to get over the bar. Lifted out at last on floats, she had gone to sea in 1780 and had a terrific fight with the *Watts,* a heavily armed British merchantman, which got away. Requiring extensive repairs and refitting, the *Trumbull* did not get to sea again until August 1781. Partly dismasted in a storm, she was overtaken and captured by the frigate *Iris* and the sloop *General Monk,* after a fight that left her too shattered for further service.

Ironically, the *Trumbull's* captors were both former American ships. The *Iris* before being captured by the British in 1777 was the *Hancock,* another of the original 13 American frigates; the *General Monk* was the ex-U.S. privateer *General Washington*. The *Iris* was later captured by de Grasse's fleet following the Battle of the Virginia Capes. The *General Monk* was captured by the Pennsylvania state ship *Hyder Ali* under Captain Joshua Barney and renamed *General Washington*.

From September 1780 until the end of the war, the frigate *Alliance* was commanded by Irish-born Captain John Barry, one of the ablest and most popular officers of the Continental Navy. In February 1781 the *Alliance* sailed for France carrying General Washington's aide, Colonel John Laurens, to plead for money, supplies, and the cooperation of a French fleet.

On the return voyage, as the *Alliance* neared the United States, she was attacked by two light British men-of-war: the ship *Atalanta,* 16, and the brig *Trepassey,* 14. In a sea as calm as a mill pond, the *Alliance* lay like a log in the water, unable to maneuver. But the two British vessels got out sweeps and rowed around to place themselves athwart the frigate's stern and quarters, out of reach of her broadsides. From this position they kept up a steady fire. Captain Barry, wounded in the shoulder by a grape shot, had to be carried below. When a panicky officer came to request permission to haul down the American flag, Barry replied indignantly, "No, sir, and if the ship cannot be fought without me, I will be brought up on deck!" Before Barry could be dressed and carried up, a puff of wind filled the *Alliance's* sails, whereupon she turned a powerful broadside on her tormentors and in a few salvoes forced them both to surrender.

In March 1783 the *Alliance* fought the last naval battle of the war. En route home from Cuba bringing money for the use of Congress and escorting a smaller vessel, she was chased by two frigates and a sloop. Captain Barry, on sighting a 50-gun French ship, was emboldened to turn on his pursuers in hopes of saving his slow consort. While two of the British ships and the Frenchman merely watched each other warily, Barry ran the *Alliance* between his consort and the frigate *Sybil*, 32, on which he opened fire. In half an hour the American frigate had silenced the *Sybil's* guns, whereupon all the British ships fled. Barry gave chase, but broke off when the French ship proved too slow to support him.

When the Treaty of Paris ended the war in September 1783, the *Alliance* was the only vessel still in commission in the Continental Navy. None were added, for the war had demonstrated that any fleet the United States was capable of producing would achieve little of consequence when opposed to a first-class naval power. Moreover, the Americans were too impoverished by postwar debt and depression to afford any navy at all. There was some sentiment for retaining at least the *Alliance*, which had served under America's two most celebrated naval officers, Jones and Barry; but the need for economy precluded even this gesture. In 1785 the *Alliance* was sold and the Continental Navy passed into history. For the next 10 years the United States was without a navy.

II

Beginnings of the U.S. Navy

As an independent nation, the United States found its formerly prosperous maritime commerce severely curtailed by British Orders in Council. These Orders barred American merchant vessels from participating in the British carrying trade, limited imports from the United States to raw materials and naval stores, and excluded American ships from the British West Indies.

To offset these restrictions, American merchant skippers wandered farther and farther afield, opening new markets not only in Europe but also in the Near and Far East. They learned what it meant to have lost the protection of the Royal Navy when, in 1785, Algerian cruisers seized two American merchant ships off the Portuguese coast. These ships had fallen victim to the notorious Barbary System. For centuries the Barbary Powers of North Africa—Morocco, Algiers, Tunis, and Tripoli—had been capturing undefended merchantmen and enslaving their crews, who were released only on payment of stiff ransoms.

Immunity from such piracy could be obtained by payment of tribute, and most nations that traded in the Mediterranean area paid—even major naval powers like Britain—partly because it was cheaper than convoy or going to war, but chiefly because the Barbary System served as a check on commercial rivals. Concerning Algiers, the most aggressive of the four pirate states, it was a maxim among cynical London merchants that "if there were no Algiers, it would be worth England's while to build one."

Congress, which had no power to tax, could not raise money to pay tribute, to ransom the American crewmen in Algerian hands, or to finance a navy to protect the nation's shipping. This painful fact proved a convincing argument leading in 1789 to the adoption of the U.S. Constitution and the founding of a strong federal government under the presidency of George Washington. Under the Constitution, Congress established preferential tariffs and harbor duties that favored American shipping. The U.S. merchant marine, thus stimulated, began a rapid expansion.

In an early experiment at unification of the services, President Washington placed all actual and potential American armed forces under a War Department, naming as first Secretary of War his former artillery officer, General Henry Knox. Knox, having in mind the Algerian menace, early looked into the problem of acquiring warships; for advice concerning what sort of fleet the new government should have, he turned to shipwrights and merchant mariners and to officers of the defunct Continental Navy. These men advised the building of frigates, and, since they expected that Congress would authorize only a few, they recommended outsize 44-gun ships. Knox agreed, but leaving himself a path of retreat, sought and obtained estimates for smaller vessels as well.

It soon appeared that there would be no United States Navy after all, for Congressional repesentatives of southern and inland districts bitterly opposed general taxes which, in their opinion, would benefit only New England shippers. Moreover, the need for maritime protection had declined because Portugal, declaring war on Algiers, had sealed the Algerian cruisers within the Straits of Gibraltar.

In 1793 the picture changed abruptly, as revolutionary France declared war on Britain, inaugurating 22 years of almost continuous warfare involving most of Europe and parts of the Near East. Wartime demands for American goods and for the services of American shipping soared, bringing a wave of prosperity to the United States. American merchant vessels, despite laws and regulations to the contrary, were now welcomed in both the French and British West Indies, where the slave populations were heavily dependent on mainland foodstuffs.

Along with prosperity came frustration for the Americans, as France and Britain each sought to cut off the seaborne trade of the other. British warships seized neutral vessels carrying goods to France or laden with French produce. France licensed privateers to capture neutral merchantmen trading with England or her possessions. In late 1793 the British government prevailed upon the Portuguese to grant Algiers a truce, whereupon Algerian cruisers swarmed out into the Atlantic Ocean and promptly captured 11 American merchantmen.

Congress, spurred by this onslaught, passed the Navy Act on March 27, 1794, after acrimonious debate. This act, which created the United States Navy, provided for six frigates—three of 44 guns and three of 36. The Act specified, however, that work on the warships should stop if peace were made with Algiers. In 1796 the United States did in fact obtain a treaty from the Algerian ruler at the cost of $525,000 in ransoms, a 36-gun frigate, and an annual tribute of $21,000. Congress nevertheless permitted the completion of the frigates *United States*, 44, *Constellation*, 36, and *Constitution*, 44. All were launched in 1797.

The new 44-gun ships, which actually carried 50 or more guns, are generally called "Humphreys frigates" because the Philadelphia shipbuilder Joshua Humphreys drew the final designs. These remarkable vessels were, however, the product of many men's ideas, notably those of Josiah Fox, a brilliant young ship designer who had studied in the leading dockyards of Europe. They were more powerful than any other existing frigate and they were able to sail faster and come closer into the wind than any ship of the line. In short, they were designed to outrun anything they could not outfight.

The *Constitution* was as long as a ship of the line but considerably less broad of beam. Her mainmast soared 180 feet from her deck. She usually carried thirty 24-pounder guns in her main battery, instead of

The Constitution.

the 18-pounders with which frigates normally were armed. On her spar deck were twenty 32-pounder carronades—stubby, short-range guns designed for close combat.

The *Constellation*, a reduced version of the 44s, had an armament about equivalent to all but the most powerfully armed contemporary foreign frigates. Although rated a 36, she usually carried twenty-eight 18-pounders on her gun deck and at least ten carronades on her spar deck. Her fine lines made her extraordinarily maneuverable.

In operations to restrict each other's maritime commerce, Britain showed considerably more foresight than France. It was clear to the British that they, as well as the French, would increasingly need American foodstuffs and the services of American shipping at home and in the colonies. Therefore they early ceased impounding neutral vessels, limiting their seizures to goods they considered contraband, and paying for the seized cargoes. The British even permitted neutrals to carry goods between French colonies and France, provided the ships stopped en route at a neutral port and paid duty. They thus gave their own trade a competitive advantage by slowing down French goods without actually stopping them. In late 1784 Britain and the United States specifically codified Anglo-American maritime relations in Jay's Treaty, which set up arbitral commissions to adjudicate complaints.

Jay's Treaty was concluded at a time when poor harvests had made France heavily dependent on grain shipments from the United States. The wrath of the French government was therefore aroused by the treaty's failure to exempt foodstuffs from the list of seizable contraband. In retaliation the French Directory sent the new American minister packing and issued a series of harsh maritime decrees culminating in that of January 18, 1798, which provided for seizure without payment of any neutral ship and its entire cargo if the ship were found carrying any goods whatever of English origin.

Few French warships were able to elude the British blockade to enforce the decrees, but scores of French privateers swarmed in the West Indies and thence cruised along the U.S. Atlantic coast seeking prey. These quasi-pirates rarely attacked British vessels, which usually sailed in convoy, but in a single year they seized more than 300 American merchantmen.

President John Adams, endeavoring to avoid hostilities, sent a commission of three eminent citizens to Paris to seek an understanding with the French government comparable to the agreement reached with Britain in Jay's Treaty. When the commissioners were received by mere political underlings who demanded a huge bribe as a preliminary to opening negotiations, the Americans refused to pay. In the United States public reaction to the French insult was voiced in the slogan "Millions for defense but not one cent for tribute!"

Congress now ordered the completion of the three unfinished 1794 frigates, *President*, 44 guns, *Congress*, 36, and *Chesapeake*, 36; also ordered were the construction, purchase, and conversion of additional ships to form a respectable naval force. On April 30, 1798, Congress established a separate Navy Department. The following month it authorized seizure of armed French vessels operating in American coastal waters; in July the authorization to capture was extended to the high seas. Thus was launched an undeclared naval war, the Quasi-War with France.

THE QUASI-WAR WITH FRANCE, 1798–1800

As Vice-President, John Adams had been influential in pushing the Navy Act of 1794 through Congress.

Commodore Thomas Truxtun.

As President and Commander in Chief, he saw to it that American sailors received good pay and wholesome food, rare in navies of that period. He thereby assured ready recruitment of seamen from the merchant marine. Adams also showed excellent discernment in appointing as first Secretary of the Navy the Maryland merchant Benjamin Stoddert. Assuming his new duties with extraordinary energy, Stoddert rapidly acquired a formidable fleet. Throughout the period of hostilities he exhibited superior judgment and a keen strategic sense.

Within a few days after the initial Congressional authorization, Stoddert had his warships patrolling the Atlantic coast. The first capture was made by the purchased 20-gun vessel *Delaware*, which took the French privateer schooner *Croyable*, 14, after a chase off Delaware Bay. The *Croyable* was renamed *Retaliation* and taken into the U.S. Navy.

After Congress extended the area of operations, Stoddert sent successive expeditions to the West Indies, where most of the French raiders were based. The first expedition, commanded by Commodore* John Barry,

* Until the Civil War the highest rank in the U.S. Navy was captain. An officer who commanded a company of ships, however, was permitted to assume the courtesy title of commodore.

senior officer in the Navy, succeeded in taking only two prizes. There was no lack of zeal, but the numerous raiders were mostly small craft, able to elude the Americans by skipping into shoal water. The warships, however, proved invaluable as convoy escorts, and their mere presence deterred the privateers from their former bold depredations.

Included in the second expedition, which reached the West Indies in the fall of 1798, was the captured *Retaliation*, now commanded by Lieutenant William Bainbridge, an officer who was to encounter more than his share of bad luck. Off Guadeloupe his vessel was recaptured by the frigates *Insurgente*, 36, and *Volontaire*, 44. She was the only U.S. naval vessel captured during the war. The following year the Americans had the satisfaction of taking her from the French once more.

As the American coast became cleared of raiders, Stoddert sent the bulk of his forces, 21 ships organized in four squadrons, to patrol in assigned sectors from Cuba around the arc of the Antilles to Curaçao. Here the Americans had the advantage of operating out of British bases and the still greater advantage, for a fledgling fleet, of close association with officers and men of the Royal Navy in its golden age of sail.

Commodore Thomas Truxtun, whose squadron was based on St. Kitts, ordered his ships to patrol singly. In early February 1799, he himself was patrolling in the *Constellation* northwest of Nevis when he sighted a sail and promptly gave chase. The strange vessel was soon recognized as a frigate; she was, in fact, the *Insurgente*, one of the captors of Bainbridge's *Retaliation*.

When a sudden squall struck both ships, the *Constellation* managed to shorten sail in time, but the *Insurgente* lost her main topmast. The *Constellation*, on coming within range, fairly danced around her opponent; easily eluding the *Insurgente*'s attempt to board, she pounded her hull from port and starboard and twice crossed her bows delivering raking fire.

When Truxtun maneuvered the *Constellation* across

The Constellation *captures the* Insurgente.

the *Insurgente*'s stern for a third raking, the French frigate struck her colors. French losses were 29 killed and 41 wounded. Three Americans were wounded and 1 was killed during the battle, not by enemy fire but by his own division officer for abandoning his gun. The captain of the *Insurgente* blamed his defeat on the early loss of his topmast and the *Constellation*'s superior firepower, but no one could deny that the Americans had put on a dazzling display of shiphandling and marksmanship.

The brilliance of this performance was largely due to Truxtun, a thoroughgoing professional officer and a stern and tireless drillmaster. He sought in his ship and squadron to equal or surpass the standards set by the Royal Navy officers, whom he rightly considered the masters of their profession. A man of wide learning in maritime matters, he had published a manual of celestial navigation and was the author of the first complete signal book used in the U.S. Navy.

Almost exactly a year after his capture of the *Insurgente*, Truxtun, again aboard the *Constellation*, sighted a large French frigate near Guadeloupe. Again he gave chase. This time Truxtun was taking his ship against a far more powerful vessel, the *Vengeance*, armed with more than 50 guns. Bound for France with passengers and specie, the *Vengeance* was anxious to avoid battle.

After a daylong pursuit, the *Constellation* drew abeam of the French frigate toward 8 P.M. There followed a five-hour running gun duel of almost unparalleled ferocity. The *Vengeance* wasted a good many shot firing at the *Constellation*'s spars and rigging in an attempt to escape. The *Constellation*, on the contrary, fired steadily at her opponent's hull, gradually silencing her fire. The captain of the *Vengeance* tried to surrender, but in the darkness and amid the roar of gunfire, the Americans neither saw his flag nor heard his hail.

Toward 1 A.M. the *Constellation*'s mainmast came crashing down, and the frigates drifted apart. Six days later the *Vengeance*, only the stumps of her foremast and mizzenmast standing, and kept afloat by furious pumping, ran her riddled hull aground at Curaçao to avoid sinking. The *Constellation*, her spars and rigging a mass of tangled wreckage, made no attempt to beat back to St. Kitts, but fell off downwind 600 miles to Jamaica; her casualties were 14 killed and 25 wounded. Casualties in the *Vengeance* were reported to be more than 150.

In 1800 two fast 12-gun schooners, the *Enterprise* and the *Experiment*, reached the West Indies. These small vessels, built especially for chasing privateers in shoal water, soon proved their worth. In six months the "lucky little *Enterprise*" captured 13 vessels. The *Experiment* was only a little less successful; in one notable battle, while becalmed with a convoy she was escorting, she beat off several hundred attackers that swarmed out from shore in barges.

In the last battle of the undeclared war on October 12, 1800, U.S. frigate *Boston*, 28, defeated the corvette *Berceau*, 24, 600 miles northeast of Guadeloupe. Unknown to the participants, a convention of peace had already been concluded between representatives of France and the United States. The French government canceled both its obnoxious decree of 1798 and the Franco-American alliance of 1778, which had become an embarrassment to the United States. The Americans canceled their claims against the French for spoliation of their maritime commerce.

In a little more than two years the U.S. fleet had grown to a respectable force of 34 ships, and these ships had captured some 80 French vessels. The value of American exports had grown to more than $200 million and the revenue from imports to more than $22 million. The cost of protecting this commerce from French depredations had amounted only to about $6 million in naval appropriations. It had been abundantly demonstrated that the Navy not only benefited New England shipping but was vital to the whole national economy.

THE WAR WITH TRIPOLI, 1801–1805

With the conclusion of hostilities between the United States and France, Congress voted to reduce the Navy to a peacetime establishment. President Thomas Jefferson, who took office in March 1801, carried out the reduction vigorously. Secretary Stoddert's plan to build six ships of the line was shelved. All ships in service were sold except for the *Enterprise* and 13 frigates, 7 of which were laid up in reserve. The naval officer corps was reduced to 9 captains, 36 lieutenants, and 150 midshipmen, and navy pay was severely cut.

When Jefferson took office, American relations with the Barbary rulers were reaching a new crisis. The Dey of Algiers, by threatening to renew warfare against American shipping, had recently forced the captain of U.S. frigate *George Washington*, unlucky William Bainbridge, to transport passengers and cargo to Constantinople. Next, the Pasha of Tripoli began demanding more tribute.

Jefferson, though an avowed pacifist, preferred war to the indignity of a purchased peace. Instead of money to buy immunity, he sent to the Mediterranean a squadron of ships to protect American trade. The Tripolitan pasha, enraged that his demands were disregarded, declared war Barbary-style by ordering the American consul's flagpole chopped down.

The following summer, the schooner *Enterprise,* on detached duty near Malta, encountered the pasha's cruiser *Tripoli,* of about equal strength. The *Enterprise* opened fire. Although the Tripolitans tried to board— their preferred mode of fighting, for which they were much feared—American shiphandling and marksmanship thwarted each attempt. The *Enterprise,* without losing a man or a spar, repeatedly raked the *Tripoli,* forcing her to surrender with more than half of her crew of 80 dead or wounded. Having not yet received authority to take prizes, the Americans stripped the pirate craft to a single mast and a rag of a sail, and set her adrift.

In 1802 the first squadron was relieved by a more powerful one, which included five frigates. The most striking achievement of this new squadron was the capture of one Tripolitan cruiser and the destruction of another with gunfire. The squadrons had from time to time blockaded the port of Tripoli, but with indifferent effect, because they lacked shallow-draft vessels to attack shoal-hugging small freighters. At the end of two years the Americans appeared little nearer to victory than at the beginning. They had certainly found no means of inducing the pasha to lower his price for peace: $200,000 and reimbursement for all expenses of the war.

President Jefferson and the new Secretary of the Navy, Robert Smith, were far from satisfied with the state of affairs. It seemed to them that their squadron commanders lacked aggressiveness; Jefferson and Smith blamed their lack of achievement in part on rivalries among the officers. Smith, hoping to get the war off dead center, had picked the hard-fighting Truxtun to head the second squadron. But Truxtun, informed that he could not have a captain for his flagship, declined the command. The Secretary, disgusted, chose to interpret his refusal as resignation from the Navy, and Truxtun was out. Smith then named Captain Richard Morris to the post, but after several months the Secretary recalled Morris for general inactivity and the President dismissed him from the service.

The third squadron, sent to the Mediterranean in 1803, was composed of five shallow-draft brigs and schooners, most of them newly built, backed by the frigates *Philadelphia* and *Constitution.* Smith now selected as commodore a very junior captain, forty-two-year-old Edward Preble, little known to the other officers and hence not involved in their rivalries. During the

Edward Preble.

Quasi-War with France Preble had cruised to the Orient and had since been on the sick list.

A dour, irascible New Englander, Preble at first made an unfavorable impression on his officers, who resented his sharp tongue and the harsh discipline he imposed. Preble, for his part, was shocked to find that all of his officers were under thirty. "They have given me nothing but a pack of boys!" he snorted. Mutual dislike gradually changed, however, to mutual respect. The young men came to recognize that their commodore, though severe, was just; that he was a sick man driving himself to the utmost; that he was an officer of high professional competence; and that his austere manner concealed a warm heart and fiery aggressiveness. Preble discovered that his officers were apt learners, quickly imbued with his own professional ideals and aggressive spirit. The term "Preble's boys" ceased to be a stigma. For the officers of the third squadron it became a proud title, especially when, in later years, most of them had risen to commanding positions in the Navy, and in the War of 1812 written their names large in history.

Preble, on reaching Gibraltar in the *Constitution,* found that the *Philadelphia,* having arrived earlier, had brought in a Moroccan cruiser caught red-handed with a captured American merchantman. Confronted with this clear violation of treaty, Preble acted with dispatch. He sent the *Philadelphia* and the schooner *Vixen* ahead under command of Captain Bainbridge to blockade Tripoli. He then assembled a powerful force, including frigates from the squadron he was relieving, and proceeded across to the Moroccan port of Tangier, where he anchored and cleared decks for action. The Emperor of Morocco, impressed by this show of strength, promptly repudiated the capture and confirmed his treaty with the United States without demanding further payment.

In late November Preble, while cruising off Sardinia, learned from the captain of a British frigate the appalling news that the *Philadelphia* had been captured by the Tripolitans. "Hard Luck Bill" Bainbridge had lost another American warship. This loss was at least partly a result of faulty judgment. Preble had sent the *Vixen* along with the *Philadelphia*, not only for inshore work, but for mutual support also. Bainbridge, informed that two Tripolitan cruisers were at sea, unwisely sent the schooner 300 miles away to patrol the strait between Tunis and Sicily on the possibility of intercepting them.

Several days later the *Philadelphia* sighted a vessel making for Tripoli harbor and gave chase, only to run aground on an uncharted shoal. Heeled sharply to port, the frigate could not use her guns against the Tripolitan gunboats that soon gathered on her starboard side. The gunboats fired mainly at the *Philadelphia*'s masts and rigging to make sure she could not escape. The Tripolitans hoped to capture the Americans for ransom; they wanted the frigate for their fleet.

Bainbridge, perceiving his situation to be hopeless, at last surrendered. He and his crew of more than 300 were conducted to the city to begin a long and harsh captivity. Two days later a shift of wind floated the *Philadelphia* free, and the Tripolitans towed her triumphantly to an anchorage under the guns of the city forts.

Although possession of the *Philadelphia* gave the Tripolitans as much naval power as the Americans now had in the Mediterranean, Preble had no thought of falling back on Gibraltar to await reinforcements. Basing his squadron on Syracuse, Sicily, he maintained as tight a blockade on the port of Tripoli as the stormy winter weather would permit. In the *Constitution* he personally reconnoitered Tripoli harbor from outside the reef and concluded that, while it would not be possible to recapture the well guarded *Philadelphia*, there was a chance that she might be destroyed.

Lieutenant Stephen Decatur, the youthful captain of the *Enterprise*, agreed with his commodore's conclusion and volunteered to lead the expedition against the frigate. Preble accepted the offer, as well as Decatur's suggestion that they use a recently captured Tripolitan ketch, renamed *Intrepid*, because her Mediterranean rig would arouse no suspicion in Tripoli harbor.

On the evening of February 16, 1804, the *Intrepid*, bearing 84 officers and men, all volunteers, entered the harbor of Tripoli under a crescent moon. At the ship's helm was Salvador Catalano, a Sicilian pilot who could speak Arabic and who knew every rock and shoal of the harbor. Next to him stood Decatur. These two, and a few sailors visible on deck, were in Maltese dress; all the rest were concealed.

At 10 P.M., as the *Intrepid* approached the *Phila-*

The Barbary States.

delphia, a voice from the frigate hailed, ordering the ketch to keep clear. Catalano replied that his ship had lost her anchors in a storm and requested permission to tie up alongside the frigate for the night. A line was passed, but as the two vessels drew together, the Tripolitan watch, suddenly suspicious, cried, *"Americanos!"*

"Board!" shouted Decatur, and the Americans, sabers flashing, swarmed over the bulwarks and up the chains onto the *Philadelphia.* The Tripolitans, seized with panic, fled. Some 20 were cut down, many jumped overboard. When the Americans had cleared the frigate's decks, they distributed combustibles from the *Intrepid,* setting them afire. As the *Philadelphia* began to blaze, they hastened back to the *Intrepid,* quickly cutting her loose to save her from igniting. Decatur was the last man off the burning frigate, leaping into the rigging of the *Intrepid* as she pulled away. The Americans, using sails and sweeps, propelled themselves rapidly out of the harbor, as shot from the city forts, which were now thoroughly aroused, splashed about them.

The fire in the *Philadelphia* spread rapidly, glowed through her ports, crept up her masts and out on her spars. As her double-shotted guns became heated, they began firing—one broadside into a nearby fort, the other into the city. Then her cable burned through and she drifted nearer to the pasha's waterside castle and blew up.

News of the American exploit caused a widespread sensation. Lord Nelson, blockading Toulon, called the burning of the *Philadelphia* "the most bold and daring act of the age." President Jefferson, on Preble's recommendation, promoted the twenty-five-year-old Decatur to captain.

The following summer Preble's squadron, aided by six gunboats and two mortar boats borrowed from the King of Naples, began a series of bombardments of the city of Tripoli, its forts, and its shipping. During the first attack on August 3, Tripolitans in nine gunboats came out through the harbor reef and converged on three gunboats manned by Americans. The Tripolitans intended to board and fight hand-to-hand, but it was the outnumbered Americans who did the boarding, and in the ensuing fierce battle across decks, they completely exploded the myth of Barbary invincibility in hand-to-hand combat. Six of the Tripolitan gunboats finally fled, leaving three in American hands.

At the height of the battle, Stephen Decatur broke off the blade of his cutlass on the pike of a giant Tripolitan. He then wrested the pike from his opponent and wrestled him to the deck. Another Tripolitan raised his scimitar to split Decatur's head, but a seaman, Daniel Frazier, who had been wounded in both arms, thrust

Stephen Decatur.

his own head under the descending weapon, which laid bare his skull. The big Tripolitan now rolled Decatur under him and drew a knife. Decatur, holding his opponent's knife hand with his own left, reached into his pocket, drew out a pistol, and wrapping his right arm around the man, fired into his back. The fellow crumpled and Decatur stepped free.

In the three gunboats captured by the Americans were 47 dead Tripolitans; of the 49 taken prisoner, 26 were wounded. Thirteen Americans had been wounded. The only American killed was Lieutenant James Decatur, Stephen Decatur's younger brother, who was treacherously shot in the head as he stepped to take possession of an enemy boat that had surrendered.

During the next month Preble's squadron bombarded Tripoli whenever weather permitted. No Tripolitan vessels again ventured outside the harbor. The only serious damage to the Americans occurred when a shot penetrated the magazine of one of the captured gunboats, causing it to blow up, killing 2 officers and 10 men. The

Decatur and his fellow Americans fight with Tripolitans after boarding their gunboats.

pasha, seeing his capital being reduced to rubble, offered to settle for $150,000 in ransoms and to demand no more tribute, but Commodore Preble rejected the offer.

As a special inducement to the pasha to bring down his price, Preble, in early September, ordered the ketch *Intrepid* loaded with gunpowder and shells and sent it by night into Tripoli harbor. The volunteer crew of 3 officers and 10 men was to place the ketch between the Tripolitan fleet and the pasha's castle, light a fuse, and row rapidly away. But from unknown causes the *Intrepid* blew up prematurely, lighting up the city and harbor with a blinding flash. There were no survivors, and no damage was done to the enemy.

Five additional American frigates, the reinforcements that Preble had repeatedly requested, were now arriving in the Mediterranean. Since by law each frigate was commanded by a captain, Preble was now outranked

and therefore superseded. On September 10, 1804, Captain Samuel Barron took over as commodore of the squadron, and Preble departed for the United States, where he received the thanks of President Jefferson and of Congress. Preble was hailed everywhere as a hero, but he had little time left to enjoy his fame. His health failed rapidly and in 1807 he died of tuberculosis at the age of forty-six.

Commodore Barron and his successor, Commodore John Rodgers, maintained a close and effective blockade of the port of Tripoli with the most powerful American naval force ever assembled. The borrowed mortar boats, which were in poor condition, were returned to the kingdom of Naples; nine new gunboats and two mortar boats were due from the United States in the summer of 1805. Rodgers planned, with the aid of these boats, to renew the frontal attacks on the city.

Meanwhile, in the absence of direct offensive action against the enemy, William Eaton, whom the Secretary of the Navy sent to the Mediterranean as Navy Agent, took matters into his own hands. This fiery veteran of the Revolution proceeded to Egypt, there located Hamet Karamanli, the deposed elder brother of the reigning pasha of Tripoli, and easily persuaded him and his followers to join an expedition to seize the Tripolitan throne from the usurper. With the help of volunteers, including nine Americans from the squadron, "General" Eaton hired an army of several hundred men, including Arab tribesmen and foreign adventurers. At the head of this motley, half-mutinous horde, he marched 600 miles across the desert into Tripolitan territory. In late April 1805, with fire support from three small American warships, Eaton's men captured the port of Derna and held the town in the face of repeated counterattacks by the Tripolitan army.

The pasha, trembling for his throne, at last capitulated. In return for abandonment of American support for Hamet's forces at Derna, he agreed to a peace treaty including no further tribute, but requiring the payment of $60,000 in ransoms for the release of the *Philadelphia*'s officers and men. Eaton, believing himself on the brink of victory, was embittered by the treaty, but it was pointed out to him that no nation had ever exacted more favorable terms from a Barbary ruler. Moreover, it was believed with good reason that the pasha, if pushed to desperation, would have massacred his American captives before relinquishing his crown.

The officers of Preble's third squadron, before leaving the Mediterranean, ordered a monument carved in Italy in memory of their fallen comrades. The "Tripoli Monument," brought to the United States in the *Constitution*, stood for many years in Washington before it was finally moved to the grounds of the U.S. Naval Academy.

III

The War of 1812

Commodore James Barron, on board the 38-gun frigate *Chesapeake* as it passed out through the capes of Virginia on June 22, 1807, had reached the peak of his career. He was en route to take command of the U.S. Mediterranean Squadron, the post his brother Samuel had held during the War with Tripoli.

A British frigate, the 44-gun *Leopard*, had put to sea from Hampton Roads at the same time as the *Chesapeake*, which she approached 10 miles off the capes. The *Leopard*'s captain hailed and sent over a boat with a lieutenant, who presented Barron with a written demand that he submit to search for deserters from the Royal Navy. Barron, suppressing his indignation, penned a dignified refusal and sent it back.

In the bitter economic warfare of blockade and counterblockade that marked the Napoleonic Wars, the British and French had resumed wholesale confiscation of ships of the U.S. merchant marine, now the world's chief neutral carrier. Despite the spoliations, there was little effective pressure for war among Americans because the influential men of the Atlantic seaboard were profiting handsomely. When, however, the chronically undermanned Royal Navy resumed its detestable practice of impressing seamen from neutral vessels, American wrath turned against Britain.

The U.S. government was partly to blame, for it did nothing to discourage British deserters to American commercial and naval vessels. These deserters, given an opportunity, jumped ship to take advantage of the better treatment and better pay offered by the Americans.

British captains were reluctant to put into U.S. ports, lest they come away dangerously undermanned. Because the Americans themselves did nothing about this distressing situation, Britain claimed the right to retrieve her deserters on the high seas. British press captains searching American merchantmen used the most arbitrary means of distinguishing between nationalities. Said one Royal Navy officer: "It is my duty to keep my ship manned, and I will do so whenever I find men that speak the same language with me." Thus thousands of American merchant seamen were forced into virtual slavery in British men-of-war. Before the *Leopard* hailed the *Chesapeake*, however, never had a British officer demanded the right to remove men from a vessel of the U.S. Navy.

Shortly after the British lieutenant left the *Chesapeake*, Barron quietly passed the word ordering his men to quarters—no simple operation, for the American frigate was utterly unready for combat, her crew was untrained, and stores were piled around her guns. Therefore, when the *Leopard* opened fire, killing 3 Americans and wounding 18, the helpless *Chesapeake* could only strike her colors. A party from the *Leopard* then came aboard, mustered the crew, and took off four men, only one of whom proved actually to be a British deserter. He was promptly hanged.

Indignation and demands for a declaration of war swept the United States. "Never since the Battle of Lexington," said President Jefferson, "have I seen this country in such a state of exasperation." Barron, tried before a court-martial of his disgusted fellow officers, was convicted of negligence and sentenced to five years' suspension without pay.

The pacifist Jefferson tried to stem the tide of war by pushing through Congress an embargo on exports. This embargo brought on such economic depression that it was replaced by less stringent nonintercourse acts. When these acts were at last suspended, spoliations and impressments at sea resumed as before.

James Madison became President in 1909, and the following year Congressional elections swept into office from the South and West militant young "war hawks," who demanded an end to pacifism and urged an invasion of Canada. On June 16, 1812, the British government, in a conciliatory move, suspended its Orders in Council. Congress, unaware of this major concession, declared war on Britain two days later.

The United States seagoing navy then consisted of 7 frigates and 9 smaller types. There were also several hundred useless little gunboats, built at the behest of Jefferson, who had the mistaken notion that they were adequate for coast defense and hence all the navy the country needed. The Royal Navy had more than 600 seagoing vessels, including 124 ships of the line and 116 frigates.

THE WAR AT SEA

Commodore John Rodgers, anticipating war, was holding in readiness at New York a squadron composed of three frigates, a sloop-of-war, and a brig. On learning that war had been declared, he immediately hove out the signal to weigh anchor, and put to sea. Rodgers' objective was a huge Jamaican convoy bound for Britain. Two days out, however, the squadron was diverted into a daylong chase of the British frigate *Belvidera*, which escaped by jettisoning boats, spare anchors and spars, and drinking water—ship-lightening measures the Americans dared not imitate at the beginning of a long cruise. The diversion cost Rodgers his original prey. Less than a day's sailing from England, he reluctantly abandoned the pursuit and headed for the Canary Islands, hoping to snap up British merchantmen in the easterly trade winds.

The arrival of the *Belvidera* at Halifax brought Vice Admiral Herbert Sawyer his first knowledge that hostilities had begun, together with the horrifying news that the New York–based squadron was at sea in convoy waters. Sawyer instantly canceled his war plan of placing a ship or two off each American port. Instead he sent the entire Halifax squadron, led by Commodore Sir Philip Broke, to cruise off New York in hopes of intercepting Rodgers' ships on their return.

Off Sandy Hook the Halifax squadron pursued and captured U.S. brig *Nautilus*, 14. It also very nearly captured U.S. frigate *Constitution*, which Captain Isaac Hull was bringing up from the Chesapeake to join Rodgers' squadron, supposing it to be still at New York. Hull recognized the enemy in time and promptly hauled to the southeast. There followed a three-day chase famous in American naval annals. On July 18 Hull, perceiving that he was heading into a squall, ordered his topmen aloft. As wind and rain hit the *Constitution*, the men, on the captain's orders, quickly brought the ship under short sail as if they feared capsizing. The British, downwind, observing what appeared to be emergency measures aboard the American, hastily shortened sail also and made everything snug before the storm should hit them. Meanwhile, the brief squall having passed over the *Constitution*, and rain concealing her from her pursuers, she hoisted all sail and darted ahead. The British, thus duped, never caught up again. Hull, barred from New York, made for Boston, where he arrived on July 26. By this time Commodore Broke, having learned of the approach of another homebound British convoy from the Caribbean, headed eastward with his squadron to rendezvous with the convoy and escort it past Newfoundland.

Isaac Hull, one of "Preble's boys," now a short and portly thirty-nine, was an outstanding shiphandler in a navy of shiphandling experts. Ardent for battle, he kept the *Constitution* in Boston only long enough to replenish. On August 2 he was again at sea, training his crew at the great guns and keeping a sharp lookout for British ships. When the master of an American privateer reported having been chased by a British man-of-war, Hull promptly shaped course to intercept the Briton, which was in fact H.M. frigate *Guerrière*, recently detached by Broke back to Halifax for refit.

Of all British ships Americans most detested the *Guerrière*, because of her flagrant impressments of seamen. She had a new captain now, James Dacres, who at the outbreak of hostilities had sent into New York by merchant vessel a challenge for Commodore Rodgers, stating that "Captain Dacres, Commander of His Britannic Majesty's frigate *Guerrière* . . . will be very happy to meet the *President*, or any other American frigate of equal force . . . for the purpose of having a few minutes' tête-à-tête." Now, in the afternoon of August 17, 1812, Captain Hull in the *Constitution*, sister to the *President*, was coming over the horizon to accept Dacres' challenge.

Dacres knew that the *Constitution* was more power-

The Constitution *versus the* Guerrière.

fully armed than his *Guerrière*, but British naval officers, long victorious over every foe, had come to scorn such odds. Announced Dacres to his crew: "There is a Yankee frigate. In 45 minutes she is certainly ours. Take her in 15 and I promise you four months' pay."

As the American frigate came down before the wind, the *Guerrière* wore three times, crossing the *Constitution*'s bows and firing broadsides. To avoid raking fire, Hull yawed ship, conforming to the movements of his opponent. Such shot as struck the thick sides of the *Constitution* bounced off harmlessly, earning her forever the nickname "Old Ironsides." The *Guerrière*, inviting close combat, now settled on a course nearly before the wind, whereupon the *Constitution* set her main topgallant sail and foresail and surged up alongside the Briton. Hull coolly held his fire until the guns of his starboard battery all bore on the enemy. Then leaping into the air he shouted, "Pour in the whole broadside!" whereupon his tight white breeches burst asunder at the seam.

In the furious cannonade that followed, American shot tore up the *Guerrière*'s sails and rigging and smashed into her hull, sending clouds of lethal splinters mast high. The enemy's mizzenmast soon began to sway and presently crashed over the side, causing the ship to lose way and pivot to starboard. The *Constitution* now forged ahead and crossed her opponent's bows, raking her fore and aft, then wore about to give the Briton another raking.

This time the *Guerrière*'s bowsprit fouled the *Constitution*'s mizzen rigging, whereupon both captains called boarders away. As the men left their guns and crowded to the point of contact, sharpshooters in the tops inflicted heavy casualties, especially in the *Guerrière*, where Captain Dacres was among the wounded. Before either crew succeeded in boarding, the frigates wrenched apart with much snapping of lines, and the weakened fore- and mainmasts of the *Guerrière* came crashing down.

The *Guerrière* now lay a helpless wreck, rolling the muzzles of her main battery under water. Hull, after making repairs to his rigging, returned to give her another raking, whereupon the British frigate, which had no flag left to strike, fired a gun to leeward in token of surrender. There were 15 killed and 63 wounded on the *Guerrière;* on the *Constitution* there were 7 killed and 7 wounded. The battle had lasted less than half an hour.

In compliance with custom, Captain Dacres, half dazed, his face stony, soon arrived by boat alongside the *Constitution* and began painfully to climb the rope ladder. Hull leaned over solicitously. "Dacres, give me your hand," said he. "I know you are hurt." When the captain of the defeated *Guerrière* offered his sword, Hull refused it, saying, "No, no, I will not take a sword from one who knows so well how to use it."

The *Guerrière* proving beyond salvage, Hull ordered the hulk set afire and returned to Boston.

Hull's victory was simply an example of a powerful frigate defeating one less powerful and less well handled. Nevertheless, news of the battle was received with astonishment on both sides of the Atlantic—astonishment mingled, in the United States, with exultation; in England, with dismay, even disbelief. Captain Dacres could never bring himself to attribute his defeat to anything but hard luck. Said he at his court-martial: "I am so well aware that the success of my opponent was owing to fortune, that it is my earnest wish to be once more opposed to the *Constitution,* with the same officers and crew under my command, in a frigate of similar force to the *Guerrière.*"

Rodgers' squadron reached Boston on August 31, two days after the *Constitution*'s triumphant return. Rodgers soon learned that in his absence the small frigate *Essex* had made a cruise in which she had cut out of convoy and made prize of a transport full of soldiers, captured a British sloop-of-war, and taken four merchantmen. In contrast, all Rodgers had to show for his 70-day transoceanic sweep was eight rather insignificant prizes. Yet his squadron had performed a profound service to the nation. By disappearing en masse into the Atlantic, it had induced the British ships based on Halifax first to concentrate before New York and then to escort the Jamaicamen past Newfoundland. All U.S. ports were thus left free of blockade long enough for hundreds of American merchant ships to reach home from abroad, and for numerous American privateers, as well as the *Constitution* and the *Essex,* to put to sea.

In the autumn of 1812, the Navy Department organized its seagoing forces into three squadrons of three ships each, under Commodores John Rodgers, Stephen Decatur, and William Bainbridge. All were to cruise against British sea-borne commerce. The sloop-of-war *Wasp,* 18, commanded by Master Commandant Jacob Jones, was ordered to leave Philadelphia and rendez-

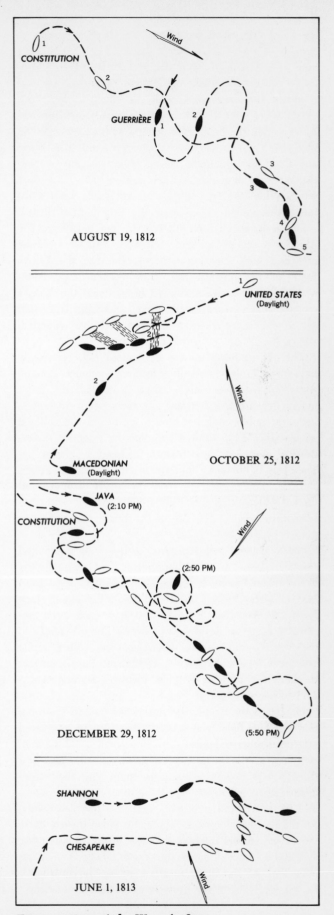

Frigate actions of the War of 1812.

vous at sea with Rodgers' frigates *President* and *Congress,* which had sailed from Boston.

Before the rendezvous could be effected, the *Wasp* encountered a small British convoy and was challenged by its escort, the brig *Frolic,* armed with 22 guns. While the merchantmen of the convoy scattered, the *Wasp* and the *Frolic* gradually closed on converging courses, the *Wasp* holding the weather position in a brisk west wind. When the two ships were 60 yards apart Captain Jones hailed, whereupon the brig hoisted British colors and opened fire with cannon and musketry. The Americans replied in kind, but at a somewhat slower rate and with superior accuracy. Because the British fired on the upward roll, they wasted many shot; nevertheless they were able to bring down the *Wasp*'s maintopgallant yard, gaff, and maintopgallant sail. All American casualties, five killed and five wounded, were among those stationed in the tops.

The *Wasp,* firing on the downward roll, repeatedly hulled the *Frolic,* gradually silencing her guns. Enough American shot went high, however, to gall the brig's masts. Because the shot also cut away her head braces, her after sails swung her bow to port, and she collided against the *Wasp* with a grinding jar. Captain Jones, quickly assessing the situation, ordered his helm up. The brig's jibboom, fouling in the *Wasp*'s mizzen shrouds, now passed just over the heads of Jones and First Lieutenant James Biddle. The *Frolic,* with her bow thrust against the side of the *Wasp,* was now in a perfect position to be raked.

Jones already had his guns loaded with grape and canister. Two of his 12-pounders fired through the *Frolic*'s bow ports, sweeping her weather deck from bow to stern. Before the *Wasp* could fire again, Jack Lang, an American seaman who had once been impressed into the Royal Navy, swung himself across to the British ship, cutlass between teeth, intent upon venting his personal grudge. Lieutenant Biddle, unable to check the ardor of his men, followed, leading over a general boarding party.

On board the *Frolic,* the Americans paused in stupefaction. The deck was a gory shambles of mutilated and dismembered bodies. Only four men could be seen standing, a courageous old tar manning the wheel and three severely wounded officers supporting themselves against uprights. Except for these men, all of the members of the *Frolic*'s crew who were able had fled below. As Biddle picked his way along the blood-slicked deck, the British officers threw down their swords in surrender, and Biddle hauled down the *Frolic*'s flag. A moment later both of the brig's masts went by the board. Of her crew of 110, at least 90 were casualties.

Before Captain Jones could get his vessel rerigged, a British ship of the line, the 74-gun *Poictiers,* came over the horizon and captured the *Wasp* and her prize. Both ships were taken to Bermuda, where the Americans were exchanged for British captives. The *Frolic* was found to be too wrecked for further service.

Commodore Decatur, in the frigate *United States,* separated at sea from his accompanying ships and sailed alone in the conviction that vessels operating individually could cover more area, escape from overwhelming force more readily, and, if defeated, cause slighter loss to the Navy. On October 25, some 650 miles west of the Canaries, Decatur's lookouts sighted a sail. The stranger was the *Macedonian,* considered the finest frigate in the Royal Navy. Both ships promptly spread all canvas and headed toward each other, intent on battle. The *United States* was the more heavily armed, having 24-pounders in her main battery as opposed to the British 18-pounders. But the *Macedonian* was fresh from having been overhauled and was much swifter than her opponent, whose lumbering slowness, a result of hull damage at launching, had earned her the nickname "Old Wagon." Captain John S. Carden, competent and experienced, had trained the *Macedonian*'s crew well, and he had the advantage of the weather gage—the upwind position—which gave him the initiative in attack.

As the *Macedonian* drew near, the *United States* suddenly wore around in an attempt to seize the weather gage. She was foiled when the *Macedonian* came closer into the wind. The *United States* thereupon wore again, and the *Macedonian* followed suit, coming to a parallel course. This time the Briton was a little too late, and the American forged ahead. Said a veteran tar in the *Macedonian,* "It's no fool of a seaman handling that ship. We've got hot work ahead of us." In fact Decatur, the firebrand of the Tripolitan War, was now maneuvering with the utmost wariness.

Carden was in a dilemma: to offset the power and range of Decatur's 24-pounders, he would have to get in close and use his carronades. Because he had turned too late, however, Carden could close the distance between ships only by turning his bow toward the *United States,* thereby exposing his frigate to diagonal fire without being able to use his main battery.

Decatur played out his advantage. He held off at a distance, cut up his opponent's sails and rigging to offset her superior speed, and forged ahead to decrease his own angle of fire. The effect on the *Macedonian* was devastating. Down came her mizzenmast and remaining topmasts; hull shots dismounted her guns and turned her decks into slaughterhouses. As the British

The United States *versus the* Macedonian.

dead and wounded piled up, their desperate comrades ridded themselves of these encumbrances by tossing the bodies into the sea.

Decatur, having steadily sharpened his angle of fire, at last put his helm over and brought the *United States* in raking position athwart the bows of the *Macedonian*. He mercifully withheld fire, however, and retired to make the slight repairs needed in his rigging. An hour later he returned to the stricken *Macedonian* and once more took a raking position across her bows, again without firing. At this demonstration Carden, at last recognizing his helplessness, ordered his colors struck. The British had suffered 104 casualties; the Americans, only 12.

There followed the usual courtesies. Carden reported by boat to the *United States* and offered his sword, which Decatur refused. In deep dejection the British captain kept repeating that he was a ruined man. "This is the first instance," said he, "of one of His Britannic Majesty's ships striking to a vessel of similar grade, and my mortification is insupportable." When Carden was informed that the *Guerrière* had earlier struck to the *Constitution*, news that had not reached England before the *Macedonian* put to sea, he was overjoyed. "Then," cried he, "I am safe!"

The *Macedonian*, after three days of repairs, set out under a prize crew for the United States. Decatur, determined to see his prize safely into port, abandoned his projected cruise and escorted her all the way.

The last of the American squadrons to sail was that of Commodore Bainbridge, which left Boston on October 26. The flagship *Constitution* and the sloop-of-war *Hornet* sailed for the Cape Verde Islands, where the *Essex*, still in Delaware Bay, was to join them.

Bainbridge, failing to make rendezvous with the *Essex* in the Cape Verdes, headed for Brazil, arriving off Salvador on December 13. In the harbor was a British sloop-of-war, the *Bonne Citoyenne*, reported to have on board a fortune in coins intended for England. After the Americans had blockaded the Briton for several days, Master Commandant James Lawrence, captain of the *Hornet*, challenged her to combat, Commodore Bainbridge pledging his honor not to intervene. The captain of the *Bonne Citoyenne* properly declined, for he was doing well enough keeping two American vessels off British shipping lanes; besides, he had the money to guard for his government.

At last Bainbridge went cruising down the coast, leaving Lawrence alone to watch the British vessel. On the morning of December 29, lookouts on the *Con-*

stitution discerned two strange sail. They were the British frigate *Java* and an American merchant vessel she had captured. Captain Henry Lambert of the *Java* signaled his prize to proceed to Salvador. He then headed for the *Constitution*, which steered out to sea to draw the enemy out of neutral waters.

Shortly after 2 P.M., as the swifter *Java* drew alongside and to windward of the *Constitution*, the latter fired a shot across the *Java*'s bows to make her show her colors, and followed this by a broadside. Each ship in a series of maneuvers next endeavored to rake and to avoid being raked, all the while firing broadsides from the main battery and musketry from the tops. Bainbridge was early wounded by a musket ball in the hip and a piece of langrage in the thigh, but he remained grimly at his station on the exposed quarterdeck.

The *Java* was handled at least as well as the *Constitution*, particularly after the latter's wheel was shot away so that she had to be steered by relieving tackles. But the British frigate was completely outclassed in gunnery. The American batteries were somewhat heavier and they were fired more rapidly and more accurately. The crew of the *Java* had drilled with the great guns only once since leaving England, whereas the Americans had been in continual practice, as was their custom, with both guns and musketry. Hence the *Constitution* gradually dismasted the *Java*, making her increasingly unmanageable.

At 2:50 the *Java*, having lost her headsails, was caught temporarily in stays, whereupon the *Constitution* crossed her stern, pouring in a heavy raking broadside. Captain Lambert, in a desperate attempt to snatch victory out of defeat, ordered boarders away, but the only result was that the *Constitution* was presented with an opportunity to cut across her opponent's bows and pour in another terrible raking broadside. Shortly

The Constitution *versus the* Java.

thereafter, Lambert received a mortal wound from marines firing from the *Constitution*'s maintop.

Shortly after 4 P.M., the *Java*, a mere dismasted hulk, ceased firing, whereupon the *Constitution* withdrew to windward and spent an hour making temporary repairs. Bainbridge then returned and placed his ship in a raking position across the *Java*'s bows. The British then struck their colors. "Hard Luck Bill" Bainbridge, though hurting in hip and thigh, at last had his hour of victory.

In this long-drawn-out, hard-fought battle, 9 Americans were killed and 25 wounded; the British loss was 22 killed and 25 wounded. The *Java*, proving beyond salvage, was burned at sea. The *Constitution* landed her prisoners under parole at Salvador and then proceeded to Boston for extensive repairs.

The *Hornet* remained off Salvador nearly three weeks longer, blockading the *Bonne Citoyenne*, which could not be persuaded to come out and fight. At length, on January 24, 1813, a British ship of the line, the *Montague*, 74, arrived from the south. Lawrence sought refuge in Salvador's neutral waters and then slipped away by night, heading for the West Indies. En route the *Hornet* captured a merchant brig, which Lawrence burned after removing prisoners and $23,000 in coins.

Off British Guiana on February 24, while chasing another merchant brig into the shoals at the mouth of the Demarara River, Lawrence discovered a small British brig-of-war, the *Espiègle*, anchored outside the bar. While the *Hornet* was maneuvering around the shallows to get at this vessel, her masthead lookouts reported another man-of-war brig approaching. Lawrence, thus confronted simultaneously with two foes, elected to attack first the brig to seaward.

Advancing on this opponent, he easily seized the windward position, and the two vessels passed on opposite tacks, exchanging broadsides within pistol shot. The British vessel, the brig *Peacock*, then wore ship and the *Hornet* swung to port to follow, advancing toward her opponent on an angle from astern. Although the *Hornet*'s approach was identical with the fatal approach of the *Macedonian* on the *United States* the preceding October, the results were utterly different. The British diagonal fire was high and wild, hitting the *Hornet*'s hull not at all and doing only small damage to her sails and rigging. The *Peacock* was in fact something of a show vessel, known widely as "The Yacht." Her crew was adept at shining brightwork but virtually untrained in gunnery. Hence the *Hornet* was able almost with impunity to take a position close under her starboard quarter, out of reach of her guns, and to pump

Captain James Lawrence.

in broadside after broadside. At the end of 11 minutes the *Peacock* struck her colors and then immediately hoisted them again union down in sign of distress, for she had six feet of water in the hold. Shortly afterward her mainmast came crashing down.

The Americans made strenuous efforts to save the sinking *Peacock* and her crew, but she went down so quickly that 9 of her own men and 3 rescuers from the *Hornet* went down with her and were drowned. British losses in action were 4 men killed, including the captain, and 29 wounded, 3 mortally. One American had been killed and 2 wounded.

Meanwhile, the *Espiègle* had remained a mere spectator at the destruction of her sister brig, and for this her captain was subsequently court-martialed. Lawrence considered attacking the *Espiègle*, but reconsidered in view of his many prisoners and a shortage of drinking water aboard. He shaped course for the United States and arrived off New York on March 24.

The British could no longer attribute to chance this long string of American victories, but they were quick to point out that the victor in most of the battles was the more heavily armed. Damages inflicted upon the

British vessels were, however, out of all proportion to their inferiority in armament. The fact is that after Lord Nelson's victory at Trafalgar in 1805 had swept the warships of Britain's European enemies from the seas, most British ship captains had neglected gunnery practice—not that the British had ever bothered much about marksmanship, their style being to get in so close that their shot were bound to hit. The Americans, on the other hand, never forgot their marksmanship tradition. Although they also often fought in close, they had the advantage of being prepared to open effective fire at maximum range.

Thus far the U.S. Navy had taken six warships. It had lost four, each to an opponent of overwhelming strength: U.S.S. *Nautilus*, 14, captured by H.M.S. *Shannon*, 38, backed by the whole Halifax squadron; U.S.S. *Wasp*, 18, captured by H.M.S. *Poictiers*, 74; U.S.S. *Vixen*, 14, taken by H.M.S. *Southampton*, 32; and U.S.S. *Viper*, 12, captured by H.M.S. *Narcissus*, 32. United States naval vessels had taken, in addition to men-of-war, at least 40 merchantmen, while American privateers, swarming out of U.S. ports and scouring the seas as far as the English Channel, had captured several hundred.

Commodore Rodgers returned to Boston on the last day of 1812 with the frigates *President* and *Congress*. He had had another disappointing cruise, having been out 85 days and covered 11,000 miles, during which time he had sighted only five British ships and captured two. His commerce raiding had been frustrated mainly by Britain's use of convoy and of evasive routing.

There was no more squadron cruising by U.S. warships. The Navy Department had come to agree with Decatur that, with pickings so slim, ships sailing independently and hence covering greater areas would have a better chance of making captures. Moreover, individual ships presumably had a better chance of slipping through the Royal Navy's ever-tightening military blockade of U.S. ports.

At the end of April 1814, easterly gales obliged the two British frigates blockading Boston to beat out to sea to avoid being blown onto the coast. Seizing this opportunity, both the *President* and the *Congress* left port, commanded respectively by Rodgers and Captain John Smith. The two frigates separated after reaching the open sea. Still at Boston was the *Chesapeake*. On May 20 James Lawrence, promoted to captain at the age of thirty-two, took command of her and prepared to follow the example of Rodgers and Smith.

Commodore Broke, who now commanded the blockade of Boston, was determined that Lawrence should

Captain Philip Broke.

do nothing of the sort. Disgusted at the escape of the *President* and *Congress*, Broke burned with desire to avenge the Royal Navy's recent defeats. Noting on his return to the waters off Boston that the *Chesapeake* was ready for sea, he pointedly dismissed his second frigate, and on the morning of June 1 took the frigate *Shannon* into Boston Bay. Broke fired a gun, which was answered by a gun from the *Chesapeake*. Then, to make his meaning clear beyond doubt, he sat down and penned a courteous challenge, sending it in to Boston by a prisoner of war in an intercepted fishing schooner. In the early afternoon Broke was gratified to see the *Chesapeake* coming out to do battle.

The *Chesapeake* and the *Shannon* were physically well matched, each rated at 38 guns and each carrying about 50. The British crew was, however, probably the most superbly trained in the Royal Navy. Broke, a most exceptional officer, had commanded the *Shannon* for seven years. Twice a day, five days a week, he drilled his men with the great guns and with small arms. He had at his own expense fitted the guns with sights and quadrants, and he had had arcs, marked off in degrees, cut into the deck behind each gun so that an entire broadside could be aimed at the same target.

The crew of the *Chesapeake* was, like other American seamen, well drilled for the most part, but expiring enlistments had recently brought in an infusion of untrained men. Moreover, most of the ship's senior officers, were new to their posts, replacing men on the sick list. The twenty-one-year old first lieutenant had, like Lawrence, just been appointed, and the acting third and fourth lieutenants were in fact midshipmen.

Lawrence's orders from the Navy Department were to take his frigate to sea at the earliest opportunity, and to proceed to the Gulf of St. Lawrence in order to intercept ships bringing supplies and reinforcements to the British army in Canada—a mission obviously more important than the defeat of a single enemy frigate. But in the atmosphere of the times, Lawrence, who had been a national hero since his defeat of the *Peacock,* could hardly disregard Broke's challenge, particularly since American newspapers had unanimously ridiculed the *Bonne Citoyenne's* refusal to take up Lawrence's

challenge at Salvador. Even before Broke's written challenge reached him, Lawrence had weighed anchor and headed out into Massachusetts Bay.

The *Shannon* led the way out to sea. A little before 5 P.M., some 30 miles east of Boston, she hove to on the starboard tack and then hoisted her jib and filled her main topsail in order to maintain enough way for maneuvering. The *Chesapeake,* sailing before the wind, headed toward the wake of the *Shannon* in order to keep out of her line of broadside fire. Lawrence had the opportunity of crossing his opponent's stern and raking him, a move that Broke expected, for he cautioned his men to "stand by to receive a raking fire from aft." Broke made no countermove, apparently feeling obliged, as the challenger, to allow Lawrence the first advantage.

Lawrence, not to be outdone in gallantry, declined the opportunity. He ordered his helmsman to luff, and

The Shannon *versus the* Chesapeake.

Lawrence mortally wounded.

the *Chesapeake* spun on her heel to starboard, coming alongside and to windward of the *Shannon* at a distance of 40 yards. Both ships fired their broadside batteries as the guns bore, while marines in the tops of each kept up a blistering fire of musketry. At such close range the effect was devastating. The *Shannon*, hulled at and below the surface, began to take water. Of 150 men on the *Chesapeake*'s weather deck, not 50 were left standing; a round shot had taken off her sailing master's head, and Captain Lawrence, wounded in the leg, was left clinging to a binnacle to support himself.

The *Chesapeake*, with too much headway, forged past the *Shannon*. Then the American frigate, her headsails shot away and her helmsman killed, swung her bow into the wind and backed down into her opponent. As she did so, she received a terrible semiraking fire which she could not return, for her guns no longer bore.

The *Shannon*'s boatswain, attempting to lash the vessels together, had his arm hacked off by an American cutlass.

Lawrence called boarders away, and then fell, mortally wounded by a bullet through the body. Carried below, he repeatedly cried out: "Don't give up the ship!" At about the same time the *Chesapeake*'s first and fourth lieutenants received mortal wounds. Her bugler, who should have sounded Lawrence's boarding order, was too paralyzed by fear to sound a note. The *Chesapeake*'s crew, virtually leaderless, began to race down the hatches in panic as Commodore Broke, sword in hand, cried, "Follow me who can!" and personally led a boarding party over from the *Shannon*.

The *Chesapeake*'s chaplain and a small group of men under her second lieutenant offered brief but futile resistance. Broke was disabled for life by a cutlass blow that laid bare his brain, but the American flag was already being hauled down by British hands.

The bloody battle had lasted only 15 minutes. Sixty-two Americans and 43 Britons were dead or dying; wounded short of mortally were 73 Americans and 39 Britons. The *Shannon,* her crew pumping steadily to keep her afloat, now headed for Halifax, as did the *Chesapeake,* under a prize crew. Lawrence died en route.

THE LATER WAR AT SEA

Captain David Porter, in the *Essex,* had failed to rendezvous with the *Constitution* and the *Hornet,* either in the Cape Verdes or at other designated meeting places. Sighting no enemy sails and running low in provisions and other supplies, Porter decided on his own initiative to round Cape Horn and enter the Pacific Ocean. Here he fell like a thunderbolt on the unsuspecting British whalers, capturing a dozen in six months and putting the others to flight. The whalers, well supplied for distant cruising, provided the *Essex* with ample stores of all kinds. Porter renamed one captured vessel *Essex Junior* and armed her with light guns as an auxiliary cruiser. His chief problem was to provide prize crews from his small ship's company. He entrusted one recaptured American vessel to the command of his twelve-year-old foster son, Midshipman David Glasgow Farragut, the future admiral.

When news reached London that an American frigate was ruining England's Pacific whale fishery, the Admiralty promptly took action. It dispatched Captain James Hillyar with the 38-gun frigate *Phoebe* and two sloops-of-war to run down the American ship, or at least chase it out of the Pacific. Hillyar set out with the understanding that nothing whatever should be allowed to interfere with his mission, not any considerations of gallantry or sportsmanship or respect for neutral waters—that his career as an officer in the Royal Navy hung on his performance.

News of Hillyar's expedition went before him on a number of hurrying sails. It was in this way that the *Essex Junior,* which had escorted prizes to Valparaiso, learned of his approach; she carried a warning to Captain Porter. Porter thereupon sailed 3,000 miles west to the Marquesas Islands for a thorough refit. He might very properly have continued on around the world and so escaped pursuit, for he was conscious that he was poorly armed; over his vehement protests the *Essex* had been furnished mostly with short-range carronades—forty 32-pounders—and only six long guns, all puny 12-pounders. As for the *Essex Junior,* she was too lightly built and armed to fight a battle. Moreover,

Porter's mission was raiding enemy commerce, not defeating warships. But Porter could not resist the challenge of Hillyar's approach, and so he proceeded with the *Essex* and the *Essex Junior* to Valparaiso, arriving February 3, 1814. Five days later the *Phoebe* arrived, accompanied only by the sloop-of-war *Cherub,* the other sloop having been ordered north to search.

Hillyar, after resting his crews and refitting, took his two ships outside of Valparaiso Bay and cruised off the port, refusing all of Porter's challenges to fight it out with him in a single-ship action. Matters were brought to a head on March 28 when the *Essex* parted her cables in a squall. Porter attempted to slip past the blockaders, and had nearly succeeded, when a gust of wind carried away his main topmast. The *Essex,* thus crippled, put about and headed back toward the coast, anchoring in neutral waters just north of Valparaiso.

The *Phoebe* and the *Cherub,* disregarding Chile's

David Porter.

neutrality, moved in to attack. What next took place discredited the carronade forever as a general naval weapon, for the British vessels simply stood off out of carronade range and pounded away at the *Essex*, first tearing up her rigging to impair her ability to maneuver, then firing at her hull. Porter did some damage to the enemy with three of his long 12s run out of his stern ports, but he had no means of effectively countering the fire of the *Phoebe*'s thirty 18-pounders. In desperation, Porter tried to run his ship aground and failed. Then, after giving all who wished to do so an opportunity to swim ashore, he at last struck his colors. From the *Essex*'s complement of 255 men there were 58 killed, 31 missing, and 65 wounded. The combined casualties of the *Phoebe* and *Cherub* were only 15.

Even had the *Essex* been victorious, it is doubtful she could have returned to the United States, for the Royal Navy had now clamped an almost inpenetrable blockade on American seaports. From the beginning of the war, British warships had taken station off major harbors to intercept American men-of-war. They were slow, however, to impose a commercial blockade, partly because the Napoleonic Wars kept most British ships in Europe, and partly because Britain hoped to reach an early settlement with the United States. Such hopes proved illusory when negotiations broke down over the issue of impressment, on which neither side would budge. Peace with France following the defeated Napoleon's abdication in April 1814 permitted Britain to send more ships and men to America. The British accordingly extended the blockade to "all the ports, harbors, bays . . . and seacoasts of the United States." American frigates were locked in port, and American sea-borne trade came to an almost complete halt. Even trade between U.S. ports had to be carried on by wagon.

In the summer of 1814 the Royal Navy brought into Chesapeake Bay an army of 4,000 men. These landed on the west bank of the Patuxent River, up which American gunboats fled. The invaders then marched on Washington. Before the steady British advance, a defending army of raw militia simply disintegrated, and government officials, including President Madison, fled in panic. The enemy troops burned the White House, the Capitol, and other public buildings, and returned to their ships.

Meanwhile a small British squadron had worked its way up the Potomac River, partly by kedging, and seized the shipping at Alexandria. Under the double threat, American authorities burned a frigate and a sloop at the Washington Navy Yard to keep them out of enemy hands. A British raid on Baltimore the fol-

lowing month was thwarted by stiff resistance on land and by the guns of Fort McHenry, which kept British warships out of Baltimore harbor—a spirited and spectacular defense which inspired Francis Scott Key to write "The Star-Spangled Banner."

In January 1814 the frigate *President*, commanded by Stephen Decatur, was attempting to slip out of New York harbor, when it was captured by the British blockading squadron. Of the American frigates only the *Constitution*, under Captain Charles Stewart, succeeded in getting to sea, slipping out of Boston harbor during a storm. In February, off the Madeiras, she performed the remarkable feat of capturing the corvette *Cyane* and the sloop *Levant* in a single action.

Some 200 American privateers managed to elude the British watchdogs, taking more than 1,300 prizes and thus imposing a severe strain on the British merchant marine. A number of the U.S. Navy's sloops and brigs also succeeded in slipping through the blockade. These ships, besides capturing numerous merchantmen, won seven victories in eight engagements with British sloops and brigs. "The fact seems to be but too clearly established," commented the London *Times* in some bewilderment, "that the Americans have some superior mode of fighting."

THE GREAT LAKES CAMPAIGNS

The planned invasion of Canada, which Jefferson had predicted would be "a mere matter of marching," got off to a wretched start. The causes were unpreparedness; apathy about, or opposition to, the war in the northeast; the employment of undependable militia, who often refused to cross the borders of their own states and who deserted at will when farms required attention; and aging senior officers, who were veterans of the American Revolution with usually no subsequent military experience. The last, according to young Lieutenant Colonel Winfield Scott, "had, very generally, sunk into either sloth, ignorance or habits of intemperate drinking."

Because Canada had few all-weather roads, the Canadian posts on or near Lakes Erie and Ontario were dependent on water transport for munitions and other supplies. Major General Henry Dearborn planned to isolate the posts by advancing on Montreal via the Lake Champlain–Richelieu River invasion route in order to seal off St. Lawrence River communications, but he could not for several months recruit enough men to carry out the operation.

In the war-minded West on July 12, 1812, Brigadier

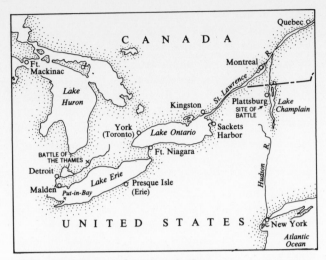

Lake campaigns of the War of 1812.

General William Hull, Isaac Hull's aging uncle, led a sizable force across the Detroit River into Canada, proclaiming, "I have a force that will break down all opposition." When he learned, however, that the British had captured Fort Mackinac and that British General Isaac Brock was approaching with reinforcements, Hull hastily retreated to Detroit. Here, on August 16, to the disgust of his officers and men, he surrendered to an inferior force without firing a shot. General Brock, having secured Detroit, marched his small army back the length of Lake Erie and, at the cost of his life, defeated and captured another American force that had invaded Canada by crossing the Niagara River.

By late November General Dearborn at last had at Lake Champlain an army of 6,000 men for his proposed march on Montreal. The invasion started bravely, but many militia stopped at the border, refusing to leave New York state. At this, Dearborn, recalling Montgomery's ill-fated winter invasion of 1775, marched his army back to winter quarters.

The following spring Dearborn transferred a carefully selected force of 1,700 men to Sackets Harbor for a descent on the British base at Kingston, at the foot of Lake Ontario. From Kingston the Americans could cut off all British supplies from the St. Lawrence and yet be out of reach of the British seagoing fleet. But Dearborn and Commodore Isaac Chauncey, the American Great Lakes naval commander, erroneously convinced themselves that Kingston was strongly defended. In late April Chauncey's squadron of 14 vessels, most of which were small, landed Dearborn's men near York (now Toronto), the capital of Upper Canada. The invaders, supported by fire from the fleet, easily captured the

lightly held town, but an exploding magazine caused some 200 casualties among the Americans. Possibly in retaliation for this, and possibly because they found a human scalp on display in the legislative hall, American sailors set fire to the Parliament building—an act of vandalism which the British used the following year to justify burning public buildings in Washington. In a few days the Americans sailed away with a captured 10-gun brig and some minor military stores. They next landed on the Canadian side of the Niagara River and with greatly superior forces captured Fort George, causing the British to pull back temporarily all along the Niagara front.

Raids such as these had no permanent effect. In order to carry out a serious invasion, it was necessary that the Americans first control Lake Ontario. Although Chauncey's squadron engaged in several skirmishes with that of the British Great Lakes naval commander, Commodore Sir James Yeo, neither would risk a real battle without decisively superior forces. To that end Chauncey and Yeo undertook a shipbuilding race which, before the end of the war, produced on both sides great 100-gun ships destined never to fire a shot in anger.

As it turned out, the decisive naval battles of the War of 1812 were fought on Lake Erie and Lake Champlain.

THE BATTLE OF LAKE ERIE

On Lake Erie, too, the British and the Americans were in a shipbuilding race. At stake here was the vast Northwest Territory, which the British, by virtue of their conquest of Detroit, proposed converting into an Indian buffer state between the United States and Canada. In the spring of 1813 General William Harrison's Kentuckians were in northern Ohio, confronting British troops and Indians under General Henry Proctor. Harrison's objective was the reconquest of Detroit. His success depended in large measure on the control of Lake Erie, for the Americans to some extent, and the British to a very great extent, relied on water transportation for provisions and other supplies.

The British, in the spring of 1813, controlled Lake Erie with a squadron commanded by Commander Robert H. Barclay, a distinguished veteran of Trafalgar. The Americans, in order to contest the British naval superiority, were building two brigs at Presque Isle (Erie); the British, in order to maintain their superiority, were building a brig at Fort Malden, Proctor's base near Detroit. Consequently the fate of Detroit and of

Oliver Hazard Perry.

Perry transferring from the Lawrence *to the* Niagara.

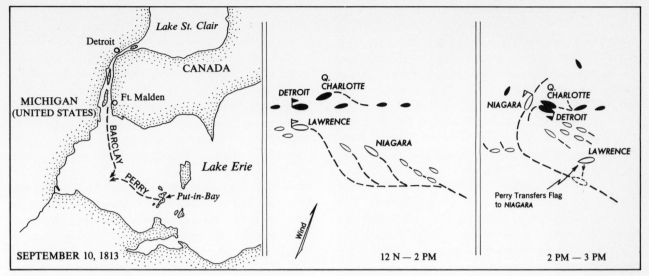

The Battle of Lake Erie.

the Northwest Territory depended to a large extent on which side won the building race. Each was perfectly aware of the other's operations, and Barclay kept the Presque Isle project under close observation.

Toward the end of March there had arrived at Presque Isle twenty-seven-year-old Master Commandant Oliver Hazard Perry, who, fretting under the strictures of coastal blockade, had volunteered his services on the lakes. Perry expedited the American building program with immense energy—procuring more shipbuilders, recruiting militia to protect his shipyard, combing the surrounding wilderness for scrap iron and blacksmiths, obtaining supplies via Pittsburgh, and overseeing the cutting of timber, which often went into construction the same day. As a result his brigs, the *Niagara* and the flagship *Lawrence*, were ready in July, each armed with two long 12-pounders and eighteen 32-pounder carronades.

On August 1, Barclay withdrew his squadron for replenishment, whereupon Perry, working nearly around the clock, lifted his brigs by means of floats over a sandbar from Presque Isle Bay into Lake Erie. Shortly afterward Lieutenant Jesse D. Elliott arrived from Lake Ontario with 100 seamen and junior officers, an addition which barely enabled Perry to sail. Perry made Elliott his second-in-command aboard the *Niagara*, but the latter was not entirely mollified by this distinction, for he had captured a British vessel on the Niagara River and had accordingly expected himself to be appointed to the Lake Erie command.

As Perry proceeded up the lake for a conference with General Harrison at Sandusky, Barclay could only fall back on Malden to await the completion of his new brig, the *Detroit*, which was to serve as his flagship. By

September the *Detroit* was ready except for armament. Because provisions at Malden were almost exhausted, it was imperative that the British restore their lake communications without delay. Barclay therefore stripped the fort to arm his new ship—17 long guns of mixed caliber and 2 carronades—and on the morning of September 10 sailed, in a mood of desperation, to do battle with the American squadron.

Meanwhile General Harrison had transferred to Perry 100 Kentucky marksmen to serve as sharpshooters in the tops. Perry, gratefully accepting them, drew up a careful plan of battle: the *Lawrence* was to fight the *Detroit;* the *Niagara* would engage Barclay's other heavy vessel, the 17-gun *Queen Charlotte;* the Americans were to advance quickly to within pistol shot of the enemy in order to make use of their sharpshooters and their heavy, short-range carronades. "If you lay your enemy close alongside," concluded Perry, in conscious paraphrase of Nelson's Trafalgar order, "you cannot be out of your place."

At dawn on the 10th, when Barclay's squadron presented itself before Perry's anchorage in Put-in-Bay, the *Detroit* and the *Queen Charlotte* were accompanied by the *Lady Prevost,* 13, and the *Hunter,* 10, as well as two vessels of little combat value carrying 1 to 4 guns. Barclay's squadron carried 67 guns and Perry's 54, but the Americans' preponderance of carronades gave them greater weight of broadside—provided they could get in close enough to use them. Luckily for the Americans, the winds were southerly, giving Perry the upwind position and therefore the choice of range.

Perry, having ordered his line, approached the enemy on a slant, his crews cheering. Aboard the British squadron the bands struck up "Rule, Britannia." At

11:50 the long guns of the *Detroit* opened up, and the *Lawrence* began to take punishment. Perry grimly held his fire while closing the range. At 12:15, when he was within pistol shot, he opened with a burst of carronade and rifle fire that swept the decks of the *Detroit* and nearly blasted her out of the water. Had Elliott, in the *Niagara*, followed orders and given the *Queen Charlotte* similar treatment, the Americans would shortly have been victorious. But, for reasons never satisfactorily explained, Elliott hugged the wind, remaining out of reach of the 14 carronades of the *Queen Charlotte*. This ship, unable to get at her adversary, sailed past the *Hunter* and joined the *Detroit* in pounding the *Lawrence*.

By 2:30 the unsupported *Lawrence* was little more than a shattered hulk, her decks covered with dead, her guns all silenced. Perry, leaving the national ensign flying, took down his commodore's pennant and his blue battle flag, which bore in white letters Lawrence's words DONT GIVE UP THE SHIP. With these flags he had himself rowed to the *Niagara*, which had forged ahead but was still at a safe distance.

Perry ordered Elliot into his rowboat to bring up the straggling gunboats, while he himself swung to starboard and steered his fresh ship straight through the British line, firing double-shotted broadsides. The *Detroit*, wearing about to avoid raking fire and to bring a new broadside to bear, fouled the *Queen Charlotte* in such a position that the *Niagara* raked both ships simultaneously until at 3 P.M. Barclay struck, thereby surrendering his entire squadron. To General Harrison, waiting anxiously on shore, Perry scribbled on the back of an old envelope: "We have met the enemy and they are ours: Two ships, two Brigs, one schooner & one sloop. Yours with the greatest respect and esteem. O. H. Perry."

After making repairs, Perry's squadron ferried Harrison's army across the lake. The Kentuckians went in pursuit of Proctor's retreating British and Indians, and defeated them in the Battle of the Thames. Detroit was thus regained, and the United States was assured continued possession of northern Ohio and the territory of the future states of Indiana, Illinois, Michigan, Wisconsin, and Minnesota.

THE BATTLE OF LAKE CHAMPLAIN

The transfer to America of Wellington's Peninsular War veterans following Napoleon's abdication enabled the British to open several new offensives. In addition to the invasion of Washington and the attempted raiding of Baltimore, it was planned that one army would advance on New Orleans from the Gulf and another would thrust southward from Montreal via the Champlain-Hudson invasion route. The general objective was to induce the Americans to accept stiff British terms for peace, terms which included transfer of territory to Canada.

Poised to begin the northern invasion in the late summer of 1814 were 11,000 troops led personally by Sir George Prevost, Governor-General of Canada. The Americans had available only 1,500 regular troops to stem this British advance. These, under Brigadier General Alexander Macomb, took a defensive position at Plattsburg on Lake Champlain and began throwing up earthworks. The chief barrier to the British advance was, however, Master Commandant Thomas Macdonough's small squadron on Lake Champlain. Macdonough's guns could dominate the lakeside road along which the British had to march; British supplies had to be brought

Thomas Macdonough.

The Battle of Lake Champlain (Crab Island at lower left, Cumberland Head at upper right).

by this route also. Hence Prevost, like Governor-General Sir Guy Carleton 38 years earlier, was forced to delay his invasion until he built superior naval strength on the lake.

The British had at the northern end of Lake Champlain a brig, the *Linnet*, 16 guns; the schooners *Chubb* and *Finch*, 11 each; and a dozen 1-gun row galleys. They were rushing to completion a 37-gun frigate, the *Confiance*, considered capable of singlehandedly defeating the whole American squadron. This squadron consisted of the corvette *Saratoga*, flagship, 27 guns; the brig *Eagle*, 20; the schooner *Ticonderoga*, 17; the sloop *Preble*, 7; and 10 row galleys mounting 1 or 2 guns each.

As Prevost advanced on the United States in early September, volunteers swarmed in from Vermont and New York to strengthen Macomb at Plattsburg. Commodore Macdonough anchored his ships in a line between the town and Cumberland Head, his van and rear protected by shoals. Because there was to be no sail handling, all of his men were available to work the guns. Macdonough had additional anchors dropped and lines rigged so that his ships could be wound about to present fresh broadsides.

On the evening of September 5, as the British army entered Plattsburg, Macomb's troops withdrew into their fortifications across the Saranac River, which divided the town. Had Prevost attacked without delay, he would almost certainly have captured the bluffs south of the Saranac, whence his long-range guns could have forced Macdonough from his defensive anchorage to probable defeat on the open lake. Instead, the governor-general cautiously halted and waited for the British squadron to come and clear his flank, meanwhile impatiently firing off a series of insulting messages to the newly arrived squadron commander, Captain George Downie. The latter, thus goaded, came out prematurely to do battle. Shipwrights were still at work aboard his flagship *Confiance*, whose crew, also newly arrived, had no opportunity to drill with her guns and sails.

In the early morning of September 11, the British ships were reported coming down the lake before a northeast wind. Macdonough beat to quarters and, paraphrasing Nelson's Trafalgar signal, hoisted a message to his fleet: IMPRESSED SEAMEN CALL ON EVERY MAN TO DO HIS DUTY. The British squadron, rounding Cumberland Head, formed line abreast and, drums rolling, advanced on the American line. Its progress was very slow in the fickle breezes in the lee of the headland. The *Finch*, unable to hug what little wind there was, failed to reach her assigned position opposite the *Preble* and drifted off to the south. The tall-masted

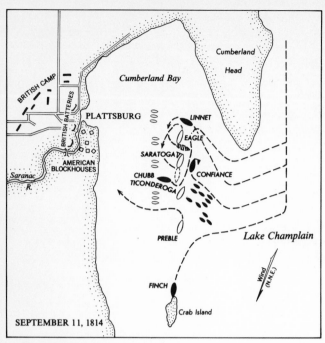

SEPTEMBER 11, 1814

The Battle of Lake Champlain.

Confiance forged ahead, receiving raking fire from the whole American line. The first shots from the *Saratoga* ranged the length of her deck, smashing her wheel and carrying away her port and spare anchors. At a distance of 500 yards from the American line, the *Confiance* swung to starboard. Anchoring opposite the *Saratoga*, she fired from her double-shotted 24-pounders half a ton of iron that violently rocked the American flagship and swept down 40 of her crew. Return fire from the *Saratoga* dismounted one of the *Confiance's* guns, and it crashed fatally into Downie.

As the other British vessels arrived to support their flagship, the weak *Preble*, under heavy fire from the British galleys, took refuge under Macomb's batteries. The *Chubb*, quickly disabled, struck to the Americans and was towed ashore. The *Eagle*, most of her starboard guns knocked out by fire from the *Linnet* and the forward batteries of the *Confiance*, cut her cables, ran down the American line, and anchored by the stern south of the *Saratoga*. She was thus able to turn her fresh port battery on the *Confiance*, but her shift of position enabled the *Linnet* to take a raking position across the bows of the *Saratoga*.

To the south the *Ticonderoga* and the American galleys engaged the British galleys, but the main battle was a thundering cannonade involving the *Saratoga* and the *Eagle* against the *Linnet* and the *Confiance*. In half an hour of steady gunfire all four were stripped of their masts and wrecked beyond repair. Macdonough was twice knocked unconscious. The fire of the *Saratoga* and the *Confiance* began gradually to slacken, as their engaged broadsides became progressively disabled. One of the *Saratoga's* guns, knocked from its fastenings, went hurtling down a hatch.

When nearly the whole of the *Saratoga's* starboard battery was dismounted or otherwise disabled, Macdonough played his trump: winding his ship about to present his port broadside. The *Confiance* attempted a like maneuver but, through loss of anchors, succeeded in turning only half way, thereby exposing her bow to raking fire from the *Saratoga's* fresh battery. Quickly reduced to a sinking hulk, her wounded men threatened with drowning, the *Confiance* at last struck her colors. The *Saratoga* now turned her port battery on the *Linnet*, which also surrendered, as did the distant *Finch*, grounded on Crab Island. A few of the British galleys avoided capture by rowing away.

Prevost, who according to plan had opened fire on Macomb's positions as the naval battle began, now disengaged his army and hastily retreated to Canada. The British thereupon restudied their position and, on the Duke of Wellington's advice, dropped their territorial demands. The Treaty of Ghent, ending the War of 1812, was signed December 24, 1814.

Word of the peace treaty did not reach America in time to halt the British attack on New Orleans. In January 1815 Major General Sir Edward Pakenham marched on the city with 9,000 Peninsular War veterans. Pakenham's army was cut to pieces and utterly routed by Major General Andrew Jackson's 4,000 sharpshooters, supported by the batteries of the naval schooners *Carolina* and *Louisiana*.

The Treaty of Ghent made no mention of impressment or spoliation of maritime trade. These grievances had, however, lost significance with the conclusion of the war in Europe. What was gained was a mutually acknowledged boundary between the United States and Canada; also gained was increased respect for the United States among foreign powers. The Americans, for their part, forgot the blockade, the raiding of their capital, and the mismanagement of their military campaigns. They remembered instead their naval victories and developed a new spirit of national unity.

IV

From Sail to Steam

During the War of 1812, the stringent British blockade had kept American ports crowded with idle shipping while cotton, grain, tobacco, and other products piled high in warehouses and on wharves. On the ratification of the Treaty of Ghent, American ships loaded with goods took to sea. At the same time sorely needed foreign goods began to arrive from England, continental Europe, the West Indies, India, and China. This was only the beginning of an unprecedented surge in American overseas commerce which, between 1815 and 1860, nearly quintupled in value.

The U.S. Navy was not permitted to decline, as had happened after earlier wars. This was partly because of the need to protect expanding trade and partly because of American pride in the Navy's accomplishments. Three ships of the line, the *Independence*, the *Franklin*, and the *Washington*, laid down during hostilities, were completed shortly after the return of peace. By 1818 eight more had been laid down, but three of these ships were never completed. In 1822 work was begun on the mighty 120-gun *Pennsylvania*, the largest sailing ship ever built for the U.S. Navy, and the largest in the world at the time of her launching in 1837. During the same period numerous frigates, sloops, and schooners were also added to what soon became a respectable oceangoing fleet. As American trade continued to expand, segments of the fleet were formed into semipermanent squadrons and dispatched to the four quarters of the world, wherever they were needed.

The first of the squadrons to be formed was actually a revival of the Mediterranean Squadron of the Tripolitan War period. Its objective was the same, to deal with the nuisance of Barbary pirates. The Dey of Algiers, complaining that the U.S. tribute money was not being promptly or fully paid, had begun in 1807 to seize American merchantmen. In 1812 the United States had broken off diplomatic relations with the dey's government. Shortly after the conclusion of peace with England, Congress declared war on Algiers, and in May 1815 Commodore Stephen Decatur sailed for the Mediterranean Sea with a force of nine vessels, including three frigates. In the Mediterranean, Decatur's squadron captured two Algerian warships, then proceeded to Algiers. There Decatur presented his terms: no further tribute, no more capturing of American ships, and a treaty to be concluded giving most-favored-nation status to the United States. When the dey hesitated to abandon his piratical practices, Decatur threatened to capture the rest of his squadron, expected soon in port. At that the dey reluctantly signed. "Why," he complained, "do they send wild young men to treat for peace with old powers?"

Decatur next proceeded to Tunis and Tripoli, where he demanded and received indemnity for American privateer prizes which, when sent into these ports during the War of 1812, had been turned over to the British. The United States, in order to impress upon the Barbary Powers its ability to maintain its rights, sent after Decatur's squadron a more powerful one which, included the new 74-gun ship of the line *Independence*, commanded by Commodore William Bainbridge. This squadron touched at the same ports.

The growing U.S. Navy and the expanding American fleet operations posed severe administrative problems, particularly since no clear distinction was drawn between operational and logistic control. Moreover, both were administered by an inexperienced Secretary of the Navy, who had no officers specifically assigned to advise him. To alleviate this situation, Secretary Benjamin Crowninshield in 1815 persuaded Congress to create a Board of Navy Commissioners, consisting of three senior captains, to administer logistics and to advise the Secretary on operations and policy. Early members of the board were Captains Porter, Decatur, and Bainbridge. In 1842, in response to increasing complications incident to the introduction of iron construction and steam propulsion, the board was replaced by five bureaus, each headed by an officer: Yards and Docks; Ordnance and Hydrography; Construction, Equipment and Repair; Provisions and Clothing; and Medicine and Surgery.

No comparative evolution occurred to establish professional control of naval operations, mainly because senior naval officers and national administrations, counting on the nation's geographical isolation and misreading the lessons of the American Revolution and the War of 1812, remained defense-minded. The Navy's main function, they believed, was the protection of maritime commerce. Its secondary function was defense against enemy invasion of coastal waters—though actual coast defense was assigned chiefly to extensive new Army-controlled coastal fortifications. Offensive naval operations were to be limited to raiding enemy commerce, for which privateers also were to be used, and attacking separated segments of a hostile fleet. With such limited concepts of the function of American sea power, Congress maintained naval appropriations at an average of $7 million annually, less than a quarter of British or French appropriations.

SUPPRESSING PIRACY IN THE WEST INDIES

The West Indies Squadron was established to safeguard shipping and to track down sea robbers in another hotbed of piracy. When the European naval powers became preoccupied with the Wars of the French Revolution and Empire, buccaneering, long suppressed, began again to flourish in the Caribbean Sea and the Gulf of Mexico. It was given a special impetus after 1810, when Mexico, Venezuela, and Colombia revolted against Spanish rule, sending out swarms of privateers who readily turned to piracy. Cuba and Puerto Rico, remaining loyal to Spain, sent out retaliatory privateers with an equal taste for marauding.

The most notorious freebooter of the period was, however, an erstwhile New Orleans master blacksmith, Jean Lafitte, who took to smuggling, then to piracy, and finally commanded a pirate fleet from an island base near the mouth of the Mississippi River. Offered a naval captaincy by the British as an inducement to assist in the attack on New Orleans, Lafitte informed American authorities of the British plan. He and his pirate gang then joined General Jackson in the successful defense of the city. President Madison rewarded the pirates with pardons, which they gratefully accepted, but they promptly resumed their profitable vocation.

With end of the war in Europe and North America, trade in the Gulf of Mexico and the Caribbean Sea flourished as never before. Because of heavy westward migration, New Orleans developed a maritime commerce second among American ports only to that of New York. The pirates fell greedily upon this commerce, attacking hundreds of merchantmen each year.

The savagery of some of the attacks is well illustrated by the case of the merchant sloop *Blessing*, which was halted by a pirate schooner south of Cuba. When the master of the *Blessing*, William Smith, failed to produce a satisfactory sum of money, the pirate captain had him thrown overboard and fired at him with a musket until he sank. The pirate then turned on Smith's screaming fourteen-year-old son, clubbed him in the head with the butt of his musket, and threw him overboard too. Finally, stripping the *Blessing* of everything of value, the pirates set fire to her and set her crew adrift in a boat.

The American government assigned to the Navy not only the job of suppressing the pirates but also the more delicate task of dealing with the Latin-American colonies from which most of the pirates came. Thus in 1819 the Secretary of the Navy sent Captain Oliver Hazard Perry on a special mission to Angostura (now Ciudad Bolívar, Venezuela) to dissuade General Simón Bolívar from issuing blank letters of marque that were in effect mere licenses to piracy. Perry had a successful interview with the Vice-President of the Colombian Republic, the general being absent from the capital; but the mission cost him his life, for he caught yellow fever and died on the return voyage.

As piracy originating from the new republics subsided, thanks to the Perry mission, the problem became intensified in the vicinity of Cuba and Puerto Rico. The Spanish authorities on these islands, resenting U.S. aid to their revolted colonies, tolerated the outrageous marauding expeditions that operated from their shores. Many of the pirates were in fact financed by leading Cuban and Puerto Rican citizens, who shared in the profits.

It was to deal with this maritime lawlessness that the Navy Department created the West Indies Squadron, first commanded by Captain James Biddle in the captured frigate *Macedonian*. Occasionally the heavy ships overtook a pirate craft at sea, but much of the pursuit was done in open boats, which navigated in shallow inlets and lagoons. The chase often ended in hand-to-hand fighting ashore. More dangerous than pirate weapons in this toilsome tropical service was yellow fever. Of flagship *Macedonian*'s crew of about 300, a third died of fever the first summer.

Captain David Porter, Biddle's successor as commodore of the squadron, sought the cooperation of the Puerto Rican governor, but with scant success. An American schooner taking a message into San Juan was fired on from guns ashore which killed her commanding officer. A lieutenant sent to Fajardo on the Puerto Rican east coast to inquire about stolen American goods was thrown into jail. For the hot-tempered Porter this latter act was too much. Landing 290 armed men, he vowed that he would have an apology from the mayor or else blow Fajardo off the map. Porter promptly received his apology but was called home to face a court-martial, which suspended him for six months for exceeding his authority. He thereupon resigned his commission in the U.S. Navy. General Jackson denounced the court-martial, praising Porter for upholding the honor of the flag. Upon becoming President, Jackson appointed him Minister to Turkey, where he died in 1843.

Meanwhile Captain Lewis Warrington, successor to Porter as commodore of the West Indies Squadron, had completed the work of his predecessors. The Americans, operating sometimes jointly with British pirate hunters, gradually made the Caribbean safe for commerce. By 1829 the American squadron was reduced to a small patrol force. The U.S. Navy had captured, in all, about 65 pirate vessels.

THE NAVY AROUND THE WORLD

Although participation of Americans in the African slave trade had been outlawed in 1807, and although the United States and Britain had agreed in the Treaty of Ghent to cooperate in suppressing it, many privateer veterans of the War of 1812 entered the traffic, continuing even after Congress in 1819 branded it piracy. In 1820 the corvette *Cyane*, first of several American

Aboard a slaver.

warships sent to cruise the African west coast, captured nine slavers. Her successors did less well, partly because they were much involved in founding and protecting the Republic of Liberia, populated mostly by freed American slaves. In 1824 the United States withdrew its patrol in a dispute with the British over rights of visit and search, a subject about which Americans were understandably sensitive. Thereafter for many years, slavers of several nations made use of false U.S. identification to foil the British patrols. In the Webster-Ashburton Treaty of 1842, the United States again agreed to cooperate with the British, this time by maintaining an 80-gun Africa Squadron. Although the squadron operated regularly until after the outbreak of the Civil War, the slave trade continued almost unabated, American ships and capital participating in it.

Of the several scientific expeditions sponsored by the U.S. Navy before the Civil War, none attracted more favorable interest or was more fruitful than the six-ship United States Exploring Expedition of 1838–42. This squadron was commanded by Lieutenant Charles Wilkes and included a group of scientists with elaborate equipment. They discovered and explored the coast of Antarctica, visited the Tuamotu, Society, and Fiji

Commodore Matthew Calbraith Perry.

Islands, surveyed portions of the west coast of North America, and brought home a wealth of oceanographic and geographic data.

After the Peace of Ghent, American commerce with the Far East not only revived but soon reached boom dimensions. The perils of such distant trade were demonstrated when in 1831 the Salem pepper trader *Friendship* was plundered and part of her crew slaughtered at Quallah Battoo, Sumatra. The following year U.S. frigate *Potomac* arrived at Quallah Battoo to take punitive measures. Her sailors and marines, with gunfire support from the ship, captured and burned the town. The natives were granted peace only upon guaranteeing safety for Americans who should visit the area thereafter.

As a more sweeping guarantee, the Navy in 1835 established a permanent East India Squadron. Commodore Lawrence Kearny, its commander from 1840 to 1842, so favorably impressed the Chinese government

by his firmness, fairness, and tact that he was able to pave the way for a general opening of China to American trade. When the expanding United States reached the Pacific coast, a transpacific steamship line to China was planned.

Squarely in the way of this line stood the still medieval Empire of Japan, which for nearly three centuries had avoided contact with foreigners, the sole exceptions being the Chinese and the Dutch, who were allowed highly restricted trading privileges through the port of Nagasaki. Shipwreck victims landing on the Japanese coast were treated as felons. The United States, with its flourishing Oriental trade and growing Pacific whaling fishery, was anxious to change all this—to open in Japan ports of fuel and refuge and hopefully also of trade. But American attempts to establish diplomatic relations with Japan were insultingly rebuffed. In the early 1850s President Fillmore sent an impressive naval expedition to try once again to negotiate some sort of treaty.

Selected as commodore of the Japan Expedition was Captain Matthew Calbraith Perry, brother of the victor of Lake Erie. The choice was an apt one. "Old Bruin" Perry at age fifty-nine was able, iron-willed, imperious, not to say pompous; he was just the man to impress the ceremonious, rank-conscious dignitaries of Japan. Perry prepared the expedition with the utmost care, learning all he could about the Japanese, seeking out top-notch officers and crews, and collecting as gifts striking examples of Western technology.

The Japan Expedition entered Tokyo Bay on July 8, 1853, the sidewheelers *Susquehanna* and *Mississippi* towing the sailing sloops *Plymouth* and *Saratoga*. Perry, styling himself "Commander in Chief United States Naval Forces Stationed in the East India, China and Japan Seas," rejected peremptory orders to depart and refused to make himself available to minor dignitaries who arrived aboard his flagship. These were met by junior officers, who announced that the commodore had come to deliver a letter from his president to officials of suitable eminence representing the emperor.

The ruling shogunate, lacking weapons to expel Perry by force and impressed by his dignified conduct and assertion of rank, decided that they could get rid of him only by meeting his demands. They therefore had a reception hall built on the shore in record time and dispatched thither two princes in gorgeous array attended by 5,000 soldiers. Commodore Perry now came ashore in stately procession, to the sound of gunfire salutes and ships' bands playing "Hail, Columbia!" The princes, in dignified silence, received the presidential letter enclosed in a rosewood box. Perry then departed

Perry delivers the President's letter.

to winter in Chinese waters, announcing that he would return the following year for the imperial reply.

When he returned to Tokyo Bay the following February with an augmented squadron, the shogunate had already come to the conclusion that Japan's only hope for peace lay in making some concessions. After lengthy negotiations in another specially built reception hall, the Japanese representatives concluded with Perry the Treaty of Kanagawa, opening two ports to American shipping but granting no trade. Now at last the Japanese dropped their reserve. Many insisted upon riding, their robes flapping in the breeze, atop the coach of a miniature steam railway, one of Perry's gifts. At a subsequent banquet aboard Perry's flagship, one of the imperial secretaries, flushed with drink and enthusiasm, threw his arms about the startled commodore's neck, exclaiming, "Nippon and America, all the same heart!"

Four years later the shogunate, realizing that Japan must have foreign trade to promote the technological revolution she needed to achieve security in the modern world, opened commercial relations with the United States.

PATHFINDER OF THE SEAS

While most naval officers were distinguishing themselves as explorers, diplomats, protectors of trade, and chasers of pirates and slavers, Lieutenant Matthew Fontaine Maury USN was diligently studying the seas for ways to improve navigation.

Shorebound by a crippling accident, Maury was appointed in 1842 to the usually humdrum post of superintendent of the Depot of Charts and Instruments in Washington, D.C. Under his vigorous superintendency the operations of the depot soon ceased to be humdrum. Noting that the charts he issued were British and nearly all long out of date, Maury and his midshipman

Lieutenant Matthew Fontaine Maury.

Title page of Maury's Explanations and Sailing Directions, *a pioneering aid to navigation.*

EXPLANATIONS AND SAILING DIRECTIONS

TO ACCOMPANY THE

WIND AND CURRENT CHARTS,

APPROVED BY

COMMODORE CHARLES MORRIS,

CHIEF OF THE BUREAU OF ORDNANCE AND HYDROGRAPHY;

AND PUBLISHED BY AUTHORITY OF

HON. WILLIAM A. GRAHAM,

SECRETARY OF THE NAVY.

BY LIEUT. M. F. MAURY, U. S. N.

SUPERINTENDENT OF THE NATIONAL OBSERVATORY.

FOURTH EDITION.

WASHINGTON:
C. ALEXANDER, PRINTER,
F STREET, NEAR NAVY DEPARTMENT.
1852.

assistants began to examine the log books of U.S. naval vessels deposited at the depot. From the logs they extracted data concerning prevailing winds and ocean currents, weather conditions, length of daily runs, and seasonal variations.

Maury became convinced that navigators often fought the forces of nature instead of using them. He was certain that, by taking account of winds and currents and avoiding storms and calms, mariners could greatly diminish hazards and speed up voyages. To extend and confirm his investigations, Maury prepared an abstract log which he sent to ship captains, requesting that in the spaces provided they record navigational, hydrographic, and meteorological observations and return the completed logs to him. At his request the Secretary of the Navy made such reports mandatory for cruising U.S. naval vessels. With this aid, Maury devised wind and current charts and determined the most efficient sea routes from point to point.

Widespread skepticism of Maury's findings was dispelled in 1849 when a Baltimore merchant skipper, following his suggested routes, cut 35 days from the usual time required for a voyage to Rio de Janeiro and back. Thereafter Maury's charts and their accompanying *Explanations and Sailing Directions* were eagerly sought, particularly by clippers which, in response to the gold rush, were plying in even greater numbers between New York and San Francisco. The use of Maury's charts and directions shortened the clippers' average sailing time from 187 to 136 days.

In recognition of his achievements, Maury was appointed superintendent of the new United States Naval Observatory, which absorbed the Depot of Charts and Instruments. Despite broadened responsibilities, Maury continued his maritime charting and pathfinding. New charts showed the best whaling grounds, the extent of iceberg drift, and water temperatures from season to season. Successive editions of the *Explanations and Sailing Directions* expanded from 10 to 1,300 pages.

Maury's charting of separate east- and westbound transatlantic steamship lanes, when generally adopted, practically eliminated the numerous collisions that were costing ships and lives; his charts and routes saved shippers in many countries uncounted millions of dollars. His book *Physical Geography of the Sea* virtually founded the science of oceanography, and his soundings and studies of the ocean depths paved the way for the laying of the Atlantic telegraphic cable.

In 1853, in response to a proposal by Maury, representatives of the major maritime nations held in Brussels the first International Maritime Meteorological Conference. On their unanimous recommendation Maury's system of observing, reporting, recording, and analyzing maritime phenomena was adopted on a worldwide scale.

THE TECHNOLOGICAL REVOLUTION

The United States was a major participant in the 1815–60 technological revolution that transformed the world's navies as they shifted from sail to steam, from wood to iron, and from shot to shell. In the process the major fleets, while not changing greatly in appearance, altered more in operational characteristics than they had done in the preceding three centuries.

When the British blockade closed down American commerce in the War of 1812, the U.S. Navy turned to Robert Fulton, the maritime engineering genius. Since 1807 Fulton had been operating on the Hudson River his commercially successful steamer *Clermont,* propelled by paddle wheels of his own invention. Could he devise a harbor defense vessel and blockade breaker powerful enough to deal with ships of the Royal Navy?

Fulton could and did. His efforts produced the *Demologos,* the first steam-propelled warship. She had twin hulls, joined above the water in catamaran fashion, and carried a paddle wheel in a channelway between the hulls. Her engines and her twenty 32-pounder guns were protected by five-foot-thick timbers, armor which no ordnance of the day could penetrate. Had she got into action, the *Demologos* would surely have caused among the British blockaders an alarm as frenzied as that later produced among the Union blockaders by the appearance of U.S.S. *Merrimack.* Her attack would have been far more decisive than that of the *Merrimack,* for she was invulnerable to anything the British could have sent against her, and her inevitable victories would probably have ushered in the naval age of steam without delay.

But before the *Demologos,* launched in the fall of 1814, was ready for action, the war had ended. Renamed the *Fulton* after the death of her designer, she saw brief peacetime service and then was tied up as a receiving ship in the Brooklyn Navy Yard.

In the next two decades business interests built hundreds of steamers, which took over most of the passenger and carrying trade in America's inland waterways. The Navy built no steam warships, although in the 1820s Commodore Porter made good use of a converted commercial sidewheeler, the *Sea Gull,* in chasing pirates in the West Indies. There were excellent reasons for the Navy's delay. Fuel and machinery took up space,

Trial run off New York of U.S.S. Fulton *(formerly* Demologos*), the first steam-propelled warship.*

which was at a premium in a man-of-war. The early, low-pressure steam engines were notoriously unreliable, and were such heavy consumers of fuel that they afforded a maximum cruising radius of only about 100 miles. The paddle wheels would cover a large part of a warship's broadside, cutting deeply into her firepower; moreover, sidewheels and machinery were highly vulnerable to shot. In battle a single hit could leave a steamer both outgunned and fatally outmaneuvered. Hence naval officers everywhere preferred to wait until commerical vessels had evolved a dependable, fuel-conserving engine, and until bigger guns were developed to offset the loss of broadside area.

Matthew Calbraith Perry, as a young officer, had seen the *Demologos* launched, and as captain of a ship in the West Indies Squadron he had observed the versatility of the *Sea Gull*. His interest aroused, he kept himself informed of progress in steam engines and boilers. In the 1830s, when he was commandant of the Brooklyn Navy Yard, he concluded that the time had come for the U.S. Navy to take the plunge. He accord-

ingly prevailed upon Navy Secretary Mahlon Dickerson to let him build a prototype steam warship.

The result was the *Fulton II*, constructed under Perry's supervision, and launched in 1837. Perry himself took command of her, in addition to his duties as navy yard commandant. A 700-ton, 180-foot-long sidewheeler, she was more conventional than the first *Fulton*, and much faster. She was awkward and barely seaworthy, but she taught Perry and the Navy what to avoid in later steamships. Equally important, she convinced Congressional skeptics that a steam navy was practical.

On Perry's recommendation, Congress appropriated funds for the steam warships *Mississippi* and *Missouri*, launched in 1841. These fine vessels, nearly 1,700 tons each, and 229 feet long, were the dreadnoughts of their day, giving the United States a temporary lead over all the other navies of the world. The *Missouri* was destroyed by fire in 1843, but the *Mississippi* had a distinguished career. She served under Perry in the Mexican War and the Japan Expedition, and during the

Civil War she played an important part in reopening the river whose name she bore.

Most of the Navy's remaining objections to steam-driven warships were overcome by the invention of a practical screw propeller. Both screw and engine were beneath the waterline, not easily reached by shot, and no broadside area was masked. Captain Robert F. Stockton USN persuaded the nautical screw's chief designer, the Swedish inventive genius John Ericsson, to come to the United States. Here Ericsson designed, and Stockton supervised, the construction of the steam sloop *Princeton*, the first screw-driven warship.

In 1855 the *Merrimack* was launched; she was the first of a series of fast screw frigates acquired by the U.S. Navy. These frigates were wooden-hulled vessels and, like all large steamers of the day, were provided with masts and sails. In appearance they rather closely resembled the frigates of the War of 1812.

In the pre–Civil War period, Britain and France made increasing use of iron for ship armor, and later also for hulls—partly to offset the growing power of gunfire and partly because they were running out of ship timber. The United States, which had ample timber, continued to build the cheaper wooden ships, both naval and commercial. For several years the speedy American sailing clippers competed favorably with European steamers, but by 1860 the steam-driven iron vessels had developed to a point where they clearly outclassed wooden vessels propelled by steam or sail.

Because paddle wheels masked so much of the broadsides of early steam warships, experimenters sought means of securing greater firepower with fewer guns. The pivot gun, which could be swung about to strengthen either broadside, was one obvious answer, but the main trend was toward bigger guns. This necessarily meant stronger guns, for charges needed to propel shot weighing much more than 32 pounds were likely to burst the old cast-iron ordnance, killing or injuring the gun crews.

Ericsson, by shifting to wrought iron, was able to build a practical 12-inch gun, the Oregon, which he mounted in the *Princeton*. A poor imitation of the Oregon, designed by Captain Stockton and also mounted in the *Princeton*, shattered during an exhibition firing, killing an officer, two congressmen, the Secretary of the Navy, and the Secretary of State. This accident put an end to experiments with wrought-iron ordnance for some time. Commander John A. Dahlgren USN developed a highly practical bottle-shaped gun, thick in proportion to pressures in the barrel. The Dahlgren gun was used widely by the Navy in the Civil War.

Naval officers had preferred solid shot for use against enemy ships until 1853, when the Russian fleet opened the Crimean War by sinking seven Turkish frigates with shellfire. That demonstration converted most navies to the use of shell for attack and iron armor for defense.

The Civil War navies used both solid shot and shell, wooden ships and ironclads. Their shells were iron spheres filled with explosive and fitted with time fuses. The shell was held in place inside the gun barrel by a round grommet, or collar; the flash of the exploding charge, passing around the shell, ignited the outward-pointing fuse.

In 1859 the British adopted the built-up rifled Armstrong gun that fired an elongated percussion-fused shell at long range with great accuracy.* The Americans, however, stuck to their Dahlgrens. At this stage of development, and at the close ranges the Americans favored, these guns were found better for penetrating armor.

THE UNITED STATES NAVAL ACADEMY

The British navy had had a naval academy for the education of its young officers since 1733. In 1802 the U.S. Army had acquired its military academy at West Point. But the U.S. Navy had nothing of the sort during the first half century of its existence. American midshipmen were expected, for the most part, to "learn by doing." Chaplains were indeed ordered to instruct them in mathematics, navigation, and French, but they were rarely qualified to do so. Ships of the line each had an underpaid, politically appointed schoolmaster. Classes afloat were, however, not taken very seriously and were subject to constant interruption as midshipmen were ordered to "more important duties."

American naval officers, if they were educated at all, were thus likely to be self-educated. Two of the most successful of the self-educated officers, Matthew Fontaine Maury and Matthew Calbraith Perry, strongly advocated the establishment of an academy ashore for training midshipmen. But Congress refused to authorize the necessary appropriations, especially as many naval officers insisted that a midshipman could learn all he needed to know by "keeping his eyes open," and that training midshipmen ashore would be like "trying to teach ducks to swim in a garret."

As it became increasingly evident that midshipmen

---

* The most common form of built-up gun has a barrel consisting of two or more tight-fitting concentric cylinders.

could not learn enough while afloat to pass their required examinations, coaching schools were established in the Boston, New York, and Norfolk navy yards, and at the Naval Asylum, a home for old sailors in Philadelphia. In these schools the midshipmen were trained by both civilian and military professors and then examined for promotion by a board of senior naval officers.

The Philadelphia school began to eclipse the others in reputation in 1842 when twenty-three-year-old William Chauvenet succeeded to the head of its small faculty. Brilliant, energetic, a recent honor graduate of Yale, Chauvenet set out to develop a two-year course at the Asylum School, but did not succeed because senior officers said that midshipmen could not be spared so long. He did, however, establish a one-year course, maintaining such high standards that the Navy Department began to phase out the other schools and send all midshipman trainees to Chauvenet at Philadelphia.

It is not clear when Chauvenet and George Bancroft, the historian and educator, first got their heads together, but when Bancroft became Secretary of the Navy in 1845, he and Chauvenet were in agreement that the time was ripe for establishing a college of the Navy. The idea may have been Chauvenet's, but Secretary Bancroft had the finesse to see it through.

Bancroft first induced the Army to transfer to the Navy an outdated post, old Fort Severn at Annapolis, Maryland. Then, when the examining board of senior officers, including Commodore Perry, met at Philadelphia in 1845, Bancroft consulted them. He recommended moving the school to a better location and proposed Annapolis. The officers concurred on both points.

The new Naval School opened at Annapolis on October 10, 1845, under the stern but fair superintendency of Commander Franklin Buchanan. Although both faculty and student body had been enlarged, it was generally assumed that this was merely the Philadelphia school transferred to Annapolis in order to remove the midshipmen from the temptations of the big city.

The school was at first, like its predecessors, a mere coaching center, with midshipmen attending on uncertain schedules between voyages. So it remained in 1846 when Bancroft left the Navy to become Minister to Great Britain, and so it remained the following year when Buchanan departed to fight in the Mexican War. Chauvenet, left behind as president of the school's academic

The United States Naval Academy in 1853. The wooden structure atop old Fort Severn (center) was a gymnasium.

board, supervised the development of the long-range plan which would carry out the intention of its founders. In 1850 the plan was adopted. The school was renamed the United States Naval Academy and its course of instruction was extended to four years.

THE MEXICAN WAR, 1846-1848

By 1845 the chronically unstable Mexican government had almost lost control of California; Texas had been independent of Mexico for nine years. At the request of the Texans, Congress voted to annex their country. Early in 1846, General Zachary Taylor marched 4,000 U.S. Army troops to the Rio Grande, over territory that Mexico had never recognized as a part of Texas. Thereupon Mexican troops crossed the river, attacked Taylor's army, and were repulsed. The United States then declared war. Taylor, supported by the U.S. Gulf Squadron, now crossed the Rio Grande, captured the town of Matamoros on the Gulf coast, and plunged inland.

Meanwhile, the U.S. Pacific Squadron, a frigate and three sloops, was operating on the coast of California. Under the command of Commodore John Sloat, parties from the squadron went ashore at Monterey and San Francisco, where they raised the U.S. flag without opposition. Sloat then fell ill and was relieved by Commodore Robert Stockton, who had arrived in the frigate *Congress*.

Marines and sailors from Stockton's squadron now joined American forces ashore. These land forces consisted of 160 scouts, frontiersmen, and California settlers led by Captain John C. Frémont, and 100 U.S. Army troops that Brigadier General Stephen W. Kearny had led across country from Fort Leavenworth, Kansas. Operating sometimes together and sometimes apart, these small forces captured Los Angeles, San Diego, Santa Barbara, and other California settlements. The Treaty of Cahuenga, signed early in 1847 between the Americans and the leaders of the weak Mexican defense force, gave California to the United States. Kearny's army force had already annexed the territory between California and Texas. Thus, since the Americans and British had now settled their dispute over the Oregon Territory, continental United States was complete except for the later purchases of Alaska and the Gadsden Tract.

The United States, having brought the misgoverned settlers of the Southwest under the protection of the American flag, had won its war. Unfortunately, however, the Mexican government did not recognize the American victory, even though General Taylor's army was penetrating ever deeper into northeastern Mexico while the Gulf Squadron maintained a close blockade of her east coast. To convince the Mexicans that they were defeated, President Polk decided to use the classical convincer, capture of their capital. He therefore ordered Lieutenant General Winfield Scott to land an army at Veracruz and march on Mexico City. The task of getting Scott's 14,000 troops ashore required the full support of the Gulf Squadron, commanded at that time by Commodore David Conner.

On March 4, 1847, U.S. Army transports joined Conner's squadron in the roadstead of Anton Lazardo, 13 miles southeast of Veracruz. Assembled in the roadstead were nearly 100 ships, including a fair number of steamers. It was the largest amphibious operation undertaken by the U.S. Navy before the North African invasion in World War II. General Scott and Commodore Conner reconnoitered the shoreline in a small steamer and selected for the landing place a stretch of beach three miles south of Veracruz.

The landing on March 9, though conducted without rehearsal, was a model of efficiency, resembling some of the smoother amphibious assaults of World War II. Off the beachhead, frigates and sloops at a distance and a line of gunboats close in, prepared to lend gunfire support. The troops went ashore in waves of surf boats, each commanded by a midshipman or petty officer and rowed by seamen. Mexican cavalry appeared briefly behind the beach, but, observing the firepower the Americans could bring to bear, they prudently retired inside the city defenses. Hence the soldiers landed to the music of ships' bands rather than the roar of gunfire.

Commodore Perry, who soon relieved the ailing Conner as commander of the squadron, arranged with General Scott for joint operations against Veracruz. After a two-day bombardment by navy guns afloat and army and navy guns ashore, the city capitulated. Scott's army now marched inland toward Mexico City, while Perry's squadron maintained the blockade and took possession of ports. The Americans permitted exports and nonmilitary imports but collected customs duties to help pay for the war.

The two U.S. armies in Mexico were consistently victorious over their ill-equipped adversaries. Scott's army entered the Mexican capital in mid-September, but no Mexican authority could be found that dared to take responsibility for ceding the territories that U.S. forces had already annexed. At length, after prolonged negotiations, peace was restored in early 1848 by the Treaty of Guadalupe Hidalgo.

V

The Civil War

When the abolitionist candidate Abraham Lincoln was elected President in November 1860, secession of at least some of the slaveholding states became a certainty. South Carolina led the way, soon followed by six other states of the Deep South. As each state seceded, its government proceeded to take over U.S. property within its borders—post offices, customhouses, arsenals, forts, navy yards.

As a rule, the officials in charge promptly surrendered rather than risk bloodshed. An exception was Major Robert Anderson, who commanded the forts in Charleston harbor and was stationed with his garrison at Fort Moultrie on the north shore. When South Carolina seceded, Anderson spiked the guns of Moultrie and transferred his 83 men at night by boat to the more defensible Fort Sumter, a masonry structure on a man-made island in the middle of the harbor. The furious Charlestonians vowed to evict these "foreigners" from what they considered South Carolina's property.

In early January 1861 the steamer *Star of the West*, chartered by the U.S. Army, entered Charleston harbor with supplies and reinforcements for Anderson. A secessionist battery set up on the south shore promptly opened fire. The *Star of the West*, after taking several hits, reversed course and hastily retreated out to sea. The first shots of the Civil War had been fired.

Although the hostile batteries surrounding Fort Sumter were being steadily strengthened, outgoing President Buchanan forbade further government intervention, for he was anxious not to present his successor with a war in progress. Militarily speaking, North and South settled down to wait out Buchanan's incumbency in order to see what Lincoln would do. In February representatives of the seceded states, meeting in Montgomery, Alabama, proclaimed the Confederate States of America and elected Jefferson Davis President. At this time Anderson and his men were still at Fort Sumter, and when President Lincoln was inaugurated in March, they were running short of food.

Nothing nettled Lincoln more than the situation at Charleston. He was therefore much interested when Gustavus Fox, a dynamic former naval officer, offered to lead an expedition to the relief of Sumter. Both General-in-Chief Winfield Scott and Navy Secretary Gideon Welles opposed the expedition, believing Sumter to be no longer tenable. Welles pointed out that even if Fox's expedition succeeded, it would have to be repeated endlessly and at ever-mounting cost. Lincoln was nevertheless determined to have a try; on his orders, Welles assembled for Fox a small squadron, its principal strength concentrated in the big paddle sloop *Powhatan*.

President Davis, informed of the relief plans, ordered Brigadier General Pierre Beauregard to take possession of Sumter without delay, using force if necessary. When Anderson rejected Beauregard's demand to surrender, the latter ordered the fort bombarded. The bombardment began in the morning of April 12, not long after Fox arrived off Charleston harbor.

Fox was powerless to intervene then, or later, because the *Powhatan* never arrived. Lincoln himself had blunderingly assigned the sloop to a second expedition, one for the relief of Fort Pickens in Pensacola Bay, and she was already far down the coast. On the afternoon of April 13, Sumter capitulated. The following day Fox's squadron, with Beauregard's permission, carried Anderson and his men away.

A day later President Lincoln, announcing that the United States would retrieve and defend its property, called for 75,000 volunteers. President Davis thereupon announced that the Confederacy would repel any attempt at invasion. The American Civil War was thus launched by Presidential proclamation.

LOSS OF THE NORFOLK NAVY YARD

The navy yard at Norfolk, Virginia, was the largest and best equipped in the nation. Here were extensive shipbuilding and repair facilities, a large drydock, and more than 1,100 guns, among which were some 300 Dahlgrens. Also at the yard were several warships, including the 50-gun screw frigate *Merrimack*, having her engines repaired.

Secretary Welles, anticipating Virginia's early secession, sent Engineer-in-Chief Benjamin Isherwood to hasten the repairs on the *Merrimack* so that she could be transferred to Philadelphia. Isherwood, working around the clock with double crews, had the frigate ready for sea on April 18, by which date Virginia had seceded. The aged commandant of the navy yard, Commodore Charles McCauley, long since befuddled by advice from Southern officers, now believed his yard surrounded by state militia ready to attack. In panic he ordered the *Merrimack*'s boiler fires extinguished.

Welles now sent Commodore Hiram Paulding to Norfolk in the screw sloop *Pawnee*, together with technicians, marines, and soldiers. Paulding was instructed to relieve McCauley, evacuate whatever ships and supplies he could, and destroy the rest. When the *Pawnee* reached the Norfolk Navy Yard at dusk on April 20, Paulding found the *Merrimack* and three other ships slowly sinking at their berths, scuttled at McCauley's direction in order to prevent their capture.

Through the night Paulding's men placed combustibles and explosives in buildings and on the decks of the sinking ships and laid powder trains. They tried to make the stored guns unusable by sledging off their trunnions, but had no success with the sturdy Dahlgrens. As the *Pawnee* slipped away down the Elizabeth River just before dawn, the navy yard blazed up and explosions rumbled. The fire proved more spectacular than destructive. Most of the repair facilities were saved; the upper decks of the *Merrimack* were burned, but her engines remained intact; the drydock was unharmed, as were the Dahlgren guns. These guns were subsequently distributed throughout the Confederacy to a score of strategic points.

RESOURCES AND STRATEGIES

Only that part of Virginia east of the Alleghenies had seceded from the Union. The western counties remained loyal and eventually formed the separate state of West Virginia. Arkansas and North Carolina seceded in May; Tennessee, in June. The strongly prosecessionist border state of Maryland was at first kept within the Union only by force of arms.

For a time Washington was isolated as troops coming

Burning of the Norfolk Navy Yard.

down from the North were turned back by mobs in Baltimore. Telegraph and rail lines were cut. Massachusetts volunteers, led by Benjamin Franklin Butler, a cross-eyed Massachusetts politician who had got himself elected brigadier general of militia, at last reached the capital via Perryville, Chesapeake Bay, and Annapolis. This was no minor feat, for citizens of Annapolis were so hostile to the Union that those midshipmen, officers, and faculty members of the United States Naval Academy who had not already gone south found it advisable to sail away in their schoolship, the old frigate *Constitution.* For the duration of the war the academy operated at Newport, Rhode Island.

The Union had tremendous military advantages over the Confederacy: 71 per cent of the population, 85 per cent of the factories, 72 per cent of the railroad mileage, 81 per cent of the bank deposits. It had a respectable navy, while the South had none. Furthermore, the Union boasted one of the world's finest merchant marines, one that could keep it supplied with everything not produced at home. The Confederacy, on the contrary, could not even feed itself because of the extensive acreage planted in cotton, its principal export crop.

As it turned out, the South's chief defensive potential, besides its immense area, lay in the abilities of the generals who elected to fight for the Confederacy: Robert E. Lee, Thomas "Stonewall" Jackson, Joseph Johnston, J. E. B. Stuart, Pierre Beauregard, James Longstreet. These were probably the ablest military men of their day.

The Confederacy.

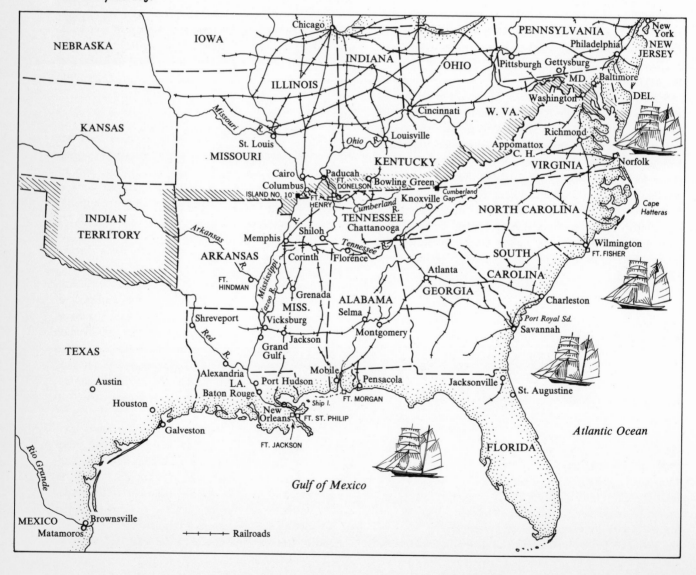

Many Confederate leaders counted on "King Cotton" to bring about the foreign intervention that alone could assure them victory. They delayed shipping the 1861 cotton crop, although there was ample time to get most of it to sea before the Union blockade closed down. It was hoped that Britain, thus deprived, would be obliged to intervene in order to save her textile industry. In fact, however, the record crop of 1860, bought up by Britain and France in anticipation of trouble, resulted in unprecedented inventories abroad that could not be worked off in two years. In any event, neither England nor France, both antislavery in sentiment, had any intention of intervening merely to assure her cotton supply. The Confederacy would have done better to ship out every bale it had, in order to build up credit abroad.

The secessionist states immediately adopted the traditional means of warring on a stronger power—commerce raiding. Two days after President Lincoln called up volunteers, President Davis by proclamation offered letters of marque and reprisal to mariners and adventurers of all nations who might wish to prey as privateers on U.S. maritime commerce. Lincoln promptly branded such privateering as piracy, and countered by proclaiming a blockade of the Confederate coasts. Secretary Welles protested that proclaiming a blockade amounted to recognizing the Confederacy as a belligerent instead of merely an area in a state of insurrection; the President, he argued, needed only to have declared the ports of the rebellious states closed. The deciding voice was that of Lord Lyons, the British minister in Washington. Lyons advised that Britain would recognize only blockade, and that any other measures might be interpreted as interference with British trade and lead to reprisals.

One curious feature of the American Civil War was that, after the Confederacy had shifted its capital from Montgomery, the opposing capital cities, Richmond and Washington, were on the national peripheries and only 100 miles apart. As a result, it was necessary that both sides maintain large armies in Virginia to guard their governments. Because these armies fought such memorable battles as Antietam, Chancellorsville, and Gettysburg, and because they were commanded by such famous soldiers as Lee, Jackson, and Grant, much of the tradition of the Civil War is concerned with their operations. But the Federal Army of the Potomac and the Confederate Army of Northern Virginia were, after all, mere holding forces. Although Lee won brilliant victories, he could never decisively defeat the Army of the Potomac with its vast manpower reserves. The Army of the Potomac, led by a succession of generals, could never

Gideon Welles, Secretary of the U.S. Navy during the Civil War.

decisively defeat Lee so long as his supplies held out. Accordingly, it became the Union's strategy to deny food and munitions to Lee through a step-by-step reduction of his base of supplies. This was the work of the blockade and of the Mississippi Valley campaign, augmented by incursions of Federal armies through the South. Union strategy, as finally developed, may be summarized by the phrase "shrinking Lee's logistic base."

Heading the Union armies was General-in-Chief Winfield Scott, seventy-four years old at the outbreak of war, gouty, and generally ailing; he was known now as "Old Fuss and Feathers" because of his predilection for fancy uniforms. Scott's poor health by no means inhibited the working of his keen mind. He shocked Cabinet members by expressing the perfectly correct opinion that the Confederacy could not be defeated in less than three years. He strongly opposed the early, headlong drive on Richmond that many Northern leaders recommended, and insisted that the South must first be weakened by a close blockade. He also suggested an advance down the Mississippi Valley in order to split the Confederacy, completing the isolation of its heartland, and to open the river as an outlet for products of the northwestern farmlands.

Scott's strategy was almost a forecast of the way

victory was finally won, but opponents of the plan derisively dubbed it "Scott's Anaconda," after the huge serpent that squeezes its victims to death. The general-in-chief did not remain in office to put his plan into effect. A combination of indignation and worsening health caused him early in the war to relinquish his command.

The Union navy had no counterpart to Scott and his successors. Navy Secretary Welles was at first the only administrator ranking between the President as commander in chief and the various naval commands. This bearded and wigged Connecticut editor and politician, who looked rather like a dirt farmer, combined keenness of judgment with complete honesty and a strong tendency to pinch pennies.

Lincoln appointed Gustavus Fox chief clerk of the Navy Department, to placate him for having been made to look ridiculous at the time of the Sumter relief expedition; Congress later created for him the post of Assistant Secretary of the Navy. Although the character of Fox, who was ebullient, generous, and gregarious, contrasted sharply with that of the silent and secretive Welles, the two men liked and respected each other and formed an effective team. In the words of the historian Richard S. West, "The two of them got on perfectly together, the one sitting quietly at the helm holding a steady course, the effervescent assistant forever darting here and yonder to seek out the best channel to steer through." The team of Welles and Fox ran the U.S. Navy throughout the war with minimum interference from President Lincoln, who was obliged repeatedly to intervene in the operations of his series of bumbling Army commanders.

Most northern politicians, in disregard of General Scott's cautious advice, held out for that quick sprint to Richmond—a dash counted upon to crush the rebellion in a single stroke. In July 1861 Lincoln, over Scott's protest, ordered Brigadier General Irvin McDowell with an ill-trained army of 35,000 volunteers to advance on Beauregard's army of 20,000 men at Manassas, Virginia. The predictable result was the disgraceful First Battle of Bull Run, fought on July 21. Beauregard's army was quickly brought up to the same strength as McDowell's by reinforcements rushed in from the Deep South and from the Valley of Virginia. The Union forces were routed and fell back on Washington in panic. The Confederate officers, losing control of their men, failed to follow up their advantage. Both armies, sobered by their experience, withdrew for a period of intensive drill and training.

From western Virginia, where he had achieved military success, Major General George B. McClellan was now summoned to Washington to relieve McDowell. McClellan did such a masterly job of training his army and also of undermining General Scott, that the latter resigned in November and McClellan succeeded him as general-in-chief. A perfectionist, never feeling that his army was honed to a sufficient degree of sharpness, McClellan, despite prodding from Lincoln, was slow to take military action. At last in March 1862 he proposed a move by water to Fortress Monroe and thence up the peninsula between the James and York rivers to Richmond.

Lincoln could see no special advantage in advancing on Richmond from the southeast instead of directly from the north, particularly since the peninsular approach would leave Washington uncovered. Nevertheless he reluctantly consented, on the ground that something was better than nothing. In order that McClellan might devote his whole attention to the forthcoming campaign, Lincoln temporarily took the Union Army command into his own hands.

THE BLOCKADE

For Secretary Welles, implementing the blockade proclaimed by President Lincoln presented a formidable challenge. The blockade, to be legal, had to be effective, a point on which the United States had always insisted when called upon to honor blockades proclaimed by England and France. However, only the most optimistic observer, studying the map and considering the means at hand, would have pronounced it possible for the U.S. Navy to impose an effective blockade on the Confederacy in less than two years. The Confederate coast stretched from Alexandria, on the Potomac River, southward around Florida to Galveston and beyond —a distance of more than 3,500 miles; along this shoreline were eight major ports and dozens of other navigable harbors. Moreover, most of the Confederacy's Atlantic coast, and much of its Gulf coast, was paralleled by offshore islands and sand barriers, between which were scores of openings for the passage of ships.

At the time of Lincoln's proclamation there were in Northern ports only three warships suitable for blockade duty. More than 250 U.S. naval officers, including such outstanding men as Matthew F. Maury and Franklin Buchanan, had elected to serve the Confederacy. Yet despite the shortage of ships and men, the U.S. Navy had stationed vessels off the chief Confederate ports in a few weeks' time and had established a reasonably effective blockade of the Confederacy within a few months.

Welles began by summoning home all but a few American naval vessels from foreign stations. He started an ambitious construction program, concentrating at first on "90-day gunboats," so called because of the speed with which they were built. He undertook a procurement program, buying or chartering almost any sort of steam vessels, including ferryboats—anything steady enough to serve as mobile gun platforms. Finding that his officer ship purchasers were being grossly overcharged, Welles assigned them other jobs and empowered business leaders to do the buying in his name. He appointed as New York purchasing agent his brother-in-law, George D. Morgan, a man as tight-fisted and as skilled at driving down prices as Welles himself. Congressional charges of nepotism he silenced by demonstrating that Morgan had saved the taxpayers many thousands of dollars. In nine months, under Welles' energetic leadership, the Navy repaired and recommissioned 76 ships, bought 136, and constructed 52.

Secretary Welles welcomed back into the Navy former officers who, like Fox, had resigned or been retired during the prewar naval doldrums when promotions were far between. His chief source of both officers and men was, however, the U.S. merchant marine, which was just going into decline because it had clung too long to sail. In one year the number of seamen in the Navy rose from 7,600 to more than 22,000, and nearly 1,000 temporary officers were added. Patriotism no doubt played its part in attracting these men to the fleet; but the lure of prize money awarded for captured vessels was not an insignificant factor.

Welles' chief manpower problem was the finding of capable engineers to handle the ships' propulsion systems. Luckily the steam engines of the day were fairly simple, but apparently they were not simple enough. It is necessary to cite only the case of the warship that steamed proudly out of New York harbor, to return presently full speed astern; her greenhorn engineers had somehow thrown her engines into reverse and had been unable to get their ship going ahead again.

Initially the U.S. fleet was organized in three squadrons: the Atlantic Blockading Squadron, the Gulf Blockading Squadron, and a Home Squadron set up to protect merchantmen from privateers and other commerce raiders. The Gulf squadron was based on Key West, the Atlantic and Home squadrons at Hampton Roads—a highly unsatisfactory arrangement for the blockading squadrons, because they were based too far away from the chief ports they were expected to watch.

The blockade closed down by stages. At first the blockaders warned away vessels that attempted to enter

Samuel F. Du Pont.

Confederate ports and sent in notices to foreign vessels that they must leave by the end of a stipulated grace period. Later the blockading vessels pounced on ships entering or leaving port or even navigating the coastal waters behind the offshore islands. For this rigorous duty every available Union vessel was used, whether steam-driven or sail. The more popular duty was of course in steamships, which, by making more captures, earned their crews more prize money.

In June 1861 Welles appointed a board, headed by Captain Samuel F. Du Pont of the Delaware powder-making family, to study means for improving the effectiveness of the blockade. This group, known generally as the Strategy Board, advised dividing the Atlantic coast blockaders into north and south blockading squadrons. They recommended sinking stone-filled hulks in the openings of the long sand barrier that separates the North Carolina sounds from the Atlantic. Through these openings skittered privateers and blockade runners based on Carolina ports such as Elizabeth City, New Bern, and Beaufort, as well as Norfolk, Virginia, which was connected with Albemarle Sound via the Dismal Swamp canal. Most important, the Strategy Board urged the capture of bases along the Confederate coasts, for without such bases the blockading vessels had to return periodically to Hampton Roads for refueling, replenishing, and minor repairs. For more ex-

Scene of amphibious assaults in North Carolina waters.

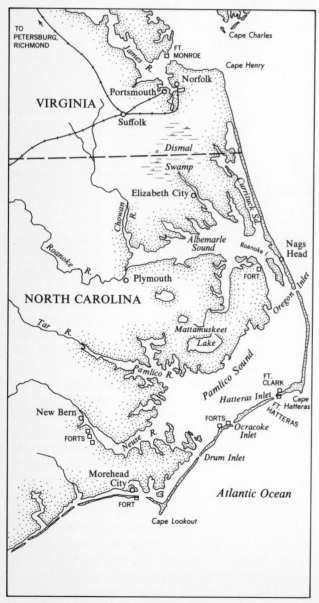

tensive refit, they were obliged to go to Washington, Philadelphia, or New York.

As the first step in implementing the recommendations of the Strategy Board, Welles ordered the closing of Hatteras Inlet, which connected Pamlico Sound with the ocean. The responsibility for this action was assigned to Flag Officer Silas Stringham, Commander Atlantic Blockading Squadron. Because this inlet was guarded by two primitive log-and-sand fortifications called Forts Clark and Hatteras, Welles requested army assistance. General Scott accordingly sent 860 men under Ben Butler, who had been promoted to major general in recognition of his operations in Maryland.

On the morning of August 28, 1861, the steam frigates *Minnesota* and *Wabash* and the sailing corvette *Cumberland*, with a total of 117 guns, opened fire on the forts, while the soldiers, supported by lighter vessels, began to go ashore three miles up the beach. Only a few more than 300 landed, for the boats, which were to return for more men, were either smashed or could not be got back through the heavy surf. As it turned out, the soldiers were not needed, for the gunnery ships, remaining out of range of the mostly antiquated Confederate guns, pounded the forts into submission. Commodore Samuel Barrow, lately of the U.S. Navy, refused to surrender to the U.S. Army, which had had no part in his defeat. At his insistence, he was conveyed out to the flagship *Minnesota*, where he handed his sword to his old friend Stringham. Barrow and nearly 700 more prisoners of war were taken away.

Scarcely less spectacular than the battle itself was the dash to Washington by separate routes of Ben Butler and Si Stringham to announce the first Union victory of the war and to claim the credit. Butler got there first and reported to Fox. Despite the lateness of the hour, the Assistant Secretary rushed with Butler to the White House and aroused the President. On hearing the news, Lincoln in his nightshirt danced a jig with Fox, while the cross-eyed politician-general sat on a sofa and roared with laughter. The next day the whole Union shared their glee at this touch of success, which alleviated the gloom of the Bull Run defeat.

In mid-September, ships of the Gulf Blockading Squadron, under Flag Officer William McKean, opened fire on Ship Island near the mouth of the Mississippi River. The Confederate garrison, unable to return an effective fire, set its quarters ablaze and destroyed as much of the island's defenses as possible before retiring to the mainland in boats. Federal troops soon occupied the island, which proved to be a useful base for blockading New Orleans and Mobile, even though a tight blockade of New Orleans was not possible because of the city's many exits to the Gulf of Mexico.

Potentially far more useful, and likely to be much more difficult to gain, was the Navy's next objective, Port Royal Sound. This was a deep, navigable indentation in the coast of South Carolina. Its outer shores were all islands and the mainland behind it was an almost impassable swamp. Between Savannah and Charleston, it was ideally located as a base for blockading both; in addition, it was virtually invulnerable from the interior. The potential danger to Union attackers was the stone-and-masonry forts flanking the entrance to the sound: Fort Walker on Hilton Head to the south and Fort Beauregard on Bay Point to the north.

The Port Royal expeditionary force, the largest assembled since the Veracruz campaign, consisted of 13 warships, 20 colliers, 6 supply vessels, and 25 transports carrying 14,000 soldiers and marines. This was to be the nucleus of the new South Atlantic Blockading Squadron. Heading the naval armada as flag officer was Captain Samuel Du Pont, formerly of the Strategy Board. It set out from Hampton Roads in orderly formation, with Du Pont's flagship, the steam frigate *Wabash*, at the head. Off Cape Hatteras it was scattered by a hurricane that sank one transport and drove two ashore.

The attack had been planned as an amphibious assault, the troops landing and storming the forts while supported by naval gunfire. After the scattering of the transports, however, and the almost complete loss of surf boats, which were swept from decks in the storm, Du Pont was obliged to reestimate the situation. He concluded that, as the only alternative to long delay, he would have to attack the forts with naval guns only.

Among the ships that had failed to join Du Pont off Port Royal was the screw sloop *Pocahantas*. Her absence must have caused some raised eyebrows in the fleet, for her captain was Percival Drayton, who came from a distinguished South Carolina family. Drayton's brother Thomas was in fact commanding the Confederates on Hilton Head, at which the fleet would presently be firing. Nevertheless, Du Pont had perfect confidence in Drayton; he had asked that the latter be given command of the *Pocahantas* as a means of proving his loyalty to the Union, which he had elected to serve.

Du Pont had intended to open the battle on the morning of November 7, 1861, with a naval attack on Walker, the stronger of the two flanking forts; but his fleet captain, Charles H. Davis, suggested another plan, which Du Pont immediately adopted. The fleet in two parallel columns, one of nine ships headed by the *Wa-*

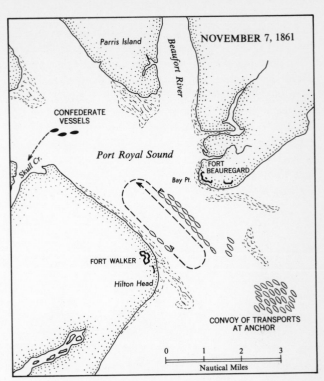

The attack on Port Royal, South Carolina.

bash, the other of five gunboats, would steam up the middle of the channel, exchanging fire with both forts. Two and a half miles past the forts, the nine-ship main battle line would reverse course to the left and head back past Fort Walker much closer than before. Firing continuously, the main line would repeatedly reverse course to the left, passing and repassing Fort Walker on an elliptical path at varying distances, thereby presenting the Confederate gunners with constantly changing problems of range and deflection. The gunboat column would remain inside the sound after its single pass, firing at Fort Walker's weak inner flank and enfilading its water faces.

In actual practice, the attack varied from the plan in three respects. First, inside the sound, the fleet encountered three small Confederate warships, which opened fire as a gesture of defiance and then fled up a creek when the 46-gun *Wabash* fired a broadside in their direction. Second, when the *Wabash* reversed course, only the *Susquehanna*, 12, and the sidewheel gunboat *Bienville*, 8, followed. Third, the *Wabash*, abandoned by most of her line, received unexpected reinforcement. As she headed back past Fort Walker, another vessel was seen approaching from the outer roadstead. It was Drayton's *Pocahantas*, which had arrived at last. When the *Pocahantas* joined the other three in firing on Fort Walker's water face, Captain Charles Steedman of

Assault on Roanoke Island.

the *Bienville*, another South Carolinian, swung his cap in the air and shouted, "Three cheers for South Carolina!" Captain Drayton shouted back, "Three cheers for South Carolina and the American flag!" Drayton's family never forgave him for firing on his native state. When he died shortly after the war, he was buried by his navy friends; none of his relatives attended the funeral.

The fleet, which had a five-to-one gunfire superiority, rapidly overwhelmed the forts. The *Wabash* alone fired 880 rounds. One observer noted that shells fell on the forts "as fast as a horse's feet beat the ground in a gallop." Another remarked that the perpendicular columns of dust cast up by the shells "looked as if we had suddenly raised from the ground groves of poplars." Before the *Wabash* and her consorts began their third loop, Fort Walker was reported abandoned, and by nightfall Fort Beauregard also had been evacuated. The Union Army had only to move in as an occupation force. Exploded was the old naval dictum that "a ship's a fool to fight a fort." Evidently the highly maneuverable new steamships could attack even powerful shore fortifications without too great risk. Nevertheless, naval

officers could not shake off their concern over what would happen if a lucky shot from a fort suddenly disabled an attacking steamer's engines.

Before the end of the year the glory of the Union's first victory, that of Hatteras Inlet, had gone sour. Hulks sunk in the openings of sand barriers were thrust aside or swept out to sea by the mighty currents. Shoals and shifting channels made Hatteras Inlet unusable, not only as a blockading base, but even as an anchorage. Stringham and Butler did not follow up their initial success, as newspapers demanded, with attacks on ports within the sounds. Journalistic criticism changed to ridicule, as writers acidly revived the story of the Stringham-Butler footrace to Washington to gather laurels. Butler, in his ruthless drive for power, had developed too thick a hide to be pricked by such barbs; besides, he had gone to New England on recruiting duty. The thinner-skinned Stringham brooded, however, and at last asked Welles to be relieved of his command. He spent the rest of the war behind a desk.

Stringham's successor, Louis M. Goldsborough, Commander North Atlantic Blockading Squadron, perceived that if Hatteras Inlet was of no use as a base, it was at least a gateway to the Carolina sounds. In mid-January 1862, accompanied by 17 shallow-draft gunboats, he made rendezvous with a large convoy of assorted transports, which were bringing 13,000 troops commanded by Brigadier General Ambrose E. Burnside. For the next three weeks gunboats and convoy fought storms as they lightened ship in order to work their way through the dangerous, shallow channel into Pamlico Sound.

In a heavy downpour on February 6, the Federal ships reached Roanoke Island, where Pamlico and Albemarle sounds meet, and promptly took the island's forts under fire. When most of the fight had been taken out of the defenders, steamers moved toward the beach, towing boatloads of soldiers. Near the shore the steamers turned away, casting off the boats, which reached land under their own momentum. By midnight the Federal troops were safely ashore. The next morning they began an advance, closely supported by Goldsborough's gunboats. By midafternoon the Federals had overrun the island, having captured 40 guns and taken 3,000 prisoners of war at a cost of 50 of their own men killed.

Goldsborough's gunboats, having Roanoke Island as a base, now proceeded to clear the sounds of armed Confederate vessels and to support Burnside's troops in capturing Elizabeth City, New Bern, and Beaufort. As a result of Federal campaigning in the sounds and their tributary rivers, North Carolina's military strength was largely diverted to local defense, and the transport of the abundant provisions of the Carolina country to General Lee's Army of Northern Virginia was thrown upon the inadequate railroad system.

Concurrently, troops operating out of Port Royal supported by Flag Officer Du Pont's South Atlantic Blockading Squadron were capturing and occupying points along the coasts of South Carolina, Georgia, and Florida. In April the Federals shattered and captured Fort Pulaski at the mouth of the Savannah River, by means of a 30-hour bombardment from guns placed on a nearby island. They thus effectively sealed off Savannah from the sea. Only Charleston and Wilmington on the Confederate Atlantic coast were now open to blockade runners.

THE BATTLE OF HAMPTON ROADS

While the Union was gradually sealing off the Confederacy with an ever-tightening blockade, the Confederates were devising a means of breaking out. They raised the sunken *Merrimack*, cut away her burned superstructure to the berth deck, got her engines running, and began building on her hull a thick, sloping casemate of more than three feet of oak and pine, topped by four inches of iron plates. This citadel was pierced for eight 9-inch rifled Dahlgren shell guns in broadside and two 7-inch Dahlgren pivot guns, fore and aft, each firing through any of three ports. In her bow was inserted a 1,500-pound, cast-iron underwater ram which was expected to be her chief weapon. Steaming with her main deck almost awash, she would have to avoid heavy seas, and because of her 22-foot draft, she had to steer clear of shoals. Although 1,500 men were assigned to the job of converting the *Merrimack*, it took eight months, partly because of lack of experience and equipment but chiefly because of difficulty in rounding up enough iron for the ship's plates.

At first neither Lincoln nor Welles considered building ironclad ships, the President because he hoped for a short war, the Secretary because he was concerned primarily with assembling a blockading fleet. Nevertheless, in the summer of 1861 Welles asked Congress for authority to set up a board of officers to advise on ironclads, as well as an appropriation to build a few of them. Receiving his authority and $1,500,000, he advertised for designs and bids and set up his Ironclad Board to make selections. The board played safe, choosing two conventional armored vessels with guns in broadside: the future *Galena*, a failure, and the future *New Ironsides*, a resounding success.

John Ericsson could not bring himself to submit a design, having never become reconciled with the Navy, which had refused to grant him full credit for the design of the *Princeton* and had blamed him in part for the explosion of Stockton's gun. He was not displeased, however, when his fellow shipwright Cornelius Bushnell asked his permission to show an ingenious Ericsson ship model to Secretary Welles. This model, a flat armored deck surmounted by a revolving gun turret and a tiny pilothouse forward, was in fact a miniature of the future *Monitor* and the most original design in the history of naval architecture. Ericsson said that the ship could be built in three months. Welles, favorably impressed, sent Bushnell and the model on to President Lincoln, who remarked, "All I can say is what the girl said when she stuck her foot in the stocking, 'It strikes me there's something in it.'"

Ericsson received his contract in early October, laid his keel at Greenpoint, Brooklyn, before the end of the month, had steam in his engines by the end of the year, and launched the unfinished hull at the end of January 1862. He never took time to draw complete plans, but merely sketched details for the workmen as construction proceeded. Ignoring the approved specifications, he improvised as he built, inventing a score of patentable devices to meet unforeseen requirements.

Because each side, North and South, knew what the other was doing, the final stage in the building of the *Monitor* and the *Merrimack* became a breathless sprint. If the *Merrimack* should get into action with any serious lead over the *Monitor,* she could, at least, smash the wooden blockade vessels in Hampton Roads and reopen Norfolk to transatlantic commerce; and, by isolating the Union forces in Newport News and Fortress Monroe, she could oblige General McClellan to abandon his plan for an advance on Richmond via the Yorktown peninsula.

The Confederates won the race. In the early afternoon of March 8, their ironclad, looking much like a floating roof topped by a smokestack, emerged from

the Elizabeth River into Hampton Roads. Commanded by Flag Officer Franklin Buchanan, erstwhile first superintendent of the Naval Academy, the *Merrimack* had been rechristened C.S.S. *Virginia,* a name that did not stick. On her first trial run she went immediately into action.

The Union ships in Hampton Roads, long forewarned, burst into instant activity. All cleared for action, tugs whistled, flag signals streamed, crews hastened to quarters. Meanwhile the lumbering ironclad, accompanied by two gunboats, headed northwest across the roads toward Newport News, where two Union sailing vessels, the corvette *Cumberland* and the frigate *Congress,* rode at anchor blockading the James River. From off Old Point Comfort the steam frigates *Minnesota* and *Roanoke* and the sailing frigate *St. Lawrence* advanced toward Newport News to rescue the *Cumberland* and

The Merrimack *undergoing conversion to an ironclad.*

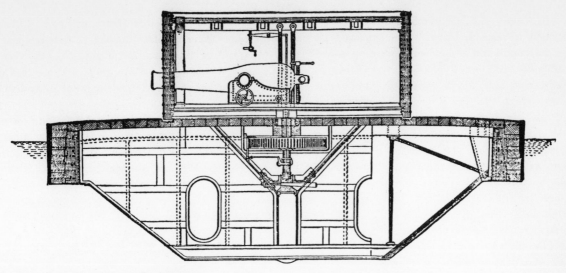

Cross section through turret of the Monitor.

the *Congress;* they hoped also to trap the *Merrimack.*
Hugging the shoals to avoid fire from Confederate
batteries on Sewell's Point, all three would-be rescuers
ran aground.

The *Merrimack,* heading for the *Cumberland,* exchanged fire with the *Congress* and repeatedly holed
the frigate's hull, while shot from the *Congress* merely
bounced off the slanting sides of the ironclad's greased
casemate and shells burst harmlessly like ripe melons
against her iron plating. The *Merrimack* bored in
through pointblank fire from the *Cumberland* and
drove her iron ram into the corvette's starboard bow.
For a minute it appeared that the ironclad would be
carried down with her victim. Then the *Merrimack*
wrenched free, leaving her ram in the corvette, which
sank rapidly, her guns firing steadily until they were
submerged. At last only the tops of the *Cumberland*'s
masts remained above water, with her flag still flying at
a masthead.

The nearby *Congress* in desperation grounded herself near the Newport News batteries. But the *Merrimack,* undeterred, circled back and, taking position
athwart the frigate's stern, poured in such murderous
raking fire that the *Congress* soon struck her colors.
Buchanan, springing atop the *Merrimack's* casemate,
ordered one of his gunboats to go alongside the frigate
and bring away her officers, but through some misunderstanding Federal guns both afloat and ashore reopened
fire. Branding this violation of truce "vile treachery,"
Buchanan ordered the *Congress* destroyed. At that moment a marksman on shore sent a bullet into his thigh.

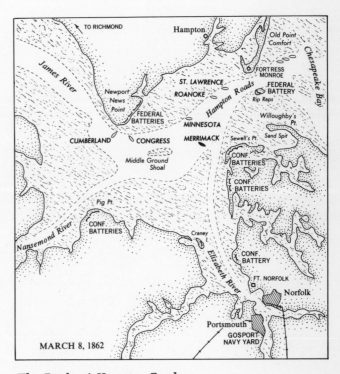

The Battle of Hampton Roads.

The Merrimack *rams the* Cumberland.

Falling back, Buchanan turned the command over to his first lieutenant, Catesby Jones. "Plug hot shot into her and don't leave her until she's afire," he ordered; "they must look after their own wounded, since they won't let us."

When the *Congress* was burning furiously, the *Merrimack's* pilots warned Jones that the ebbing tide made it dangerous for the deep-draft ironclad to remain in the roads. So Jones reluctantly turned away from the *Merrimack's* next scheduled victim, the *Minnesota.* The ironclad, cheered by spectators lining the Confederate shores, anchored for the night in the Elizabeth River.

News of the events in Hampton Roads spread panic in Northern ports and caused near hysteria in Washing-ton. At a special Sunday meeting of the Cabinet on March 9, the President and the Secretary of War, Edwin Stanton, took turns going to a window overlooking the Potomac to see whether the *Merrimack* had arrived. Stanton predicted that the ram would disperse Congress and destroy the Capitol and other government buildings, or that it would bombard New York and Boston, extorting from those cities, under threat of destruction, money to carry on the war. He sent telegrams to governors of seaboard states urging them to seal off their harbors with obstructions.

Meanwhile, the *Monitor* had arrived in Hampton Roads after a harrowing voyage under tow, in which she had barely avoided foundering. She had entered Chesapeake Bay on the afternoon of March 8 as the

The Merrimack *bombards the* Congress.

Merrimack was breaking off action. She reached the *Roanoke* at 9 P.M., her way lighted by the burning *Congress*, which blew up shortly after midnight. The captain of the *Roanoke* directed the *Monitor's* commanding officer, Lieutenant John L. Worden, to place his ironclad alongside the still grounded *Minnesota.*

Soon after dawn on the 9th, the *Merrimack* weighed anchor and headed out across Hampton Roads toward the *Minnesota.* Out came the *Monitor* to meet her. The two ironclads, banging away, fought a four-hour circling battle in which neither did the other any serious harm. Once the nearby *Minnesota* fired a whole broadside at the *Merrimack* without effect. The Confederate ram replied with a shell from her bow gun that wrecked four compartments in the frigate. The decisive shot came at

11:30 A.M.: a shell from the *Merrimack* which exploded against the eye slit of the *Monitor's* pilothouse, temporarily blinding Worden. Before Worden's first lieutenant could take command, the helmsman, obeying the captain's last order to "sheer off," steered the shallow-draft *Monitor* over the shoals where the *Merrimack* could not follow. Because Catesby Jones' pilots were warning him of the receding tide, and because the *Monitor* showed no inclination to resume the fight, Jones ordered the *Merrimack* taken to Norfolk for repairs. The first battle of ironclads thus ended without a victor.

Although the *Merrimack* came out twice more, the *Monitor,* in obedience to orders, remained under the guns of Fortress Monroe, helping to guard the transports that were landing General McClellan's army of

The battle of the ironclads.

Officers of the Monitor.

120,000 men. As the Federals began their advance up the peninsula toward Richmond, the outflanked Confederate forces evacuated Norfolk and its navy yard, and Federal troops from Fortress Monroe promptly moved in. To prevent capture of the *Merrimack*, the Confederates set her afire. She blew up when the flames reached her magazine.

The Union Navy, not to be outdone by the Army, tried to capture Richmond by using ships alone. To this end the *Monitor*, the new ironclad *Galena*, and three gunboats made a run up the James River, planning to bombard the Confederate capital into surrender. At Drewry's Bluff, eight miles short of their goal, they were stopped by a barrier of pilings, sunken ships and barges, stones, and scrap iron. From the heights Confederate batteries rained down shot and shell. These had no visible effect on the *Monitor* but penetrated the *Galena* 18 times. The little squadron took four hours of punishment at the barrier, which it could not penetrate, and then returned the way it had come.

McClellan also advanced to within a few miles of Richmond and then retreated. Although his Army of the Potomac outnumbered its opposition five to three, after a series of costly skirmishes, McClellan concluded that it was he who was outnumbered. He hastily withdrew to a bend in the James River where he could be supported by Federal gunboats and ironclads. Before the summer was over, McClellan abandoned the peninsula and returned with his army to Washington, the bloodless occupation of Norfolk having been his only conquest. Thus the peninsular campaign, which had aroused such hopeful expectations in the North, turned out to be just one of the several costly and fruitless Federal advances on the Confederate capital.

THE CHARLESTON CAMPAIGN

The invulnerability demonstrated by the *Monitor* in Hampton Roads and at Drewry's Bluff encouraged the Union Navy to build more "monitors." The first of these, the *Passaic* class, also designed by Ericsson, was an enlarged version of his original *Monitor,* with such obvious improvements as placing the pilothouse atop the turret.

These and other Union ironclads, including the *New Ironsides*, Secretary Welles earmarked for Rear Admiral Du Pont's South Atlantic Blockading Squadron for use against Charleston. From the beginning of the war a major Union objective was the capture of this "Cradle of the Rebellion." Welles was ambitious to see Charleston taken by the Navy alone, as ships had conquered

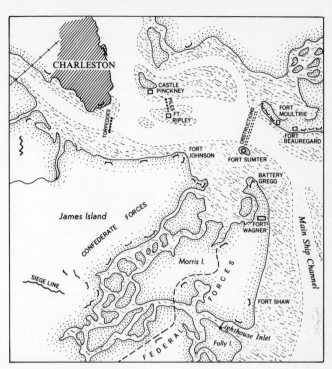

Charleston harbor, 1863.

Hatteras Inlet, Port Royal, and, more lately, New Orleans. The first ironclads sent south were the *Monitor* and the *Passaic*. Leaving Hampton Roads under tow at the end of 1862, they ran into a storm off Cape Hatteras. The *Passaic* was heavily damaged; the *Monitor* foundered, drowning 16 of her crew.

As Du Pont well knew, the defenses of Charleston were infinitely more formidable than those of positions previously taken by naval attack. The city was moreover to the Confederacy a cherished symbol, under no circumstances to be surrendered. Hence the fortifications covering the seaward approaches to the city had been steadily augmented. By 1863 the harbor was surrounded by more than a dozen batteries armed with about 150 heavy guns and many more of lesser caliber. The channel was partly obstructed by floating and underwater obstacles, many bearing "torpedoes"—as mines were then called. Moreover, the Charlestonians were building ironclads of their own. One misty morning early in 1863, two of these, the *Chicora* and the *Palmetto State*, miniature *Merrimacks*, slipped in among the wooden blockade vessels off the harbor and severely damaged two of them.

By spring 1863 Du Pont had at Charleston the *New Ironsides*, seven monitors, and the *Keokuk*, a lightly armored turtlebacked ship surmounted by two barbettes. Prodded by Welles and Fox, Du Pont on April 7 at last took his ironclad squadron into Charleston harbor. As the defenders had intended, the Union ironclads were halted by obstructions at the focus of all the heavier Confederate guns, which opened up on them with devastating fire. The *Keokuk,* hit 90 times, soon limped away in a sinking condition. The other ships withstood the onslaught for half an hour, when at turn of tide Du Pont signaled withdrawal. The ironclads had concentrated much of their fire against Fort Sumter but without achieving any serious destruction.

Du Pont had intended to resume the attack the following day, but, on receiving the reports of his captains, he changed his mind. Even though each ship had taken scores of hits, none but the sinking *Keokuk* was severely damaged. Yet there were enough jammed turrets, armor penetrations, loosened plates, and bolt heads sheared off by concussion to make him conclude that a return to the attack without extensive repairs might prove fatal.

When the local Federal Army commander requested naval fire support, Du Pont curtly replied that he "would not fire another shot." Welles, demanding action and underestimating the difficulties, soon afterward relieved him of his command. His successor, Rear Admiral John A. Dahlgren, the ordnance expert, arrived in early July with orders to operate jointly with troops under Brigadier General Quincy A. Gillmore in the capture of Morris Island. From here guns could be turned on the harbor forts and on Charleston itself.

On the morning of July 10 Gillmore's 11,000 troops, supported by their own guns and by fire from Dahlgren's ironclads, began to cross by boat from Folly Island to Morris Island. The fewer than 1,000 Confederate defenders, under continuous fire from the ships, fell back rapidly. Within a few hours the Federals occupied all of Morris Island except the northeast peninsula, where the Confederates had fallen back into their strongholds, Fort Wagner and Battery Gregg.

It cost the Federals 1,600 casualties in two months of desperate fighting to advance across the last few hundred yards to Fort Wagner. They lurked and trenched among the hot sand dunes, constantly menaced by mortars and sharpshooters and by gunfire from several Confederate forts. Each time they attempted to storm Wagner they were thrown back by murderous volleys of grape shot and canister.

The Confederates in Fort Wagner lived like trapped animals, under almost constant fire from land and sea, for long periods not daring to venture out of their bombproof shelters. Their dead they buried in the sand where they fell, until the odor of death almost overcame the survivors and the water in the shallow water holes became undrinkable. In the first week of September a prolonged bombardment, clearly heralding another attempted Federal assault, began to penetrate the Confederate bombproofs. During the night of September 6 the defenders, having reached the limits of human endurance, evacuated both Fort Wagner and Battery Gregg, slipping away to Charleston by boat.

For weeks Federal troops on Morris Island had been bombarding Charleston and joining the ironclads in shelling the harbor forts. Now Gillmore turned the abandoned guns of Wagner and Gregg on the other forts. Sumter, by this time reduced to rubble, had only one

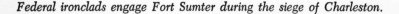

Federal ironclads engage Fort Sumter during the siege of Charleston.

Rear Admiral John A. Dahlgren (center) and staff aboard the Pawnee *off Charleston.*

operational cannon. Both Gillmore and Dahlgren were determined to take the fort, because of its symbolic value and because it could function as a platform for guns to cover the clearing of obstructions from the harbor. On the evening of September 8 both Gillmore and Dahlgren, with little attempt at coordination, prepared to send in landing parties by boat. Only Dahlgren's boats arrived, and the Confederates were ready for them. The defenders inside Sumter poured down on the invaders rifle fire and grenades, as well as fireballs that provided a point of aim for the surrounding forts and the ironclad *Chicora*. Most of the Federals managed to escape in their boats, but 124 were killed or captured.

The bombardments continued, but crumbling Fort Sumter and battered Charleston remained in Confederate hands. The defenders devised ingenious means for harassing the Union fleet. One of them was the night-running David, a cigar-shaped, steam-driven semisubmersible craft which carried a torpedo ahead at the end of a spar. In October 1863 a four-man crew in a David succeeded in exploding its torpedo against the starboard quarter of the *New Ironsides*, which had to be withdrawn from the war for a year to undergo extensive repairs. After this attack all the ironclads doubled their night watches and all were provided with outriggers and submerged nettings.

A potentially more dangerous weapon than the David was the submarine *Hunley*. Driven by eight men turning a crank, she could approach a ship while submerged. After the *Hunley* had drowned two of her crews, however, General Beauregard decreed that she should operate only on the surface. One evening in February 1864 she was taken out past the well-guarded ironclads to the wooden blockaders anchored beyond the bar. Here she thrust her 95-pound spar torpedo into the new screw sloop, the U.S.S. *Housatonic*. There was a flash and a roar, and sloop and submarine went down together.

BLOCKADE-RUNNING

For several months, before Secretary Welles had organized an effective blockade of the Confederacy, ships moved fairly freely in and out of Southern ports. More than 500 merchant vessels came and went between the date of Lincoln's proclamation and the end of 1861. Despite this lack of effectiveness, Britain, the world's leading wartime blockader, chose to issue no protest over the Union's sporadic interference with British merchantmen approaching or leaving Confederate harbors.

C.S.S. Hunley *under construction.*

In August 1861 the Liverpool subsidiary of John Fraser and Company of Charleston, as a means of testing the blockade and of encouraging blockade-runners, sent to Savannah a ship loaded partly with munitions for the Confederate government and partly with private cargo consigned to the parent company. The vessel achieved its mission without interference, and Fraser and Company realized such a handsome profit that they promptly acquired and operated a fleet of blockade-runners.

In November the iron screw steamer *Fingal*, acquired in Liverpool by James D. Bulloch, the Confederate Navy's purchasing agent in Britain, arrived in Savannah loaded with munitions. Because of the chaotic state of Southern railroads, an export cargo of cotton could

not be assembled for the *Fingal* until December. The U.S. Navy by that time having established its blockading base at nearby Port Royal Sound, escape to sea from Savannah had become nearly impossible. The Confederates therefore converted the *Fingal* into the ironclad ram *Atlanta*. When she attempted to break the blockade, the *Atlanta* ran aground and was captured by the Federal monitor *Weehawken*.

By 1863 the movement of freight through the ever-tightening blockade had become a highly specialized operation. Cargoes destined for the Confederacy were usually shipped in regular merchantmen from Europe to Bermuda, Havana, or Nassau. Here the freight was transferred to blockade-runners, typically speedy side-wheelers—long, low, shallow-draft, painted gray. These vessels hovered off Southern ports awaiting an opportunity to dart past the blockaders in storms, fogs, or darkness. Or they would make landfall some distance from a blockaded port and at night race through the shallows along the coast to the protection of Confederate harbor forts. Although blockade-running became increasingly risky as Welles added more and faster vessels to his blockading fleet, the rich rewards attainable brought quick replacements for runners captured or destroyed. By 1863 a blockade-runner making a monthly run was able to clear $1 million a year, fantastic earnings for those times.

Most of the blockade-runners were of British registry and many were British built and owned. Not a few were commanded by British naval officers who were temporarily retired and operating under assumed names. Because most of those involved in blockade-running were in the business solely to make money, they specialized in luxury goods such as coffee, tea, wines, perfumes, silks, linens, corsets, and Paris gowns. These goods, which fetched a high price in proportion to cargo space, were exchanged for gold or cotton. The commercial runners thus stimulated inflation in the South without relieving the Confederacy's serious needs.

To remedy this situation, the Confederate government acquired more blockade-running vessels of its own and began to regulate imports and exports, requiring the commercial runners to allocate up to half of their cargo space to government account. The blockade-runners thus began to make a growing contribution to the Confederate effort, bringing in foodstuffs, drugs, ammunition, and weapons, among which were about 600,000 small arms and many larger guns. Without these supplies the Confederate armed forces could not have carried on the war.

CONFEDERATE RAIDERS

Privateers, issued letters of marque by the central Confederate government or by the governments of several Confederate states, had a brief success. Some 80 of them captured nearly 60 Union merchantmen, while only two of the privateers were captured. In little more than a year, however, Confederate privateering came to an end, for the simple reason that it ceased to show a profit. The tightening Union blockade made it increasingly difficult to bring prizes into Confederate ports, and most foreign countries, having signed the Declaration of Paris of 1856, which outlawed privateering, had closed their ports to prizes. Private shipowners willing to take risks in return for quick gains therefore switched to blockade-running.

Captain Raphael Semmes CSN.

The Confederacy, however, by no means abandoned commerce raiding; supplementing and eventually replacing the privateers were naval cruisers. The first of the dozen Confederate government raiders to get to sea was the *Sumter*, an erstwhile passenger steamer rebuilt and armed at New Orleans. Confederate Navy Secretary Stephen B. Mallory turned her over to Commander Raphael Semmes CSN. Semmes, tall, angular, fiercely mustached, looked the part of the genteel semipirate he was to become. A sea lawyer with legal training, he could talk his way past the brushes with international law that his shadowy vocation entailed. With wily skill he evaded most of the risks inseparable from his daring and emerged the nemesis of the Union merchant marine, as well as the most successful commerce raider of the war.

In June 1861 Semmes, eluding the blockader *Brooklyn* at the mouth of the Mississippi River, began cruising in the West Indies. He early learned what the privateers already knew, that sending captured vessels into port was fruitless: off Confederate ports they would be captured by the blockaders, and in foreign ports they would be seized by the local authorities. In either case, the vessels would be restored to their owners with forfeiture of prize money. Hence Semmes set the custom, followed by later Confederate raiders, of destroying Union merchant vessels at sea. After removing passengers, crew, and anything he could use, he put the ships to the torch. When the *Sumter* became overcrowded, he disembarked his captives at an obscure port or else transferred them to one of his prizes, which he released under bond—a signed agreement in which the captain promised to pay ransom six months after the Confederacy achieved independence.

By the time that word of the *Sumter's* operations in any given area had reached the United States and Federal warships could be dispatched in pursuit, Semmes, by neatly calculated timing, had shifted to a new area. He thus worked his way through the West Indies and down the South American coast to Brazil, everywhere talking local authorities into letting him purchase coal and other supplies, despite efforts of U.S. consuls to prevent it.

At length Semmes doubled back to Martinique, where he barely eluded U.S.S. *Iroquois,* one of several armed vessels sent out by Welles to hunt him down. He next headed for Europe, where he hoped to have much-needed repairs made on his ship. In January 1862 the *Sumter,* after having captured her eighteenth prize, limped into Gibraltar, where she was promptly blockaded by three Union warships. Semmes, seeing no prospect of escape, paid off his crew, put the *Sumter* up for sale, and with his fellow officers headed back toward the Confederacy.

Meanwhile, Bulloch had arranged for the construction of two screw sloops in commercial shipyards in the Liverpool area. The U.S. Minister to Great Britain, Charles Francis Adams, correctly surmising that these vessels were destined for the Confederacy, demanded that they be impounded. He could produce no legal proof, however, for Bulloch had cannily concealed his interest in the transaction by means of dummy ownerships.

In March 1862 the first of Bulloch's ships, provisionally named the *Oreto,* put to sea unarmed, with British officers and crew. In the Bahamas she was turned over to Captain John Maffitt csn, who armed her with guns brought from Scotland in another ship and rechristened her C.S.S. *Florida.* Maffitt lacked an adequate crew and soon discovered, moreover, that critically important gun parts had been left behind by mistake. To remedy these deficiencies, he ran the gantlet of blockaders into Mobile, the *Florida* receiving severe damage from gunfire. Four months later, fully manned, equipped, and repaired, she slipped out to sea again on a stormy night.

Ranging the Atlantic, the *Florida* captured 37 merchantmen, 2 of which were afterward armed and sent off under junior officers on raiding cruises of their own. In October 1864 she entered the harbor of Salvador,

Brazil. Here she found one of her hunters, the powerful screw sloop *Wachusett*. The *Wachusett's* skipper, Commander Napoleon Collins, could not resist the opportunity to embellish his hitherto undistinguished career with a flash of glory. In violation of Brazilian neutrality he rammed and opened fire on the Confederate raider, forcing her to surrender. He then towed her triumphantly out of the harbor and escorted her as a prize to Hampton Roads.

Although this capture was hailed by both press and public in the Union states, the Federal government properly disavowed Collins' illegal action. Before the *Florida* could be returned to Brazil, however, she was rammed and sunk by an Army transport, in what may have been an accident.

Bulloch resorted to subterfuge in order to get his second sloop, the *Enrica,* to sea. At the end of July 1862, he had the ship dressed in flags and, with guests aboard, took her down the Mersey River for a trial run. In the Irish Sea, Bulloch transferred with his guests to a tugboat and returned to Liverpool. The *Enrica* proceeded to the Azores, where she was met by her future tender, the bark *Agrippina,* bringing guns, ammunition, and coal. She was met, also, by the chartered steamer *Bahama,* bringing her new commander, Raphael Semmes, now promoted to captain.

When the sloop had been armed with six 32-pounders and two huge pivot guns, fore and aft, Semmes took her out into neutral waters. The band played "Dixie," the Confederate flag was unfurled at the ship's peak, and Semmes commissioned her C.S.S. *Alabama.* He then addressed the assembled crews of the *Bahama* and the *Alabama.* Picturing the Confederacy as the unhappy victim of aggression, he urged the men to join him in wreaking vengeance; more to the point, he offered them high pay and promised them abundant prize money. Eighty-five seamen promptly enlisted. Semmes later enlisted others from captured vessels until he had his full complement. Provided with a crew and with a ship worthy of his mettle, he now set out on the most destructive commerce-raiding cruise in history.

Semmes first went after the New England whaling fleet operating near the Azores, burning 8 ships in two weeks. Then heading westward along the North Atlantic commercial shipping route, he captured 11 more vessels, putting 3 under bond and burning the rest. Only a shortage of coal kept him from spreading terror off Long Island and New Jersey. Instead, he headed south for a coaling rendezvous with the *Agrippina* at Martinique.

Learning from a captured newspaper of a Union expedition against Galveston, Semmes proceeded thither.

The Alabama *sinking the* Hatteras.

The sidewheeler U.S.S. *Hatteras* came out of Galveston Bay to investigate the stranger, whereupon the *Alabama* adroitly lured her out to sea in the gathering darkness. When the *Hatteras* was too far out for prompt support from the other Federal warships, Semmes' first lieutenant bellowed, "This is the Confederate States' steamer *Alabama!*" and with six quick broadsides the raider sent the *Hatteras* down. The *Alabama*, after rescuing all survivors, headed southeast and put them ashore at Jamaica.

During the remainder of 1863, the *Alabama* cruised in the Atlantic and Indian oceans, as far as the South China Sea. But spoils grew progressively more scarce, for Semmes had almost literally driven the U.S. merchant marine off the high seas. In April 1864, the *Alabama* made her 69th and final capture while en route to Europe for repairs to her boilers and sheathing.

On June 11 the raider, considerably the worse for wear after two years of almost continuous cruising, dropped anchor off Cherbourg. News of her arrival

promptly crackled over the telegraph wires of Europe, attracting from Holland U.S. screw sloop *Kearsarge*, commanded by Captain John Winslow, Semmes' old friend and cabinmate. When the *Kearsarge* arrived off Cherbourg, Semmes sent out a challenge to battle—a quixotic act in view of the *Alabama*'s deteriorated powder and serious need of repairs. He might have hesitated had he known that the *Kearsarge*'s vital midsection was protected by heavy chains bolted to her sides and concealed by boards painted to match the hull.

On the morning of June 19, the *Alabama*, refueled but without repairs or fresh ammunition, weighed anchor and steamed out to where her opponent was waiting. Accompanying the challenger were several vessels, including the English yacht *Deerhound* and a French ironclad steam frigate, which took station at the three-mile limit to ensure that France's neutral waters would not be violated.

Because both Semmes and Winslow intended to fight with their starboard batteries, they passed each other on opposite courses, opening fire, and then circled to avoid drawing apart. Thus firing and circling, they were carried westward by the current through seven complete revolutions.

The *Alabama*'s gunfire produced little effect upon her armored opponent, but the guns of the *Kearsarge,* particularly her two 11-inch Dahlgrens, blasted jagged holes in the *Alabama*'s hull and swept away her bulkheads. So great was the carnage among the latter's crew that the coxswain was obliged to clear the working spaces around the guns by shoveling dismembered bodies over the side.

As the *Alabama* began to sink, Semmes ordered her colors struck so that her wounded might be saved, but because of a misunderstanding, the *Kearsarge* failed to send immediate aid. Crying, "Every man save himself who can," Semmes threw his sword overboard and leapt into the sea. Then, as the ship upended and sank stern first, the yacht *Deerhound* approached and picked up Semmes, along with some 40 of his officers and men. To the intense chagrin of Captain Winslow, who had expected to make a prisoner of war of the famous Confederate raider, the *Deerhound* conveyed all her passengers to England.

The *Alabama* and the other Confederate cruisers, for all their spectacular feats of destruction, had little effect on the outcome of the war. They failed to attain their main objective, which was to weaken the blockade. Canny old Secretary Welles, who had a proper appreciation of military priorities, did not direct blockaders in significant numbers to hunt down the raiders.

To be sure, the raiders destroyed some five per cent of Union merchantmen. Union shipowners, to avoid further losses, had most of the rest of their vessels either laid up, sold abroad, or transferred to foreign registry. The principal sufferers were, besides the shipowners, the stranded passengers of captured vessels. The Union was in no way weakened, and its foreign commerce actually expanded, as goods were carried increasingly in neutral bottoms.

The last of the Confederate raiders, the *Shenandoah,* appears to have been sent out in a spirit of mere vindictiveness. This former East Indiaman, purchased by Bulloch following the loss of the *Alabama,* was ordered to the Pacific Ocean to destroy Yankee whalers. Cruising as far north as Bering Strait, the *Shenandoah* burned 38 ships. Most of this destruction was, however, carried out after the war was over, because news of the Confederate surrender was slow to reach those distant waters.

BEGINNING THE MISSISSIPPI VALLEY CAMPAIGN

From the beginning of the Civil War, General Scott had proposed Union capture of the Mississippi River as an extension of the blockade. Federal control of the great river would cut off the heartland of the Con-

The Kearsarge *sinking the* Alabama.

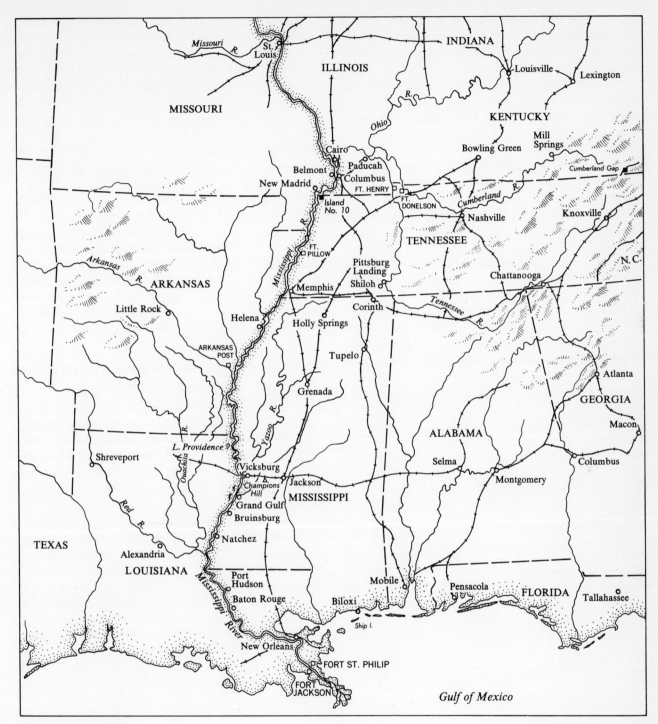

The Mississippi Valley.

federacy from the food-producing states of Arkansas and Texas and from most of Louisiana. It would block the not inconsiderable flow of supplies entering the Confederacy via Matamoros, the Mexican port just across the Rio Grande from Brownsville, Texas. And it would preserve the economy of the Northwest, which depended far more on the rivers for shipment of its products than on the few existing railroads. On this last point, the Federal government did not have confidence in Confederate guarantees that the Mississippi would be kept open for peaceful use by all the river states.

Scott estimated that conquest of the Mississippi would require 12 to 20 gunboats and a sufficient number of transports to carry 60,000 men. The first Union gunboats on the river were timberclad vessels, the converted wooden sidewheelers *Tyler*, *Lexington*, and *Conestoga*, all provided with five-inch oak bulwarks impenetrable by musket fire. These vessels were followed by seven ironclads designed by Naval Constructor Samuel Pook and built by James Eads of St. Louis. Called "Pook Turtles" or "Eads Ironclads," they were 175 feet long, 51 feet wide, and drew only 6 feet of water. They were propelled by covered sternwheels, and each carried 13 guns inside a slope-sided, two-foot-thick oak casemate, which was armored in front and over the engine spaces with two and a half inches of sheet iron. Named for river towns, they were the *St. Louis*, the *Carondelet*, the *Cincinnati*, the *Louisville*, the *Mound City*, the *Cairo*, and the *Pittsburg*. Eads later converted two snag boats into the supergunboats *Benton* and *Essex*. The 12 squat, ugly craft were the nucleus of a growing Western Flotilla.

Originally neither General Scott nor Secretary Welles thought of the flotilla as anything but the floating wing of the Army. Welles, for his part, could not conceive of anything called naval operations being carried out 1,000 miles upstream from the sea. He saw nothing strange in boat crews composed of soldiers and recruited rivermen, the latter also serving as junior officers. He was ready to cooperate, however, and willingly loaned the Army seamen to assist and instruct its amateur sailors, naval officers to command the individual gunboats, and his old friend and schoolmate Flag Officer Andrew H. Foote to command the flotilla. Welles thus implemented the sort of unified command that became standard in World War II. The growing Union flotilla caused considerable alarm in the South, for the gunboats could penetrate the Confederacy by way of the Cumberland and Tennessee rivers as well as the Mississippi; and the Confederates utterly lacked the facilities to match the Federal riverboat-building program, modest as it was.

The Ohio River might have provided a defensible frontier for the Confederate Northwest, had not the Kentucky government chosen to remain neutral. Accordingly, the Confederates began to build Forts Henry and Donelson on the Tennessee and Cumberland rivers in Tennessee, just south of the Kentucky border. In studying how to block the Union gunboats from advancing down the Mississippi, the Confederates could not resist the defensive possibilities of Columbus, Kentucky, 18 miles downstream from the Federal base at Cairo, Illinois. On September 3, 1861, Leonidas Polk, a Confederate major general and Episcopal Bishop of Louisiana, violated Kentucky's neutrality by occupying Columbus with 10,000 troops. Two days later, Union Brigadier General Ulysses S. Grant crossed the Ohio River into Kentucky at Paducah with 20,000 troops. A Confederate army then moved into Bowling Green, while a much smaller Southern force blocked Cumberland Gap on the Kentucky-Virginia border. The Confederacy thus established in the Northwest a rough barrier against invasion.

BREACHING THE CONFEDERATE NORTHWEST BARRIER

In January 1862 General Grant and Flag Officer Foote, both dogged and bellicose, together requested from their common senior, Major General Henry W. Halleck, permission to get an offensive rolling by jointly assaulting Forts Henry and Donelson. When the hesitant Halleck reluctantly consented, they quickly organized an expeditionary force.

In early February Foote's four available ironclads and his three timberclads led the way up the Tennessee River, now swollen out of its banks by rains and melting snow. Grant with 18,000 troops disembarked from transports four miles below Fort Henry, while the gunboats continued on upstream to take the fort's river face under attack.

The Confederate commander of Fort Henry, Brigadier General Lloyd Tilghman, was aware that he was outnumbered on land and outgunned on the river; in addition, he was not unmindful of the wretched design of Fort Henry, which had been built so low that it was now partly flooded. He therefore sent most of his garrison to Fort Donelson, retaining 75 gunners to cover their retirement with a delaying action. These gunners gave an excellent account of themselves, repeatedly hitting all four of the Union ironclads, which advanced to within 600 yards of the fort, and disabling two. One of their shells, entering through a port of the *Essex*, decapitated a sailor and pierced a boiler. Steam escaping from the boiler scalded a dozen men to death; many

Foote's gunboats attack Fort Henry.

Andrew H. Foote.

others leapt overboard in terror and agony and were drowned in the icy water. One shell thus cost 32 lives.

Nevertheless, the superior firepower of the flotilla rapidly took the fight out of Fort Henry, chiefly by knocking out its heavy ordnance. When at length the fort was reduced to four serviceable guns that could be aimed at the gunboats, Tilghman hauled down his flag and surrendered to Foote. Only then did the first of Grant's troops, delayed by flooded roads and hip-deep mire, arrive on the landward side of Fort Henry.

The three timberclads now went raiding up the Tennessee River as far as Alabama. They seized military stores, destroyed government property, and captured three steamers, including the 280-foot *Eastport*, which the Confederates were converting into an ironclad.

Grant, meanwhile, had marched his army across to Fort Donelson on the Cumberland River, whither also came Foote, on February 14, with four ironclads and two timberclads. At long range Foote had the advantage over Donelson, for the fort's guns were mostly small caliber and their crews poor marksmen. Deciding to repeat the aggressive tactics that had made short work of Fort Henry, he led his ironclads to within 400 yards of Donelson's water batteries. At this range the fort was able to inflict damaging hits on the Union boats, particularly from its upper battery. Atop a high bluff, it sent plunging fire down through the unarmored overheads. Foote, struck in the foot, was among the wounded. Soon the ironclads, all more or less disabled, retired in confusion.

Two days later, however, Fort Donelson capitulated

The gunboats attack Fort Donelson.

to Grant's army, producing jubilation in the North and panic in the South. Grant, promoted to major general for his victory, now proposed advancing south along the Tennessee River in order to outflank General Polk at Columbus and General Albert Sydney Johnston, who had 18,000 troops near Nashville. With his superior numbers Grant expected to defeat first one, then the other. But the cautious General Halleck, anticipating a Confederate counterattack that never came, immobilized him for three weeks. At last he permitted Grant's troops, reinforced to 35,000, to advance to Pittsburg Landing on the Tennessee River, where they were to be joined by 50,000 more men under Brigadier General Don Buell.

Grant's enforced delay enabled Polk and Johnston to retire from their untenable positions and to combine forces at Corinth, Mississippi. Here they were joined by General Pierre Beauregard and by reinforcements from as far away as Mobile and New Orleans. Johnston now had 40,000 troops. In early April he advanced and, at the cost of his life, attacked Grant at nearby Pittsburg Landing. In the ensuing Battle of Shiloh, so named from a local country church, the Confederates, now led by Beauregard, in a daylong fight forced the Federals to the river's edge. There, however, two Federal timber-clads fired up the ravines, obliging the Confederates to draw back. During the night the Union Army was strengthened by the arrival of 20,000 of Buell's troops. The now outnumbered Confederates could only retire, but the Federals were too exhausted to pursue them. Union losses in this bloody battle were nearly 14,000; Confederate losses were a little under 11,000.

That same day, April 7, 1862, saw Confederate forces defeated at Island No. 10 on an S-curve of the Mississippi River 40 miles downstream from Columbus. Here Bishop Polk, on withdrawing to Corinth, had left 7,000 troops and 120 guns. The artillery had been emplaced on the island and on nearby high river banks to bar the Mississippi to Union military traffic. In order to deal with this situation, Halleck retained in Missouri an army of 20,000 men under Brigadier General John Pope.

In mid-February Pope's army, as well as Foote's gunboats and new mortar boats, had reached the vicinity of Island No. 10, where there were far more Confederate guns than had been assembled at either Fort Henry or Fort Donelson. A Federal gunboat disabled here would be carried by the current downstream to certain capture or destruction. Foote, stumping about on crutches because of his unhealed foot wound, therefore took the Confederate fortifications under fire from long range.

Because the Island No. 10 complex was nearly surrounded by swamps and flooded forests, an attacking army could reach it only by crossing the river downstream. Hence Pope needed transports below Island No. 10 and one or two ironclads to protect the transports from Confederate shore batteries and armed steamers.

The Army engineers made a passage for the transports by sawing a shallow channel through a drowned forest at the base of the loop behind No. 10. The flotilla then sent two of its ironclads dashing past the Confederate batteries in thunderstorms. One of the ironclads, Captain Henry Walke's *Carondelet,* ran the gantlet on the night

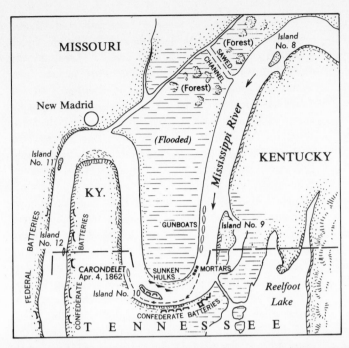

Island No. 10.

The Carondelet *passes Confederate batteries on Island No. 10.*

of April 4, its casemate draped in chains and piled with cordwood, and with a coal barge lashed alongside. Two nights later the *Pittsburg,* piled high with bales of hay, got safely past. Pope's army, covered by the two gunboats, crossed the river and blocked the Confederates' only possible retreat. Among the thousands of Confederate captives taken were three generals. The Mississippi was now open to the Federal gunboats almost as far as Memphis.

THE CAPTURE OF NEW ORLEANS

While the lower Mississippi River country was stripping its defenses of troops to stop Grant's army and Foote's gunboats from coming down from the north, the Federals were planning an advance from the south on New Orleans, the Confederacy's largest and richest city.

The Confederates considered New Orleans, surrounded by swamps, to be invulnerable except from the Mississippi. Hence they had rigged floating barriers across the river above and below the city. They had also assembled a small River Defense Fleet of armed vessels spearheaded by the ironclad *Manassas,* a steam tug cut down to the waterline and provided with a ram, an armored turtleback, and a single gun at the bow. At New Orleans two larger ironclads, the *Louisiana* and the *Mississippi,* were under construction.

The downstream river barrier, a line of hulks and logs anchored and chained together, was protected by two powerful masonry forts, Jackson and St. Philip, which were on opposite sides of the river. A break in the barrier directly under the guns of Fort Jackson permitted Confederate ships to pass. In October 1861 the River Defense Fleet had slipped through this opening for a night attack on a Union squadron that had entered the Mississippi. When the *Manassas* rammed the Federal flagship, other Confederate steamers released fire rafts, whereupon all the Union vessels retreated ignominiously to the Gulf.

This Union setback convinced the Confederate government that New Orleans was safe from any forces approaching from downstream. Union Assistant Navy Secretary Fox insisted, however, that the city could be taken by naval attack from the Gulf. He was supported in this conviction by Commander David Dixon Porter, firebrand son of the famous captain of the *Essex.* Together they sold the scheme to Secretary Welles, General McClellan, and President Lincoln. To head the expedition Welles selected the sixty-year-old Tennessean David Glasgow Farragut, an officer with a reputation for good judgment and meticulous attention to detail.

Farragut, designated flag officer, with his flag in the new screw sloop *Hartford,* assembled his attack squadron of wooden steamers at Ship Island, the base off Biloxi captured by the Federals. Here he was joined by a flotilla of 21 mortar schooners and 7 gunboats commanded by Porter, and by transports bringing occupation troops under General Ben Butler.

The New Orleans campaign, 1862.

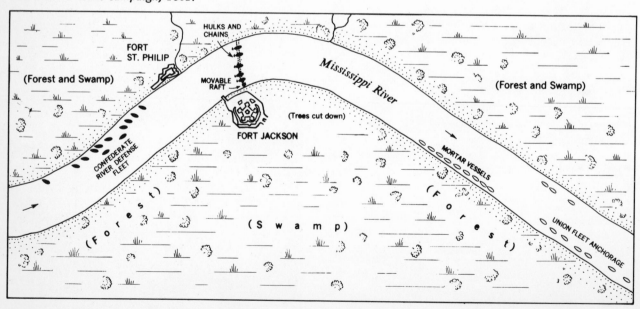

Porter's flotilla and Farragut's 3 corvettes and 9 gunboats entered the Mississippi without much difficulty, but it took a month of pushing, tugging, and swearing to haul Farragut's 4 sloops and his veteran sidewheeler *Mississippi* over the bar, which was heavily silted because of the scarcity of river traffic. The last of his ships entered the river at the end of the first week in April 1862, just as the battle ended at Shiloh, 400 miles to the north.

Farragut was already overseeing final preparations for his attack. Heavy chains were draped over the sides of the vessels to protect engines and boilers, hulls were camouflaged with mud, decks were whitewashed to make guns visible in darkness, and ships were trimmed by the head so that they would not be swung about by the current if they ran aground under fire.

Porter took his mortar schooners upriver and on April 18 began to exchange fire with Forts Jackson and St. Philip. He had convinced Washington authorities, but not Farragut, that he could knock out both forts in 48 hours. It was soon apparent that the schooners could not reach St. Philip without exposing themselves to murderous fire from the other fort. Porter therefore concealed them behind trees on the south shore, where they were able to concentrate on Fort Jackson.

The mortar schooners, expending more than 1,000 rounds of shell a day, scarred the face of the fort and set fire to wooden structures inside, but it was quickly obvious that Porter's flotilla was not going to reduce even one fort in 48 hours—or in thrice that time. Farragut, not in the least surprised, calmly prepared to run the gantlet with his squadron before Porter should run out of ammunition. On the evening of April 20 the flag officer sent forward two gunboats to blow up the barricade. The explosives failed to go off, but one of the gunboats succeeded in poking a hole in the middle of the barrier wide enough for ships to pass through in single file.

Above the forts the small Confederate River Defense Fleet was preparing for action with naval vessels, army-controlled craft, and a couple of Louisiana-owned sidewheelers—13 armed ships in all. To these were added the unfinished ironclad *Louisiana*, which was towed down from New Orleans and anchored near Fort St. Philip. The ironclad *Mississippi* was not yet in a condition to be moved.

By nightfall on April 23, Farragut had his squadron in readiness for the attack. At 2 o'clock the next morning two red lanterns hoisted to the peak of the *Hartford* signaled his ships to get underway. An hour and a half

David Glasgow Farragut.

Porter's mortar schooners in action.

later, as the vessels began to file through the barrier, in intense darkness, a rising moon in their rear made them visible to lookouts in Fort Jackson. Up soared a signal rocket, and both forts opened fire. Farragut's advancing ships returned the fire as their guns found targets. At the same time Porter's schooners, stepping up their bombardment, streaked the night sky with glowing shell fuses. Above the forts, the Confederate warships moved out into the river towing fire rafts, which were ignited and which floated down toward Farragut's approaching squadron.

The poorly trained gunners in the forts, having only the flash of gunfire to aim at in the dark, tended to fire high, killing men in the passing ships and shattering masts and yards, but rarely touching hulls. Soon Union gunners and helmsmen were blinded by the smoke of the cannonade mingling with fog. Their ships, groping about in the murk and thrown off course by the four-knot current, passed sometimes so close to a fort or to the anchored *Louisiana* that Federals and Confederates could snarl oaths at each other.

The *Hartford*, after passing the forts when the smoke was thickest, ran ashore and was set ablaze by a fire raft. As the flames crackled up her rigging, even stout-hearted Farragut's courage momentarily failed. "My God," he cried, "is it to end this way?" But the crew soon extinguished the fire, and the flagship backed off the shore and again pointed her bow upstream.

Before the Federals' battle with the forts ended, their fight with the Confederate ships had begun. This was a brawling melee in which both sides fired in the darkness at friend and foe. The *Manassas* lumbered about, attempting repeatedly to ram Union vessels. She succeeded only in landing glancing blows on the sloop *Brooklyn* and on the *Mississippi*. The latter, piloted by Lieutenant George Dewey, chased the Confederate ironclad ashore and so riddled her with shot that she slid off the bank and sank.

By dawn most of the Confederate vessels had been sunk, burned, or otherwise put out of action. Exceptions were the *Louisiana*, the oceangoing sidewheeler *Governor Moore*, and a few gunboats that had fled upstream or had taken refuge under the guns of Fort St. Philip. The *Governor Moore*, still full of fight, was hotly pursuing the Union corvette *Varuna*, while being pursued by several other Union vessels. As the *Governor*

Farragut's fleet passing between Forts Jackson and St. Philip.

Moore surged up on the corvette, her captain fired the forward gun down through his own bow to rake his opponent, which he then sank by ramming. But the other Union vessels, drawing near and firing steadily, soon drove the *Governor Moore* ashore disabled. Her captain, after seeing his wounded removed, set his ship afire to prevent her capture. The *Varuna* was the only ship that Farragut lost, but three of his gunboats were turned back by the forts. Union losses in the battle were 37 killed and 149 wounded; Confederate losses were 84 and 110.

The next day Farragut's squadron proceeded up the Mississippi. Batteries just below New Orleans opened fire, but the big ships silenced them with a few salvos. As the squadron approached the city, the crews were appalled to see mountains of blazing cotton bales stacked on the levee. Ships, some loaded with cotton, were burning at the quays or afloat on the river. Conspicuous among the latter was the unfinished ironclad *Mississippi*. The Confederates had labored all night to insure that nothing of value would fall into Federal hands. Helpless but defiant, a mob ashore shouted anathemas at the fleet as, a little after noon, it anchored off the city. No Confederate soldiers were to be seen, for General Mansfield Lovell, realizing that his 3,000 poorly armed militia were utterly incapable of defending New Orleans against naval gunfire, had sent them out of the city rather than risk hostilities. Because no official could be found who was willing to surrender New Orleans, fleet and city settled down to a period of malevolent armistice.

Forts Jackson and St. Philip, though now cut off from supplies, still held out. On the night of April 27, however, the men in Fort Jackson, anticipating an overwhelming attack from the swamps, mutinied against their officers rather than put up what seemed to them a hopeless resistance. The next day the commanding officer of the forts surrendered them to Porter. The captain of the *Louisiana*, rather than surrender, set fire to his ship, which presently blew up, killing a man in St. Philip.

On May 1 General Butler came up the river to New Orleans with 2,500 troops to occupy the rebellious city of 170,000 inhabitants. He proved extraordinarily effective, but his stern measures made his name detested all over the Confederacy. He at once declared martial law and convinced the unruly mob that he was prepared to meet defiance with gunfire. The mayor and other city officials proving uncooperative, he ordered them locked in the dungeons of Fort Jackson. He hanged a man who tore down the U.S. flag from a public building. On May 15, he issued his notorious General Order No. 28: ". . . when any female shall . . . insult or show contempt for any officer or soldier of the United States, she shall be regarded and held liable to be treated as a woman of the town plying her avocation." At this, President Jefferson Davis proclaimed Butler "an outlaw and common enemy of mankind," and directed that he was, if captured, "to be immediately executed by hanging."

RENDEZVOUS AT VICKSBURG

General Halleck, shocked by the bloodletting at Shiloh, assumed personal command of the newly designated Army of the Tennessee, which he rapidly built up to a strength of 110,000 men. Then, after a supercautious, month-long 20-mile advance, he occupied Corinth, while Beauregard slipped away with 52,000 troops to Tupelo, 70 miles farther south.

After the capture of Island No. 10, the Union gunboat flotilla steamed down the Mississippi and with mortar fire attacked the next Confederate strong point, Fort Pillow. Here Flag Officer Foote reluctantly turned his command over to Flag Officer Charles H. Davis and went home to nurse his wound, from which, however, he was not to recover. The morning following the change of command, eight small Confederate gunboats darted out briefly from the protection of the fort and rammed two of the seven Union ironclads, sinking one and obliging the other to run aground in the shallows to avoid sinking.

On Halleck's occupation of Corinth, the outflanked Confederate garrison evacuated Fort Pillow and the Confederate gunboats withdrew down the Mississippi. Davis' remaining five ironclads followed, backed now by eight swift wooden rams. On June 6 the rebel gunboats took a stand before the city of Memphis, while thousands of townspeople watched from the bluffs. Shortly after the opposing lines of gunboats had opened fire, two of the wooden rams, the *Queen of the West* and the *Monarch*, dashed through the Union column. The *Queen* plunged her beak into an enemy gunboat, which sank like a stone. Two rebel boats aimed their rams at opposite sides of the *Monarch*, which slipped nimbly from between them, and they crashed into each other. In the ensuing confusion, the Federal ironclads closed in with devastating gunfire. Only one Confederate vessel escaped; the rest were sunk, blown up, or captured.

Davis, after accepting the surrender of defenseless Memphis, turned the city over to occupation troops that had accompanied his flotilla. Shortly afterward he took his rams and gunboats 400 miles down the Mississippi

The Battle of Memphis, June 6, 1862.

without meeting any opposition. On July 1, just above Vicksburg, the flotilla joined Farragut's squadron which, on Departmental orders, had steamed the 400 miles up from New Orleans.

Farragut's big seagoing vessels, not designed for river navigation, had repeatedly collided and run aground. His men, tormented by heat and mosquitoes, were laid low in large numbers with dysentery and malaria. The small river towns of Baton Rouge and Natchez had readily surrendered to his guns, but Vicksburg, situated on a high bluff at a hairpin turn, had bidden Farragut defiance. Guns emplaced atop the bluff could enfilade ships coming and going but could not be reached by the ships' guns.

Farragut, supported by Porter's mortar schooners, which remained below Vicksburg, ran most of his ships past the city. It was a futile gesture. Vicksburg, unlike Island No. 10 and the forts below New Orleans, was not dependent on the river for supplies. Farragut wrote to Halleck suggesting a joint attack, but the general, who was still at Corinth, replied that he could spare no troops. Beauregard, however, sent a division under Major General Earl Van Dorn to strengthen Vicksburg's defenses.

The Mississippi, long at the flood, now began to subside so rapidly that Farragut's deep-draft ships were in danger of being stranded. Up the nearby Yazoo River a powerful new Confederate ironclad, the *Arkansas,* was in similar danger. On July 15 the *Arkansas* came chugging down the Yazoo chasing three Union vessels that had been sent up to investigate her. Entering the Mississippi, the rebel ironclad steamed through the surprised Union fleets, firing and being fired at. Before the Federals could get up steam, she had found refuge under the guns of Vicksburg.

That night Farragut, alarmed at the new threat to Union vessels below Vicksburg, again ran his squadron past the city. He had hoped, while passing, to destroy the *Arkansas,* but his gunners could not make her out in the darkness. Not long afterward, he was elated to receive discretionary orders to return to the Gulf. Thither he proceeded with his larger ships, leaving a few gunboats behind to help guard against the *Arkansas.* At New Orleans he was gratified to receive word that he had been promoted to the newly created rank of rear admiral.

In August General Van Dorn ordered the *Arkansas* down the Mississippi to support a Confederate Army attack on Baton Rouge. She was nearly there when one of her engines broke down and she was swept against the shore. Threatened with capture by approaching Union gunboats, she was set afire by her crew and presently blew up. Davis now took his gunboats upstream to base at Helena, Arkansas. Porter's flotilla had already retired to the south. Thus 500 miles of the Mississippi were restored to Confederate use.

WINTER ON THE MISSISSIPPI

Halleck's failure to join Davis, Farragut, and Porter in a joint assault on Vicksburg stands out as a major blunder of the war. The Confederates steadily reinforced this strong point and erected batteries on the bluffs at Port Hudson 250 miles downstream. They thus regained control of that segment of the Mississippi into which flows the Red River, the principal route over which the meat and grain of the Southwest moved to sustain Confederate military forces on the Mississippi River and eastward.

In the summer of 1862 Halleck went to Washington as general-in-chief, leaving Grant again in command of the Army of the Tennessee. In October Davis became chief of the Bureau of Navigation. His flotilla, renamed the Mississippi Squadron, was transferred to the Navy under the command of Porter, now an acting rear admiral. Porter at once began to strengthen his squadron, chiefly by acquiring "tinclads," which were lightly armored river steamers.

It took Grant several months to assemble forces in order to restore in part the fine army that Halleck had scattered in pursuit of secondary objectives. At last, in late November, Grant resumed his southward advance, moving along the railroad almost to Grenada, Mississippi. He found the task of supplying his army more difficult and more dangerous than during his advance on Pittsburg Landing. At that time he had used the Tennessee River, which had been patrolled by Foote's gunboats; now he was dependent on the integrity of every mile of railroad between his army and his main base at Columbus.

Grant, increasingly aware of his supply problem and meeting increasing enemy resistance, suddenly changed his strategy. He divided his army with Brigadier General William Tecumseh Sherman, whom he ordered to advance on Vicksburg by way of Memphis and the Mississippi River. Grant counted on the threat of the 40,000 men he retained to hold the main part of the Confederate Army away from Vicksburg while Sherman attacked it from the river.

The campaign did not work out at all as Grant had planned. Confederate cavalry got around behind his army, tore up his railroad supply line, and burned his supply dump at Holly Springs. Grant had no choice but to retreat, with his men living off the land. Because the Confederates had also cut the telegraph wires, he could not warn Sherman.

Sherman and his army of 32,000 steamed down the

David Dixon Porter.

Mississippi, escorted by Porter's gunboats. At the same time the Confederates, relieved of the threat of Grant's army, were shifting forces in order to bolster the defenses of Vicksburg. When on December 29 Sherman undertook to storm the bluffs north of the city, he was bloodily repulsed. This defeat ended the campaign.

Grant reassembled his forces and established headquarters on the west bank of the Mississippi, a little above Vicksburg. He and Porter spent the rest of the winter attempting to block the inflow of Confederate foodstuffs via the Red River and to place an army on the high ground behind Vicksburg.

In early February 1862 Porter ordered the ram *Queen of the West* to make a dash past the Vicksburg batteries and to run down the Mississippi River to blockade the Red. The ram got past the city with some damage but no casualties, and in the next fortnight she captured and destroyed several heavily loaded freighters. Porter, encouraged by this success, sent the ironclad *Indianola* down to join her. Before the vessels could meet, the *Queen of the West* was disabled by a shore battery and captured.

The *Queen* was quickly repaired and, manned by a Confederate crew, teamed up with the fast ram C.S.S. *Webb*; the two went in pursuit of the *Indianola*, which they overtook not far below Vicksburg. The clumsy ironclad turned to fight, but, despite her superior firepower, she was no match for the agile rams. The *Webb* stove in one of her wheelhouses, causing such dangerous leaks that her captain ran her aground and surrendered. This surrender Porter called "the most humiliating that has occurred during the war."

Although his squadron was scattered on various missions, Porter nevertheless took prompt action. The *Queen of the West,* sent upriver by the Confederates for salvage gear, came steaming back with the horrifying news that she was being chased by an enormous black monitor. In panic the salvage crew that was trying to refloat the *Indianola* blew her up to prevent her recapture, and the *Queen* retreated into the Louisiana swamps, where she was found and sunk by Farragut's gunboats.

The monitor was a hoax. Porter had ordered a coal barge fitted with fake wheelhouses, a wooden turret, log guns, pork barrels piled up to resemble smokestacks, and, according to one Confederate source, a purloined privy for a pilothouse. His men smeared her with tar to make her look like an ironclad, painted the words DELUDED PEOPLE, CAVE IN on her "wheelhouses," and pushed her at night out into the Mississippi current. The barge passed by the guns of Vicksburg in dignified silence, suffering little visible damage. "She was," said Porter, "a much better looking vessel than the *Indianola.*" Certainly no vessel of the Civil War more completely attained her objectives.

When Farragut learned of Porter's loss of the *Queen* and the *Indianola,* he decided that it was up to himself to blockade the Red River traffic. On the night of March 14 he attempted to run upriver past the Port Hudson batteries with seven of his vessels—three screw sloops, each with a gunboat lashed to her port side, trailed by the sidewheeler *Mississippi.* "I expect all to go by who are able," he announced, "and I think the best protection against the enemy's fire is a well-directed fire from our own guns."

Farragut had hoped to make his approach undetected, but when his flagship *Hartford* at 11 P.M. came within 800 yards of Port Hudson, the Confederates, not at all surprised, opened fire from the bluff. At the same time they illuminated the Union vessels with locomotive headlights from the east bank and silhouetted them with prepared bonfires on the west bank. The *Hartford's* guns replied, as did the deep-throated mortars of the Union flotilla concealed by trees downstream. Within minutes the river was obscured in smoke.

Only the flagship and her consort managed to run past the Confederate guns and around the bend. The two following sloops were driven back damaged. The venerable *Mississippi* ran aground directly opposite the Confederate batteries, which set her afire with shell. After her crew had escaped, she floated free and drifted blazing down the river until the flames reached her magazines, whereupon she blew up and sank. With his two vessels above Port Hudson, Farragut set about vigorously patrolling. Porter cooperated by floating down to him barges loaded with coal and other supplies.

THE CAPTURE OF VICKSBURG AND PORT HUDSON

Sherman's repulse had demonstrated that Vicksburg was invulnerable to attack from the Mississippi River. Operations in early 1863 revealed that the city was equally unassailable from the maze of swamps and streams to its north. Twice Porter's gunboats attempted to escort troops across this region to the Yazoo River and the high ground beyond. Both expeditions were defeated by a combination of natural obstacles and Confederate defenses.

Sherman and Porter recommended that the Union forces return to the Tennessee border and drive south through central Mississippi—the strategy that Grant had adopted and then abandoned the preceding December. "There is but one thing now to be done," said Porter, "and that is to start an army of 150,000 men from Memphis, via Grenada, and let them go supplied with everything required to take Vicksburg." Grant rejected the proposal, saying that a return of his army to Tennessee would look like another retreat and would be another blow to Union morale.

This left only one practical route to the high ground behind Vicksburg: southward west of the city, then back up through Mississippi. A canal cut across the peninsula opposite Vicksburg would provide the shortest route southward. Troops accompanying Farragut's squadron had begun digging there the preceding summer, and the work had been resumed before Grant reached the area. Grant let the digging proceed, for he knew that President Lincoln expected great results from the canal route. He himself, however, had little enthusiasm for it, because Confederate guns could reach its lower end from the bluffs on the opposite shore. The project was brought to an end when high water inundated the peninsula and filled the canal with mud.

Another plan tried by the Federals was to open the levee between the Mississippi River and Lake Providence, which was just west of the river, after sawing a channel from the lake through cypress swamps to the tributaries of the Red River. Still another scheme was to cut the levee and to flood the bayous west of the Mississippi; these bayous were curved, stagnant lakes occupying former channels of the ever-shifting river.

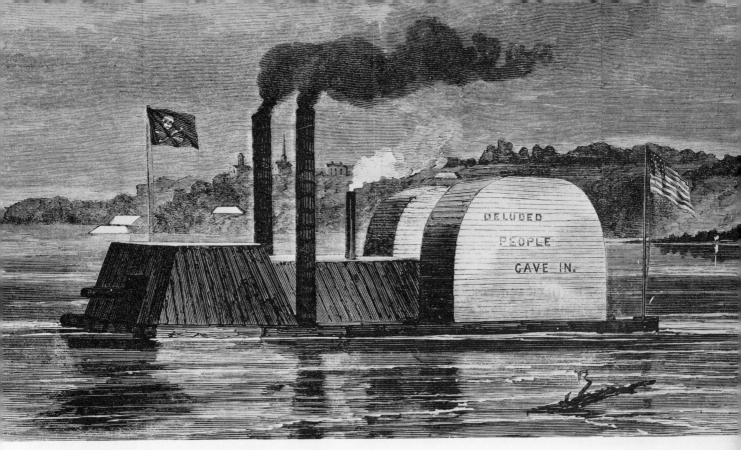

Porter's dummy ironclad running past Vicksburg at night.

Before either of these routes could be opened, receding waters exposed a rough but usable road behind the bayou levees. Along this road at the end of March 1863 Grant started his troops marching. Their advance was initially a mere crawl, because there were flooded stretches to be bridged or to be filled in and laid with corduroy road. For supplies and for transportation across the Mississippi, Grant looked to the Navy.

Admiral Porter was ready and able to cooperate. On the evening of April 16, leaving gunboats behind, he ran past Vicksburg seven of his ironclads towing coal barges and shepherding three transports loaded with stores for the Army. To absorb enemy shot, he piled his decks and casemates with logs and with bales of cotton and wet hay. As the column in darkness approached the hairpin bend, Confederate pickets at the tip of the peninsula warned Vicksburg by setting fire to a house. Promptly a calcium flare gleamed from the bluff opposite, lighting the river below, and along the city waterfront a row of tar barrels began to blaze.

As the squadron came within range, the whole amphitheater of Vicksburg, from the heights to the water's edge, blossomed with gunflashes. The vessels replied with shell, shrapnel, and canister, but they were at a disadvantage because eddies at the bend had set them spinning out of control. The flagship *Benton*, instead of hugging the Louisiana shore as planned, whirled so close to the city wharves that Porter could hear the crash of brick walls knocked over by his ships' guns. In the long, slow passage past the batteries, one of the transports caught fire and had to be abandoned. The rest of the vessels came through with minor damage, and only one man was killed. A major contribution of the operation was its demonstration of the fact that, despite Vicksburg's growing firepower, the town could still be passed. Six nights later six more transports attempted the run and five were successful.

Grant had planned to cross the Mississippi at Grand Gulf, but Porter's ironclads, in a long bombardment on April 29, failed to knock out a battery on a bluff there. Army, squadron, and transports accordingly moved several miles downstream to Bruinsburg, where the troops crossed the next day. Meanwhile, the gunboats that Porter had left behind were supporting General Sherman and 10,000 troops in a realistic feint at the bluffs above Vicksburg. While the vessels fired, blew whistles, and made smoke, Sherman's soldiers disembarked, circled through the woods, slipped back aboard their transports, and then ostentatiously disembarked again. The deceived Confederates, gazing in awe from the bluffs, estimated the attacking enemy in scores of thousands. Their commander telegraphed to headquarters: "The demonstration at Grand Gulf must be only a feint. Here is the real attack. The enemy are in front of me in force such as I have never seen before at Vicksburg. Send me reinforcements." By the time the Confederates discovered their error, Grant's 30,000 men were ashore at Bruinsburg and Sherman was marching his troops down the levee road to join them.

Lieutenant General John C. Pemberton had 32,000 soldiers in and near Vicksburg. General Joseph E. Johnston, over-all Confederate commander in the West, was assembling another army near Jackson, the capital of Mississippi. It was Grant's intention to place his army between Pemberton and Johnston before they could unite. Recalling his difficulties in supplying his forces in December, Grant now made probably the most audacious move of the war. He commandeered all vehicles for miles around, including fancy carriages, and had them loaded with munitions to accompany his troops, who were issued three days' rations. He then hastened with his army to the northeast, breaking off all connection with the river base. When his men had consumed their rations, they were to subsist off the land.

Grant first struck Johnston, who was now at Jackson, defeating his army and driving it out of the city. Johnston ordered Pemberton to attack Grant from behind, but Pemberton instead probed southward in order to cut Grant's nonexistent communications. Grant, turning, routed Pemberton's army at Champion's Hill and chased it back into Vicksburg. Frantically Johnston ordered Pemberton to evacuate Vicksburg and join him to the north, but Sherman's corps, on Grant's right, cut off escape in that direction by seizing the bluffs above the city. The Federal gunboats in the river below saw Sherman's cavalry chasing the enemy from the very heights from which his men had been repulsed the preceding December, and toward which they had recently feinted.

With fire support from the gunboats, Grant twice assaulted Vicksburg and was twice turned back. He then entrenched for a siege. His men were amply supplied by way of the river, but Vicksburg, isolated by Porter's squadron in the Mississippi and Grant's army ashore, slowly starved. For several weeks gunboats and artillery, in a steady bombardment, turned the city into rubble, obliging the famished citizens to seek refuge in cellars and caves.

Farther down the Mississippi a similar campaign, though on a smaller scale, was being waged against Port Hudson. Here Major General Nathaniel P. Banks, with 20,000 troops and supported by Admiral Farragut's squadron on the river, had first assaulted and then closely invested the Confederate garrison of 6,000.

In early July 1863 the Civil War reached a decisive turning point. On the 3rd at Gettysburg, Pennsylvania, General Lee suffered his first defeat. On the 4th starving Vicksburg surrendered to General Grant, and on the 8th equally starving Port Hudson surrendered to General Banks. A great burden was thus removed from the minds of Union leaders, for although the war would continue many months, victory for the Union now appeared inevitable.

The "Anaconda" at last extended from New Orleans to Cairo: the heart of the Confederacy was decisively cut off from the foodstuffs of its Southwest. "The Father of Waters," said Lincoln, "now rolled unvexed to the sea." On July 16 the merchant steamer *Imperial* arrived at New Orleans from St. Louis, the first of many merchant vessels to ply again the Mississippi north and south.

THE BATTLE OF MOBILE BAY

After the capture of New Orleans, Farragut had proposed an immediate attack on Mobile, the next most active blockade-running port on the Gulf. More than two years passed, however, before the Federal government ordered active operations in the Mobile area, and then only because of two compelling situations. Threatening to break out of Mobile Bay and to disrupt

The Battle of Mobile Bay.

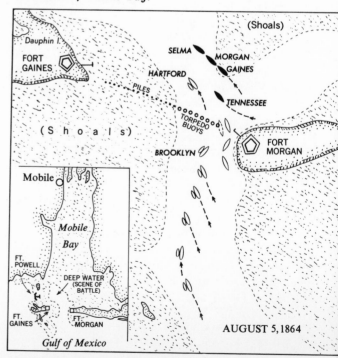

The Battle of Mobile Bay.

the blockade was a new ironclad, the *Tennessee*, commanded by Admiral Franklin Buchanan, first captain of the *Merrimack*, which the *Tennessee* resembled. At the same time, General Sherman was urgently requesting an attack on Mobile to draw forces away from Atlanta, toward which his army was advancing.

Mobile, situated at the head of Mobile Bay, was, like New Orleans, protected by distant forts. Thirty miles to the south, Fort Gaines on Dauphin Island and Fort Morgan on Mobile Point flanked the main entrance to the bay. From Dauphin Island to the ship channel were lines of obstructing piles, which were extended by lines of submerged torpedoes, leaving a narrow passage for blockade-runners directly under the guns of Fort Morgan. At the western end of Dauphin Island and guarded by tiny Fort Powell was a shallow secondary entrance, navigable only by small craft.

The manpower requirements of the climactic Virginia campaigns initially limited the Mobile operations to an attack on the *Tennessee* and the forts. Farragut, who had learned to respect ironclads from his experience with the *Arkansas*, demanded, and finally got, four monitors to supplement his wooden vessels. Major General Gordon Granger arrived with 2,400 soldiers, whose first task was to land on Dauphin Island and to establish a line of communication between the Gulf and

the Union fleet, after the ships had fought their way past Fort Morgan into the bay.

At dawn on August 5, 1864, Farragut's attack force got underway, moving in on a flood tide in a southwest wind that would blow smoke into the fort. The 14 wooden ships were lashed together in pairs, the weaker ships on the left. The sloop *Brooklyn*, accompanied by the *Octorara*, led the way because she carried at her bow four guns and an antitorpedo fender. Next came the flagship *Hartford* and the *Metacomet*. A little ahead and to the right of the wooden vessels, the monitors *Tecumseh*, *Manhattan*, *Winnebago*, and *Chickasaw* advanced to neutralize the fort and to fend off the *Tennessee* during the passage into the bay. Farragut had warned all his captains to keep to eastward of a buoy which he had reason to believe marked the edge of the minefield.

At about 7 A.M. the approaching attack force began to exchange fire with Fort Morgan. In order to see above the smoke, first the *Hartford*'s pilot, then Farragut, climbed up the ship's main rigging. Captain Drayton, concerned for the admiral's safety, sent Quartermaster Knowles aloft with a line to lash him fast.

In the pilothouse atop the *Tecumseh*'s turret, Captain Craven saw the *Tennessee* and three wooden gunboats emerge from behind Fort Morgan on a westerly

Farragut, in the rigging of the Hartford, *directs the attack on the Confederate ironclad* Tennessee.

course, and promptly steered left to intercept the ironclad. "The Admiral ordered me to go inside that buoy,"
he said to Pilot John Collins, "but it must be a mistake."
As Collins was protesting that there was depth enough
for the *Tecumseh* east of the buoy, a deafening blast
almost lifted the monitor out of the water. It then
started to go down by the bow.

Both men dropped through a hatchway into the turret. At the foot of the escape ladder, Captain Craven
stepped back. "After you, pilot," he said. Collins sprang
up the ladder and felt the ship drop away from him as
he reached the top rung. He was one of 21 officers
and men to escape from the sinking vessel. For the
other 93, including Craven, the *Tecumseh* became an
iron coffin. Farragut, shouting from his lofty perch, ordered a launch sent to rescue survivors, a mercy mission

from which the Confederates were careful to withhold
fire.

Suddenly the whole expedition faced disaster. Captain Alden of the *Brooklyn*, warned that he was heading into a line of buoys, which were actually floating
empty cartridge boxes, ordered his ship to back water.
As following vessels pressed on those that had stopped
ahead, a monumental pile-up became imminent. In the
confusion the Union ships slackened fire, while the
gunners ashore improved in rapidity and accuracy. The
Hartford, stalled under Morgan's guns, took broadside
fire from the fort and raking fire from the Confederate
vessels on the far side of the minefield. In seconds her
deck was a shambles of broken bodies and mangled
limbs. The wounded struggled, or were carried, below
to the surgeon's quarters. The still active men hastily

lined up the bodies of the dead out of the way on the port side. A solid shot took off a gunner's head. A cannon ball tore off the legs of a seaman, who threw up his arms, only to have them carried away by another shot. Miraculously he survived.

Farragut, in agonizing uncertainty, breathed a prayer for guidance, and a voice seemed to command, "Go on!" He ascertained from the pilot, just above him, that the channel was wide enough to let him pass the stalled *Brooklyn*. Said he, "I will take the lead."

At Farragut's order the *Hartford* now forged ahead, while the *Metacomet*, alongside, briefly backed water, thereby swinging both vessels to port around the *Brooklyn*. Someone shouted a warning that they were heading into lines of torpedoes. "Damn the torpedoes," cried Farragut, "full speed ahead!" The *Hartford* and her consort passed through the minefield, and the rest of the column followed. Men thought they heard primers snapping, but no more torpedoes exploded. As Farragut had suspected, most of them had been corroded into harmlessness through long immersion.

The lumbering *Tennessee* lunged first at the *Hartford* and then at the *Brooklyn*, missing both. She then exchanged fire with the other Union ships as they passed into the bay. One of the Confederate gunboats, the *Selma*, continued to rake the *Hartford* and the *Metacomet* while they were advancing through the narrow channel. When the Union vessels reached deep water where they could turn and aim their broadsides, they quickly dispersed the gunboats. One gunboat caught fire and was abandoned. Another found refuge under the guns of Fort Morgan and escaped to Mobile after dark.

The *Metacomet*, casting off from the *Hartford*, went in pursuit of the *Selma* and soon forced her into submission, inflicting heavy casualties. The *Selma*'s captain, Lieutenant Murphy, boarded the *Metacomet* and drew himself up to rigid attention before her commanding officer, his friend of happier times. "Captain Jouett," said he, "the fortunes of war compel me to tender my sword to you." Replied Jouett, smiling, "Pat, don't make a damned fool of yourself. I've had a bottle on ice for you for the last half hour."

While Farragut's crews were having a rest and a second breakfast, the admiral was considering how to strike at the *Tennessee*, now safe under Fort Morgan's guns. He had decided on a night attack with his monitors, when he was astonished to learn that Admiral Buchanan was advancing into deep water in broad daylight to engage the 17 heavily armed vessels of the Union force. Said Farragut grimly, "I did not think old Buck was such a fool."

Farragut's sloops, swifter and more maneuverable than his monitors, had the first round with the *Tennessee*, ramming her with their specially armored bows and firing shot and shell. They received far more damage than they inflicted. The *Hartford* had just rammed the ironclad when the *Lackawanna*, heading a second time to ram the Confederate, drove into the *Hartford* instead, cutting her down to within two feet of the waterline. Farragut, standing on the port quarter rail, angrily turned to a signal officer and asked, "Can you say 'for God's sake' by signal?"

"Yes, sir," replied the officer.

"Then say to the *Lackawanna*, 'For God's sake get out of our way and anchor!'"

By now the monitors were arriving on the scene. The *Manhattan*, armed with two 15-inch guns, fired steel bolts that finally penetrated the *Tennessee*'s armor. Other shot jarred loose and scattered metal fragments inside her casemate, and one of them broke Buchanan's leg. The Confederate's port shutters jammed. Down came her smokestack, and choking fumes filled her casemate. The *Chickasaw*, following her relentlessly, shot away her steering chains.

The *Tennessee*, no longer able to aim her guns by turning ship, was gradually pounded into submission. With Buchanan's consent, Captain Johnston at last climbed out atop the casemate to show the white flag. Union casualties were 52 killed and 170 wounded, not counting the losses in the *Tecumseh;* of the other Federal vessels the *Hartford* sustained the heaviest losses: 25 killed and 28 wounded.

The evening following the battle, the Confederates evacuated and blew up Fort Powell. On August 7 Fort Gaines surrendered to Granger's troops, who then transferred to Mobile Point and, before the end of the month, starved Fort Morgan into submission. It was not until the following spring that sufficient troops were available for operations against the city of Mobile, which was occupied by Federal troops three days after Lee's surrender at Appomattox.

SHERMAN'S MARCH

In recognition of his capture of Vicksburg, Grant was made supreme army commander in the West. For his subsequent relief of Federal forces besieged at Chattanooga, Congress voted him the rank of lieutenant general, a title held previously in the U.S. Army only by Washington and Scott. In March 1864, Lincoln summoned Grant to Washington to assume command of all the Union armies. Sherman succeeded to Grant's western command.

Now at long last Union forces were given a coherent strategy. In early May, Grant, attaching himself to Major General George G. Meade's Army of the Potomac, advanced on Lee's Army of Northern Virginia. Simultaneously Sherman advanced on General Johnston's Army of Tennessee, which Grant had forced into northern Georgia. The first and second soldiers of the Union were thus pitted against the first and second soldiers of the Confederacy.

Although Grant, with 119,000 troops, and Sherman, with 98,000, were twice as strong as their adversaries, neither, despite skillful maneuvering, could for several weeks outflank his wily opponent. They were able, nevertheless, to force back their adversaries by sheer power—Lee on Richmond and Johnston on Atlanta. Finally, in mid-June, Grant, by secretly transferring his army across the James River, managed to get around Lee's right flank. His indecisive subordinates, however, allowed Lee time to rotate his front and entrench. Thus denied a smashing victory, Grant at least contained the

Army of Northern Virginia, thereby simplifying Sherman's problems in Georgia.

An impatient President Davis further eased Sherman's problems by replacing General Johnston with the reckless John B. Hood, whom Sherman defeated three times in 10 days. When Hood took refuge in Atlanta, the Union Army forced him out into the open by circling the city and cutting the railroads that supplied him. Sherman next detached Major General George H. Thomas with enough force to deal with Hood. Then, leaving Atlanta in flames, he daringly set out across Georgia with 62,000 troops to secure a base for seaborne supply. His hungry army, advancing on a 60-mile front through this last great granary of the Confederacy, picked it clean of foodstuffs, ripped up the railroads, and seized or destroyed everything of any conceivable military value.

For 33 days Sherman's army was completely out of contact with the Federal government. Union officials became alarmed for its fate. Confederate newspapers, to heighten the mystery and keep the North worrying, avoided reporting Sherman's moves. At last, in mid-

Surrender of the Tennessee *(center).*

December, a ship of Admiral Dahlgren's blockading squadron, probing up the Ogeechee River south of Savannah, caught sight of troops attacking Fort McAlister while a group of officers observed operations from atop a rice mill. "Who are you?" inquired the ship's signal flags.

"General Sherman," replied a wigwag flag from the mill.

Asked the ship, "Is Fort McAlister taken yet?"

"No, but it will be in a minute."

Shortly afterward blue-clad soldiers appeared on the fort's ramparts, dancing and showing the Union flag.

Before Sherman's army could surround and isolate Savannah, the Confederate garrison of 15,000 had slipped away to the north. The general sent President Lincoln a message: "I beg to present you as a Christmas gift, the city of Savannah."

In early February 1865, Sherman began his march northward through the Carolinas in order to join Grant in clamping the pincers on Lee. From Charleston, the outflanked Confederates promptly retreated. Dahlgren's sailors at last raised the Union flag over the rubble of Fort Sumter and walked the nearly empty streets of the city they had strived so long to capture.

Sherman's northward march, even more destructive than his devastation of Georgia, was now recognized as the logical extension of the Mississippi Valley campaign. It was an 800-mile outflanking of the Army of Northern Virginia, a further dismemberment of the Confederacy, and a steady and inexorable shrinking of Lee's logistic base.

THE ASSAULT ON FORT FISHER

In October 1864 Admiral Porter assumed command of the North Atlantic Blockading Squadron with orders to close Wilmington, North Carolina, the last major Confederate port open to blockade-runners. This port was a favorite of the runners, for the Cape Fear River, on which the city was located, had shallow approaches and several mouths; it was hence difficult to blockade. Connected by rail to Richmond via Petersburg, Wilmington had become the port of the Confederate capital and chief supplier of the Army of Northern Virginia. General Lee had warned that, without materials flowing from abroad through Wilmington, he could not hold Richmond.

A secondary but important objective assigned to Porter was the destruction of the rebel ironclad *Albemarle,* which threatened Union vessels operating in the North Carolina sounds. Soon after Porter took command at Hampton Roads, there came aboard his flagship a long-haired, hatchet-faced young lieutenant named William Cushing, who announced that he was prepared to sink the ironclad. Cushing, kicked out of Annapolis for academic deficiency and general hell raising, had since earned a reputation as a daredevil.

With Porter's blessing, Cushing and 14 volunteers one rainy night steamed unobserved up the Roanoke River in a launch equipped with a spar torpedo. They discovered the *Albemarle* alongside a wharf, surrounded by an antitorpedo pen of floating logs. Signaling for speed, Cushing rode his launch over the slippery logs and, with bullets ripping through his clothes, thrust his torpedo-tipped spar under the ironclad's overhang. He then pulled the lanyard. The resulting blast sank the ironclad and swamped the launch, but Cushing swam away and, in a stolen boat, got back to the fleet. Only one other man from the launch returned.

The key to the closing of Wilmington was Fort Fisher, a huge sand-and-log fortification on the end of the peninsula at one of the mouths of the Cape Fear River. Because this fort could be taken only by large-scale amphibious assault, Secretary Welles stripped the block-

Second attack on Fort Fisher, January 13–15, 1865.

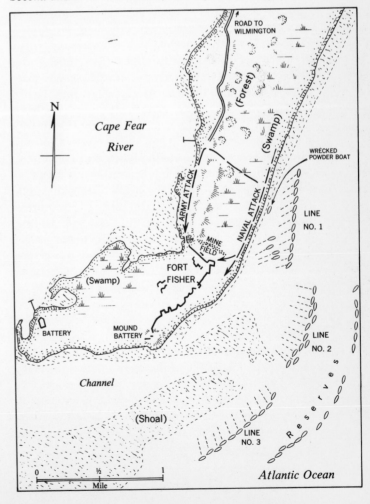

ading squadrons in order to provide Porter with 55 bombardment vessels and nearly as many transports and auxiliary craft—much the largest naval force so far assembled in the war. General Grant appointed Major General Godfrey Weitzel to command the landing force, assigning to him 6,500 troops from the Army of the James. General Ben Butler, then commanding the Army of the James, typically intruded himself into the act. He suggested that a ship loaded with gunpowder be exploded near Fort Fisher the night before the landing. If the explosion did not blow the fort to pieces, he insisted, it would at least take the fight out of the defenders. Porter, a born experimenter, agreed to give the plan a try, but he was horrified when Butler announced that he was coming along on the expedition. The lawyer general was a meddler and a military blunderer, but he was also a master politician with powerful connections, and he was a candidate for the Presidency. Because he could be ruthlessly vindictive, neither Porter nor Grant, nor even President Lincoln, cared to cross swords with him.

The powder ship proved a fizzle. A half-rotten erstwhile blockade-runner was packed with 215 tons of black powder and anchored at night off Fort Fisher. Volunteers lighted fuses and started a fire on the ship. The powder, instead of exploding, merely burned, providing a gorgeous spectacle and disturbing the defenders in the fort scarcely a whit.

At dawn the next day, Christmas Eve 1864, Porter opened the naval bombardment, pouring great quantities of shell into the fort, which replied only feebly. On Christmas Day, after another high-speed bombardment from the fleet, General Weitzel went ashore with the first echelons of his troops. After about 2,300 soldiers had landed, he reported to Butler that Fort Fisher, far from being demolished by the fleet bombardment, as Porter had predicted, was only slightly damaged. A little later the officer in charge of the landing craft warned Butler that a storm was threatening. "General," he said, "you have got either to provide for these troops tonight on shore some way, or get them off; because it is getting so rough that we cannot land much longer." Butler, after thinking over the situation, recalled the landing force, notified Porter that the operation was canceled, and sailed away, leaving on the storm-lashed beach 700 stranded soldiers for the Navy to retrieve.

Porter, exasperated, fired off an indignant report to Welles, who released it to the press to clear the Navy of blame. In the anti-Butler furor that resulted, the general's superiors at last found their opportunity to dump him. At Grant's request, and on Lincoln's orders, the Secretary of War relieved Butler of his command

and ordered him home to Massachusetts. Grant then wrote to Porter, "Hold on if you please a few days longer, and I will send you more troops with a different general."

Porter, for all his denunciation of Butler, must eventually have realized that the general's refusal to assault Fort Fisher had not been entirely unjustified. Reconnaissance revealed that the fort was indeed only superficially damaged. In fact, only 3 guns out of 75 had been dismounted, and only 3 men of the 1,800-man garrison had been killed; the bombproofs and magazines remained intact. The fort had fired slowly merely to conserve ammunition.

The meager results of the naval bombardment demonstrated that unaimed area fire is ineffective against fortified positions. Porter, no fool, saw his mistake and revised his tactics accordingly. He and Grant were grimly determined that the second assault should succeed, not only for military reasons, but because a second failure would vindicate Butler and possibly set his feet on the road to the White House.

The Second Fort Fisher Expedition arrived off the fort on the morning of January 13, 1865. The attack force, now enlarged to 62 gunnery vessels, promptly renewed its bombardment, this time deliberately, from close range, each ship aiming at an assigned target until it was destroyed and then shifting to the next, according to plan. By 2 P.M. the landing force, increased to 8,000 troops, was ashore. Their new commander was tough, energetic Brigadier General A. H. Terry. During the day Terry's soldiers busily entrenched. Throughout the night the monitors and the *New Ironsides* kept up the bombardment. On January 14 the landing force cut off Fort Fisher completely from the mainland and extended their trench system to within 500 yards of its land face.

On the morning of the 15th Porter began sending ashore a naval landing force of 2,000 sailors and marines to participate in the assault. At 3 P.M. the fleet shifted fire and blew whistles, at which signal the naval landing force raced along the beach toward the fort's eastern salient. Few men reached it, for from the parapet, Confederate sharpshooters discharged a devastating rifle fire that mowed down the attackers by the score. More than 300 fell; the rest dug into the sand or retreated.

The Confederates atop the salient gave a triumphant cheer, only to receive a volley of rifle fire in their backs. While their attention had been distracted by the naval assault, Terry's soldiers had stormed into the fort at the opposite end of the land face. The Confederates, despite their surprise, put up a desperate fight. Not until 10 P.M. could Terry fire his rocket announcing victory.

Bombardment of Fort Fisher, January 14, 1865.

The fleet replied with cheers, rockets, and steam whistles. The Navy's war was over.

On his way home General Butler paused in Washington to testify before the Congressional Committee on the Conduct of the War, insisting that Fort Fisher was impregnable. Just as he finished his testimony, newsboys were heard outside crying an extra edition announcing that the fort had fallen. Butler joined in the general laughter—somewhat wryly, one may suspect.

THE SURRENDER

Throughout the winter of 1864–65, while mud held the entrenched armies of Grant and Lee immobile in the Richmond-Petersburg area, the military posture of the Confederacy steadily deteriorated. At Nashville in mid-December Thomas shattered the impetuous Hood's Army of Tennessee. After the fall of Fort Fisher, an enlarged Union Army, supported by a greatly reduced fleet under Porter, advanced on Wilmington by way of the Cape Fear River. Once more Porter made use of a dummy monitor, piloted up the river on a flood tide by none other than daredevil Lieutenant Cushing. On February 22 the Confederates evacuated Wilmington and the Federals occupied it. The city proved to be an invaluable supply base for Sherman's army coming up from the south.

At the end of January the Confederate Congress, dissatisfied with President Davis' conduct of the war, created for General Lee the post Commander in Chief of All Confederate Forces. Lee could do little with his increased authority, for supplying and commanding the Army of Northern Virginia consumed all his attention and energy. He did, however, rectify one serious consequence of Davis' misjudgment by restoring General Johnston to active duty. To Johnston Lee gave the hopeless task of stopping Sherman with a force of only 27,000 men, which included the remnant of the Army of Tennessee. Sherman, by absorbing the Federal troops at Wilmington, had brought his own strength to more than 80,000. Johnston, therefore, could only fall back through North Carolina as he had earlier fallen back through Georgia.

The Confederate soldiers, unpaid, ill supplied, ill clothed, ill fed, became disillusioned with their "rich man's war but poor man's fight," and deserted in increasing numbers. By April 1845, the Army of the Potomac had swelled to 125,000 soldiers, while the Army of Northern Virginia had shrunk to 57,000. Hence when Grant attacked Richmond and Petersburg on April 2, Lee was obliged to evacuate both cities. In order to keep Confederate tobacco out of Federal hands, Lee's provost marshal ordered Richmond warehouses set afire, but the fires got out of control and spread to much of the city. When General Weitzel's occupation troops entered, they found the industrial heart of Richmond little more than a charred shell.

Lee retreated westward, hoping to swing southwest at Amelia Courthouse and to advance along the Richmond & Danville Railroad, joining forces with Johnston south of Danville. But Grant, moving parallel to Lee and south of him, blocked the railroad. Lee consequently continued west toward Lynchburg. Finally, three of Grant's corps outdistanced Lee and at Appomattox Courthouse placed themselves athwart his line of march, while two more Union corps came up behind him. Lee, surrounded, his army reduced by captures and desertions to 28,000 men, his logistic base reduced to zero, on April 9 surrendered his army to Grant. Before the end of the month, Johnston, reduced to 15,000 troops, surrendered to Sherman.

VI

The New Navy

In 1867 Farragut, promoted to the newly created rank of admiral, took command of the U.S. European squadron. Honored and entertained by military and naval leaders, as well as crowned heads of Europe, he must have been embarrassed to receive dignitaries aboard his wooden flagship *Franklin*. This vessel was something of an oddity when compared with the iron or ironclad warships of England, France, and Italy.

After the Civil War the U.S. Navy had quickly reverted to wood and sail. One reason was that Secretary Welles had reinstated the prewar worldwide system of squadrons, which naturally had to be made up of seagoing vessels. The Navy's only truly seagoing ironclad had been the *New Ironsides*, which was accidentally destroyed by fire in 1866. The rest—shallow-draft gunboats and monitors suitable only for river and harbor work—were laid up or disposed of. Without bases the Navy had no adequate means of fueling its squadrons. Hence the wooden steamers were rerigged for full sail power, their engines were altered for greater economy and less speed and range, and their four-bladed propellers were replaced by less efficient two-bladed ones, which could be lined up vertically with the keel to reduce drag under sail. Use of steam was forbidden except in emergencies.

During the war the Union navy had laid down a class of fast cruisers to chase Confederate raiders and, in the event of foreign intervention, to raid enemy commerce. The first of these vessels to be completed, the *Wampanoag*, was launched in 1868; she achieved a world speed record of nearly 18 knots. Well armed, she and her sisters were perfect commerce raiders and, like the Humphreys frigates, able to outrun anything they could not outfight. Yet the design was discontinued and the *Wampanoag* was radically altered to make her slower and less expensive to operate, speed being deemed a useless luxury in time of peace.

Because Congress did not vote adequate appropriations for the Navy, U.S. warships remained armed with obsolete smoothbore muzzle loaders, and vessels beyond repair were not replaced. A fleet that in 1865 had in some respects been the most powerful in the world rapidly became contemptible. The fact was that the American people and their political representatives had lost interest in the Navy. Their attention was focused on reconstruction, on developing the nation's commerce and industry, on opening the West, and on spanning the continent with railroads.

Congress could indeed see little use for a navy. The squadrons had initially been established to protect an American merchant marine that now no longer existed. The country was at peace with the world, it had no nearby naval rivals, and it was insulated from the chronic troubles of the Old World by the broad Atlantic. Even naval leaders saw no use for capital ships, for they assumed that in event of a foreign war the U.S. Navy would return to its traditional roles of coast and harbor defender and commerce raider. Anyway, ship and gun design obviously was going through a period of rapid evolution. Why not let other countries make the costly experiments that would lead eventually to new types?

INTELLECTUAL PROGRESS

Despite the hopes and hard work of the Naval Academy's founders, the generally poor preparation of recruits arriving at Annapolis kept its educational level low. The academy remained a kind of rough barracks with classrooms attached. Rowdyism was followed by harsh repression. Perhaps it was out of sheer frustration that William Chauvenet in 1859 left Annapolis to accept a professorship at Washington University. At the outbreak of the Civil War, Professor Henry Lockwood, another faculty luminary, left the academy to join the Army. A West Point graduate, he became a brigadier general. Most of the academy's officer instructors, assigned to combat duty, were replaced by civilians with doubtful qualifications.

Hence the educational standards of the academy, while it was operating at Newport during the war, reached rock bottom. In an attempt to provide more ensigns, the school lowered its entrance requirements to bare literacy, a self-defeating measure which produced more failures instead of more graduates.

To the academy at Newport came two midshipmen with important connections: Tom, son of Secretary Welles, and Carlisle, son of Admiral Porter. Tom, as a plebe, was the victim of such rough, even sadistic, hazing that, with his father's reluctant permission, he resigned from the academy and joined the Army. Carlisle lasted a little longer but was finally expelled for academic deficiency. Joining the Marine Corps, he displayed conspicuous gallantry at the storming of Fort Fisher. During the war the Secretary and the admiral were too busy to look into the causes of their sons' troubles, but each filed away his grievance for future action.

A month after the end of hostilities, Welles sent to Newport a blue-ribbon board of visitors, with Farragut as president and Porter as his second, to inspect and report on conditions at the Naval Academy. Afterward Welles consulted long and earnestly with his top admirals. He then appointed Porter academy superintendent.

Porter took over his new duties with all the vigor and enthusiasm he had shown in his wartime commands. While workmen at Annapolis were restoring the academy buildings and grounds, which the Army had used as a hospital center, Porter assembled as administrators and instructors a brilliant group of young naval officers, all veterans of the war. As commandant of midshipmen he

Stephen B. Luce.

secured Lieutenant Commander Stephen B. Luce, a gifted teacher, who had been a student at the Naval Academy, had twice returned as an officer instructor, and was the author of the academy's textbook on seamanship.

After the midshipmen reported to Annapolis in October 1865, Porter began to weed out the undersirables by raising academic standards and standards of conduct and expelling those who failed to measure up in either category. With equal ruthlessness he forced out faculty members whom he considered less than fully qualified. Having thus purged student body and faculty, Porter instituted an honor system, set up a program of athletics, scheduled regular dances, encouraged dramatics and other creative means of expression, and organized a curriculum that at last showed recognition of the fact that iron and steam had arrived in the Navy. In short, he found the Naval Academy a disorderly barracks and

The United States Naval Academy at Annapolis following the Civil War, as restored and enlarged by Superintendent David Dixon Porter.

left it a respected college. In an eminent career, this was his greatest achievement.

In 1869 the fame of the academy's steam engineering department under Porter was such as to attract from Nevada young Albert Michelson, the science-oriented son of a Polish immigrant. After graduation, Ensign Michelson returned to the academy as an instructor, and there in 1878 measured the speed of light more accurately than it had ever been measured before. This was a major step in a distinguished career in which Michelson became the first American to win the Nobel Prize in Physics, and the first to perform the experiment on which the Einstein Theory of Relativity is based.

Although, in the Navy's lean years of the 1870s, the Naval Academy suffered for lack of adequate funds, it continued to be a source of ideas. In 1873 a group of academy officers and professors founded the United States Naval Institute, which met regularly to discuss professional and scientific matters. Papers read at these meetings were from time to time issued in pamphlet form—the *U.S. Naval Institute Proceedings,* later issued quarterly and ultimately, after 1917, monthly. Over the years the *Proceedings* has been the main public forum for discussion and debate of subjects affecting the Navy.

When Luce left the Naval Academy in 1869 and returned to sea, he was shocked to discover how the quality of seamen as a class had deteriorated. Most of the sailors in American warships were now foreign mercenaries who spoke little English: waterfront drifters with little knowledge of seamanship and no interest in a naval career. Luce persuaded the Secretary of the Navy and Congress to provide, first, a training ship, and later a training squadron under his command, to prepare young Americans for careers at sea. This effec-

Alfred Thayer Mahan.

structor whom he wanted most, Commander Alfred Thayer Mahan, was not made available until 1886. At that time, however, Luce was ordered to sea, whereupon Mahan took over from him as president of the War College. In 1890 the enemies of the college succeeded in closing its doors. That same year, however, Mahan's early War College lectures appeared in book form, under the title *The Influence of Sea Power upon History, 1660–1783.* This work so lucidly vindicated the new imperialism stirring the major industrial nations that it attracted worldwide attention. Together with Mahan's next book, *The Influence of Sea Power upon the French Revolution and Empire, 1793–1812,* which appeared in 1892, it assured the continuing existence of the Naval War College. The college has proved to be a constant source of creative thought in the fields of naval strategy and tactics, as well as the philosophy of war.

BUILDING THE NEW NAVY

By the 1880s the American people's intense preoccupation with internal affairs had come to an end. Post–Civil War adjustments had almost been concluded, and the main problems of reconstruction had been solved. The most desirable western lands had been settled. Railroads spanned the continent. American industry was thriving as never before, exports were increasing, and manufacturers were seeking more and more foreign markets for their products. The federal treasury was showing annual surpluses of more than $100 million. In a heady atmosphere of prosperity and growing consciousness of national strength and importance, the U.S. government began to retire its old wooden navy and to build a new navy of steel.

Naval expansionists in Congress argued that the merchant marine should be revived to carry the country's rapidly increasing trade, and that the Navy should be made strong enough to protect it. Other arguments followed as corollaries: A big navy would require overseas bases for fueling and servicing. It would be necessary to dig a United States–controlled Isthmian canal to enable that navy readily to operate on both coasts. Possession of a canal would necessitate the securing of outlying islands to protect its approaches—islands such as Cuba, the Danish West Indies, Samoa, and Hawaii. Through such thinking, the United States was swept into the new wave of imperialism in which the chief industrial states of Europe scrambled to secure new markets and new sources of raw materials. This aggressive contest was supported by a philosophical per-

tive training system was eventually, however, brought to an end by advancing technology. Luce continued to believe that the sailing ship was the best school for apprentice seamen, but in this conviction he ceased to be supported by the Navy Department. As the day of even auxiliary sail power passed, and engines, guns, and instruments became ever more complex and sophisticated, it became necessary for seamen to receive most of their training in properly equipped schools ashore.

More lasting was Luce's concept of a war college on the postgraduate level for teaching the science of warfare to officers destined for high command. After a long campaign of persuasion, Commodore Luce received authorization in 1884 to establish the United States Naval War College in a former almshouse on Coasters Harbor Island off Newport. Said he at the opening ceremony, "Poor little Poor House, I christen thee the United States Naval War College." Such was the opposition from Congress and from senior naval officers, that nearly a year passed before Luce could collect a small faculty and eight student officers and begin classes. The inversion that applied to nations Darwin's theory of the survival of the fittest. According to this view, national survival depended on national power, and national power, in the popular mind, meant military power. Writers and orators won respectful attention by pointing out the historical preeminence in dominion, civilization, and wealth of those nations that maintained powerful navies.

Popular support for a revived navy derived in part also from a new feeling of defenselessness. Faster and faster crossings of the Atlantic made it seem less a moat for security than a highway for possible attack. Yet, without adequate means, the United States was committed through the Monroe Doctrine to defend the whole Western Hemisphere. The War of the Pacific of 1879–84, involving Chile, Bolivia, and Peru, revealed to a startled American public that some South American countries had stronger and more up-to-date navies than their own. The Sino-Japanese War of 1894–95 brought to American attention the fact that even backward China had two armored battleships.

With the advent of steel hulls and rifled, built-up, breechloading guns, the time to build seemed at hand. The evolution of warships appeared to have reached a plateau. Ships could be built without fear of rapid obsolescence. In 1881, therefore, Secretary of the Navy William M. Hunt took the first step toward launching a new naval program by appointing a board of officers to study needs and make recommendations.

Hunt's board, inclined at first to be conservative, at length accepted the proposals of a minority, which included Benjamin Isherwood, and recommended the building of swift cruisers—steam-and-steel versions of the Humphreys frigates. The first of the new ships, authorized by Congress in 1883, were the protected cruisers *Atlanta, Boston,* and *Chicago* and the smaller *Dolphin,* a so-called dispatch boat. They were painted white and publicized by the Navy as the "White Squadron," but they became popularly known as the Navy's "ABCDs." The *Chicago,* largest of the four, displaced 4,500 tons, steamed at 18 knots, and carried four 8-inch and fourteen 5-inch guns. None of the ships were armored, but the vital parts were "protected" by a thick steel deck overhead. All the vessels were provided with masts and rigging for sail power. Also in 1883 Congress, in order to assure early retirement of the old navy, limited repairs on wooden ships to 20 per cent of the cost of a new vessel of similar type and class.

Beginning in 1885 Congress every year for more than a decade authorized some naval shipbuilding, decreeing that insofar as possible American materials should be used in constructing and arming new warships. One anticipated result was the laying of foundations for domestic steel, munitions, and related industries. Perhaps less generally anticipated were the subsequent activities of these same industries as potent progagandists and lobbyists for continued naval building and development.

After the authorization of the ABCDs, sentiment began to grow in Congress in favor of building seagoing armored ships—vessels that could break up an enemy blockade of American harbors. Otherwise, as Isherwood pointed out, the Navy's commerce raiders would, like the privateers of the War of 1812, be unable to get their prizes into port. South Carolina's Senator Matthew C. Butler carried the argument a step further by denouncing commerce raiding as an "insignificant kind of guerrilla, bushwhacking warfare." He condemned the policy of passive coast defense, demanding instead a fleet of battleships in the face of which no enemy would hazard blockade or amphibious invasion of the American coasts. Congress as a whole was not ready to go so far, but in 1886 it appropriated funds for the *Maine* (6,680 tons) and the *Texas* (6,315 tons), originally called second-class battleships but later more properly reclassified as armored cruisers. That year and the following one, Congress, as if not quite able to break with the past, also appropriated funds for outdated monitors. The only other armored vessel authorized in that decade was the armored cruiser *New York,* of the 1888 authorization.

Gradually, however, national leaders developed a reasonable understanding of the capital-ship strategy of control of the sea, that is, denying the sea to the enemy's ships while reserving it to one's own use. The argument for capital ships was forcefully set forth in Navy Secretary Benjamin F. Tracy's annual report for 1889, a document believed to have been written partly by Mahan. In response to the Secretary's report a convinced Congress in 1889 at last appropriated funds for three battleships: the *Oregon,* the *Massachusetts,* and the *Indiana,* each displacing 10,288 tons and armed with four 13-inch, eight 8-inch, and four 6-inch guns.

The following year Mahan's *Influence of Sea Power upon History* appeared. It shifted naval thinking from abstract theorizing to the contemplation of a specific example, that of England. The book demonstrated how England, with inherent advantages, had by the judicious use of naval power achieved security and gained wealth, dominance, and a worldwide empire. *The Influence of Sea Power upon the French Revolution and Empire* carried the analysis to the point of Britain's triumph in the defeat of Napoleonic France. Mahan showed that England's rise to world power grew out of the capital-ship doctrine, which Englishmen had employed without entirely understanding, and toward which Americans were now groping. He thus provided both a justification and a blueprint for the new imperialism.

Using examples from history, Mahan systematized the theories of naval strategy. By tracing the evolution of tactics under sail, he provided insight into the tactical problems, not only of his own day, but also of later times. He decried such inconclusive measures as commerce raiding and passive coast defense and preached the propaganda of a big navy as the instrument not only of national defense but also of national prosperity and greatness.

Mahan's ideas won immediate and enthusiastic reception in Britain, Germany, and Japan, leaders in the new imperialism. Americans were at first hesitant to apply concepts of such magnitude to themselves, but Mahan, by means of magazine articles and such influential political friends as Theodore Roosevelt and Henry Cabot Lodge, at last aroused in his countrymen a renewed sense of manifest destiny and a realization that a powerful navy, more powerful than any they had envisaged, was needed to implement it.

THE SPANISH-AMERICAN WAR

Captain Charles Sigsbee sat in his cabin in U.S.S. *Maine* quietly writing. His ship was at anchor in Havana harbor, having been sent there in response to a riot in which U.S. citizens in Cuba had been threatened. The disturbance was an effect of the Cuban Civil War, then in its third year.

Officials at Havana had received the *Maine* politely but coldly. Sigsbee, in order to gage the attitude of the people, attended a bullfight with several of his officers. They found the populace unfriendly but not overtly hostile. Now, on the evening of February 15, 1898, Sigsbee was preparing a report of the situation for the Navy Department. At 9:40 there was a terrific blast, then another. The ship almost leapt from the water. All electric lights went out. Sigsbee groped his way from his cabin and found the forward part of the *Maine* missing, the rest blazing and going down fast. Fewer than 100 of the ship's 350-man complement were saved; they were rescued mainly by boats from an American passenger liner and a Spanish cruiser.

Spanish authorities expressed deep sympathy, and made every effort to be helpful. Captain Sigsbee, convinced of their sincerity, urged, in his report to the Secretary of the Navy, that public opinion in the United States be suspended until after an investigation could be made. At first most Americans appeared willing to wait and see, but the yellow journals with "war extras" and scare headlines soon stirred the public to near hysteria. Chanting the slogan "Remember the Maine! To hell with Spain!" Americans demanded retaliation. Congress responded on March 9 by unanimously voting $50 million for war preparations.

The Maine *entering Havana harbor.*

From the early days of the republic, the United States had been sensitive about Cuba, only 90 miles from Key West, commanding the eastern approaches to a future Isthmian canal, and flanking the Straits of Florida, through which flowed shipping that linked the U.S. Atlantic and Gulf coasts. Before the American Civil War the United States had made several attempts to purchase the island from Spain, and when these attempts failed she had threatened other means of annexing it. With the linking of the American coasts by railroad, interest in annexation died down; but with the outbreak in 1895 of a rebellion of the Cubans against their Spanish rulers, the Americans became emotionally involved.

The rebels were no less cruel and reckless than the Spanish authorities, but because they were fighting to gain their independence, Americans understandably gave them their sympathy. The Spaniards, as a means of denying aid and comfort to the guerrillas, crowded Cuban women, children, and old people into concentration camps. These camps, wretchedly equipped and poorly supplied, quickly became places of filth, disease, and starvation, where inmates died by the hundreds. American newspapers vied with one another in arousing public feelings with luridly exaggerated stories of the camps and of atrocities committed by the Spaniards.

By the end of 1897 the rebellion had almost been suppressed. The government had moderated its concentration policy, improved conditions in the camps, and granted the Cubans a measure of autonomy. Americans began to lose interest in the Cuban cause. Then

came the sinking of the *Maine*, whereupon the American public was aroused against the Spaniards as never before.

It is puzzling, in retrospect, that the Americans clung to the notion that Spaniards sank the vessel, for Spain had at least Cuba to lose and nothing to gain by provoking the United States into declaring war. Spanish and American boards of inquiry studied the wreck, sending down divers. According to the Spanish report, the ship was sunk by the internal explosion of a magazine. According to the Americans, the *Maine* was destroyed by the external explosion of a submarine mine. The New York *Journal* offered $50,000 for information leading to the arrest and conviction of the persons responsible. The reward was never claimed.

Because, despite continued negotiations with Spain, the American people appeared determined to go to war, both countries stepped up military preparations. The battleship *Oregon*, at Puget Sound, was ordered to the East Coast. She made the 15,000-mile cruise in 66 days at a record average speed of 11.6 knots. A new Spanish ministry, discovering with horror the poor state of Spain's armed forces, risked civil war at home in yielding to American demands that the Cuban rebels be granted an armistice and that the concentration camp system be abandoned.

It was too late. The rebels would now accept nothing short of complete freedom, and the Americans were resolved to see that they got it. On April 11 President McKinley, fearful of imminent Republican defeat if he

The Maine *on the bottom of Havana harbor.*

did otherwise, asked Congress for authority to use the Army and Navy. On the 19th Congress passed resolutions declaring Cuba free and independent, demanding the withdrawal of Spanish forces, and directing the President to use the nations's armed forces to put the resolution into effect. A fourth resolution astonished the cynical statesmen of Europe by guaranteeing that the United States would under no circumstances annex Cuba.

On April 22, the U.S. Navy Department ordered Acting Rear Admiral William T. Sampson, Commander North Atlantic Squadron, to blockade Havana and western Cuba. On the 24th Spain declared war on the United States. On the 29th the Spanish Home Fleet, under Admiral Pasquale Cervera, left the Cape Verde Islands, where it had been stationed awaiting developments, and headed for the Caribbean Sea.

The chief strength of Sampson's north Atlantic squadron lay in the battleships *Iowa, Indiana,* and *Massachusetts* and the armored cruisers *Texas, Brooklyn,* and *New York.* Cervera was crossing the Atlantic with the armored cruisers *Maria Teresa, Oquendo, Vizcaya,* and *Cristóbal Colón,* and three destroyers. The Spanish ships were rated swifter than those of the Americans. Some European commentators regarded this advantage as offsetting American superiority of armament and predicted a long war which the Spaniards had a good chance of winning. Captain Mahan more accurately predicted an American victory in "about three months." In fact, as a result of corruption and inefficiency, Cervera's fleet was hopelessly outclassed. It had sacrificed its speed advantage because of failure to clean hulls and to maintain the boilers of the destroyers in a reasonable state of repair. The Spanish fleet's inferiority in armament was aggravated by the fact that the *Colón* had not received her two big guns, that about half of the secondary guns of the other cruisers were inoperable, that the ships had not held target practice in a year, and that 85 per cent of their ammunition was defective. When Cervera had pointed out these shortcomings to the naval ministry, he received the extraordinary reply: "In these moments of international crisis nothing can be formulated or decided." As he headed for the Caribbean, he faced the fact that there were only two probable outcomes: destruction of his fleet or a humiliating return to Spain.

When news of the Spanish sortie was flashed by cable to the United States, panic seized the East Coast. The War and Navy departments were inundated by demands from worried citizens and their political representatives, who wanted mines in every river, warships in every harbor, troops and guns at every point along the coast. Although the Navy Department recognized the risk of dividing the fleet in the face of possible attack, it had, in order to calm the people's fears, retained a Flying Squadron of a battleship and three cruisers at Hampton Roads under the command of Commodore Winfield Scott Schley. It now organized a North Squadron of old monitors and other vessels to guard the coast from the Delaware capes northward.

OPERATIONS IN THE PHILIPPINES

Theodore Roosevelt, the energetic and bellicose Assistant Secretary of the Navy, frequently dismayed President McKinley and John Long, McKinley's able but conservative Navy Secretary. The President and the Secretary believed the time had come to curtail the naval building program, but Roosevelt, a friend and disciple of Mahan, argued that it should be expanded. McKinley and Long hoped and believed almost to the last that war with Spain could be averted. Roosevelt

George Dewey.

The Olympia, *Dewey's flagship.*

was convinced that it was inevitable and eagerly antic-ipated it. Despite their differences, Long greatly es-teemed his young assistant. Roosevelt had early shown a firm grasp of naval principles in his book *The Naval War of 1812*, published when he was twenty-four years old. With such background, his vigor, enthusi-asm, and quick mind enabled him, in long days extend-ing far into the night, to do the work of several men.

McKinley and Long expected that, if war came, it would be confined to Cuba, with some action in nearby Spanish Puerto Rico. Roosevelt, taking a global view, fixed his attention on the Pacific Ocean area. At that time few Americans were aware that Spain had posses-sions in the Pacific, but Roosevelt knew that the Philip-pines were a Spanish colony and that the Spaniards had a small fleet in Philippine waters. Whether his objective was empire building or merely hitting Spain a secondary blow, we cannot be sure, but he personally

decided that the U.S. Asiatic Fleet should attack the Spanish squadron in the Philippines.

Although he had no authority to do so, Roosevelt picked Commodore George Dewey, as aggressive and independent as himself, to command the Asiatic Fleet. He prevailed upon Dewey to request his senator to speak on his behalf directly to the President. At the same time he pigeonholed a letter favoring another candidate until Dewey's appointment was assured.

After the sinking of the *Maine*, Roosevelt chafed at the Navy Secretary's deliberateness of action. On the afternoon of February 25, Long happened to be away, leaving his assistant as Acting Secretary. Roosevelt seized the opportunity to fire off a whole series of pe-remptory orders that put the Navy on a full war footing. To Dewey, now at Hong Kong, he cabled: "Keep full of coal. In event of declaration of war Spain, your duty will be to see that the Spanish Squadron does not leave the Asiatic coast, and then offensive operations in the Philippine Islands."

Dewey, on his own authority, had transferred the Asiatic Fleet from Yokohama to Hong Kong to be nearer the Philippines. He bought 3,000 tons of coal and then purchased the collier that brought it. He also acquired a supply vessel, to serve as fleet train. He had all engines overhauled, personally inspected all equipment and engine spaces, and conducted regular gunnery drills. He had underwater hulls scraped, ordered the white sides of his vessels to be painted battle gray, and made provisions for jettisoning wooden bulkheads and other combustibles. Lacking information about Philippine defenses, he got in touch with the U.S. consul at Manila, who at considerable risk undertook espionage activities and cabled or mailed his findings to Hong Kong. In short, Commodore Dewey prepared for action with all the meticulous attention to detail that he had seen exercised by his Civil War commander and idol, Admiral Farragut.

On the eve of war, the commodore prepared to avoid conflicts with British neutrality regulations by shifting his fleet to Mirs Bay, 30 miles up the Chinese coast. The general conviction at Hong Kong was that the Americans were going straight to destruction. After a farewell dinner tendered Dewey and his officers by a local British regiment, one of the hosts expressed the sentiment of all by remarking, "A fine set of fellows, but unhappily we shall never see them again."

On April 25 came a cable from Secretary Long: "War has commenced between the United States and Spain. Proceed at once to the Philippine Islands. Commence operations particularly against the Spanish fleet. You must capture vessels or destroy. Use utmost endeavor." Dewey waited 36 hours in order to get from the American consul, then en route from Manila, the latest information on the state of Spanish defenses. On the 27th he headed for the Philippines.

Dewey's combat vessels comprised four protected crusiers: the flagship *Olympia* (5,780 tons), the *Baltimore,* the *Raleigh,* and the *Boston;* and the gunboats *Concord* and *Petrel.* The squadron was armed with 53 guns ranging from five to eight inches. Six hundred miles away in the Philippines, Rear Admiral Don Patricio Montojo, well informed by his Hong Kong spies concerning the characteristics of the American squadron, estimated the American firepower at twice that of his own fleet. He therefore decided to fight near land, where shore batteries could supplement the inadequate fire of his ships.

On the evening of April 30, the American squadron was off the entrance to Manila Bay. Dewey had been informed that the channel was mined and that it was flanked by powerful batteries. In Hong Kong newspapers he had read stories from Europe about the power and effectiveness of the Spanish guns and minefield. The European news commentators concluded that Manila, so well shielded, was clearly impregnable. If Dewey should lose a ship or two going into the bay, the rest might well be destroyed inside. With home base 7,000 miles away, he could not be rescued or reinforced, nor could he be resupplied with ammunition. The decision on whether to enter was thus an appalling responsibility.

In fact, fleets do not normally enter harbors looking for enemy warships. The usual action in a situation such as Dewey faced was to blockade—a perfectly feasible operation for the commodore because his collier and supply ship were with him. A blockade would at least keep the Spanish fleet in port and out of mischief, and by causing shortages in Manila, would possibly wring extra concessions from the Spaniards.

On the other hand, Dewey was not worried about the minefield. He doubted that local engineers had the skill to plant mines in deep water. Furthermore, in tropical climates mines deteriorated rapidly. The batteries were another matter, for they could readily punch holes in his unarmored ships. As was his wont when faced with a perplexing situation, Dewey now asked himself, "What would Farragut do?" He knew perfectly well what Farragut would do. If the Admiral had dared to run past Fort Morgan and over a minefield by day, Dewey would certainly risk running past a few batteries by night. So, in the spirit of "Damn the torpedoes, full speed ahead!" he led the way into Manila Bay.

As the column of blacked-out ships entered the channel, Dewey's gunners grew tense at their guns, but nothing happened. A little after midnight a stoker in one of the ships threw a shovelful of coal dust into a furnace, whereupon sparks spurted like fireworks out of the ship's smokestack. One of the Spanish batteries then opened fire.

"Well, well," said the commodore to Captain Charles Gridley, captain of the *Olympia,* "they did wake up at last."

The Spaniards made no hits, and their battery was quickly silenced by gunfire from the ships. The entire American column passed into the bay unscathed. The squadron then slowed down to four knots in order not to reach Manila before dawn.

At first light Commodore Dewey could make out the city's spires against a dim sky. Many merchant ships were present, but Montojo's fleet, which Dewey had expected to find at Manila, was not there. The Spanish admiral had taken his ships south to Cavite in order to spare the city a bombardment. As the American squadron

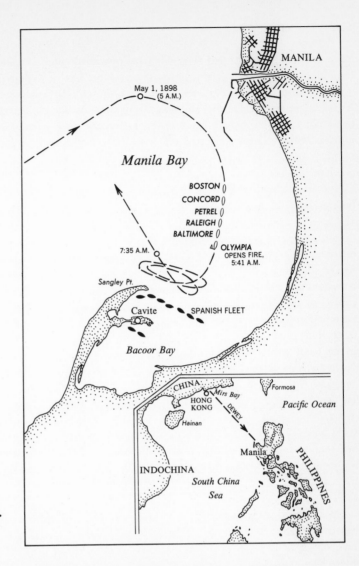

The Battle of Manila Bay.

The Battle of Manila Bay, May 1, 1898.

wheeled to starboard and headed south, the Manila batteries opened fire with shell that passed harmlessly over the ships.

Shortly after 5 A.M., by the light of the rising sun, lookouts in the *Olympia*'s tops sighted the Spanish fleet —six cruisers and a gunboat—stretching in a rough crescent from Sangley Point across to shoal water near the mainland. In fact, all but two of the so-called cruisers were smaller than U.S. gunboat *Concord*. The two largest Spanish vessels were the *Reina Cristina*, Montojo's flagship (3,520 tons), and the wooden *Castilla*, which was protected but also immobilized behind lighters filled with stones. Of the other vessels some were moored, others not.

Long before the Americans came within range, the nervous Spaniards opened fire. On the *Olympia*, up went the signal "Engage the enemy," whereupon the national colors were hoisted on each American ship and bands struck up "The Star-Spangled Banner." At the last note a lusty cheer sounded from every vessel, followed by the cry "Remember the *Maine*!"

On the exposed bridge of the *Olympia* stood Dewey in white uniform, stroking his white mustache and estimating ranges. His impressive paunch and imperturbable bearing made him a figure of calm authority, rendered just a bit jaunty by the fact that he was wearing a golf cap. It seems that in jettisoning the wooden bulkheads somebody had inadvertently tossed over the commodore's uniform cap.

When Spanish shells began to fly overhead and splash near the flagship, Dewey, still estimating ranges, remarked to Lieutenant Corwin Rees, the executive officer, "About 5,000 yards, I should say, eh, Rees?"

"Between that and 6,000, I should think, sir."

Dewey then turned to the *Olympia*'s commanding officer and said almost casually, "You may fire when you are ready, Gridley."

For the Americans the Battle of Manila Bay proved something of an anticlimax. Dewey's squadron, firing steadily, paraded back and forth past the Spanish fleet, hurling back attempts by two of Montojo's ships to charge the American line. At 7:35 the Americans hauled off to check ammunition and eat breakfast, and then resumed the battle. By a little past noon all of the Spanish ships were sunk, burned, or abandoned, the shore batteries were silenced, and a white flag of surrender flew over the main government building at Cavite. The carnage and devastation in the Spanish ships were almost unparalleled in the history of fleet battles. The American squadron, on the contrary, was scarcely damaged. No Americans had been killed and only eight were slightly wounded. The Spaniards had fought gallantly but were

Admiral Montojo's flagship Reina Cristina *wrecked and abandoned.*

defeated by their inferior firepower, inferior ammunition, and their almost complete lack of training. Dewey's careful preparations had paid off. "The Battle of Manila," he said, "was won at Hong Kong."

OPERATIONS IN THE CARIBBEAN

When Admiral Sampson learned that Admiral Cervera had left the Cape Verde Islands, he assumed that the latter would put in for coal at Puerto Rico, the only Spanish base between the Cape Verdes and Cuba. On May 3, therefore, Sampson lifted the blockade of a considerable stretch of Cuban coast, and with the *Indiana,* the *Iowa,* his flagship *New York,* two monitors, and several lesser craft, headed for the other Spanish island. Speed was deemed essential, because Cervera was expected to arrive in the West Indies on May 8. On that date, however, a deeply frustrated Sampson was off Haiti struggling with his monitors, which were so slow that they had to be towed; moreover, they kept breaking down or parting their tow lines. When the Americans arrived off San Juan, Puerto Rico, on the 12th, they found no sign of Cervera, who was a little too wily to make so obvious a landfall.

While Sampson was venting his frustrations and, incidentally, risking his ships and men in a useless bombardment of San Juan's defenses, a cablegram reached the Navy Department from the U.S. consul on Martinique reporting that Cervera's squadron had appeared off that island. This was shocking news, for not only was the north Atlantic squadron divided into several sections, but the *Oregon,* having circumnavigated South America, was now headed for the very waters where Cervera was reported to be.

The Navy Department promptly ordered the Flying Squadron to Key West, whither Sampson also sped with his swiftest vessels, leaving the cumbersome monitors to get back to base as best they could. Schley and Sampson both arrived at Key West on May 18, to learn that Cervera had dropped off at Martinique a destroyer that had been disabled by the Atlantic crossing, and then had touched at the Dutch island of Curaçao.

This news meant that the *Oregon* was safe, but it provided no clue to Cervera's destination. The Navy Department, basing its estimate on information that the Spanish squadron was bringing munitions for the defense of the Cuban capital, concluded that Cervera would attempt to reach Havana, or that he was bound for the southern port of Cienfuegos, which was connected to the capital by rail. Sampson therefore ordered

William T. Sampson.

the Flying Squadron, reinforced by the *Iowa,* to pass around west of Cuba to blockade Cienfuegos, while he himself guarded the approaches to Havana.

Both the department's information and its conclusion were erroneous. Cervera was bringing no munitions for Havana. Short of coal, he had steamed straight from Curaçao to the nearest harbor of refuge, the relatively isolated southeastern port of Santiago de Cuba, which he entered on May 19.

Schley's operations during the next few days have been the subject of so much controversy that it is difficult to know how to describe them fairly. A postwar court of inquiry pronounced them "characterized with dilatoriness, vacillation, and lack of enterprise," but this verdict has not won universal concurrence.

Because the Navy's overriding objective was locating and destroying Cervera's squadron, or at the very least blockading it tightly in port, one might have expected Schley to dash to his destination. Instead, the Flying Squadron, belying its name, poked around to Cienfuegos at an average speed of 10 knots. The commodore's explanation was that, anticipating a lengthy blockade, and possibly a battle, he was sensibly conserving coal.

Arriving off Cienfuegos on May 22, Schley could not see inside the harbor, but observing smoke and hearing what he took to be a gun salute, he concluded that the enemy squadron was inside. Meanwhile, evidence was piling up in Washington that the Spanish ships were at Santiago. Sampson rushed this information to Schley by fast dispatch boat, adding: "If you are satisfied that they are not in Cienfuegos, proceed with all dispatch, but cautiously, to Santiago de Cuba, and if the enemy is there, blockade him in port."

Because the Cienfuegos area was strongly held by the Spaniards, who would probably capture any spies he sent ashore, Schley was at a loss how to get the information he needed. Among reinforcements arriving on May 24, however, was the cruiser *Marblehead*, whose commanding officer had earlier made contact with rebels ashore. From these reinforcements Schley now learned that the Spanish squadron was definitely not present.

Within a few hours Schley's squadron was en route to Santiago. The 315-mile run took two days because his gunboats, which were slow, had additional difficulty riding the rough seas; Schley had not felt justified in leaving them behind in waters where Cervera's ships might be prowling. Some 22 miles from Santiago, he made contact with three American scout cruisers, which reported that, although they had been in the area several days, they had seen nothing of the Spanish squadron.

Schley, feeling that he had come on a wild goose chase, now began to worry about his coal supply. Although he had a collier with him, he considered the weather too rough for coaling at sea. He therefore signaled his ships to get underway on a westerly course for a return to Key West. This was the beginning of the famous "Retrograde Movement," for which Schley was later sharply criticized.

Progress at first was exceedingly slow because the collier developed engine trouble and had to be taken in tow. Hence the next morning a scout cruiser was able to overtake the squadron and to deliver a cable from Washington via Haiti: "All Department's information indicates Spanish division is still at Santiago de Cuba. The Department looks to you to ascertain facts, and

Operations in the Caribbean.

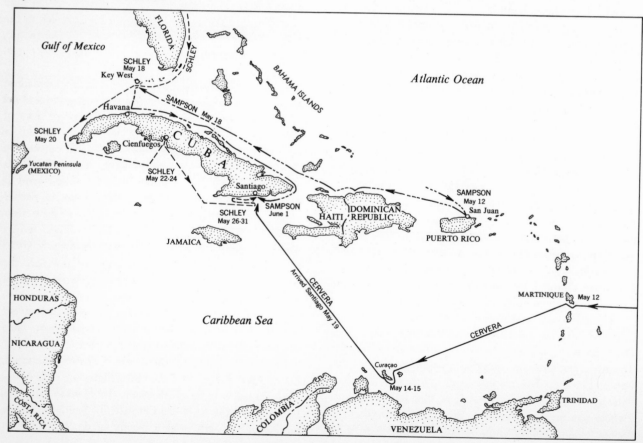

Winfield Scott Schley.

that the enemy, if therein, does not leave without a decisive action."

Schley sent back a reply in which he stressed his coaling difficulties and concluded with the regret that the "Department's orders cannot be obeyed, earnestly as we have all striven to that end. I am obliged to return to Key West, via Yucatan Passage for coal. Can ascertain nothing concerning enemy." When this reply, so shocking to the Navy Department, was relayed to Sampson, he decided that if Schley was coming back to Key West, he himself had better go to Santiago.

The Flying Squadron steamed westward until the evening of May 27 when, the wind having abated, Schley ordered his ships to coal at sea. The squadron then headed back to Santiago. There, on the morning of the 29th, the *Cristóbal Colón*, Cervera's best cruiser, was clearly visible, awnings spread, at the harbor entrance, where she had been for the past four days. On the 31st, Schley conducted an eight-minute bombardment of the

Colón and the harbor forts at such extreme ranges that no damage was done. The next day Sampson reached Santiago with reinforcements, including the newly arrived *Oregon*, whereupon the *Colón* withdrew into the inner harbor. The Americans then established a close blockade.

Sampson had known of the Flying Squadron's return to Santiago, but he decided, in view of Schley's recent actions, that he had better come anyway and take personal command of operations. On his arrival Sampson expressed no disapproval of Schley's conduct, but afterward, in a secret message to Secretary Long, he characterized it as "reprehensible."

Sampson arranged his blockaders in a semicircle off the harbor entrance, the battleships in the center and the smaller vessels in the wings. At night all the ships drew in closer and a searchlight was directed into the channel. On the night of June 3, in order to prevent the escape of the Spanish squadron should the blockaders be blown off station by a storm, Lieutenant Richard P. Hobson attempted, with a volunteer crew, to seal the ships inside the harbor by sinking a collier athwart the narrow, winding entrance channel. But fire from the flanking Spanish batteries smashed the collier's steering gear so that she drifted past the narrows and sank at a point where she presented no serious obstacle. On June 18 American marines went ashore some 40 miles to the east of Santiago and, in the first fighting on Cuban soil, seized Guantanamo Bay for use as a coaling and operational base.

Sampson at last concluded that, if Cervera's squadron would not come out of the harbor, he must go in and get it. First, however, the channel had to be swept clear of mines, lest one of his ships in midcolumn should be sunk and block those inside from those still outside. So he called on the Army for troops to capture the batteries at the channel mouth in order that he might send in boats to clear the mines. The Army, eager to participate in the campaign, readily complied, sending from Tampa an expeditionary force of 16,000 soldiers led by Major General William R. Shafter, a sixty-three-year-old Civil War veteran. With naval support and aid, the soldiers began to go ashore with their equipment at Daiquiri, 16 miles east of Santiago. The landing, which began on June 22, took four days and was carried out in such wild disarray that it surely would have been thrown back had there been any opposition.

During the landing Sampson and Shafter conferred, but succeeded only in thoroughly confusing each other. The general, instead of attacking the Spanish batteries, plunged into the jungle and headed for Santiago. At the outskirts of the city after a bloody battle, Shafter, who

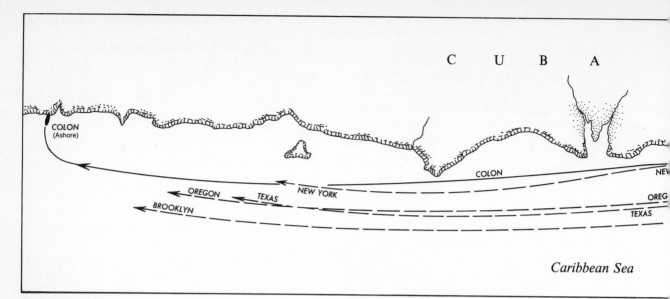

C U B A

COLON
(Ashore)

COLON

NEW

OREG

NEW YORK

OREGON   TEXAS

BROOKLYN

TEXAS

Caribbean Sea

The Battle of Santiago, July 3, 1898.

weighed 300 pounds, and was feverish from the heat, fired off a hysterical message to Sampson urging him to "force the entrance" and to bring his ships into Santiago harbor in order to support the Army. Sampson, exasperated by this reversal of assigned Army-Navy roles and unable to reach an understanding with the general by messenger, on July 3 turned the tactical command over to Schley. He then headed east along the coast in the *New York* for a personal interview with Shafter. The blockade was further weakened that morning by the absence of the battleship *Massachusetts,* then coaling at Guantanamo Bay.

Cervera, ordered to get his ships out of Santiago harbor before they were captured or destroyed by the U.S. Army, chose this opportunity to sortie, leading the way out of the channel at 9:35 A.M. in the *Maria*

Teresa. The *Iowa* fired a warning shot, whereupon all the blockaders, opening fire, steamed toward the head of the emerging Spanish column. The *Teresa* turned west, hugging the shore and firing at the swift *Brooklyn,* Schley's flagship. Crossing the *Brooklyn's* bows, she broke out of the blockade. The *Brooklyn,* instead of immediately turning westward with the *Teresa,* turned east, on Schley's orders, and made a complete loop. This clockwise revolution, never satisfactorily explained, not only cost the *Brooklyn* priceless time but very nearly brought her into collision with the *Texas.*

The battle quickly stretched out into a chase, with the *Brooklyn* and the *Oregon* forging out ahead of the other American vessels, and the *New York* far behind and vainly attempting to catch up. The two Spanish destroyers were almost blown out of the water by fire from the

Schley's flagship Brooklyn.

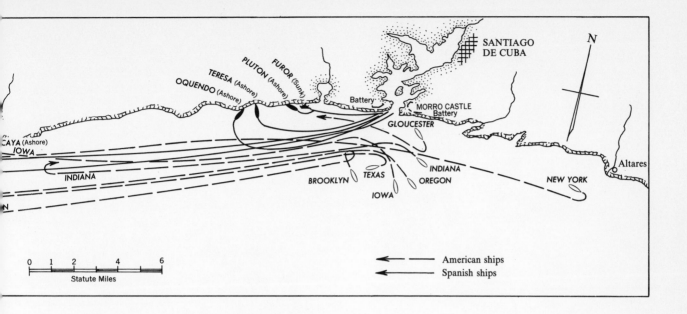

SANTIAGO DE CUBA

Battery
GLOUCESTER
MORRO CASTLE
Battery
Altares

TERESA (Ashore)
PLUTON (Ashore)
FUROR (Sunk)
OQUENDO (Ashore)
CAYA (Ashore)
IOWA
INDIANA

BROOKLYN   TEXAS   INDIANA
            OREGON
        IOWA

NEW YORK

N

0 1 2   4   6
Statute Miles

⟵ — — — — American ships
⟵ ———— Spanish ships

converted yacht *Gloucester* and by shells fired from the *Indiana* as she sped past. The *Teresa,* the *Oquendo,* and the *Vizcaya* were put out of action, not so much by direct American gunfire, which was less than remarkable, as by burning decks and other woodwork, with which they were too amply provided. All aflame, one after the other they turned toward shore and beached themselves. Only the *Colón,* swiftest of Cervera's cruisers, continued in flight, speeding westward at 14 knots, hotly pursued by the *Brooklyn* and the *Oregon,* which gradually overtook her and began making hits. At that the *Colón,* only slightly damaged, struck her colors and ran onto the beach. The Battle of Santiago was over. The Spaniards had lost 260 men, killed or drowned; some 1,800 others, including Cervera, were taken prisoner. American casualties were 1 man killed and 1 wounded.

Operations following the destruction of Spain's Asiatic and Atlantic squadrons were militarily anticlimactic but far-reaching in their consequences. An American convoy bringing troops to occupy Manila made a bloodless capture of Spanish Guam, where the governor did not know that a war was in progress. Both Santiago and Manila capitulated after naval bombardments. With naval support, the U.S. Army took possession of the principal towns of Puerto Rico. The Navy next laid plans for a cruise against Spain itself. The Spaniards thereupon promptly sued for peace, relinquishing all claims to Cuba and ceding Puerto Rico, Guam, and the Philippines to the United States. Cuba granted the United States a permanent naval base at Guantanamo Bay.

The gross errors made by the U.S. Army and Navy were more than offset by the far greater mistakes made by the armed forces of Spain. "We cannot expect ever again," warned Mahan, "to have an enemy so entirely inapt as Spain showed herself to be." Despite the flaws in the American performance, the war marked a turning point for the American people. The United States emerged as a major world power, and Americans thenceforth participated more generally in international affairs. More ominously, the accession of Guam and the Philippines projected American concerns into the area of interest of another expanding sea-power—Japan.

THE UNITED STATES BECOMES A NAVAL POWER

The year of the Spanish-American War, 1898, was the watershed of American naval, as well as foreign, policy. That year Congress authorized three 18-knot battleships and four 12-knot monitors. The monitors, obsolete when built, were the final gasp of the old passive coast-defense strategy. Every year thereafter until the end of World War I, at least one battleship was authorized—the sole exception being 1901, and that only because of congestion in the shipyards. The new naval policy and the acquisition of the Philippines prompted the United States in 1898, after long hesitation, to annex the Hawaiian Islands, chiefly for a naval base. The following year the United States annexed Wake Island and American Samoa. In the glow of pride in the Navy's accomplishments during the war with Spain, Congress also authorized the expansion and complete rebuilding of the United States Naval Academy. Down came the old red-brick buildings, most dating back

The "Great White Fleet" entering San Francisco Bay, 1908.

to pre–Civil War times; up went sparkling new French Renaissance–style buildings of granite and gray brick, including Bancroft Hall, the world's largest dormitory.

The new ship construction, acquisition of bases, and building reflected the acceptance by Congress of the policy that the United States should have a navy powerful enough to defeat the main naval force of any potential enemy. The widely accepted national goal was to acquire a navy second only to that of Great Britain, which was no longer considered a potential enemy but a nation closely tied to the United States by a growing community of interests. America's chief rivals in the new era were Germany, which was challenging British naval supremacy with an ambitious ship-construction program, and Japan, which by destroying Russia's fleets in the Russo-Japanese War of 1904–05, had established a world position as a first-rate sea power.

Theodore Roosevelt, who, as Assistant Secretary of the Navy and as Vice President, had campaigned for the capital-ship policy, presided over its implementation from 1901 to 1909 as President. In a gesture of pride and muscle flexing, he sent his 16 first-line battle-ships, the "Great White Fleet," on an unprecedented 14-month voyage around the world. It was a triumphant feat of shiphandling, but the British took the edge off Roosevelt's display of strength and skill. On the eve of the fleet's departure from Hampton Roads, at the end of 1907, they revealed the characteristics of their new *Dreadnought*, which rendered every other battleship in the world obsolete.

TECHNOLOGICAL DEVELOPMENTS

Some writers have given the impression that the *Dreadnought* was first a gleam in the eye exclusively of Sir John Fisher, Britain's First Sea Lord. In fact, the special characteristics of this ship were the inevitable consequence of improvements in large-caliber gunnery. Before the *Dreadnought* was secretly launched in 1906, the U.S. Navy had under construction two ships with similar characteristics.

The development of smokeless powder and improved methods of fire control meant that naval battles would be fought at increasingly greater ranges, ultimately at ranges at which only the heaviest guns could reach the enemy. Then why not, it was argued, eliminate all but the largest caliber guns and add more of them? In 1901 Lieutenant Homer Poundstone did design such an "all-big-gun" ship for the U.S. Navy, but it was not then accepted. Battleships continued for some time to carry guns of as many as six different calibers, and no more than four apiece of the largest.

In 1905, however, Congress authorized construction of the *Michigan* and the *South Carolina*, each armed only with eight 12-inch guns in four two-gun turrets in pairs at the ends of the ship, and having one turret elevated so as to fire over the other. These ships were followed in the next two years by the *Delaware* and the *North Dakota*, each having main batteries of ten 12-inch guns and anti-torpedo-boat batteries of fourteen 5-inch guns. Long before any of the above-mentioned vessels were completed, the British revealed their *Dreadnought*, which also carried ten 12-inch guns and had a battery of 12-pounders to fight off torpedo-boat attacks. The

Dreadnought's main battery firepower was two and a half times as great as that of any other battleship then afloat, but she could fire no heavier broadside than the *Michigan* or *South Carolina* because her turrets were all on deck level—three centerline, one on each beam. She carried 11 inches of armor on her belt and over her turrets, displaced 17,900 tons, and could make 21.5 knots.

Paralleling and stimulating the change in battleship design in the United States was a steady improvement in American gunnery. This was the achievement mainly of William S. Sims, who as a junior naval officer had observed with dismay the wretched showing of the U.S. Navy's gunners in comparison with those of European navies. Unable to get a hearing for his reform plans in

Midshipmen of the class of 1902 aboard the Navy's first submarine, the Holland.

Commander Marc A. Mitscher in an early naval seaplane at Pensacola.

Ely lands aboard the Pennsylvania.

the Navy Department, he had appealed directly to President Roosevelt, who gave them a favorable endorsement. Rear Admiral Henry C. Taylor, the progressive new chief of the Bureau of Navigation, appointed Sims inspector of target practice, a post which he held from 1902 to 1909. The U.S. Navy, using methods that Sims borrowed from the British navy, achieved a true revolution in gunnery, and at length rivaled the best navies in the world.

The 1898 Naval Appropriations Act provided for 16 destroyers, the first in the U.S. Navy. Two years later the Navy commissioned its first submarine, the 54-foot-long *Holland.* For several years the *Holland* was based during the winter at the Naval Academy, where it was used to train midshipmen, including Chester W. Nimitz.

NAVAL AVIATION

The U.S. Navy early took an interest in the newly invented airplane, seeing its possibilities for reconnaissance and the spotting of gunfire. At Norfolk in 1910 a civilian flyer, Eugene Ely, demonstrated the possibility of teaming planes and ships by flying a plane off a specially constructed launching deck on the cruiser *Birmingham.* Two months later he took off from shore at San Francisco, landed on an improvised flight deck on the cruiser *Pennsylvania,* and was brought to a halt by hooks under his aircraft that caught on to lines stretched athwartships between sandbags. He thus proved the practicability of the aircraft carrier.

In 1911 the Navy, on the strength of a $25,000 Congressional appropriation, contracted for two land planes, a Curtiss and a Wright, and one of Glenn Curtiss' newly developed amphibians. Four officers were then sent to the Curtiss and the Wright brothers factories to learn how to fly them. The next spring these officers, Lieutenants Theodore Ellyson, John Rodgers, and John Towers, and Ensign Victor Herbster, along with some beginners, set up a primitive aviation camp at Annapolis. Ellyson flew a plane shot from a compressed-air catapult mounted on a barge; and Towers gave Lieutenant Ernest J. King, then the executive officer of the Annapolis Engineering Experiment Station, his first airplane ride, a 20-minute flight at 60 miles an hour. Both Towers and King were later carrier commanders and chiefs of the Bureau of Aeronautics. In 1913 the aviation camp was transferred to Florida, where it became the nucleus of the Pensacola Naval Air Station, the Navy's "academy of the air."

For lack of adequate appropriations, little more was achieved in naval aviation during the next few years. When the United States entered World War I, the Navy had only 39 qualified aviators and some 50 planes.

VII

World War I

When World War I broke out in Europe, American military and naval leaders studied it carefully for its lessons, but in general believed that it had little bearing upon the United States. President Wilson had expressed the national policy in declaring the country to be "impartial in thought as well as in action."

The Navy seemed satisfied with the two-battleships-a-year plan—wrung out of Congress by Roosevelt in 1908 and continued in the Taft and Wilson administrations—particularly since Congress was authorizing such giants, for those days, as the *Idaho* class, each with a 32,000-ton displacement, a 21-knot speed, and twelve 14-inch rifles. The opening of the Panama Canal under U.S. control, an event which coincided with the European declarations of war in August 1914, had the effect of further strengthening the U.S. Navy by increasing its ability to redirect its power rapidly from one distant area to another.

Wilson's Secretary of the Navy, Josephus Daniels, regarding the European conflict as remote, neglected war preparations in favor of long-needed reforms in training and personnel policies. He introduced schools both ashore and afloat for basic education as well as naval training, built up a system of naval libraries, provided the means for better selection of enlisted men, and paved the way for them to obtain commissions, either directly or by attending the Naval Academy; he added civilians to the faculty of the Naval Academy and an additional course at the Naval War College. Daniels' most controversial decision was to forbid "the

use or introduction for drinking purposes of alcoholic liquors on board any vessel."

Britain, abandoning her traditional peripheral strategy based on sea power, had sent to France an expeditionary force which held the Allied left flank and thereby helped to halt the German drive on Paris. The opposing armies then, in a series of outflanking maneuvers, stretched themselves farther and farther, finally tying down their entire available strength within entrenched lines all the way across France—lines that scarcely moved one way or the other throughout the four years of conflict. Continental strategy having thus produced a stalemate, the peripheral strategists, headed by the First Lord of the Admiralty, young Winston Churchill, proposed outflanking this Western Front by opening a route by way of the Black Sea to supply munitions to the faltering Russian army on the Eastern Front. The plan, though brilliant in concept, came to grief in 1915 through wretched execution in the rugged steeps of Gallipoli peninsula. This failure, costing a quarter million Allied casualties, convinced many observers that in the face of modern defenses amphibious assault had ceased to be possible. A great spoiler of reputations, the Gallipoli fiasco caused Churchill, among others, to be relieved of office.

Meanwhile, Britain's Grand Fleet and Germany's High Seas Fleet, the latter a little more than half as strong as the former, had remained at their bases, mere fleets-in-being, warily watching each other across the North Sea. Because the Grand Fleet would naturally

German U-boat of World War I, showing rapid development over the Holland *type.*

have liked nothing better than to destroy the High Seas Fleet, and the High Seas Fleet had no intention of coming out and offering itself for destruction, North Sea operations settled down to a campaign of decoy and ambush. Such maneuvers brought about the inconclusive Heligoland Bight Action of August 1914 and the Dogger Bank Action of January 1915.

In mid-1916 the decoy-and-ambush policy at last resulted in the great Battle of Jutland, in which the opposing battle-cruiser fleets on May 31 lured the opposing battleship fleets into contact with each other. Admiral Reinhart von Scheer, the High Seas Fleet commander, promptly headed for home. Admiral Sir John Jellicoe, who led the Grand Fleet, declined to pursue lest his battleships be led over mines and submarines; instead,

he twice blocked the High Seas Fleet from its bases. After dark, however, Scheer broke through the British rear and succeeded in returning to Wilhelmshaven. In the several contacts between fleets, the Germans, despite their numerical inferiority, inflicted nearly twice as much damage as they received. This highly atypical battle, studied closely by all navies for the next two decades, had far greater influence on tactical development than it merited.

A more immediate effect was the profound shock that it gave American naval and government leaders. Britain's poor showing profoundly alarmed the Americans, whose sympathies lay with the Allies and who had counted on the Grand Fleet to destroy the High Seas Fleet, or at least keep it bottled up. Now it appeared that the

United States might yet be vulnerable to an expansionist Germany. Hence, within 60 days after Jutland, Congress passed the Naval Act of 1916 that authorized the building within three years of 10 battleships, 6 battle cruisers, 10 scout cruisers, 50 destroyers, and 67 submarines.

NEUTRAL RIGHTS AGAIN

"Madison and I," moaned Wilson, "are the only two Princeton men that have become President. The circumstances of the War of 1812 and the present war now run parallel. I sincerely hope they will go no further." Wilson was referring to interference, by the belligerents, with U.S. shipping. As in previous European wars, an American economic depression had been converted into a boom by trade with the belligerents, and as in previous wars, American neutral trade on the high seas had come under attack.

In addition to the naval blockade, the British had imposed on Germany an economic blockade. This was not an old-fashioned close blockade, which submarines and aircraft had made impractical, but one made sufficiently effective by mines in the Straits of Dover and off the German coast, as well as by patrols in the English Channel and in the Atlantic Ocean between Scotland and Iceland. Neutral ships were ordered into British ports for inspection. They were not permitted to transport to neutral Scandinavia and Holland more of the items that Britain chose to label contraband than those countries had imported before the war, lest they transship the excess to Germany.

England and France, meanwhile, imported freely from the United States and other neutrals. Germany at first could impose no restriction on this trade except by means of surface raiders, which were quickly run down by the Allies when their movements were reported by radio. In February 1915, therefore, Germany proclaimed the approaches to Britain and France a barred zone wherein all enemy merchant vessels would be sunk without warning—a manifest breach of international law.

The United States protested this proclamation, and the American protests became threats of war upon the U-boat sinking of the British liner *Lusitania*, in which 128 American lives were lost. Further war threats were made upon the subsequent submarine sinkings of the British *Arabic* and the French *Sussex*, when more Americans were killed or wounded. The German government thereupon pledged itself to abide by international law.

By the end of 1916, however, when it became obvious that Germany was not winning the war, a desperate German government decided to gamble on starving England into defeat before the United States could come to her aid militarily. On February 1, 1917, on orders of the Kaiser, U-boats began to sink without warning all ships, Allied or neutral, found in barred zones around Britain, France, and Italy and in the eastern Mediterranean. Wilson promptly severed diplomatic relations with Germany and ordered American merchantmen bound for the war zone to be armed. When the Germans sank four American merchant ships, Wilson called for a declaration of war, which Congress passed by a heavy majority on April 6, 1917.

Once again the United States had elected to go to war in defense of its neutral shipping. A contributing factor, however, was an intercepted and published German message to Mexico seeking an alliance in event of war between the United States and Germany, in return for the restoration to Mexico of Texas, New Mexico, and Arizona. In addition, there was among Americans a feeling of kinship for Britain, of gratitude to France, and of apprehension at the specter of a Europe dominated by imperial Germany.

THE CONVOY QUESTION

Among the officers who had strongly advocated that the Navy prepare for war were Rear Admirals William S. Sims, President of the Naval War College, and Bradley A. Fiske, inventor of the torpedo plane and currently Aide for Operations. In March 1915 Fiske, with the backing of the Navy League, an organization of friends of the Navy, had induced Congress to create the Office of Chief of Naval Operations. This long-needed office, functioning as a naval general staff, would "under the direction of the Secretary" control fleet operations and prepare war plans. Fiske, serving as acting chief, got the office off to a good start despite the limitations of a meager staff. He resigned when he was not permitted to make what he considered adequate preparations for war.

Fiske's successor, the first actual Chief of Naval Operations, was Admiral William S. Benson, a conservative officer who was not above compromise when it was inevitable. He probably achieved all that was possible in view of the powerful opposition in the Navy Department and in Congress. If he could not sufficiently strengthen the Navy, he could and did make sure that correct and current reports were prepared and made available on the state of naval and merchant marine ships and equipment. Nevertheless, when war came, only a third of the Navy's vessels were materially fit and 90 per cent

William S. Sims.

eyes," Admiral Benson warned Sims. "It is none of our business pulling their chestnuts out of the fire."

Sims arrived in London on April 9, 1917, three days after the U.S. declaration of war. He was cordially received by Sir John Jellicoe, now First Sea Lord. In complete frankness, Jellicoe revealed a shocking situation: German submarines were weekly sinking 20 per cent of Britain's ships engaged in ocean trade. In February the U-boats had sunk more than half a million tons of shipping. They had increased this figure in March, and the daily rate of sinkings had risen still more in April. Unless some drastic remedy were found, Britain would be starved into defeat by November.

Sims did a little investigating into the situation before making his report on it. He found that the principal means used by the British for combatting the U-boats were blockade, knocking out enemy submarine bases, patrolling sea routes, mining, and evasive routing. The Admiralty had lost faith in the first two, which had produced only meager results. Patrolling routes in advance of merchant ships and the use of minefields with their swept channels merely restricted the merchantmen into well-defined lanes and gave notice to lurking U-boats that their prey was on the way. Evasive routing was also meaningless if advance patrolling made the evasion obvious. In short, the British system, instead of protecting the ships that were bringing in not only the nation's military supplies but its very means of subsistence, merely exposed them to the enemy.

At the British Admiralty a group of younger officers was studying the use of convoy, greatly effective in the Napoleonic Wars, but supposedly outmoded in the age of steam. Convoy grouped merchantmen but also brought together warships to escort and screen them. Objections raised against convoy were many: it bunched targets, caused collisions, delayed sailings, disrupted timetables, reduced all ships to the speed of the slowest, and crowded ports on their arrival. The overriding objection was that a convoy was only defensive, and warships could not be spared from offensive duties.

Yet despite lack of interest among the high echelons of the Admiralty, convoy was being tried in cross-Channel coal shipments and in the trade with Norway. In the former, losses were reduced from 20 to 0.19 per cent; in the latter from 25 to 0.24 per cent. Sims studied these figures and listened to the arguments of the young officers, which in his opinion outweighed the polemics of their seniors. He then decided on a measure as outrageous as the one he had used as a junior officer, years before, to press for his theories concerning improved gunnery. Sims now sought out Prime Minister David Lloyd George and argued strongly for convoy. As he

were severely undermanned. The fleet, moreover, was topheavy with battleships and cruisers, when destroyers and smaller craft were needed for antisubmarine patrol and the escort of convoys.

After the United States had severed diplomatic relations with Germany, Secretary Daniels sent Admiral Sims as the U.S. naval representative to London. Here Sims' initial assignment was to consult the British and then to recommend to the U.S. Navy Department ways in which the Navy might most effectively be used in event of war. "Don't let them pull the wool over your had earlier convinced President Roosevelt, he now convinced the Prime Minister. Lloyd George put pressure on the Admiralty, which at last invited the young convoy enthusiasts to make still more thorough studies, and on April 30 agreed to experiment with ocean convoys.

Sims now found he had an almost equally skeptical U.S. Navy Department to convince. Daniels and Benson, who suspected Sims of being hopelessly anglophile, doubted his reports of England's extremity. As a gesture, they dispatched six destroyers overseas, but they expected to retain at home the main part of the fleet, which was by no means to serve as a mere appendage of the Royal Navy. American strategic planners, influenced by the United States' most recent war, were concerned with the Caribbean Sea and the approaches to the Panama Canal. A painful rethinking of the situation was required before the professionals could accept the idea of moving a sizable portion of the fleet abroad to operate in European waters.

Moreover, American naval leaders were as wedded to the theory of defending routes as were the British. Secretary Daniels cabled to Sims on June 2: "In regard to convoy, I consider that American vessels having armed guard are safer when sailing independently." A month later, the Navy Department tentatively accepted the idea of convoy, but still insisted that the main function of the Navy was "safeguarding the lines of communication."

Sims, in his new capacity as Commander United States Naval Forces Operating in European Waters, exerted every effort with his slowly growing forces to combat the U-boat by all methods, not the least of which was escort of convoy. Despite doubts on both sides of the Atlantic, the success of the convoy system confounded all objections. Convoy did indeed bunch targets, but these often proved fatal bait for the U-boats. Escorts sank more submarines in company with merchantmen than when sailing independently on patrol. Merchant skippers proved perfectly capable of sailing in convoy, and there were few collisions. When ships were divided into slow and fast convoys, the problem of slowing down the fast vessels was largely avoided. Ports, when warned of the impending arrival of a convoy, could plan unloading more efficiently than when single vessels arrived independently after zigzag voyages under radio silence.

Above all, the convoys saved ships and men. In April 1917, the month in which the United States entered the war and in which Sims began to argue his case, British losses were nearly 900,000 tons. Thereafter they fell off rapidly, almost in direct proportion to the increasing use of convoy. It is no exaggeration to state that the adoption of convoy saved Britain from defeat in World War I.

THE U.S. FLEET REPORTS FOR DUTY

The token force of destroyers sent abroad was Division 8, commanded by Commander Joseph K. Taussig. Sailing from Boston on April 24, the six vessels encountered such tumultuous seas that it was impossible to eat meals at table. On the ninth day out, in moderating weather off the Irish south coast, the crews were gladdened to see a British destroyer flying the signal "Welcome to the American colors" and prepared to conduct them into the port of Queenstown (now Cobh). Here, the next day, crowds cheered the Americans as they marched to the U.S. consulate, where they found awaiting them a letter of welcome from Admiral Jellicoe.

That evening the destroyer captains were dinner guests of their new commanding officer, Vice Admiral Sir Lewis Bayly, a gruff old bachelor. Bayly, famed as "the father of destroyer tactics," had been kept on beyond retirement age as Commander in Chief of the Coasts of Ireland.

"When will you be ready to go to sea?" asked Bayly, expecting bad news as a result of the tempestuous crossing.

"We are ready now, sir," replied Taussig in some surprise, "that is, as soon as we finish refueling."

Bayly's stern old face creased in a smile. This reply and the subsequent conduct of the Americans so pleased Sir Lewis that he raised British eyebrows by referring to them as "my boys."

The U.S. Navy Department, convinced at last of the need, dispatched more divisions abroad each month; by July 1917 there were 34 American destroyers patrolling the wreckage-strewn waters of the Queenstown area. Each destroyer, avoiding a fixed pattern, patrolled one or more areas, each 10 miles square, sometimes picking up survivors of a submarine attack, and occasionally escorting an especially valuable vessel across its square to hand on to the next destroyer. For the most part, however, the patrol duty was deadly monotonous and must have seemed futile, for the U-boats could always see the patrol vessels before they themselves were sighted, and hence could easily slip away. Sometimes a submarine would tauntingly remain on the surface as a destroyer charged toward it at flank speed, then crash-dive and be off in time to escape depth-charge attack.

After the adoption of convoy, Queenstown remained a major base for American destroyers, which were now

Destroyer Division 8, first U.S. naval force in European Waters during World War I, nears Queenstown (now Cobh).

used mainly for escort duty, although a certain amount of independent patrolling continued. Sinkings of merchantmen declined rapidly, but so did opportunities for sinking submarines, for U-boat skippers were loath to launch torpedoes at merchant ships when nearby were swift destroyers with depth-charge racks and Y-guns. The patrollers off Queenstown had at least damaged a few U-boats. The escorting destroyers, on the contrary, had no luck at all until mid-November 1917. That bit of luck was worth waiting for.

In the late morning on the 17th, the *Nicholson* led five other destroyers out of Queenstown to sweep the area where a convoy was due presently to leave the harbor. Watching intermittently by periscope was Lieutenant Gustav Amberger in *U-58*. Amberger had

been assigned the task of sinking S.S. *Welshman*, a large merchantman known to be sailing with this convoy. He maneuvered his U-boat into a position where he thought he could not miss.

Out came the convoy from the inner harbor and assumed rectangular cruising formation with three of the destroyers on each flank. Lieutenant Amberger, watching intently, ordered: "Stand by to fire torpedoes!" Almost simultaneously a bridge lookout on the destroyer *Fanning* at the end of the port wing shouted, "Periscope off the port beam!" Only he had seen the periscope, the exposed section of which was no bigger than the tip of a walking stick. Nevertheless, the *Fanning's* executive officer, who had the conn, took the lookout's word for it, ordered left full rudder, and dropped a depth charge with 300 pounds of TNT off the fantail. The flagship *Nicholson* next came dashing through the convoy to drop another charge. By now crews were shouting in excitemennt as the stern of *U-58* bobbed above the surface, sank, and rose again. As more and more of the submarine came into view and the *Fanning's* gunners began to make hits, Captain Arthur Carpender suddenly cried, "Cease fire! Cease fire!" The U-boat's conning-tower hatch had flown open and out popped Lieutenant Amberger, hands up, shouting, "*Kamerad! Kamerad!*"

Out climbed the rest of *U-58's* crew, also with hands up. The Americans, with German help, tried to take the U-boat in tow, but the last two men to come through the hatch had opened her seacocks, and she began to sink with much snapping of Manila lines. The Germans had

to be fished out of the water. One was drowned; 4 officers and 35 men were captured. From the Admiralty came congratulations, and Admiral Sims sent a message: "Go out and do it again."

Queenstown was only one of the 15 antisubmarine bases established by the United States in the European theater. Other important bases were at Portsmouth, Brest, and Gibraltar. Because of the destroyer shortage, the first American vessels sent to all the bases except Queenstown were converted yachts manned by reservists. Although Queenstown continued to operate throughout the war as a chiefly American antisubmarine station, Brest, as the principal port of disembarkation for American troops, in time became the main U.S. naval headquarters in Europe.

The Navy's first U-boat capture: U-58 *surrenders to the destroyers* Fanning *and* Nicholson.

More effective than the converted yachts, and costing about a quarter of the price of the destroyers, were the 200-foot eagle boats built on an assembly line by the Ford Motor Company. The real workhorses of the American antisubmarine force were, however, the 100-foot submarine chasers, called "Cinderellas," "mosquitoes," or "the splinter fleet." They were built of wood and cost only $80,000 apiece, in contrast to the $1,800,000 required for a destroyer. When it came to antisubmarine work, the subchaser could do nearly everything that a destroyer could do, and it could do one vitally important thing that a destroyer then could not do—locate an underwater submarine. Each subchaser was equipped with a hydrophone, an underwater listening device that indicated direction but not range. Because, however, the subchasers operated in pairs or, more commonly, in threes, they could pinpoint and track a U-boat by triangulation, closing in inexorably on converging courses to drop depth charges on their unlucky prey.

The subchasers, fanning out across the Atlantic and into the Mediterranean, escorted convoys and maintained patrols, all the while—even in moderate seas—bucking and rolling enough to shake a man loose from his false teeth; but their college-boy crews nevertheless seemed to thrive on the rough life. The most useful service of the subchasers was performed in coastal waters, notably in the English Channel, where convoys broke up in order to distribute ships among several ports. Before the arrival of the subchasers, such areas had been happy hunting grounds for the U-boats; afterward, they were areas to be scrupulously shunned.

In order to seal up in their Adriatic lair the German and Austrian submarines that were wreaking havoc against Allied shipping in the Mediterranean, the British and Italians spread underwater nets across the Strait of Otranto and kept its approaches under observation with destroyers and observation balloons. In summer 1918, 36 subchasers, based on Corfu, added their tracking capabilities to this effort. The result was a seal so tight, and destruction or severe damage so certain, for any submarine trying to penetrate the barrier, that Austrian submariners, in a spirit of mutiny, flatly refused to attempt the transit. The better-disciplined Germans tried it, but those who returned brought back hair-raising stories of narrow escapes.

In early October, 11 of the subchasers acted as an antisubmarine screen for 6 British and Italian cruisers in an attack on the Austrian naval base and supply depot of Durazzo on the Dalmatian coast. While the cruisers smashed the defenses and port facilities and damaged harbor shipping with shellfire, the subchasers protected them from submarines, and were credited with sinking two that came out to attack. This was the sole fleet engagement in which the U.S. Navy participated, in the entire war.

In proportion to numbers involved, no anti–U-boat weapon employed in World War I proved half so effective as the Allied submarine. The U-boat, surrounded by enemies on the surface, usually had to submerge in order to attack or to escape being attacked. Hence, to keep its batteries charged and its hull full of fresh air for meeting such opportunities or emergencies, it had to spend as much time surfaced as considerations of safety permitted. The Allied submarine, on the contrary, having no enemies on the surface, could remain submerged much longer, for the simple reason that it dared to come up for air and recharging as often as necessary. It was a mere matter of statistics, therefore, that a submerged Allied submarine was more likely to encounter a surfaced U-boat as a target for its torpedoes than vice versa. "We got used to your depth charges and did not fear them," said a captured German submarine officer, "but we lived in constant fear of your submarines."

Although another breakout of the German High Seas Fleet seemed unlikely, the mere possibility of it influenced the Allied high command to buttress Britain's Grand Fleet, floating idly at Scapa Flow, by adding a squadron of American dreadnoughts, the coal burners *New York*, *Wyoming*, *Florida*, and *Delaware*—chosen because of a shortage of fuel oil in Britain. On the morning of December 6, 1917, these vessels, under the command of Rear Admiral Hugh Rodman in the *New York*, entered Scapa Flow and, to the sound of band music and enthusiastic cheering, took their places alongside the British men-of-war. Rodman paid a call on Grand Admiral Sir David Beatty, Commander in Chief Grand Fleet, in the *Queen Elizabeth*. Reading a carefully prepared, modest little speech, he offered the services of himself, his ships, and his men—to which Beatty replied: "Today marks an epoch in the history of England and America!" Rear Admiral Rodman, a superb shiphandler who had never quite outgrown the rusticity of his Kentucky upbringing, then somewhat marred the solemnity of the occasion by turning to Beatty, one of the world's four ranking naval officers, and remarking, "I don't believe much in paper work. Whenever you have anything to bring to my attention, come and see me."

Toward the end of the war the U.S. Navy, concerned lest German battle cruisers elude the blockade and strike at American troop convoys en route to France, stationed at Bantry Bay in southwest Ireland the dreadnoughts *Nevada*, *Oklahoma*, and *Utah*, under Rear

Rear Admiral Hugh Rodman's dreadnoughts welcomed by the British Grand Fleet at Scapa Flow.

Admiral Thomas S. Rodgers. How these vessels could have overtaken the Germans and forced a battle with them is open to question, since the battle cruisers could outspeed the American battleships by several knots.

FENCING IN THE U-BOATS

Close blockade of the ports from which the U-boats issued proved impractical. Certain officials, particularly in the U.S. Navy, therefore suggested simply locking the submarines inside the North Sea, with minefields planted in the Strait of Dover and across the broad stretch of sea from Norway to the Orkney Islands.

Although the Dover project had been tried earlier in the war, it had been unsuccessful because of currents, tides, and a shifting ocean floor. Royal Navy officers were nevertheless willing to try it again, and this time they were successful. They stoutly opposed the northern barrage, however, chiefly because there were not enough

mines, and those available were not good enough for so enormous and difficult a project.

Rear Admiral Ralph Earle of the U.S. Bureau of Ordnance was of a different opinion. He had a mine that would do the work of half a dozen of the old contact type, an antenna mine that would explode lethally, if one of its tentacles was touched, as far away as 50 feet. Earle was building a factory near Norfolk to manufacture it in quantity. His plan for blockading the North Sea was at length accepted, winning official approval in early November 1917 of the U.S. government and—somewhat reluctantly, one gathers—the British government. By mid-October Admiral Henry T. Mayo, Commander in Chief Atlantic Fleet, having reviewed on-the-scene estimates, was able to outline the project: 100,000 mines to be planted in three sections, each 35 by 230 miles, with the mines in layers from just beneath the surface to 240 feet deep.

The United States responded to this gigantic challenge with the typically American sort of teamwork that put men on the moon half a century later. Contracts for mine parts were distributed among some 500 contractors. The Norfolk plant assembled the major components and charged 1,000 mines a day. Twenty-four cargo steamers carried them across the Atlantic Ocean, landing them on the Scottish west coast to avoid U-boat waters. The mines were then transported, day and night, to the east coast through the newly enlarged and lighted Caledonia Canal. Here, at two large plants, they were put through the final assembly process at the rate of 2,000 a day and delivered to 10 specially converted outsize minelayers.

Under the over-all command of Rear Admiral Joseph Strauss, minelayers, and their antisubmarine escorts, proceeded to an assigned area, where, on June 8, 1918, the project was begun auspiciously by the laying of nearly 5,000 mines in four hours. The British, who were handicapped by small vessels, by an old type of mine requiring closer spacing, and by a less elaborately planned organization, laid far fewer. British observers with the American minelayers were amazed at the machinery devised for the operation and the clockwork precision with which it was performed.

The first line across the North Sea was completed on September 20, 1918, the date of the ninth excursion, in which the Americans planted 5,520 mines in a record 3 hours 50 minutes. The following excursions added to the density and extent of the minefield. This work was still proceeding when the Armistice ended the war. By then the Americans had planted 56,600 mines; the British, 13,600.

The number of U-boats destroyed by the North Sea Mine Barrage is still a matter of question. Estimates range from "possibly 1" to "probably 20." Yet it is clear from prisoner interrogations that the effect on the German submariners was enormous. On July 9, 1918, *U-86* radioed that she was returning, after having been damaged by a new and dangerous minefield. A month later *U-113* was forced back to port heavily damaged. Other U-boats came in gravely impaired, and still others disappeared completely. Morale among the submariners plummeted. Attempts by the German Admiralty at this point to force men out of the idle High Seas Fleet into the U-boat service set off the mutinies that eventually undermined the whole German defense posture.

THE FERRY TO FRANCE

The most pressing problem faced by the United States on entering World War I was getting troops and supplies to France, and the chief difficulty was in finding the needed transportation. The Central Powers had sunk 7 million tons of Allied ships. The neglected U.S. merchant marine could make available only 1 million tons.

For troop transports the United States commandeered 20 American liners and all the suitable Dutch and German ships in American ports. The interned Germans did an expert job of sabotaging their engines, but American workmen quickly repaired them by the new technique of electric welding. Twenty German ships, including the giant *Leviathan*, were to carry some half million American soldiers to Europe. In all, 45 ships, including the U.S. Navy's 2 transports, were assembled for carrying troops across the ocean. These vessels, together with escort craft that included 24 cruisers, formed the Cruiser and Transport Force, commanded by Rear Admiral Albert Gleaves. Of more than 2 million soldiers sent abroad, 46 per cent were carried in American ships, most of the rest by British. The U.S. Navy provided about 86 per cent of the escort vessels.

Not a single troop ship in convoy was sunk en route to France. The reason was threefold. The troop convoys were heavily escorted, they sailed a course south of the main shipping lines, and, most important, they were neglected by the U-boats, for the Germans gambled on starving Britain into surrender before the Americans could get sufficient men and supplies to Europe to turn the tide.

The amount of tonnage required to carry the troops' supplies and equipment was four times that needed for the troops themselves. The transporting agency for these supplies was the Naval Overseas Transportation Service. To acquire vessels for this purpose, the Shipping Board set up an Emergency Fleet Corporation, which, by requisition, purchase, and the construction of steel, wooden, prefabricated, and even concrete vessels, at length made available 10 million tons of ships.

The U.S. Navy's efforts, heavily expended in transportation and in the protection of shipping, did not stop at the shoreline of Europe. At the request of General John J. Pershing, the Navy mounted five 14-inch naval guns on railroad cars and shipped them to France along with navy crews. These guns, effective far beyond the range of army guns, destroyed distant enemy communications, bridges, supply dumps, and railroad centers, and induced the Germans to withdraw "Big Bertha," a 75-mile-range gun that had been raining shells on Paris.

Some 30,000 marines fought in France, serving in such critical sectors as Château Thierry, Belleau Wood, St.-Mihiel, and the Meuse-Argonne. Although the marines displayed their accustomed valor in France and won their well-deserved laurels as usual, marine and naval leaders later had reason to regret the nature of their operations in World War I. Critics asked: if ma-

Railway-mounted naval gun at the front.

rines performed exactly the same duties as soldiers, then why a separate Marine Corps?

END OF THE GERMAN FLEET

The Germans lost their gamble. The Americans arrived not only in time to turn the tide; they more than made up for the withdrawal of the armies of revolutionary Russia, which had concluded an armistice with Germany in December 1917. On October 4, 1918, the German and Austrian governments, acting through neutral Switzerland, requested an armistice of the Allies. General Erich Ludendorff ordered his exhausted and depleted forces to strike again, hoping by fighting bitterly to the end to obtain better peace terms. His orders were countermanded, and he was dismissed.

In the same spirit as Ludendorff, Admiral von Scheer, now Chief of the Naval Staff, ordered the High Seas Fleet to sortie and raid British ports in order to draw out the Grand Fleet into one last, cataclysmic battle. The sailors refused to obey the order, and extinguished the ships' fires. Admiral Franz von Hipper, Commander High Seas Fleet, reluctantly signaled: "Sailing canceled."

As a means of breaking up the mutiny and quelling it piecemeal, Hipper divided the fleet among several ports. At Kiel, a lieutenant ordered his squad to fire into a street mob of rioting sailors and was himself shot dead. Mutiny now turned into revolution, and at night Kiel fell into the hands of seamen turned Communist. Sailors and dockworkers swarmed aboard the battleship *König*, killed the executive officer and the watch officer, and gravely wounded the captain.

From Kiel the contagion spread to the other seaports and to the interior, across Germany to the Western Front. Soldiers deserted and straggled to the rear by thousands, tens of thousands, and finally by hundreds of thousands. On November 9 Berlin was in the throes of a general strike, and that evening the Kaiser abdicated and fled to Holland. At 5:40 A.M. on Monday, November 11, the German government, now headed by an obscure tailor, Friedrich Ebert, accepted the sweeping terms of the Armistice, which included the surrender of all submarines and the internment in a neutral harbor of most of the High Seas Fleet. At 11 A.M. that day the firing ceased.

The submarines reported in groups to Rear Admiral Reginald Tyrwhitt's force at Harwich. The ships to be interned—9 battleships, 5 battle cruisers, 7 light cruisers, and 50 destroyers—were to disarm themselves and report to Admiral Sir David Beatty at the Firth of Forth for inspection. The fleet not only disarmed; it stripped itself of its matchless optical instruments and all other expendable German inventions, leaving the ships barely able to navigate.

Ten days after the signing of the Armistice, the High Seas Fleet steamed into the Firth of Forth between parallel lines of ships of the Grand Fleet, which included the U.S. dreadnoughts. The next morning Allied inspection units searched the alien ships and found everything in order. That day Rear Admiral Ludwig von Reuter, who commanded the internment fleet, was informed that his ships would be interned not in a neutral port but at Scapa Flow, the Grand Fleet's wartime anchorage in the Orkney Islands.

For seven months the internment fleet rode at anchor with skeleton crews in Scapa Flow, under the eyes of a guard squadron. Its only sources of information were letters from home and an occasional belated London newspaper. From these sources von Reuter and his officers learned that the High Seas Fleet was to be turned over to the Allies for reparations, that the Germans had raised strong objections to the harsh terms of the peace treaty, and that the Allies had given them five days to accept it under threat of renewed warfare. To the Germans at Scapa Flow it seemed that war was imminent and that the High Seas Fleet would be used against the Fatherland. Determined that this should never happen, they loosened seacocks and removed watertight doors.

On June 21, 1919, the final day of the ultimatum, the guard squadron left Scapa Flow for target practice. To the Germans of the internment fleet the departure meant that war had been renewed. On the flagship *Emden* up went the secret signal: "Paragraph 11. Acknowledge." By the time the Britons remaining at Scapa Flow noticed that the German ships were settling and listing, most of them were beyond salvage.

Ships of the interned German fleet scuttled at Scapa Flow.

VIII

The Twenty-Year Truce

During World War I all of the Allied powers except Japan shelved their capital-ship building programs to allow for rapid construction of destroyers and other antisubmarine craft. At the end of the war Britain, in a drastic economy move, scrapped half of her fleet, including ships no more than seven years old. In all, she sent to the junkyard 38 battleships, 2 battle cruisers, 87 light cruisers, 300 destroyers and torpedo boats, and 106 submarines. France and Italy scrapped few ships, but were too impoverished by the war to build new ones.

Only the United States and Japan contemplated strengthening their navies. The United States revived the ambitious program of 1916 for the building of 16 capital ships, and in 1919 President Wilson asked Congress for a second program identical with the first. He thus proposed to make the U.S. Navy by all odds the world's most powerful. Britain's prospect of being relegated to second, or even third, place on the seas was infuriating to her citizens, who felt that they deserved more consideration in view of their heavy wartime sacrifices and subsequent naval retrenchment.

By 1921 both Japan and the United States, suffering from postwar financial depression, were beginning to have second thoughts about their expensive naval programs. In the United States, Congress had vetoed Wilson's 1919 building plan and rejected his League of Nations, and the people had repudiated his party at the polls. Pacifism was increasing in the country, and with it demands for economy in military preparations. In the context of this mood, President Harding invited Britain, France, Italy, and Japan to send representatives to Washington to confer on arms limitations. Because the proposed agenda included discussion of problems of the Pacific and the Far East, Harding also invited Belgium, China, the Netherlands, and Portugal.

On November 12, 1921, in Washington's Memorial Continental Hall, American Secretary of State Charles Evans Hughes opened the conference with a thunderclap heard round the world. Instead of speaking in polite generalities, as expected at an opening meeting, he came immediately to the point with concrete proposals, among them a 10-year holiday in capital-ship construction, and scrapping battleships, including those then being built, to achieve a ratio of 5:5:3 for the United States, Great Britain, and Japan. "Thus," said Hughes, "the number of capital ships to be scrapped by the United States, if the plan is accepted, is 30, with an aggregate tonnage (including that of ships in construction, if completed) of 845,740 tons." The delegates gasped at this apparently sacrificial offer, and still more at the utter candor, so contrary to diplomatic practice, with which Hughes had laid his cards face up on the table. But he was not through. He next proceeded to spell out to the British and Japanese delegates just what the United States expected them to sacrifice. The total for all three powers was 66 ships displacing 1,878,043 tons. In 15 minutes Hughes had verbally sunk more weight in warships than all the admirals in all the battles of history.

Delegates of the major powers, after considering

Hughes' proposals for several weeks, produced the Five-Power Naval Disarmament Treaty. The 10-year holiday in capital-ship construction was adopted, and tonnage was eventually stabilized for the United States, Britain, Japan, France, and Italy at 500,000, 500,000, 300,000, 175,000, and 175,000 tons respectively for battleships, and 135,000, 135,000, 81,000, 60,000, and 60,000 tons for aircraft carriers. Replacement in both types of ships was to be permitted after 20 years. Individual battleships were limited to 35,000 tons, carriers to 27,000, and cruisers to 10,000. Battleships might carry nine 16-inch guns. Carriers and cruisers were permitted no armament larger than 8-inch guns.

These restrictions fell far short of those desired by Secretary Hughes, but France rejected out of hand any suggestion for limiting land forces, and no agreement could be reached concerning over-all tonnages for naval vessels other than capital ships. As a special inducement to the Japanese to accept inferiority in this category, the United States agreed not to further fortify her bases west of Hawaii, and Britain engaged not to strengthen her bases north of Australia or east of Singapore.

A prime motive of the U.S. government in calling the Washington Conference was abrogation of the Anglo-Japanese Alliance, signed in 1902 in response to Russian aggression. The alliance had since then become a source of alarm to the United States and of embarrassment to Britain. Senator Lodge now proposed substituting for that alliance a Four-Power Treaty whereby Britain, France, Japan, and the United States agreed to respect one another's rights and possessions in the Pacific area. Japan would have much preferred the continuance of the alliance to so vague a compromise, but she accepted the agreement when the alternative was obviously nothing at all. Lastly, all the nations represented at the conference signed a Nine-Power Treaty guaranteeing the territorial integrity of China—in effect endorsing the U.S. "Open Door" policy.

United States historians have tended to congratulate their fellow Americans on the brilliant attainment of their aims in the Four-Power and Nine-Power treaties, while bemoaning the poor deal they got in the Five-Power Treaty as the result of misplaced generosity or simple gullibility. In fact, however, the Americans got pretty much what they wanted in all of the agreements. A major reason for this success was that the U.S. delegates were privy to the instructions which the other delegates were receiving from their governments, while, as a rule, it is believed, the other delegates had no such advantage. Cryptanalysts of the so-called "American Black Chamber" were breaking down and transcribing secret radio messages from the foreign governments to their representatives in Washington and serving them to the American delegates each day with their morning coffee.

Of the 18 battleships retained by the United States in accordance with provisions of the Five-Power Treaty, 8 were less than six years old. This was true of only 3 of the 16 battleships retained by Britain, and of 5 of the 6 battleships retained by Japan. Britain and Japan each canceled the construction of eight 18-inch-gun battleships then in the blueprint stage. As to the exceptions permitted in over-all tonnage, the United States got by far the most favorable concession in the right to build the 33,000-ton carriers *Lexington* and *Saratoga* on the hulls of unfinished battle cruisers that had been destined for the scrap heap.

Perhaps the greatest benefit the United States derived from the Five-Power Treaty is that she was saved from wasting money and manpower in building up a great fleet of battleships—an obsolescent, not to say obsolete, type, though not generally so recognized at the time. It is true that the failure to limit over-all cruiser tonnages diverted the British and the Japanese to increased construction in this category. The United States was left behind in this expansion, but the fault lay in American neglect of an opportunity, not in the treaty.

As for the nonfortification clause, Japan—mistress of Formosa and the island groups of the Pescadores, the Ryukyus, the Kuriles, the Bonins, the Carolines, and the Marshalls, as well as all the Marianas except Guam— was pledged not to fortify hundreds of potential bases. In comparison, the pledge made by the United States and Britain not to fortify the few Pacific Ocean positions which they controlled was insignificant. At any rate, the American delegates must have felt that they were bargaining away an empty right, for in 23 years Congress had done little to develop Guam and the Philippines as bases. After the Five-Power Treaty was abrogated, Congress, as was freely predicted, did nothing to strengthen Guam and almost nothing to fortify the Philippines.

In 1924 Congress, noting the degree to which the U.S. Navy was falling behind, authorized eight 10,000-ton cruisers, but President Coolidge, a strict economizer and no Navy enthusiast, suspended funds for the construction of all but two, the *Pensacola* and the *Salt Lake City*. In 1927 Coolidge tackled the problem from a different angle by calling another naval conference, this time at Geneva, with the specific aim of applying tthe 5:5:3 ratio to cruisers.

The Geneva Conference was a total failure. France and Italy refused to participate. Britain was willing to accept parity with the United States in cruisers but

The Five-Power Naval Disarmament Treaty cancelled construction of U.S. battleships of the North Carolina *class, here shown as originally planned.*

insisted that to police her worldwide empire she needed a tonnage which, in the opinion of the American delegates, was prohibitive. The American position was in any event weak compared to that of 1922, when Hughes could call for a capital-ship tonnage based on the existing strength of the U.S. Navy. Not least among the fairly complex causes of failure were the skillful efforts of one William B. Shearer, who was hired by American shipbuilding interests to wreck the conference and to disrupt moves toward further naval limitations.

Coolidge, nettled, permitted the construction of the rest of the 1924 class of cruisers and induced the chairman of the House Committee on Naval Affairs to introduce legislation that would bring the U.S. Navy to full parity with Britain's Royal Navy. The proposed program called for 71 new ships, including 5 aircraft carriers and 25 cruisers. On publication of these figures, pacifists and disgruntled taxpayers raised such protests that Congress whittled the program down to 15 heavy cruisers and 1 carrier.

Agreement among the three chief naval powers was reached in the more carefully prepared 1930 London Conference, in which France and Italy again refused to participate. The United States, Britain, and Japan concurred on a 10:10:7 ratio in cruisers—339,000, 339,000, and 236,600 tons—and parity in submarines, with 52,700 tons permitted each nation. The ban on capital-ship construction was extended to 1936. These agreements had no immediate effect upon the U.S. Navy. During the Hoover administration not a single combat vessel was laid down. At the end of 1932, the United States had 153,400 tons of modern cruisers, while Britain had

297,600 and Japan 252,250. Of all types of modern vessels, the three nations had respectively 101, 140, and 184.

The Quaker President Hoover trusted the curious Kellogg-Briand Pact to keep the peace. This pact was a kind of international exorcism outlawing all but defensive war—as if all wars were not billed as "defensive" by their participants. Another oddity of the Hoover administration was the cutting off, by Secretary of State Henry L. Stimson, of a vital source of diplomatic and military intelligence. Stimson, informed of the cryptanalytic activities of the American Black Chamber, was deeply shocked and instantly ordered it closed and disbanded.* "Gentlemen," he asserted, "do not read each other's mail."

When the naval treaty limitations expired at the end of 1936, the U.S. Navy was at last being built up to treaty strength. In 1933, as a corollary to President Franklin Roosevelt's National Industrial Act to relieve unemployment, Congress had authorized the *Brooklyn*-class light cruisers, the *Craven*-class destroyers, the carriers *Enterprise* and *Yorktown,* and four submarines. The following year the Vinson-Trammel Act authorized an eight-year replacement program amounting to 102 ships. The Second Vincent Act of 1938 authorized a tonnage increase of 20 per cent above the former treaty limits.

* It was just as well. Herbert O. Yardley, Director of the American Black Chamber, had turned traitor and sold out to the Japanese for $7,000. By that time, however, the Army and Navy had established their own cryptographic sections. In 1940 the Army section broke Japan's PURPLE diplomatic code. Early in 1942, the Navy's section made possible the American victory in the Battle of Midway by breaking JN25b, the current variation of the Japanese naval code.

A much-improved North Carolina, *ordered in 1937, launched in 1940, and commissioned in April 1941.*

At the time of the Pearl Harbor attack in 1941, the U.S. Navy's combatant ship strength was as follows:

Type of Vessels	In Commission	Under Construction
Battleships	17	15
Carriers	7	11
Cruisers	37	54
Destroyers	171	191
Submarines	111	73

AMPHIBIOUS DOCTRINE

The policies of the United States with respect to the Pacific islands have not always been distinguished by foresight. After the Battle of Manila Bay, when the U.S. government was trying to decide what, if anything, to do with the Philippines, Commodore Dewey was annoyed at the presence of a German squadron standing by, ready to take over if the Americans did not. After the United States had annexed the Philippines, the Spaniards still owned a thousand small Pacific islands and atolls—the Carolines, the Marshalls, and the Marianas. Of these, the United States chose to annex only one, the island of Guam, largest and southernmost of the Marianas. Spain, anxious to divest herself of the cares of empire, sold the rest to Germany at bargain rates. This sale put hundreds of potential bases between the United States and the Philippines into the hands of an expansionist and aggressive power. Yet few Americans, least of all Alfred Thayer Mahan, gave much thought to the possible threat.

In 1914, after World War I had broken out in Europe,

Britain invoked her 1902 alliance with Japan, requesting the Japanese to rid the Pacific of German cruisers. As it turned out, the British themselves destroyed the enemy cruisers when the Germans entered the Atlantic, but Japan seized the opportunity to occupy key positions in Germany's Pacific Ocean islands. To all protests the Japanese blandly replied that this was only a temporary wartime measure to prevent the bases from being used by German ships. At the end of the war, however, they made a deal with the British whereby, under League of Nations mandate, Britain would control the former German islands south of the equator and Japan would retain control of those north of the equator. When Japan left the League in 1933, she held on to her share of the islands as national property and proceeded to fortify them, probably before the expiration of the Five-Power Treaty.

The United States, whose relations with Japan had been moving from crisis to crisis since 1905, recognized the danger, but not vividly enough. American protests kept the Japanese from annexing the islands outright at the end of World War I, but protest was as far as the government was prepared to go. Hence U.S. Navy strategists grimly took up the problem of what to do in event of war between the United States and Japan.

It was assumed that the Japanese, with their geographic advantages, would capture the Philippines and Guam. The U.S. Navy would then have to fight its way to the rescue across the Pacific, operating for long periods far from permanent bases and seizing enemy bases for conversion to its own use. This sort of warfare raised three problems: (1) how to free the fleet from dependence on established bases, (2) how to isolate and attack enemy bases protected by land-based air units, and (3) how to invade and occupy heavily defended enemy bases.

The U.S. Marine Corps took as its special problem number 3, which it interpreted as assault from the sea into the teeth of enemy defenses. At the end of World War I, the marines had been in need of a specialty with which to identify themselves. The nature of naval warfare and the conduct of the sailor had so changed as to cost the Marine Corps most of its traditional roles, those of boarding enemy ships at sea, sharpshooting from the tops, and assisting naval officers in the discipline of unruly seamen. Although marines were also traditional protectors of bases, in World War I, as we have seen, they had fought like soldiers and had thus, to some degree, lost their identity and hence their claim to a separate existence.

In the early 1920s, Navy and Marine Corps units tested amphibious techniques in exercises conducted in the Panama Canal Zone and at the tiny island of Culebra east of Puerto Rico. Trial of British amphibious doctrine in the Hawaiian Islands in 1925 convinced both the Navy and the Marine Corps that dividing the command between the general and the admiral, a time-honored European technique, would not prove satisfactory in carrying out the U.S. Pacific Ocean war plan.

Beginning in early 1927, the energies of the Marine Corps were for several years largely employed in quelling disorders in Nicaragua. Out of this experience, however, came two important concepts applicable to amphibious assault: close cooperation of air units with ground elements of the same force, a tactic which was to become a Marine Corps specialty; and the efficacy of small, closely knit, semi-independent patrols, the originals of the battalion landing teams of World War II.

In the early 1930s, the Marine Corps schools at Quantico operated in close coordination with Marine Corps headquarters and the Naval War College to devise a suitable organization and specific techniques for amphibious assault. An action that was thoroughly investigated was the ill-fated Gallipoli Expedition of 1915, a near-perfect example of how not to conduct landing operations. The organizational studies led to the establishment, in December 1933, of the Fleet Marine Force, which was to operate as an integral part of the U.S. fleet. A year later, both organization and techniques were incorporated into the first American textbook of amphibious doctrine, the *Landing Operations Manual.*

From 1935 to 1941, annual training exercises tested the procedures set forth in the *Landing Operations Manual* and provided the basis for revisions and refinements. In 1938 the Navy adopted the book as *Fleet Training Publication 167,* and subsequently the Army adopted a slightly modified version as a field manual. Wartime experience brought about only two major

An "alligator," forerunner of the amtrac, or LVT.

changes in the basic book. In the *Landing Operations Manual* and *FTP 167*, amphibious assault was regarded as part of a naval campaign with all forces continuously under command of the admiral. During wartime, once the landing force was established ashore, the landing force commander, usually a general, ceased to be under the admiral's command and reported directly to theater headquarters. Again, writers of the original manual believed that the danger of enemy air and submarine attack was such that ships would have to deliver support fire for landings at extreme range, while maneuvering radically at high speed. In fact, deliberate, aimed fire from ships close to shore proved not only practicable but vitally essential to keep landing-force casualties within bounds.

Meanwhile, suitable landing craft were being developed. The two main prototypes were the Higgins boat, a shallow-draft vessel designed and made by shipbuilder Andrew Higgins for use by trappers and oil drillers, and the "alligator," a swamp vehicle. The former evolved into the LCVP (Landing Craft, Vehicle and Personnel), the American landing craft most widely used during World War II. The latter developed into the LVT (Landing Vehicle, Tracked), or amtrac, which proved indispensable in that war for crawling across coral reefs. Such equipment, combined with special attack transports and support weapons and the procedures laboriously worked out between world wars, produced

well-nigh irresistible assaults from the sea. Major General J. F. C. Fuller shortly after World War II called these assault techniques "the most far-reaching tactical innovation of the war."

CARRIER DOCTRINE

The aircraft carriers came into being partly as a result of the confusions of the Battle of Jutland, in which admirals had to make instant decisions based on inadequate cruiser reconnaissance. To give the fast-moving steam fleet far-seeing eyes, the British Admiralty ordered several ships converted into carriers for land-based planes.

In the U.S. armed services, opinion after World War I regarding the future of the Navy was widely varied. Conservative naval officers asserted that nothing had really been changed by the introduction of air power. Planes might sink an occasional small vessel, but the battleship remained the queen of battles, unsinkable from the air. At the opposite end of the spectrum of opinion were those who insisted that future wars would be decided by air power alone, and that armies would be useful only to occupy the space conquered by planes; surface fleets would be of no use whatever. In between were those who saw a greater role for the carrier than mere reconnaissance. Extremists in this group conceived

A Higgins boat, the ship-to-shore craft that evolved into the LCVP, most widely used landing craft of World War II.

After sinking the Ostfriesland, *General Billy Mitchell's flyers continue their demonstration by bombing and sinking the anchored ex-German cruiser* Frankfurt.

U.S.S. Langley, *first U.S. aircraft carrier, was converted from a collier.*

of the carrier as a true weapon of attack, nothing less than the capital ship of the future, rendering the battleship obsolete.

The loudest, if possibly not the most astute, of the air enthusiasts was the Army Air Service's Brigadier General William ("Billy") Mitchell, who asserted: "If a naval war were attempted against Japan, for instance, the Japanese submarines and aircraft would sink the enemy fleet long before it came anywhere near their coast." Mitchell's day of triumph came in 1921 when, in a demonstration outside the Virginia capes before an international audience of dignitaries, his army planes attacked the anchored former German battleship *Ostfriesland*. On the second day of attack the aircraft, using specially built 2,000-pound bombs, flew at low altitudes and at last succeeded in sinking the tired old battlewagon. With no antiaircraft fire to oppose them and no damage control parties aboard the ship, the exhibition was utterly unrealistic. Nevertheless, some befuddled Navy observers are said to have wept openly. General Charles T. Menoher, Chief of the Army Air Service, came closer to the point when he said, "I guess the Navy will get its airplane carriers now." He was quite correct. The Navy promptly began to convert a collier into its first carrier, the *Langley*, and secured consent from the treaty powers to build the carriers *Lexington* and *Saratoga*.

Mitchell had indeed demonstrated that battleships were vulnerable to air power, but so was everything else, on both land and sea. Henceforth, fleets in wartime would have to employ antiaircraft fire and combat air patrols of fighter planes in order to protect themselves from air attack. Instead of cruising in columns or rectangles, they would have to move by day in circular formations in order to mass antiaircraft fire and keep to a minimum the area to be covered by fighters. No battleship thus protected was ever sunk or even severely damaged. What cost the battleships their traditional function was not increased vulnerability, but the fact that in the usual conditions of World War II, fleets in battle remained hundreds of miles apart, far beyond the range of guns.

One of the most important technical developments worked out in the early days of carrier experimentation was dive bombing. When planes at high altitudes dropped bombs, ships had time to maneuver out of the way; but it was another matter to elude bombs practically fired from planes that dived to within 300 feet of the vessels.

Not everyone appreciated the wisdom of U.S. Navy planners in refusing to mass-produce planes too soon. It meant that in days before World War II, flyers had to make do with a variety of obsolescent planes; but those available in quantity when war came to the United States incorporated all the latest advances in aircraft engineering and weaponry. In use in late 1941

U.S.S. Lexington, *canceled as a battle cruiser by the Five-Power Treaty, reordered in 1922 as an aircraft carrier.*

Douglas Dauntless dive bombers (SBDs).

Grumman Wildcat fighters (F4Fs).

were the Grumman Wildcat fighter (F4F) and the Douglas Dauntless dive bomber (SBD). The Grumman Avenger torpedo plane (TBF) reached the fleet the following summer.

The first American vessel built as an aircraft carrier from the keel up was the *Ranger*, commissioned in 1934. A compromise ship, she was designed in accordance with a plan to build greater numbers of ships, rather than a few of the highest quality, within the tonnage limitations specified by treaty. The *Ranger* was early recognized as something of a failure. Too slow and light to serve as an attack carrier, she spent her career in the Atlantic, mostly in antisubmarine work. Another carrier, the *Langley*, also too light for fleet combat, was converted into a tender. By the time the United States entered World War II, however, the attack carriers *Yorktown, Enterprise, Wasp,* and *Hornet* had joined the fleet, and 19 more were on order.

Several fleet exercises had demonstrated the feasibility of the carrier as an attack vessel, particularly against land bases. In 1929 planes from the *Saratoga* in a simulated attack theoretically destroyed two locks of the Panama Canal. Carrier planes later made successful mock attacks on Pearl Harbor and Mare Island. Prior to the American entry into World War II, however, the carriers were never assigned permanent cruiser-destroyer screens. Official doctrine still limited their employment to reconnaissance and shadowing, spotting of fleet gunfire, protecting the fleet from enemy submarines and aircraft, and slowing down a fleeing enemy. It was assumed, on the highest decision-making level, that naval battles would consist of Jutland-style gunnery duels between columns of heavy ships.

LOGISTIC DOCTRINE

In prewar days the U.S. armed forces, spearheaded by the Marine Corps, had largely solved the problem of invading strongly defended bases. Also, though this fact was not fully recognized, the aircraft carrier had provided the means for isolating and attacking enemy bases protected by land-based air defenses. There remained the question of how to free the fleet from dependence on established bases, essentially a logis-

U.S. fleet carrier Hornet, *built as a carrier from the keel up.*

tic problem. The solution was found late, but it was found in time.

Sailing ships had been able to remain at sea for months, but with each adoption of the fruits of the industrial revolution, ships became—until the nuclear age—more dependent on land bases for fuel, ammunition, repairs, and general upkeep. A notable exception to this trend was the shift from coal to oil. Alongside-refueling with oil, an American specialty developed after World War I, proved much simpler, quicker, and more practical than coaling at sea. Nevertheless, a steam fleet could not move far from base without provision for servicing overseas or by its own train of service vessels.

By 1941 many of the U.S. wartime problems of stepped-up manufacture, distribution, and shipping had perforce been at least partially solved in order to meet the needs of England and China. At the same time, however, Pearl Harbor, the nation's chief Pacific naval base, was barely able to support the Pacific Fleet, and, as the Japanese raid demonstrated, it was utterly unprepared to protect the ships. After the raid brought the United States into World War II, not only were steps taken immediately to strengthen Pearl Harbor, but work on additional bases was begun at Bora Bora in the Society Islands, at Samoa, at Tongatabu in the Tonga Islands, at Efate and Espiritu Santo in the New Hebrides, at Noumea on New Caledonia, and at Auckland, New Zealand. These points were already in Allied hands, but it was obvious that as the Allies advanced westward they would have to capture Japanese positions and convert them into bases for their own use. The solution to this problem was threefold.

First was the recruiting and establishment of Construction Battalions ("Seabees"), men trained in base construction, given uniforms and some military status, taught the use of weapons, and landed with assault troops. Initially the Seabees all performed the same tasks, but they were eventually organized into such specialized groups as Base Aircraft Service Units (BASUs) and Carrier Aircraft Service Units (CASUs).

Second was the development of standardized base components, including all the materials and personnel needed to set up various sorts of bases. Groups of components were designated "Lions" for major naval bases, "Cubs" for secondary bases, and "Acorns" for naval air bases. Flexibility was achieved through the *Catalogue for Advanced Base Functional Components,* a kind of multivolume mail order catalogue from which base components could be ordered.

Third, and in some ways the most important, were the mobile service squadrons of Service Force Pacific,

the logistic arm of the U.S. Pacific Fleet. The service squadrons were nothing less than floating bases comprising tenders, oilers, and repair and supply ships of all kinds. They moved with the fleet and dropped anchor in any suitable harbor, ready to supply and maintain the warships. Originally established at Funafuti in the Ellice Islands in October 1943, the squadrons subsequently went to work in the calm lagoons of such Central Pacific atolls as Majuro, Kwajalein, and Ulithi and in the waters of the Admiralty Islands and of Kerama Retto off Okinawa.

THE LAND-POWER THEORISTS

The German geographer Karl Haushofer believed that Germany's defeat in World War I was caused by her leaders' failure to appreciate the influence of geography. To overcome this deficiency Haushofer founded in 1922, in Munich, the *Institut für Geopolitik,* which comprised geographers, political scientists, and economists. With these men he studied, among others, the works of Alfred T. Mahan, the sea-power historian, and Halford J. Mackinder, the British geographer and land-power theorist. Mahan attributed Britain's imperial predominance to her sea power, and her sea power to such geographical factors as her insularity and her position athwart the sea communications of western Europe. Mackinder pointed out that sea and land power had dominated alternately in history. Mahan explained England's rise; Mackinder explained her decline in relation to the continental powers.

The rising influence of land power was ascribed by Mackinder to steam and gasoline engines and the expanding networks of railroads and all-weather roads. Land transporation at last competed with sea transportation in cost and safety; moreover, distances were usually shorter and speed was greater. Hence, the interiors of continents became as accessible and exploitable as the rimlands, and they had the added advantage of being less vulnerable in time of war.

Mackinder called the Europe-Asia-Africa land mass the World-Island. Other lands, including the Americas, Britain, Japan, and Australia, he called satellites, because of their smaller areas and populations. The hinterland of Eurasia, including most of Siberia and European Russia, he called the Heartland, the earth's largest and least vulnerable continental interior.

Writing in 1919, Mackinder did not believe that the Russians themselves would be able fully to reap the unique advantages of their Heartland. Germany, however, which he called a "going concern," was in his

Service squadron in the lagoon of an atoll.

opinion the nation geographically best placed and militarily most likely to capture and exploit the Heartland. Possessed of this base and its masses and resources, Germany could thrust outward to the oceans, seizing the seafaring nations and their ports from the landward side. Then, controlling all the resources of the World-Island, she could take to sea to conquer the rest of the world. Mackinder, in his book *Democratic Ideals and Reality,* expressed his views in a formula:

Who rules East Europe commands the Heartland:
Who rules the Heartland commands the World-Island:
Who rules the World-Island commands the World.

The analysis that Mackinder intended as a warning to England Haushofer and his colleagues adopted as a blueprint for German aggression. From Haushofer's pseudoscientific geopolitics Adolf Hitler derived most of his *Lebensraum* notions. Luckily for the Allies Hitler would not, or could not, heed Haushofer's admonition to conquer the Heartland first and at all costs to avoid a second front. When the Germans invaded Russia in 1941, they were simultaneously engaged on several fronts. Thus overextended, they were defeated on all.

THE ROAD TO WORLD WAR II

In the early 1930s, at a time of worldwide economic depression, Germany, Italy, and Japan, each under a military dictatorship, set out to win prosperity and dominion through aggression against their neighbors. The failure of the major powers, particularly France and Britain, to take effective countermeasures destroyed the League of Nations and brought on World War II.

In the latter part of 1931 Japanese military leaders, in defiance of the Nine-Power Treaty, in defiance of the Kellogg-Briand Pact, in defiance indeed of their own government, launched an attack on the Chinese province of Manchuria, which they overran in a little more than three months. Protests from the United States and the League of Nations had no effect whatever on the aggressors. Secretary of State Stimson announced at last that the United States would not recognize Japan's seizure of Manchuria. After Japan, in retaliation for a Chinese boycott of Japanese trade, landed troops at Shanghai and savagely massacred soldiers and civilians alike, the League adopted Stimson's nonrecognition policy and demanded that the Japanese withdraw from Manchuria. Japan withdrew instead from membership in the League, and her militarists made good their control of the Japanese government by a process of selective assassination.

The spectacle of Japan defying international authority with utter impunity was not lost on Germany and Italy. Hitler withdrew Germany from the League of Nations; in 1935 he denounced all treaty limitations on German armaments and reestablished universal military service in the empire. That year the Italians, under the dictatorship of Benito Mussolini, invaded Ethiopia, which they annexed in 1936. The League of Nations denounced this act of bald aggression and temporarily imposed economic sanctions on Italy. Thenceforth Italy purchased from Germany the war-making materials which she could not buy from League members. She withdrew from the League and with Germany formed a Rome-Berlin Axis.

In 1936 Germany, in defiance of the Versailles Treaty and the Locarno Pact, remilitarized the Rhineland. In 1937 Japan launched a full-scale, though undeclared, war on China and quickly subdued most of the eastern half of that immense country. Japanese airplanes unerringly bombed American hospitals, schools, and churches in China. The Japanese government apologized for the sinking of U.S. gunboat *Panay* in the Yangtze River, but evidence suggests that it was no accident. In 1938 German troops poured across the border into Austria, which Hitler seized and annexed as a province of his Nazi empire. Already the battle lines were being drawn in Spain, where a civil war, which flared up in 1936, had been expanded into a European conflict in miniature, with Germany and Italy actively supporting the rebel Nationalist Party, and Britain, France, and the Soviet Union directly or indirectly supporting the Loyalist government.

Whatever stiffness Britain had shown toward the aggressors from 1935 to 1938 had resulted chiefly from the influence of Anthony Eden, Britain's tough-minded foreign secretary. The consequences had not been encouraging, for England had been repeatedly humiliated, and neither China, Ethiopia, nor Austria had been saved. Germany, Italy, and Japan were becoming more firmly aligned on one side, and France, Britain, and Russia were aligning themselves on the other. War impended. Prime Minister Neville Chamberlain therefore decided to jettison Eden and his policies and to try another tack. Reasoning that a tougher attitude might hasten war, he decided to try a little appeasement.

At once Chamberlain initiated a series of agreements with Italy. In return for promises by the Italians to muffle their anti-British propaganda and to withdraw their armed forces from Spain, Britain agreed to persuade the League of Nations to recognize Italy's Ethiopian conquest. Consequently, League members recognized the King of Italy as Emperor of Ethiopia. This humiliating surrender by the League cost it its last remaining shreds of authority.

Chamberlain now prepared to bend the back to Hitler, who was making noisy declarations about German minorities in the Sudeten region of Czechoslovakia. The Sudeten Germans, who had been stirred up by Nazi agents and by Hitler's speeches, were demanding nothing less than outright annexation to the German empire, and Hitler was declaring his determination to take the Sudetenland, if not peacefully, then by force. The Czechs mobilized and turned to France and Russia for help. Italy championed Germany because they were allies; Poland and Hungary did the same, because they hoped to get a piece of dismembered Czechoslovakia.

Prime Minister Chamberlain and Prime Minister Edouard Daladier of France flew to Munich to petition Hitler to keep the peace. Here they signed the notorious Munich Agreement of September 29, 1938, which gave Hitler the Sudetenland in return for an empty promise: "This is the last territorial demand I have to make in Europe."

On Chamberlain's return to England, he announced: "It is peace in our time." Six months later Hitler coolly annexed the greater part of Czechoslovakia, leaving the remainder for Poland and Hungary as a reward for their support. He then seized Memel from Lithuania and demanded Danzig from the Poles. Britain and France now abandoned their discredited appeasement policy and allied themselves with Poland. Russia, alienated by the Franco-British sell-out of Czechoslovakia, in August 1939 signed a nonaggression pact with Germany. Hitler, thus freed of threats from the east, on September 1 marched his armies into Polish territory. Two days later Britain and France declared war on Germany.

IX

World War II

The United States, inadequately supported by Britain and France in its early peace-keeping endeavors, retreated into isolationism in the spirit of "a plague o' both your houses." At the same time the country took steps to insulate itself from the coming war. In a series of extraordinary measures, the government renounced rights that the United States had three times gone to war to defend. An Act of Congress in 1935 forbade the sale or delivery of munitions to a belligerent nation and empowered the President to prohibit Americans from travel on the ships of belligerents. An amendment the following year forbade loans to belligerents, and a new Congressional Act in 1937 required that all sales to them be paid for before export and be carried away in other than American ships. This last was the notorious "Cash-and-Carry Act." To avoid being challenged on the seas, Americans planned to retreat from the seas.

Upon the declaration of war in Europe, President Roosevelt promptly established a Neutrality Patrol, which had a stated purpose of reporting and tracking belligerent aircraft, ships, or submarines approaching the United States or the West Indies. A month later the United States, in concert with the republics of Latin America, proclaimed a safety zone 300 miles wide off the coasts of the Americas south of Canada. Inside this zone warlike operations were forbidden.

Despite the apparent determination of the United States to sit out this war, the Americans were never, to use President Wilson's phrase, "impartial in thought as well as in action." American traditions opposed the totalitarian and aggressive governments of Germany, Italy, and Japan. The American people were outraged by the mistreatment of minorities in Germany and by atrocities committed by the Japanese army against Chinese civilians. Concerning Hitler's systematic persecution of the Jews, President Roosevelt in November 1938 declared: "The news of the past few days from Germany has deeply shocked public opinion in the United States. . . . I myself could scarcely believe that such things could occur in a twentieth-century civilization."

Even the Neutrality Acts were less than strictly neutral, for the British, having command of the seas, could purchase and take home goods from the United States, while Germany could not. The U.S. government, by not recognizing Japan's undeclared war, permitted Americans to sell and deliver materials to embattled China via Hanoi or the Burma Road. At the outbreak of hostilities in Europe, the United States lifted the embargo on munitions specifically for the benefit of Britain and France.

President Roosevelt realized more fully than most others that the United States could not afford to see victory for a gangster nation like Hitler's Germany. He therefore began by devious means to lead his country into rearmament and to increase aid to Germany's antagonists. In his eyes the Neutrality Patrol was chiefly a means of preparing for war. As the patrol was expanded, ships were refitted and pressed into service, and reserves were called to the colors and given training that prepared them admirably for convoy escort duty.

The Nazi blitzkrieg quickly rolled over Poland, which Germany divided with Russia. The following spring,

At the Atlantic Conference, August 1941: General Marshall is conversing with President Roosevelt; behind Prime Minister Churchill, Admirals King and Stark are in consultation. Signed by and for President Roosevelt.

German armies overran Denmark and Norway and plunged through the Low Countries into France. The British army, overwhelmed by German aircraft and armored columns, barely escaped from French soil. Italy declared war on Britain and France, Paris fell, and France appealed for an armistice. Hitler, with access presumably to the combined naval power of Germany, France, and Italy, now stood with his armies poised on the English Channel, threatening to invade Britain. It thus seemed a distinct possibility that the Royal Navy also might be added to the Axis fleet. Roosevelt asked the new prime minister, Winston Churchill, for assurances that the British fleet would not be surrendered to Germany. Churchill replied that he himself would never relinquish the ships, but that, in the event of a British defeat, his government might be turned out and its successor might trade the fleet for better terms at the armistice table.

Now at last the American people, faced with losing the Royal Navy as their first line of naval defense, came into agreement with their President on the issue of possible war. Congress appropriated funds for a two-ocean navy and passed the first peacetime draft in American history. President Roosevelt notified Berlin and Rome that the orphaned colonies of Denmark, Holland, and France in the Western Hemisphere were not subject to transfer from one non-American power to another. With Canada the United States set up a permanent board to propose joint action against threats from overseas.

Despite the possibility of a surrender of the British fleet to Germany, Roosevelt decided to do something about Britain's shortage of escort vessels. This shortage had been rendered critical by losses in the Allied attempt to oust the Germans from Norway and during the evacuation of the British army from France by way of Dunkirk. In September 1940, Roosevelt and Churchill made a deal whereby Britain granted the United States 99-year leases of sites for bases in the West Indies in return for 50 U.S. destroyers built during, or shortly after, World War I. Britain also granted to the United States as gifts bases on Newfoundland and Bermuda; the United States gave to Britain 10 Coast Guard cutters equipped for antisubmarine duty.

To circumvent the "cash" part of the U.S. "cash-and-carry" policy and to avoid the war-debts problems that had followed World War I, Congress, at the President's urging, in March 1941 passed the Lend-Lease Act. This act permitted the United States to go into high gear in the production of war materials and to transfer all that could be spared to Britain, and later Russia, on a loan basis. "We must," said Roosevelt, "be the great arsenal of democracy." The United States soon engaged in further unneutral acts—seizing Axis ships in American ports, freezing German and Italian assets in the United States, occupying Greenland, and relieving Britain in the defense of Iceland.

Early in 1941 high-ranking American and British officers, meeting secretly in Washington, concluded the ABC-1 Staff Agreement, whereby the U.S. Navy would share responsibility for escorting transatlantic convoys. In the event that the United States entered the war, the American Joint Chiefs of Staff would meet periodically with the British Chiefs of Staff under the designation Combined Chiefs of Staff to make strategic plans and decisions; the United States would exert its principal military effort in the European theater, even if Japan should make war on America. The decision to "beat Hitler first" was based on Germany's greater military potential, on her greater threat to the United States because of her control of the Atlantic coast of Europe, and on the fact that Germany was already fighting England, which could be helped at once, whereas Japan had now sealed off China from the outside world.

The Neutrality Patrol was expanded and reorganized as the U.S. Atlantic Fleet so that it could handle the Navy's new assignment. Appointed as its commander in chief was Admiral Ernest J. King, a stern, demanding, and dedicated officer who was to become a principal architect of Allied victory.

In August 1941 President Roosevelt and Prime Minister Churchill met at Placentia Bay, Newfoundland, with their top-ranking officers. Here they discussed problems of common defense and issued an Atlantic Charter setting forth the joint war aims of their countries.

OPENING HOSTILITIES IN THE ATLANTIC

The undeclared war between the United States and Germany opened on September 4, 1941. The German submarine U-652, tracked for three hours by U.S. destroyer Greer, at last fired a torpedo. The Greer counterattacked with depth charges. Both missed.

In mid-September, the U.S. Navy began regular escort of convoy, relieving Canadian escorts off Newfoundland and handing the Britain-bound merchant ships over to Royal Navy escorts at a Mid-Ocean Meeting Point (MOMP), south of Iceland. Here the American escort vessels usually picked up a westbound convoy, which they delivered to Canadian escorts in the Newfoundland area.

Blood was first drawn by the undeclared enemies on the dark night of October 16, when a U-boat "wolfpack" attacked an eastbound convoy, sinking seven merchantmen. One of these merchantmen, while ablaze, silhouetted U.S. destroyer Kearny, which was struck by a torpedo. Eleven Americans on board the destroyer were killed, but the heavily damaged vessel made port in nearby Iceland. Two weeks later the naval tanker

The Reuben James, *torpedoed by a U-boat in October 1941, was the first U.S. warship sunk during World War II.*

Salinas and the destroyer *Reuben James* were torpedoed on successive nights. The *Salinas*, buoyed by empty compartments, survived. The torpedo that hit the *Reuben James* probably set off her forward magazine, for the entire fore part of the ship, including the bridge, was blown off. More than 100 of her company were lost; no officers survived.

In response to these hostile acts, Congress removed the "carry" feature of the U.S. neutrality policy. American merchant ships might now be armed and sent with lend-lease materials directly to British ports. The formal plunge into full-scale war, however, came as a result of the Japanese raid on Pearl Harbor. The following day, December 8, 1941, Congress declared war on Japan. Three days later, Germany and Italy declared war on the United States, and that same day the United States declared war on those countries.

U-BOATS IN AMERICAN WATERS

In the reorganization of commands following the Pearl Harbor attack and the declarations of war, Admiral King was ordered to Washington as Commander in Chief, U.S. Fleet (COMINCH). Admiral Royal E. Ingersoll succeeded King as Commander in Chief, Atlantic Fleet (CINCLANT). Because Admiral King's responsibilities were found to overlap those of Admiral Harold R. Stark, Chief of Naval Operations (CNO), President Roosevelt, in March 1942, sent Stark to London as Commander, U.S. Naval Forces, Europe, and appointed King CNO as well as COMINCH.

The Joint Chiefs of Staff were Admiral King; General George C. Marshall, U.S. Army Chief of Staff; and General Henry M. Arnold, Chief of Staff of the U.S. Army Air Corps. All were also members, with their British counterparts, of the Combined Chiefs of Staff. In July 1942 Admiral William D. Leahy was appointed to the post Chief of Staff to the Commander in Chief of the Army and the Navy, President Roosevelt. In that capacity Leahy was a member of both the Joint and the Combined Chiefs of Staff and was their presiding officer.

For the U.S. Navy, World War II was three interrelated wars, each with its special problems: the war against enemy submarines, known as the Battle of the Atlantic; the war against the European Axis; and the war against Japan. Although these wars were in progress simultaneously, they are treated separately in this narrative for the sake of clarity, in the order given above.

Admiral Karl Dönitz, commanding German submarines, was surprised by the Pearl Harbor attack and

Admiral Ernest J. King.

therefore did not get U-boats into American waters until mid-January 1942. Even then, he could send only five. These submarines and their successors, never more than a dozen at a time, played havoc with coastal and Caribbean shipping. They sank 26 vessels of 146,000 gross tons in January, 36 ships totaling 192,000 tons in February, and 47 vessels of 276,000 tons in March. Surfacing after dark, the U-boats found targets in ships that were often fully lighted or were silhouetted by shore lights or the glow of brightly illuminated cities. Burning vessels became a familiar sight off East Coast resorts, and the beaches were gradually covered with black oil from torpedoed tankers. This dreadful slaughter of shipping, which the government tried to keep secret, caused a far greater setback to the American war effort than the partly publicized Pearl Harbor attack.

To meet the U-boat onslaught, Vice Admiral Adolphus Andrews, Commander Eastern Sea Frontier, had only a handful of patrol craft. Such vessels had been neglected in favor of building larger ships, on the assumption that they could be built quickly enough when needed. In February the British came to the rescue with 24 trawlers and 10 corvettes. As these and other

Sub-hunting crew of a Coast Guard cutter looses a depth charge in battle practice.

Plane from escort carrier in a U.S. hunter-killer group depth-bombs a U-boat.

patrol craft became available, small, lightly escorted convoys called "bucket brigades" began running along the coast during the daylight hours and putting into protected anchorages for the night. At the same time, for the benefit of faster ships that still ran at night, the government ordered a blackout of waterfront lights and a dimout of all port cities.

By May a regular coastal convoy system was in operation, and nearly 200 planes were on antisubmarine patrol from 19 airfields along the U.S. East Coast. Dönitz, retreating before these countermeasures, ordered his U-boats to concentrate in the Caribbean Sea and the Gulf of Mexico. Here in May they sank 85 ships, mostly tankers, while only 5 were sunk off the East Coast. As more escorts became available, an interlocking system was established whereby ships could transfer from convoy to convoy in order to serve the complex pattern of shipping in the Gulf and Caribbean.

The U-boats now retreated to the waters off Panama, Trinidad, Salvador, and Rio de Janeiro in search of unprotected ships. Their stay was lengthened by the presence of new supply submarines known as "milk cows." The sinking of five Brazilian freighters off Salvador in late summer provoked Brazil into declaring war on Germany. By the end of 1942, convoys were in full operation as far south as Rio de Janeiro, and the U-boats had retreated to the convoy routes of the mid-Atlantic.

THE TENTH FLEET AND HUNTER-KILLER OPERATIONS

Combatting U-boats was far more difficult in World War II than it had been in World War I. The submarines could no longer be penned in by mines, because Germany early gained control of all the European coast from North Cape to the Pyrenees. They could not be destroyed at their Bay of Biscay bases, because, while the Royal Air Force had been busy protecting England from invasion, the Germans had built on the French coast submarine pens with concrete overheads so thick as to be virtually impenetrable by bombs. The U-boats, moreover, were controlled by the intuitive genius of Dönitz, who, using radio, massed them in wolfpacks against convoys and coached them into action.

Convoy continued to be the best means of protecting shipping, although a great deal more was now required. Early in the war the British and Americans operated convoys together, but Admiral King was dissatisfied with the way the Admiralty directed British-American convoys to northern Russia. At his suggestion, the British

and Canadians, after March 1, 1943, retained control of the North Atlantic convoys, while the Americans controlled convoys sailing from one American port to another and those in the Central and South Atlantic.

On May 1, Admiral King brought together all American antisubmarine control and intelligence activities into an organization called the U.S. Tenth Fleet. To give the new fleet authority, he himself assumed command, but he delegated operations to the fleet chief of staff, Rear Admiral Francis S. Low. The Tenth Fleet was unique in that it had no ships of its own but could order any ship of any U.S. fleet to go anywhere.

Improved antisubmarine techniques cost the Germans a record 41 U-boats in May 1943, mostly in the North Atlantic. Dönitz, badly shaken, ordered most of his submarines southward into the Central Atlantic. This move was scarcely for the better, for here American hunter-killer groups were just going into operation. These groups consisted of an escort aircraft carrier (CVE) screened by old destroyers or destroyer escorts.

First of the new antisubmarine groups to operate in the Central Atlantic was that of Captain Giles E. Short, in the escort carrier *Bogue*. On June 5, a Wildcat and an Avenger from this carrier attacked and sank *U-217*. On the 8th, well-armed *U-758* fought back against *Bogue* planes and dived to safety. Four days later, seven planes from the carrier sank the milk cow *U-118*. Next to arrive in the Central Atlantic were groups centered on the escort carriers *Core, Santee,* and *Card*. In less than three weeks the hunter-killers had sunk 15 U-boats with a loss of only three planes.

The operations of these groups were a far cry from the needle-in-haystack searches of World War I's Queenstown patrols. The U-boats, in order to keep in touch with Dönitz as he required, were continually breaking radio silence. The U.S. Navy's Atlantic arc of high frequency radio direction finders (HF/DF, pronounced "huffduff") picked up German transmissions and flashed the bearings to Washington headquarters, which established a fix and radioed it out to the hunter-killer groups. The group nearest to the transmitting submarine immediately sent planes to sink it. All this took place so swiftly that the attacking aircraft often arrived over the U-boat before it could close down transmission and submerge. Dönitz's boats were thus talking themselves to death.

THE FINAL CAMPAIGNS

While improved antisubmarine techniques were decimating Dönitz's U-boats in the North and Central

Atlantic, aircraft and ships based on southwest England were attacking them in the Bay of Biscay, across the surface of which the boats passed by night to and from their French bases. Air Vice Marshal Sir John Slessor called the bay "the trunk of the Atlantic U-boat menace, the roots being in the Biscay ports and the branches spreading far and wide." Planes of the Royal Air Force Coastal Command had been patrolling this "trunk" since 1940. They had, however, sunk no U-boats for lack of long-range bombers, none of which could be spared from the strategic bombing of Germany.

In early 1943 the U.S. Army loaned the Coastal Command 36 radar-equipped B-24 bombers, but because these bombers succeeded in sinking only one submarine in a month's time, the Joint Chiefs transferred them to Morocco to support the North African campaign. The B-24s had been foiled by Metox, a German radar detector that outranged the planes' radar and hence gave early warning.

Coastal Command next obtained a few Wellington bombers equipped with 80-million-candlepower searchlights and new ultrahigh frequency radar which Metox could not detect. The Wellingtons were thus able to surprise and blind the night-running U-boats, which however usually managed to crash-dive and escape. In April, 27 bomber attacks achieved only one kill.

Dönitz nevertheless made the fatal mistake of arming his submarines with powerful antiaircraft guns and ordering them to surface by day to recharge batteries and to fight back if surprised. As a result the Wellingtons, aided by a few newly arrived Halifax heavy bombers and Sunderland flying boats, in May sank

Boarding party on U-505.

Captain Gallery on the Guadalcanal, *with his prize in the background.*

seven boats and damaged seven. Admiral King, impressed by this score, sent to the bay offensive several squadrons of B-24s and one of PBY patrol bombers, and the Royal Navy added five sloops, two of which promptly sank a U-boat apiece.

The improving scores reached spectacular heights in the "Big Bay Slaughter" of the week of July 28, when nine boats were sunk in six days. Thereafter the rate of sinkings decreased as many U-boats shifted to new submarine bases in Norway; those that continued to be based on France came and went hugging the Spanish coast, where the mountain backdrop made them invisible to radar. Nevertheless, between May 1 and the end of 1943, 32 U-boats had been sunk in the Bay of Biscay and its approaches.

Out in the Central Atlantic the American hunter-killer groups, aided by huffduff and by cryptanalysis of radio messages sent to and from the garrulous U-boats, had developed a specialty of catching the submarines fueling from their milk cows. With the pipeline stretched between them, neither submarine could dive, and hence the attacking planes often got both. Loss of milk cows obliged Dönitz in September 1943 to cease active operations in the Central Atlantic. But U-boats en route to assignments off Capetown or in the Indian Ocean had to pass through the area and refuel near the Azores or the Cape Verdes. In March 1944 the *Block Island* group sank two U-boats at each of these fueling stops; one sub was a milk cow.

A striking example of the coordination between huffduff and the killer groups was the hounding of *U-66*, which was en route from South Africa and was short of fuel. On April 19 the submarine's captain, Lieutenant Seehausen, radioed a request, monitored by huffduff, for instructions on where to rendezvous with a milk cow. In the predawn darkness of the 26th, as Seehausen approached the appointed spot, he was horrified to see four American destroyer escorts already there, attacking the milk cow *U-488*, which they destroyed. Seehausen dived and slipped away, but after he had requested another rendezvous, huffduff and the hunter-killers were soon again on his track. On May 5 the badly frustrated U-boat captain despairingly radioed Berlin: "Refueling impossible under constant stalking. Mid-Atlantic worse than Bay of Biscay." This message, spurt-transmitted— that is, recorded on tape and radioed at high speed —was on the air only a few seconds, but 26 huffduff stations took bearings on it. Within an hour the *Block Island* had the fix and sent the destroyer escort *Buckley* to run down the bearing. The *Buckley* found *U-66*, opened fire, dodged a torpedo, and then rammed the U-boat, which began to blaze, whereupon desperate Germans tried to clamber aboard the *Buckley*. The Americans, taking them to be a boarding party, beat them off with anything handy, including coffee cups and shell cases. After *U-66* had gone down hissing, the *Buckley* rescued 36 survivors.

Even more spectacular was the June 1944 capture of *U-505* by Captain Daniel V. Gallery's group built around the escort carrier *Guadalcanal*. The Germans, blasted to the surface by depth charges and ahead-thrown projectiles called hedgehogs, hastily abandoned *U-505*, whereupon a specially trained American boarding party plunged down the conning tower hatch, disconnected demolition charges, and closed seacocks. They brought out code books and a cipher machine, for which Ameri-

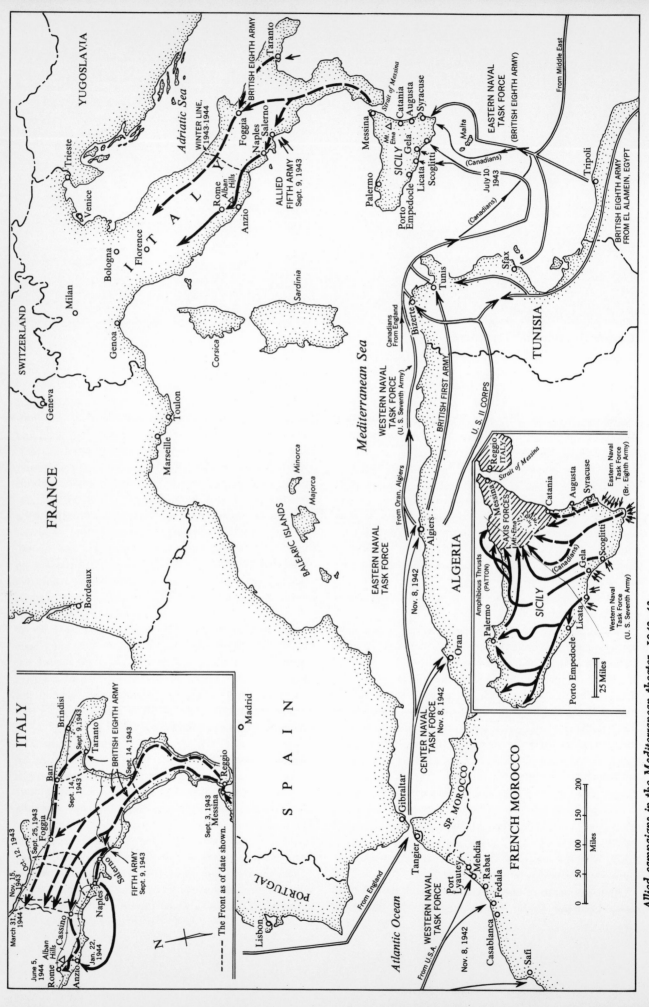

Allied campaigns in the Mediterranean theater, 1942–43.

Western Naval Task Force en route to Morocco.

can cryptanalysts were grateful, since these acquisitions greatly simplified their brain-cracking labors. Gallery, after pumping out the partly flooded U-boat, put a line on her and towed her to Bermuda.

In the last months of the war, when U-boats had become little more than a nuisance, new German snorkel boats, whose breathing tubes permitted them to remain submerged with diesels running, staged a blitz in British coastal waters. Reports from spies that seven snorkelers were about to cross the Atlantic to launch rockets at East Coast cities caused such apprehension that CIN-CLANT set up a barrier of ships to intercept them. The barrier sank five of the U-boats. The others reached the American coast after Germany's defeat and quietly surrendered. These submarines were found to be carrying no rockets.

THE ALLIED INVASION OF NORTH AFRICA

On October 22, 1942, Rear Admiral H. Kent Hewitt called together at Norfolk a group of senior naval and army officers and revealed to them their destination: French Morocco. Major General George S. Patton, who was to command the landing force, followed up with his usual fighting speech. When, during the next two days, the Western Naval Task Force sortied from Hampton Roads, only the select few who had been at the meeting knew whither they were bound.

Other segments of the task force joined the fleet at sea—a Covering Group, which included the new fast

battleship *Massachusetts* and two heavy cruisers, and an Air Group, including the carrier *Ranger* and four escort carriers. When assembled, the force contained 102 ships covering more than 500 square miles of ocean. Admiral Hewitt, Commander Western Naval Task Force, in the heavy cruiser *Augusta*, was senior officer present; he commanded even General Patton and his 35,000-troop landing force. After the landing, and until Patton had secured his beachhead, the general would be senior to the admiral. Unity of command was thus maintained.

Hewitt's task force was only one of three moving on French North Africa. Out of the British Isles came two more: a Center Naval Task Force, carrying 39,000 American troops with British naval support, bound for the Algerian port of Oran; and an Eastern Naval Task Force, with 23,000 British and 10,000 American troops, heading for Algiers. Commanding the whole three-part expedition was Lieutenant General Dwight D. Eisenhower USA; the overall naval commander was Admiral Sir Andrew B. Cunningham RN. The code name for the expedition was Operation TORCH.

Nothing quite like Hewitt's expedition against Morocco had ever been attempted—an amphibious assault on an oceanic front staged directly from bases on the far side of the ocean. The crossing, moreover, was through seas infested with U-boats. But huffduff and the Tenth Fleet had done their work well; each submarine had been spotted, so that the Western Naval Task Force, despite its size, was able to evade them all.

The specific function of the Western Force was to seize Casablanca for use as a supply port, particularly if the Nazis should advance through nominally neutral

Spain and close the Straits of Gibraltar. How much resistance the French would put up to the landings was an unanswered question. All of French North Africa—Morocco, Algeria, and Tunisia—was controlled by the Vichy government of Marshal Henri Pétain in southeast France, which the Germans dominated but did not occupy. The French, by the terms of their armistice with Germany, were bound to resist invasion. If the African French cooperated with the invaders, the Germans were sure to retaliate against Vichy France. Moreover, many Frenchmen had a special grudge against the British, who in 1940 had sunk French warships in the port of Oran to make sure that they did not get into Axis hands.

As the Western Task Force approached the coast of Africa, it split apart. A Northern Attack Group headed for Mehdia with 9,000 troops to capture a nearby airfield, and a Southern Attack Group with 6,500 troops shaped course for a landing at the small port of Safi. The Center Attack Group, with Hewitt and Patton and accompanied by the Covering Group and the *Ranger*, advanced toward Fedala, a tiny port 15 miles northeast of Casablanca. Hewitt approached the landings with misgivings. In the post Commander Amphibious Force Atlantic Fleet, he had been responsible for training the Morocco landing force. He was sharply aware that there had not been enough time. The Combined Chiefs of Staff had not reached the decision to invade northwestern Africa until July 25, 1942. Seasonal weather had dictated that the invasion be scheduled not later than November 8.

The long delay was the result of disagreements between American and British leaders. The U.S. Joint Chiefs of Staff had proposed seizing a beachhead in France in late summer 1942, to be followed in 1943 with a drive into Germany. The British, who had lost 1 million men on the Western Front in World War I, and who in World War II had already been evicted from Norway, France, and Greece, had no intention of risking a fourth costly expulsion. They refused to re-enter the Continent until the Axis powers should be sufficiently weakened to assure the success of a cross-Channel attack without too great a cost in lives.

Yet something had to be done. The Germans in Russia were driving on Stalingrad; those in Egypt were threatening the Suez Canal. A vigorous thrust, somewhere, against the dangerously overextended Germans might turn both of their advances into retreats. Churchill, who in World War I had sponsored the Dardanelles-Gallipoli expedition as a means of outflanking the Western Front, now suggested invading northwestern Africa

Follow-up troops coming ashore at Fedala.

as a means of outflanking western France. Northwestern Africa provided the least formidable opening into the Axis-controlled empire, and a landing here would clamp the pincers on General Erwin Rommel's *Afrika Korps*, which was in contact with General Sir Bernard Montgomery's British Eighth Army at the far end of North Africa. The Joint Chiefs were shocked. Such diversion of forces from the strategic center, they said, would delay the cross-Channel attack until 1944. They were perfectly correct, but since the British remained adamant, they at last agreed to go along. Northwestern Africa it was.

A little after midnight on November 8, the cruisers *Augusta* and *Brooklyn* and 10 destroyers shepherded the 15 transports of the Center Attack Group to their anchorage some seven miles off the Fedala landing beach. As Hewitt had feared, there was mounting confusion. Some of the transports straggled and were slow in lowering their landing craft. The soldiers, overloaded, climbed slowly down the nets to the pitching boats. In the darkness some of the boats became lost, and most were late in reaching the rendezvous area. By the time they had arrived at the line of departure, the ship-to-shore movement was an hour behind schedule. The run to the beach was hampered by high seas, the inexperience of the coxswains, and the fact that some of the advance scout boats with their seaward-flashing lights were out of place. Many of the landing craft collided, crashed into rocks, or were carried by the surf high onto the beach, where they were left stranded by the receding tide. Nevertheless, at dawn, 3,500 Americans were ashore and had seized control of the town.

By this time, French batteries flanking the beachhead had opened fire on the follow-up landing craft and on nearby destroyers. Captain R. R. M. Emmet, commanding the Center Group in the transport *Leonard Wood*, had ordered by voice radio: "Play ball!" thereby putting the American attack plan into effect. By 0700* the Center Group gunnery ships had the Fedala batteries under fire, the *Ranger*'s aircraft were battling with French planes over Casablanca, and the Covering Group was exchanging fire with the 15-inch guns of the unfinished battleship *Jean Bart* in Casablanca harbor and with the El Hank battery nearby. Beginning at 0815 Vice Admiral François Michelier, who was directing the defense of Casablanca, sent out from the harbor a cruiser and seven destroyers in a series of sorties against the Center Group. By noon all but one of the French ships had been sunk or disabled, having been attacked

* The remainder of this narrative uses 24-hour time, which came into almost universal use by military forces in World War II.

General George S. Patton and Admiral H. Kent Hewitt watch the Battle off Casablanca from the flag bridge of U.S.S. Augusta.

by the gunnery ships of the Center and Covering groups and by planes from the *Ranger*. By that time, also, the Fedala batteries were in American hands. The march on Casablanca could not, however, begin that day, because not enough troops and supplies were ashore and half of the landing craft had been destroyed.

Meanwhile, at Safi, 150 miles down the coast, the Southern Attack Group had achieved an impressive success. Two old four-stack destroyers, blazing away at French gun positions, had led the landing craft by night directly into the breakwater-protected harbor. While the old battleship *New York* and the light cruiser *Philadelphia* pounded the shore batteries, American troops took over key positions in town. After dawn, planes from the escort carrier with this group smashed most of the local French planes on the ground. Next, in came a converted train ferry bringing medium tanks, and the American parade from Safi to Casablanca began. The *Philadelphia* and several destroyers kept pace along the coast in order to provide fire support.

The Northern Attack Group landings at Mehdia were even more confused than those at Fedala. Here navy guns definitely saved the beachhead. The light cruiser *Savannah* silenced the guns of the town's ancient but well-armed fortress, the Kasba. A French armored column advancing along the coast road was forced back by cruiser and destroyer fire, and a column of troop-filled trucks approaching from the interior was dispersed

Luncheon conference at Fedala, November 11, 1943. Admiral Hewitt is at the head of the table; at his right is Admiral François Michelier, recent defender of Casablanca; at Hewitt's left is General Patton.

by 14-inch shells from the old battleship *Texas*. By November 10 some of the invading troops had broken through the defense lines and seized the airfield at nearby Port Lyautey. Others arrived at the airdrome by way of the winding Sebou River aboard the destroyer *Dallas*, which had broken through a boom near the river mouth. Bombers, prepared to operate against Casablanca, flew in to the field from one of the escort carriers, only to learn that a cease-fire had been ordered.

By sheer chance Admiral Jean Darlan, head of the French armed forces and number-two man in the Vichy French government, happened to be in Algiers visiting an ailing son when the Allies invaded French North Africa. It was he who ordered the cease-fire, with the secret concurrence of Marshal Pétain. On the morning of November 11, American troops from Fedala had nearly surrounded Casablanca and were about to open an all-out attack with sea and air support when Admiral Michelier received his orders to cease resistance. Later that day, French and American leaders met at a cordial luncheon conference. To Michelier, Admiral Hewitt expressed regret at having had to fire on French ships. Replied Michelier, taking Hewitt's proffered hand, "I had my orders and did my duty, you had yours and did your duty; now that is over, we are ready to co-

operate." The rejoicing over this happy conclusion turned to dismay during the next two days, for two of the U-boats that Hewitt's force had evaded in transit got in among the Center Group transports at their exposed anchorage off Fedala and sank four of them.

The invasions of Oran and Algiers, in some respects far different in execution, were planned alike: night landings on beaches flanking the cities, and dashes by pairs of destroyers or cutters into the inner harbor to prevent sabotage. Neither harbor dash was successful; three of the attacking vessels were sunk with heavy casualties. The best-trained American troops had been assigned to the capture of Oran, where the heaviest resistance was correctly anticipated. Here relatively smooth landings were followed by an orderly advance. The invasion at Algiers, on the contrary, was wildly confused. Poor boat handling cost 90 per cent of the landing craft. Luckily the resistance at Algiers was the lightest of all. This and the other landings provided valuable training, as well as a grim warning that far more training was needed before the Allies could attempt to assault a truly hostile coast.

The Nazis, as predicted, retaliated for the cooperation of the French North Africans with the Allies by occupying all of France. When they broke into Toulon to seize the French fleet, however, they found nothing they could use. The ships had all been scuttled by order of the fleet commander.

Shortly before the northwestern Africa landings, the British Eighth Army had defeated the *Afrika Korps* in the Battle of El Alamein. The Germans were fleeing westward, closely pursued. The British and American invaders, with some French forces, began moving eastward to join with the Eighth Army in trapping the Germans in Tunisia. But errors, supply problems, and adverse weather held up effective Allied operations until spring of 1943. By then 200,000 Axis reinforcements had been rushed to Tunisia. The more heavily reinforced Allies, coming from Algeria and Egypt, met in Tunisia, having crossed 2,000 miles of Africa between them. They trapped 275,000 Axis troops and took them prisoner. At Stalingrad the Nazis were retreating from a Russian offensive. This retreat was to end in the heart of Berlin.

In January, Roosevelt and Churchill and their staffs had met in conference at Casablanca. Here it was decided that if Allied offensives anywhere were to succeed, the antisubmarine warfare must be given top priority. The Americans now argued for a cross-Channel attack into France in 1943, but the British produced statistics to demonstrate that Germany, at that time, could have 44 divisions in France, while the Anglo-Americans would have available for a landing no more than 25. The British insisted that further peripheral operations were desirable in order to draw out more Germans from western Europe. At last the Americans acquiesced to British proposals for an invasion of Sicily in July 1943. In return, the British agreed to allocate more forces to the Pacific theater so that the Americans might retain the initiative they had won by capturing Guadalcanal. At the conclusion of the conference Roosevelt, with Churchill's concurrence, announced that the Allies would accept nothing short of the unconditional surrender of Germany, Italy, and Japan. This inflexible position was much criticized and may have prolonged the war.

THE INVASION OF SICILY

The Americans, while agreeing to the invasion of Sicily, declined at that time to commit themselves to further operations in the Mediterranean. Much depended on the outcome of this invasion. The taking of Sicily was expected to make Allied Mediterranean communications more secure, to divert Germans from the Russian front, to demonstrate to Italy the futility of continuing in the war, and to enable the Allies to capture another big bag of Axis war prisoners. The last could be assured only by quickly blocking Sicily's back door, the Strait of Messina.

The Combined Chiefs, impressed with Eisenhower's conduct of the North African campaign, kept him in supreme command with the new rank of full general. Cunningham, promoted to fleet admiral, was to command the naval forces: Vice Admiral Hewitt's Western Naval Task Force and Vice Admiral Sir Bertram Ramsay's Eastern Naval Task Force. General Sir Harold Alexander was given command of the ground forces: Lieutenant General Patton's U.S. Seventh Army and Lieutenant General Montgomery's British Eighth Army. Air Chief Marshal Sir Arthur Tedder headed the Mediterranean Air Command, and Lieutenant General Carl Spaatz the subsidiary Northwest African Air Forces. The approaching Sicilian operation was code-named HUSKY.

Eisenhower was too much involved in the Tunisian campaign to give HUSKY much thought. Most of the planning for the latter was therefore done at Hewitt's and Cunningham's headquarters in Algiers and at Patton's base, 165 miles away. The suggestion was made that the surest way to trap the enemy in Sicily would be to land at Messina. It was, however, rejected, because Africa and Malta were too far away to provide fighter cover. Not that it made much difference, for General Spaatz, who was not present, did not believe in tactical air support. He favored fighting the *Luftwaffe* and the Royal Italian Air Force, and indeed his aviators were very good at it. They temporarily knocked out the dozen airfields in Sicily before D-day.

The army-navy planners, unaware of Spaatz's policies, finally selected a line of beaches that stretched around the southeast corner of Sicily. Hewitt's Western Naval Task Force would land Patton's Seventh Army on the southwest coast near the small ports of Licata, Gela, and Scoglitti, while Ramsay's Eastern Naval Task Force landed Montgomery's Eighth Army at the southern tip of the island and just north of it on the east coast. These were positions from which the Axis forces were more likely to be pushed out of Sicily than trapped inside.

July 10, 1943, was selected for D-day, 0245 for H-hour. The date and hour would permit a paratroop drop by moonlight, with the moon setting in time for the task forces to approach the beach and land the armies in darkness. Hewitt suggested delaying the landing so that the fleet could approach in darkness and support the assault waves at dawn. But Patton and Alexander objected, saying that the factor of surprise was too important to sacrifice for the dubious advantages of naval gunfire support. They had not seen what navy guns had done at Mehdia.

The supplying of invading armies without harbors at the beachhead was made possible only by the arrival in the Mediterranean of new beaching craft that could transport men, vehicles, and supplies directly to an open beach. These craft were the Landing Ship Tank (LST), the Landing Craft Tank (LCT), and the Landing Craft Infantry (LCI). They, as well as the smaller LCVP, were used in training for the coming invasion. The training, thorough and realistic, involved rehearsals on a divisional scale. At the same time, every effort was made to mislead the enemy in regard to Allied intentions, including dropping off the coast of Spain an anonymous corpse, called "Major William Martin," whose briefcase was stuffed with misinformation.

Mussolini and Field Marshal Albert Kesselring, the German army commander in Italy, were not misled. They expected the next Allied assault to come against Sicily, but they relied on General Alfredo Guzzoni, commanding the Sicilian defense forces, to destroy the invaders at the water's edge. From the standpoint of sheer numbers Guzzoni had the means—350,000 troops, including more than 50,000 Germans. To meet this force the Allies could muster only 470,000 invaders, a number far short of the three-to-one superiority traditionally deemed necessary for the success of an assault. Yet Guzzoni was far from optimistic. The Germans, he was sure, would put up a good fight. So might some of the imported Italians. But the Sicilian natives, almost to a man, hated Mussolini, hated the Germans, hated the war, and admired the United States, where many of their friends and relatives had found happiness and prosperity. With this sort of defenders, Guzzoni realized, Sicily was a hollow shell.

The Allies were not counting on anything of the sort. They planned to send in their whole invasion force at one time in nearly 1,400 ships and beaching craft, landing simultaneously along 100 miles of beaches. In sheer size for a single operation, the Sicily landings dwarfed every amphibious assault in history, including that on Normandy, in 1944, which built up gradually through a series of reinforcements.

Out of the teeming ports of North Africa and the Middle East steamed various elements of the Sicilian expeditionary force. A convoy bringing the 1st Canadian Division of the Eastern Task Force came directly from England. All were intricately routed to keep out of one another's way, to mislead observers as to their destination, and to arrive on schedule at the points off Malta from which they would make the final run to the Sicily beaches. On July 9 rough seas caused concern among the commanders and their staffs, but Admirals Hewitt and Ramsay, trusting their aerologists' assurances that the wind would abate in time, decided to press on. (See map, page 168.)

After midnight on July 10, Hewitt's Western Naval Task Force approached the Sicilian coast. The hills were outlined here and there by conflagrations ignited by a recent Allied air raid. Off Gela, the distant crackle of small arms fire announced that U.S. paratroops, dropped earlier, had made contact with the enemy. The assigned beaches were marked by the blinking of infrared lights from surfaced British submarines.

Axis planes had sighted and reported the approaching convoys. Rome knew that the invasion was imminent but, incredibly, the Sicilian reservists defending the beaches were not alerted. Many of their officers, not expecting an invasion in the foul weather, had abandoned their posts and gone to bed. Some of the gunners were asleep in their pillboxes.

The storm abated as predicted, but the water remained so rough that many of the invaders, tossed in the landing craft, became seasick en route to the beach. No two landings were exactly alike, but for the most part the LCVPs, lowered from transports or disgorged fully loaded from beaching craft, led the way in, and the beaching craft followed. The first waves of landing craft were accompanied by rocket-firing support boats that laid down a barrage on the beaches just before the invaders stepped ashore. Whenever this treatment failed to subdue the defenders, Allied gunboats, destroyers, and cruisers opened up and blasted them into silence. When those few defenders who were still resisting at dawn beheld the immense size of the offshore armada that completely concealed the horizon, they either fled or surrendered.

The Eastern Naval Task Force at the southern point of Sicily and off the east coast met similar light resistance, although it was later severely harassed by air raids from Italy. At both beachheads LSTs had difficulty in landing tanks because of offshore sandbars, but naval gunfire repeatedly pounded back columns of enemy tanks heading for the beaches. On July 11, General Patton at last saw for himself the kind of support that navy guns could provide land forces. From a rooftop in Gela he was dismayed to observe some sixty 30-ton German tanks leading an advance in his direction. An ensign with a walkie-talkie asked the general if he would like a little help from the fleet. "Sure!" replied Patton, whereupon the ensign passed the word and the cruiser *Boise* fired 38 six-inch shells, which provided the supplement to army artillery that was necessary to turn back the German advance.

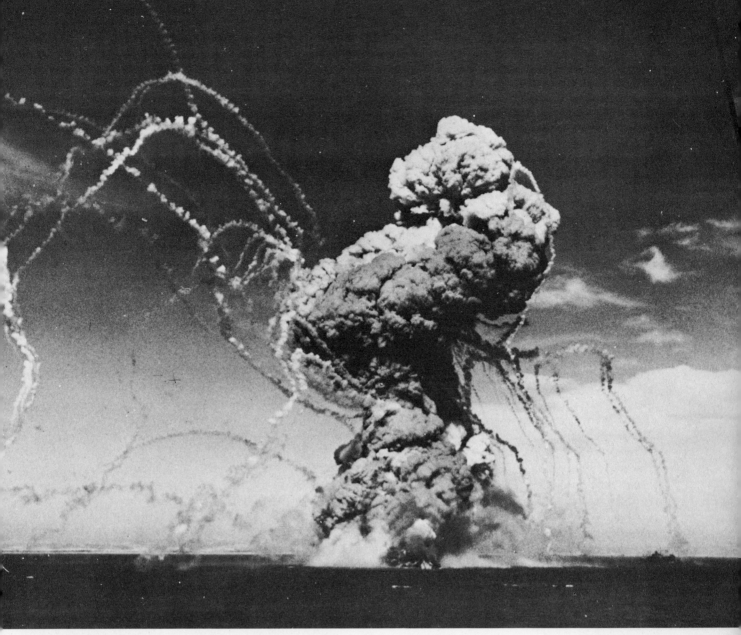

U.S. ammunition ship blows up during the invasion of Sicily.

The absence of tactical air support was keenly felt by fleet and army. Moreover, the lack of adequate liaison between land and sea forces and the air force had tragic consequences. On the evening of July 11, more American paratroops headed toward Sicily in 144 transport planes for a second drop. A little before midnight these planes flew over the Western Task Force immediately after the 24th enemy air raid of the day. Trigger-happy American gunners, both afloat and ashore, shot down 23 of the American planes. Two nights later, under similar circumstances, 11 Allied transport planes were shot down over the British task force.

Montgomery's Eighth Army quickly captured Syracuse and Augusta, two of Sicily's best ports, which were invaluable in easing the Allied supply problem. Mont-

gomery's main task, assigned by General Alexander, was to dash up the east coast and seize the Strait of Messina, thereby bottling up the Axis forces on the island. Alexander, because of his poor opinion of American troops, assigned to Patton a supporting role, that of overrunning central and western Sicily. There has rarely been a more obvious piece of military miscasting.

Sir Bernard had looked dashing enough while chasing the desperate, poorly supplied Rommel across the African desert, but in Sicily, when he came up against strong resistance at Catania, he turned slow and cautious. Instead of calling on the Navy to blast the enemy out of his path or to transport his forces by sea beyond the enemy strong point, he rotated his army inland in order to pass around west of Mount Etna. Consequently, he was soon brought almost to a halt in the rugged terrain at the base of the volcano.

Meanwhile, Patton, aptly named "the Great Ground Gainer," had sped west and seized Porto Empedocle. Thence his Seventh Army troops trotted across to Palermo, which they entered triumphantly on July 22, greeted by shouts of "Down with Mussolini!" and "Long live America!" Two days later, all of western Sicily was in American hands. By this time Patton, accompanied by cruisers and beaching craft, which provided fire support and supplies, was speeding eastward along the north coast, with the enemy retiring before him. Three times he used his little navy to hurl troops forward into the path of the retreating Axis forces, but the only effect was to speed the enemy's gallop to the strait.

By August 3 the Germans and Italians, crowded into the northeastern tip of Sicily, were being ferried with their supplies across to Italy, while elite Axis forces held back Patton's and Montgomery's armies, now almost abreast. On August 17, the Axis evacuation was completed and the U.S. Seventh Army, having sped around two sides of the Sicilian triangle, entered Messina. Two hours later a column of British Eighth Army tanks rattled into town to be greeted by the Americans with: "Where you tourists been?"

Though the Allies had failed to capture the bulk of the Axis forces in Sicily, the Italian King was sufficiently impressed to depose Mussolini. The latter's successor, Marshal Pietro Badoglio, while announcing that he would continue the war, in fact began to put out peace feelers.

SALERNO

The British, in order to induce the reluctant Americans to join them in an invasion of Italy, at last definitely committed themselves to a 1944 cross-Channel attack and gave their blessing to the opening of a new American offensive against Japan in the Central Pacific. The main attack against Italy, scheduled for September 9, 1943, was to be in the Gulf of Salerno, which was the gateway to Naples and just barely within the attack radius of Sicily-based fighter planes. The assault would be carried out by the newly formed Anglo-American Fifth Army commanded by Lieutenant General Mark Clark USA. (See map, page 168.)

In support of Clark's army, Montgomery's Eighth Army was to invade Italy at the "toe" and hasten up the "boot." Monty, however, refused to cross the Strait of Messina until enough massed artillery could be assembled to assure him an unopposed crossing. He then

proceeded up the peninsula at such a leisurely pace that General Alexander sent him orders to speed up, but to no avail.

On the evening of September 8, as transports carrying the Fifth Army approached the Gulf of Salerno, the troops on board rejoiced to hear General Eisenhower's broadcast announcing an Italian armistice. To most of the men it meant that the war was over in Italy and that they could simply walk ashore. In vain their officers tried to explain that they still had Germans to fight.

The terms of the armistice required the Italians to surrender, placing their armed forces under Allied control to fight the Germans. But the Germans got wind of the negotiations and poured troops into Italy. They rescued Mussolini and put him at the head of a puppet state in northern Italy. They disarmed the Italian soldiers, most of whom submitted and then vanished, blending into the civilian population. The Germans and the Allies could have at each other as long as they pleased; for the Italian soldier the war was over. The Italian fleet got away and made it to Malta, but the ships, lacking radar and other modern equipment, were of little use to the Allies.

To Marshal Kesselring, commanding the German forces in southern Italy, the choice of Salerno for the next Allied assault was perfectly obvious. He rushed thither a panzer division and set to work to prepare the hottest possible reception for the invaders, deploying tanks, mining the gulf and its beaches, and siting guns from the hilltops to the water's edge.

Admiral Hewitt, who commanded the Salerno support and amphibious forces, had again pleaded for a chance to give the beachhead a good pounding at dawn before the men went ashore. Complete surprise in even a night landing, he pointed out, was rendered impossible by the noisy engines of the landing craft. But the Army rejected the idea of any preliminary bombardment, contending that a little surprise was better than none. However, the Navy was bringing along plenty of muscle to back up the invasion when the opportunity came. The British provided four battleships, two fleet carriers, five escort carriers, four cruisers, and two monitors; the Americans, three cruisers. Both brought numerous destroyers.

At midnight on July 8, transports bringing American troops anchored in calm water a dozen miles off the southern half of the Gulf of Salerno and began to rail-load LCVPs. Minesweepers led the way into the gulf, followed by scout boats that located the assigned beaches and blinked signals seaward. Crews in the scout boats heard the rumble of motors and saw moving headlights, as German motorized units took final dispositions to repel the invasion. At the line of departure 6,000 yards offshore, the American coxswains opened full throttle, and the landing craft sped toward the beach. As the first wave approached the shore, an enemy loudspeaker thundered: "Come on in and give up! We have you covered!"

Dawn was graying the skies when the first LCVPs hit the beach and dropped their ramps. At that instant the Germans opened up with rifle, machine gun, mortar, cannon, and tank fire, while German aircraft swept over the beach, bombing and strafing. The Americans, responding to their training rather than to their fears, rushed ashore, taking heavy casualties. Bypassing enemy strong points, they sought their assigned assembly areas. The British landings on the beaches to the north were somewhat less costly because here the Germans had fired prematurely at beaching craft, thereby freeing the fleet to open up with a prelanding bombardment. It was in fact naval guns more than anything else that made the landings possible and that subsequently saved the beachhead.

The Germans, after seeing naval gunfire silence their batteries, blast their machine gun positions, and disable their tanks, shifted their main air attack to the fleet. They now introduced a radio-directed glide bomb, a lethal weapon which disabled the cruisers *Savannah* and *Uganda* and the battleship *Warspite*. By September 12 the Germans had on Salerno Plain three divisions armed with 600 tanks and mobile guns. With this power they made repeated drives to force the Fifth Army into the sea and were narrowly thwarted by Allied infantry, field artillery, and naval guns. At last, on the 16th, Marshal Kesselring gave up and ordered a general withdrawal from the coast, "in order," he afterward wrote, "to evade the effective shelling from warships." That afternoon, advance elements of Montgomery's Eighth Army at last made contact with Clark's Fifth.

The Fifth and Eighth armies now began advancing abreast up the Italian peninsula. Their progress was slow, for the Germans took full advantage of the mountainous terrain to delay them with mobile artillery emplaced on hillsides and in passes. The Allies found that

GIs hug the beach at Salerno as German planes bomb and strafe.

the enemy had blown every bridge and reduced key towns to impassable rubble, sown with mines. Nevertheless, before the end of September, the Eighth Army had captured the important airdrome at Foggia. On October 1 the Fifth Army entered Naples. Here the Nazis had sunk ships, cranes, trucks, and locomotives in the harbor to make it unusable, and had blown up a good part of the city to avenge themselves on the turncoat Italians.

While an Anglo-American salvage team set about clearing Naples harbor, the Fifth and Eighth armies, drawing supplies precariously through Salerno, pushed on to the Volturno River, where the Germans had taken a stand. Fighting their way the next 100 miles to Rome was to take the Allies eight months and cost them thousands of lives and mountains of material. Yet it would draw no German reserves from France and would tie down in Italy twice as many Allied troops as German. In retrospect, the British and Americans would have done well to stop at Naples.

ANZIO

By November the Allied advance had stalled before positions shrewdly contrived by Marshal Kesselring in the mountains 40 miles north of Naples. Generals Eisenhower, Alexander, and Clark planned to outflank the German line with a landing on the coast at Anzio, near Rome. From Anzio the invaders were expected to dash to the Alban Hills, whence they could intercept supplies flowing down to Kesselring's defense line. So many beaching and landing craft had been earmarked for transfer to Britain, however, that only a one-division assault could be mounted. Such an assault would be hopelessly weak unless the Allies at the main front could roll rapidly forward and join hands with it. But the Allied drive bogged down in December rains, and so the Anzio project was dropped.

Prime Minister Churchill promptly picked it up again, insisting that a landing at Anzio would at least divert strength from the German line. He then obtained President Roosevelt's consent to check the outflow of beaching craft long enough to mount a two-division assault. General Eisenhower, declaring that two divisions were still inadequate for an independent operation, departed to prepare for the cross-Channel assault. He left in his place General Sir Henry ("Jumbo") Wilson, whom Churchill easily browbeat into adopting the Anzio plan.

The assault was scheduled for January 22, 1944. Major General John Lucas USA was to command the troops, and Rear Admiral Frank Lowry USN the naval forces. After only three weeks of planning, organizing, and rehearsal, the men were dispatched from Naples, mostly in beaching craft. The Air Force reported that it had completely sealed off the beachhead by demolishing all bridges, roads, and railroads leading to it.

Although the Army had decreed that the landing should be at night, its execution was almost flawless. Rocket-firing beaching craft laid down a barrage on the beach to detonate mines. Then the first wave of LCVPs touched down precisely on schedule at 0200. There was no immediate opposition. For once the enemy had been taken by surprise. (See map, page 168.)

General Lucas was the next to be surprised, for the beachhead had not been sealed off after all. His landing force was quickly surrounded by Germans. Lucas first postponed his dash to the Alban Hills, then abandoned it altogether when he perceived that the Germans could be more rapidly reinforced than he could. "I had hoped," said Churchill sadly, "that we were hurling a wildcat onto the shore, but all we got was a stranded whale."

The situation at Anzio degenerated into a miserable five-month stalemate, with both sides sending in a steady stream of reinforcements. By March, 90,200 Americans and 35,500 British were crammed into the shrinking beachhead, surrounded by 135,000 Germans. Day and night the invaders and their support ships were subjected to almost continuous bombardment and to repeated bombings. Denied the protection of entrenchments because of steady rains that raised the ground water level, the men built crude surface shelters made from sandbags.

At last in May the rains ceased, and hardening roads enabled the Allies on the main front to resume their offensive. On May 25 the Fifth Army broke through to the Anzio beachhead, where casualties had reached 59,000. A third of the total resulted from disease, exhaustion, and neuroses; some 5,000 had been killed, 17,000 wounded, and about 6,800 captured. In the fleet supporting the beachhead, 10 ships and 10 beaching craft had been sunk and more than 500 men killed.

On June 4 the Allies marched unopposed into Rome, where they were greeted by joyful crowds. Two days later Allied forces crossed from England into France, and the war in Italy became a mere secondary front.

NORMANDY

As early as summer 1943, photographic air reconnaissance had revealed suspicious construction in the Pas-de-Calais area, directly across the Strait of Dover from England. The structures were soon identified as launching sites for Germany's new "vengeance" (*Vergeltungs*) weapons, the flying bomb (V-1) and the supersonic rocket (V-2). With these weapons the Germans hoped to devastate cities and military bases in southern England. Though the Allies underestimated the destructive power of the new weapons, they gave top priority to bombing plants suspected of manufacturing them and to bombing the Pas-de-Calais launching sites. They thereby delayed operation of the V-weapons by several months.

Despite the misestimate, awareness of the new menace put additional urgency into preparations for Operation OVERLORD, the scheduled Allied invasion of western Europe. Perhaps Britain's greatest strategic contribution to the war was the delaying of OVERLORD until it could be executed with near certainty of success and without prohibitive losses. Undoubtedly, however, a major contribution of American strategists was inducing the British, finally, to join them in crossing the Channel in time to prevent Hitler from getting his V-weapons into full operation. "I feel sure," wrote General Eisenhower, "that if he had succeeded in using these weapons over a six-month period, and particularly if he had made the Portsmouth-Southampton area one of his principal targets, OVERLORD might have been written off."

Eisenhower was appointed Supreme Commander, Allied Expeditionary Force, in late December 1943. After a brief visit to the United States, he arrived in London in mid-January 1944. Most of the planning for OVERLORD was already done. In accordance with decisions reached at the January 1943 Casablanca Conference, Lieutenant General Sir Frederick Morgan had been appointed COSSAC—Chief of Staff to the Supreme Allied Commander (designate)—with the task of organizing and directing a staff to plan for the invasion of western Europe. When, at the end of 1943, General Morgan's planning staff was absorbed into SHAEF (Supreme Headquarters Allied Expeditionary Force), it numbered 489 officers and 614 enlisted men.

The area selected for the assault was a stretch of Normandy coast between the ports of Cherbourg and Le Havre. Three paratroop divisions were to be dropped at night behind the beaches, chiefly to seize and hold bridges and causeways. At first light, warships would open fire on the beach defenses, for the Army was at last convinced of the value of a preliminary naval bombardment. Just before the troops went ashore, bombers would sweep over the beaches for a final pounding of the defenses. In contrast to the broad invasion of Sicily, the assault on Normandy was to be made by only five divisions—two American, on beaches code-named Utah and Omaha; and, to the east of these, three British, on

General Eisenhower with Admirals Kirk and Deyo.

beaches designated Gold, Juno, and Sword. Following this comparatively narrow assault, 50 divisions would be poured in before the coming of winter.

D-day was to be June 5, 1944, a date that provided moonlight for the paratroop drop and time for the dawn naval bombardment before the desired tidal condition was reached. On the American beaches, this would come an hour after low tide. Then offshore antiboat obstacles would be exposed for destruction by teams of American demolition experts. Landing craft could be unloaded without danger of becoming stranded, and follow-up troops would have less and less beach to cross. June 6 and 7 would also provide satisfactory conditions, which would not occur again for two weeks.

Heading the naval, ground, and air forces under Eisenhower were Admiral Ramsay, General Montgomery, and Air Chief Marshal Sir Trafford Leigh-Mallory. The largely American Western Naval Task Force, which was to support Utah and Omaha beaches, was commanded by Rear Admiral Alan G. Kirk USN. Beginning in December 1943 the Western Naval Task Force and the British Eastern Naval Task Force began training exercises that culminated, in the spring of 1944, in full-scale mock invasions on the south coast of England. These invasions closely simulated Operation NEPTUNE, the amphibious phase of Operation OVERLORD.

Hitler estimated that the Allies would attempt an invasion of western Europe not later than the spring of 1944. He consequently ordered his commander in the west, Marshal Gerd von Rundstedt, to build an "Atlantic Wall" consisting of concrete strong points pro-

Infantry landing craft bound for Normandy, each carrying a barrage balloon as protection against low-flying strafing planes.

viding interlocking fire on beaches from Denmark to Spain. Rundstedt, aware that he could never hope to arm so extensive a coast, concentrated on the Pas-de-Calais, the most likely invasion area because it was the nearest to England, as well as to the Rhine and the Ruhr, and because it was the site of most of the V-weapon launching devices. Having, from his study of the Salerno invasion, become convinced of the futility of static shore defenses against naval gunfire, Rundstedt organized mobile divisions in the hinterland which were to be rushed to the invasion area to contain the invaders within the beachhead.

Rundstedt's second-in-command, Marshal Rommel, was, for his part, convinced that Allied air power would hold the German mobile divisions at bay, never letting them reach the invasion area. He believed that, unless the invaders were hurled back into the sea within 24

hours, Germany faced defeat. Rommel therefore grimly concentrated on beach defenses, although he was sent only a small percentage of the mines that he believed he needed. Studying the developing pattern of Allied bombing, minesweeping, and port activities, he concluded that the Allies might be preparing for an invasion, not at the Pas-de-Calais, but farther west. Hence he began to concentrate on the Normandy beaches.

While the Allied air forces had been supporting the Mediterranean operations, the *Luftwaffe* had been built up. In 1944 therefore the Allies resumed sustained air raids on Germany, this time stressing attacks on planes, aircraft factories, storage parks, and repair depots. In the week of February 19–25, 3,300 heavy bombers out of England and some 500 out of Italy burned out aircraft factories as far south as Augsburg and Regensburg, and shot down about 600 German planes. This was achieved at a cost of 226 bombers, 28 fighters, and 2,600 men. When the campaign ended in mid-April, the Allied air forces had gained a 30-to-1 superiority over the *Luftwaffe*. There would be no enemy air interference with Operation OVERLORD.

The Allied air forces now shifted to sealing off the beachhead and succeeded to a far greater degree than ever before. The bombers began by smashing railroad marshaling yards; they then hit the bridges, knocking out all those spanning the Seine between Paris and the Channel. Next they bombed and strafed the trains, strewing the tracks with wreckage, and then blew up the tracks. By this time the Germans had no real substitute for trains, since they had few trucks left and little gasoline to operate them. Those trucks that were available they dared to move only at night. For the most part, the inventors of the blitzkrieg moved now by bicycle or on foot.

Meanwhile, the invasion troops were assembling in ports and along the coast of southern England. The Americans, finally numbering 1,600,000, had spread out from their first base at Londonderry to occupy western Britain. Now most of them, like their British brothers in the eastern portion, were heading south, marching along the country roads by day, moving by truck and tank at night. The principal exception to this movement was an encampment in the Dover area. Here forces, said to be General Patton's 1st U.S. Army Group, were apparently making vigorous preparations to invade France by way of the Pas-de-Calais. To the occasional German observer who managed to fly that far, it was an impressive sight. Actually, it was no American army group but a British hoax, involving dummy landing craft, dummy tanks, and mostly empty tents. This monumental fake served its purpose well, keeping the whole German Fifteenth Army frozen on the opposite shore for six weeks after D-day.

From Milford Haven in Wales around to Felixstowe on the North Sea, the British harbors filled with ships, more than 900 of which were bound for the beaches that were to be invaded by the Americans; there were nearly twice as many for the British beaches. They were to move by intricate patterns of departure, time, course, and speed to Area Zebra, the big rendezvous area south of Portsmouth. From Area Zebra they would cross over in darkness to Normandy. On May 28 Admiral Ramsay signaled from his headquarters in southern England: "Carry out Operation NEPTUNE," whereupon crews were confined to their ships, and troops, already behind barbed wire in long marshaling camps, prepared to embark.

By Saturday, June 3, the embarkation of troops was complete, the fire-support ships had put to sea from Scapa Flow, Belfast, and the River Clyde, and minesweepers were in the Channel clearing a passage for convoys, which were forming off the ports. That evening General Eisenhower met with his top commanders in Admiral Ramsay's headquarters, a country mansion near Portsmouth, to hear the latest weather forecasts. They were most discouraging. At the next meeting, held at 0400 on June 4, the meteorologists predicted impossible weather for the 5th—a ceiling too low for air support, and heavy seas that could swamp landing craft. The Supreme Commander had no choice but to postpone the invasion for 24 hours. Ships were recalled from the sea. The whole far-flung operation, so ponderously put in motion, was temporarily reversed.

When the commanders met on the evening of June 4, the weather was foul outside, but the staff meteorologist predicted clearing weather for the 6th. Eisenhower thereupon set the invasion forces again in motion, but deferred his final decision until he received another report early the next morning. Learning that the clearing weather would last until the afternoon of the 6th, at 0415 he gave the irrevocable order: "O.K. We'll go."

The foul weather that had so worried the Allied leaders completely deceived the Germans, who had no advance information of its clearing. Marshal Rommel felt secure enough to head for home in Germany in order to join his family in celebrating his wife's birthday, which happened to be June 6. Most of the German coastal radar stations had been bombed from the air or were being jammed. The Allied paratroops that were dropped behind Utah and Sword beaches were assessed as diversionary operations to draw attention away from the Pas-de-Calais. Although the Allied fire-support ships were off the French coast at 0200, more than an hour passed before they were picked up by German search radar. Orders were then passed and batteries were manned. For most of the defenders, however, the first convincing evidence that an invasion was impending came when dawn revealed the vast armada lying off the Normandy beaches.

Of the five assaults, that on Utah Beach on the Contentin peninsula was the easiest. Here the shore was lightly armed, and the defenders were green reservists and unwilling foreign conscripts; moreover, most of the infantry had been drawn into the interior to engage the American paratroops. By 1800 on D-day, more than 21,000 troops and 1,700 vehicles were ashore with fewer than 200 casualties, but off this beach several vessels, including two destroyers, were sunk by mines. At the other end of the line, the British had little difficulty capturing Gold, Juno, and Sword beaches. The defenses here were stronger than at Utah Beach, but the enemy troops were no better, and the delays necessary to let the rising tide cover offshore reefs permitted a thorough naval bombardment of more than two hours' duration.

The difficult landing was at Omaha Beach. Here abandoned masonry villas had been turned into fortresses. The bluffs rising behind them were covered top to bottom with machine guns and casemated artillery. Manning these defenses were crack German troops who had not been distracted by any paratroop landings in their rear. Here the desired tidal conditions came so soon after dawn that the fire-support ships—the old battleships *Arkansas* and *Texas*, 2 British and 2 French cruisers, and 12 destroyers—achieved only 35 minutes of preliminary bombardment. Because of cloud cover, the

480 bombers that swept over the landing completely missed the beach, scattering their bombs among cattle and crops as far as three miles inland.

The amphibious tanks that led the landing craft to the beach nearly all sank in the choppy seas or were knocked out by artillery. Many of the LCVPs were badly shot up before they dropped their ramps. The troops, under intense fire, had to wade 75 yards to the beach and then work their way through the maze of antiboat obstacles, many of them mined and all interlaced with barbed wire. Most of the wounded were drowned by the incoming tide. The survivors at last reached the uncertain protection of a sea wall, behind which they huddled. Following them onto the beach underwater demolition teams, taking fearful losses,

The Normandy invasion, June 6, 1944.

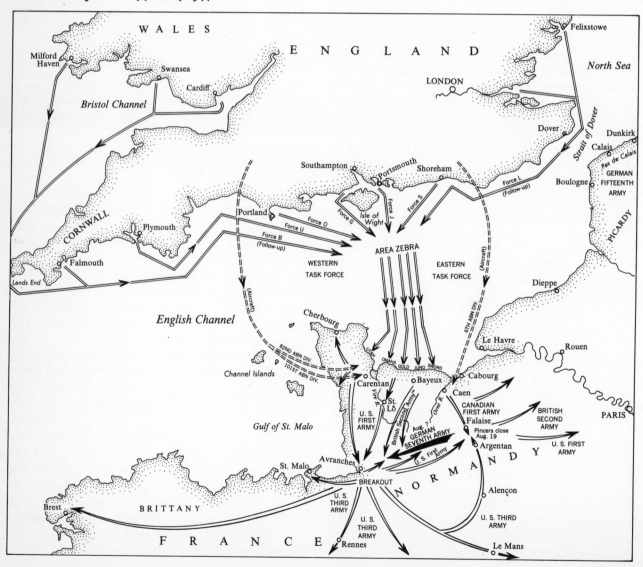

Landing at Omaha Beach on D-day, June 6, 1944.

blasted channels through the obstacles so that landing craft could be brought nearer to the shore on the rising tide.

So many company officers had been killed or wounded in the dash from the landing craft that the men at the sea wall lacked guidance as to what they should do next. When, finally, army engineers blasted gaps in the barbed wire behind the wall, the men began to set up machine gun positions and, under the leadership of the few surviving officers, to crawl up onto the sand flats. What they most seriously lacked were tanks and artillery; the beaching craft and amphibious trucks bringing these to shore had been sunk or disabled by the rough seas and enemy fire.

Rear Admiral C. F. Bryant, Commander Bombardment Group, perceiving the invaders' critical need of fire support, called his ships by voice radio: "Get on them, men! Get on them! They are raising hell with the men on the beach, and we can't have any more of that! We must stop it!" Promptly the battleships and cruisers, using air spot by Britain-based Spitfires, put a ring of fire around Omaha Beach that prevented enemy reinforcement, and concentrated on the strong points that guarded the ravines leading from the beach. The destroyers, lacking spotter contacts, moved to within 1,000 yards of the beach, sometimes scraping bottom, and taking visual aim, turned the gun-studded bluffs into a shooting gallery. So effective and steady was this fire support that the invaders crossed the beach in increasing numbers and mounted the ravines. By nightfall 34,000 American troops were ashore and had established a beachhead more than a mile deep. The cost had been high: 2,000 casualties.

Pending the capture of ports, the Allies made use of artificial harbors which they called mulberries and gooseberries. The mulberries were composed of concrete caissons towed across from England and sunk off the Normandy coast to form a breakwater enclosing pontoon piers. The gooseberries, tired old merchant ships, were sunk nearer shore to provide sheltered harbors for small craft. By June 16, Mulberry A, off Omaha Beach, was receiving ships. Three days later, the worst storm in half a century hit the English Channel and battered Mulberry A to pieces. Mulberry B, off Gold Beach, held fast because it was protected by reefs and by the cape north of Le Havre. Thereafter, unloading at Omaha

The Arkansas *delivering gunfire support at Omaha Beach.*

was done directly from LSTs to the beach, by which means 15,000 tons of supplies and 15,000 troops were being landed there daily at the end of June.

The storm emphasized the need to capture the port of Cherbourg, the chief goal of that part of Lieutenant General Omar Bradley's U.S. First Army that had landed at Utah Beach. By June 18 a drive across to the Gulf of St.-Malo had sealed off the Contentin peninsula. By the 24th the First Army had surrounded 40,000 Germans at Cherbourg and was calling on the Navy to knock out powerful batteries protecting the harbor and flanking the city. On June 25 an Anglo-American bombardment force, commanded by Rear Admiral Morton L. Deyo USN, crossed the Channel to comply. While the Army attacked Cherbourg from the landward side, the battleships *Nevada, Texas,* and *Arkansas,* 4 cruisers, and 11 destroyers pounded the enemy batteries from the sea, directing their fire with the help of shore-based fire-control parties and spotter aircraft. Most of the batteries, up to 280-mm (11-inch) caliber, were heavily casemated, and some were in steel turrets. This was formidable ordnance for ships to stand up against. Despite rapid maneuvering and the use of smoke, three of Deyo's destroyers were hit, and a 280-mm shell wrecked the bridge of the *Texas.* The next day, however, the Germans at Cherbourg surrendered. They had done a spectacular job of ruining the harbor, but the experienced Allied salvage engineers had it ready to receive limited cargo within two weeks.

On the Fourth of July the millionth Allied soldier landed in France. The time was approaching for the long-planned breakthrough on the Allied right flank. On the left flank, on July 9, Montgomery's British troops entered Caen, after it had been shattered by 2,500 tons of aerial bombs. As anticipated, this advance attracted the greater part of the German Seventh Army, for an Allied drive from Caen would cut off the Seventh from the Fifteenth Army, which was still at the Pas-de-Calais waiting to repulse Patton's phantom army group situated at Dover. But Patton had abandoned his ghostly duties and was in France with Bradley, whose First Army, taking advantage of the German massing before Caen, broke through light enemy defenses to Avranches. Here, on August 1, Patton took command of the U.S. Third Army, which had split off from the overgrown First, and turned Bradley's breakthrough into a breakout. Elements of the new Third Army, fanning out, captured the ports of Brittany and, surging east and north, met the British out of Caen. They thereby trapped 50,000 troops of the German Seventh Army, which Hitler had ordered westward in an attempt to cut Patton's supply line.

On September 1, General Eisenhower assumed command of the Allied ground forces, which were now in full pursuit of fleeing German armies. On the right flank was Bradley's 12th Army Group (U.S. First and Third armies). Moving along the Channel and North Sea coasts was Montgomery's 21st Army Group (Canadian First and British Second armies). Bradley's forces had liberated Paris. Montgomery's forces were about to capture the missile-launching sites in the Pas-de-Calais—and none too soon, for, since mid-June, 2,340 V-1s had reached London, and the first of the more deadly V-2s was about to be launched.

SOUTHERN FRANCE

General Morgan, in his original OVERLORD plan, had recommended an invasion of France's Mediterranean coast, to be carried out simultaneously with the assault on Normandy. The southern assault would serve as a diversion and it would open Marseille as an additional port of supply for the Allied armies. Moreover, troops advancing up the Rhone Valley could take over the

right flank of the drive into Germany and at the same time isolate Germans in southwestern France.

The Combined Chiefs of Staff at first adopted Morgan's recommendation for a southern invasion, which was given the code name ANVIL. As D-day approached, however, it became increasingly obvious that there would not be enough landing and beaching craft for simultaneous landings in southern and northwestern France. Operation ANVIL would have to be carried out with the craft that had been used in NEPTUNE. That would mean a lapse of several weeks between assaults. Eisenhower nevertheless insisted upon the Mediterranean invasion in order to have the use of a major port for supply and reinforcement.

Almost from the beginning, Churchill and some of the

Omaha Beach two days after D-day.

British generals had opposed Operation Anvil, because it would entail the withdrawal of troops from the Italian campaign for the purpose of invading southern France. They favored exploiting the momentum achieved in Italy for a landing across the Adriatic at Trieste, followed by a drive via the Ljubljana Gap to the Danube River. Although Churchill presented his plan as a military concept, his aim was evidently political: to beat the Russians into Austria and Hungary. Eisenhower strongly opposed the Ljubljana operation as militarily unsound, a view in which he was supported by Roosevelt. After many protests, Churchill finally backed down. He insisted, however, upon changing the code name of the southern assault to Operation Dragoon—because he felt he had been dragooned into consenting to it.

During the high level debate, planning for Dragoon had gone on as though there were no question of its being mounted. Final preparations and rehearsals were carried out at Naples and at nearby beaches. Admiral Hewitt, working closely with his subordinates and his army associates and making use of the accumulated amphibious experience of the war, organized a flawless assault. It was scheduled for France's Côte d'Azur between Cannes and Toulon on the morning of August 15, 1944. At long last Hewitt was to have the daylight landing for which he had been arguing since before his invasion of North Africa.

As at Normandy, the assault area was sealed off in advance by Allied aircraft, which, in the three months preceding D-day, pounded enemy airfields and strong points in the area with 12,000 tons of bombs. Before dawn on August 15, paratroops landed behind the beachhead and commandos landed on its flanks to set up roadblocks against enemy reinforcement. At dawn, Hewitt's Western Naval Task Force appeared off the coast. Its main divisions were the attack groups Alpha, Delta, and Camel and an aircraft carrier group which included seven British and two American escort carriers. Planes from these carriers would spot for the fire-support vessels and disrupt enemy communications and troop concentrations. Groups Alpha, Delta, and Camel were to land troops on three sets of similarly designated beaches, and the individual beaches in each set were designated by colors, as Delta Red, Delta Green, and so on.

The aerial bombing of the beach defenses was done by 1,300 bombers from Italy, Sardinia, and Corsica, which attacked the shore positions almost continuously from 0550 to 0730. The ships, which had been firing at the shore between bomber flights, then gave the beaches a thunderous half-hour prelanding bombardment. As the

U.S. Coast Guard rushes drums of gasoline ashore past sunken vessels at Toulon to keep recently landed French troops moving.

landing craft headed shoreward, the battleships and cruisers checked fire, and the destroyers moved in to give the area behind the beaches a final pounding. Moving in ahead of the first wave of landing craft, LCIs fired rockets into the beach to detonate land mines. All along the 30-mile invasion front, the invading troops stepped ashore against little more than token resistance.

The bombing and bombardment had killed or wounded many of the defenders and had knocked out most of their guns. In any case, the beaches had generally been lightly defended, because the most experienced troops had been summoned north in an attempt to hold back the Allied armies from Normandy. Many of the remaining soldiers were discouraged Czech conscripts and Polish prisoners of war in German uniform. Nevertheless, at one beach, Camel Red in the Gulf of Fréjus, a little band of determined resisters kept up a lively fire. Hewitt, forewarned of this situation by intelligence, had deferred the landing here until 1400, but the minesweepers had not by that time been able, in the face of the persistent fire, to clear the approach channel. Hence the landing was shifted to Camel Green, over which supplies were flowing to forces that had gone ashore that morning. That the shift caused little confusion attests to the thoroughness with which the assault had been planned.

The 5,000 British and American paratroops that had been dropped behind the beaches now marched eastward along the coast and, with naval support, liberated both Cannes and Nice before the end of August. Marching westward, also with naval support, were two French divisions. They had come ashore not with, but following, the Americans because Hewitt refused to complicate the assault with language problems. The French troops, with ample help from the air and from naval guns, attacked German positions at Toulon and Marseille. The Navy's principal contribution was to knock out the powerful harbor batteries, including one of 340 mm at Toulon. At last, on August 28, the German garrisons in both cities surrendered.

The capture of these ports was ahead of schedule and fortunately so, for immense quantities of supplies were needed for the two armies that had invaded France by way of the Dragoon beaches. These armies, the U.S. Seventh Army of Lieutenant General Alexander Patch and the newly formed French First Army of General of the Army Jean de Lattre de Tassigny, were hotly pursuing the Germans up the Rhone Valley. They constituted the 6th Army Group, which was commanded by Lieutenant General Jacob L. Devers.

On September 11, near Dijon, Patch's Seventh Army made contact with elements of Patton's Third Army from

The invasion of southern France, August 15, 1944.

Normandy, and thus Operation Dragoon merged with Operation Overlord. Devers' 6th Army Group now wheeled right and, with Bradley's 12th Army Group and Montgomery's 21st Army Group, drew up in a line stretching from Switzerland to the North Sea on the frontiers of Germany and German-occupied Holland.

THE GERMAN DEFEAT

The speed with which the Allies advanced through France and Belgium was made possible mainly by their nearly absolute mastery of the air. Poor winter flying weather, however, brought all their advances to a standstill. It also permitted Rundstedt to surprise Bradley with a brief counterattack in the Ardennes, an operation popularly known as the "Battle of the Bulge."

Early in 1945 the Russians, Americans, British, and French resumed their offensives, advancing on Germany from east, south, and west. In March, Eisenhower's armies reached the barrier of the Rhine. Here the U.S. Navy made its last direct contribution to the European war. LCVPs and LCMs, furnished by the Navy and manned by Navy crews, ferried Bradley's armies over the river in most of their initial crossings. The Allies were thus enabled to capture the Ruhr industrial areas by double envelopment, as well as 325,000 prisoners of war, including 30 generals.

On April 28, Mussolini, fleeing toward Switzerland,

was captured and killed by anti-Fascists, who displayed his body in Milan hung by the heels. Two days later Hitler, having named Dönitz his successor, took poison in a bunker under his chancellery as the Russian army entered Berlin.

Individual German armies were now surrendering. On May 5, representatives of Dönitz arrived at Eisenhower's Reims headquarters seeking terms for a general surrender. Dönitz, after learning that nothing short of unconditional surrender would be accepted, capitulated by wire. His senior representative, Field Marshal Alfred Jodl, signed the surrender instrument early on May 7, 1945. Hostilities ceased in Europe at midnight on May 8.

THE ATTACK ON PEARL HARBOR

For sheer audacity the Japanese raid on Pearl Harbor, December 7, 1941, is almost without parallel in naval warfare. It required the conducting of a carrier force undetected across 3,500 miles of open sea to within striking range of America's most powerful Pacific base. For it to succeed, the Americans had to re-

Japanese air raids on Pearl Harbor, December 7, 1941.

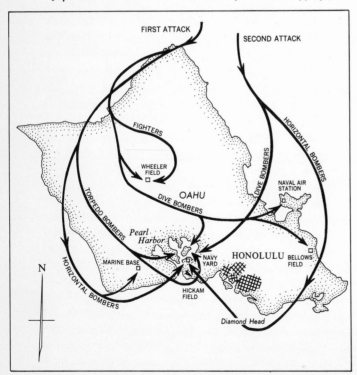

main uninformed and unprepared, their fleet in the harbor and their planes on the ground, until the attack was upon them. Incredibly enough, that is exactly what happened.

Yet the attack came not without warning. Through radio intercepts and cryptanalysis American leaders knew that Japan planned to break off diplomatic relations with the United States on December 7. In two previous wars Japan had established a pattern of breaking off relations and then attacking the enemy's fleet without a declaration of war. An hour before the attack, an American destroyer reported and sank a midget submarine off the entrance to Pearl Harbor. At the opposite end of the island of Oahu, a pair of army radar operators began plotting a large flight of planes coming in from the north.

Why did neither Washington nor Pearl Harbor anticipate a raid on the Pacific fleet? Chiefly because the attention of American leaders was focused on another Japanese advance, which was in fact the main thrust. Aircraft had reported a powerful expeditionary force heading south from Japan and rounding the southern point of Indochina as it headed for the Malay peninsula.

Such a southward move had been anticipated for months. Japan had depended heavily on the United States for the oil needed to carry on her undeclared war with China. When the American government began restricting sales of oil to Japan, the Japanese made plans to assure themselves of an alternate supply in the Netherlands East Indies. In July 1941, they occupied southern Indochina, whence their planes could threaten the Philippines, Singapore, and Borneo. The United States, Britain, and the Netherlands East Indies countered by freezing Japanese assets, making it difficult for Japan to buy oil or other needed materials anywhere. Hence Washington anticipated not only that the Japanese would advance into the East Indies, but that they might also attempt to seize Singapore and the Philippines to protect their communications. American strategists discounted the possibility that Japan would also take the risk of attacking Pearl Harbor.

The Japanese Naval General Staff held exactly the same view. When Admiral Isoroku Yamamoto, Commander in Chief of Japan's Combined Fleet, recommended an attack on Pearl Harbor, they vigorously opposed weakening the impending southern thrust to carry out so hazardous an operation. Yamamoto insisted that the elimination of the U.S. Pacific Fleet was essential to the success of the southern advance. He threatened to resign unless his plan were adopted. At last, in early November 1941, the General Staff gave in. The Pearl Harbor Striking Force, comprising the carriers *Akagi,*

The Arizona *afire at Pearl Harbor.*

Kaga, Hiryu, Soryu, Shokaku, and *Zuikaku,* escorted by the battleships *Hiei* and *Kirishima,* three cruisers, and nine destroyers, moved to a secret base in the Kurile Islands to await further orders.

By late November, the Japanese leaders had concluded that negotiations with the United States toward unfreezing Japanese assets were futile. They saw no acceptable alternatives to broadening the war. The time seemed propitious, for the Germans were at the gates of Moscow and Alexandria and the U.S. Navy was engaged in an undeclared war in the Atlantic. On December 1 an imperial conference decided on war, whereupon Yamamoto radioed the Striking Force: "Climb Mount Niitaka," meaning "Proceed with the attack."

On December 7, an hour after midnight, Vice Admiral Chuichi Nagumo, who commanded the Striking Force, received from Tokyo an intelligence report that no carriers were at Pearl Harbor. This was a disappointment, but there were in the harbor eight battleships, which now became the primary targets. To forestall counterattack, the Japanese would also strike American aircraft and airfields. Just before dawn, Nagumo's carriers reached the launching point, 200 miles north of

Pearl Harbor, and turned into the wind. At 0600 the first wave of 183 planes took off. After a tense wait of nearly two hours, flagship *Akagi* picked up from the flight leader the code word: "*Tora . . . tora . . . tora.*" Remarkably enough, Yamamoto's flagship off Japan also picked it up. The word meant "Surprise achieved." In this moment of vindication, Yamamoto showed no sign of emotion. Nagumo's force had launched a second wave, of 170 planes, at 0715. By 1300 all surviving aircraft were back on their carriers; only 29 were missing. Half an hour later, the Striking Force set a retirement course NNW. There was no counterattack.

When the smoke lifted over Oahu, more than 2,400 Americans, most of them naval personnel, were dead or dying, and 1,300 more were wounded. Some 230 aircraft had been destroyed or heavily damaged, and in Pearl Harbor 18 ships had been sunk. "Battleship Row" was a shambles: the *Arizona* was a total loss; the *Oklahoma* had capsized; the *California* and *West Virginia* were sunk at their moorings; and the *Nevada,* the *Maryland,* the *Tennessee,* and the *Pennsylvania* were more or less heavily damaged. But the repair facilities, which later returned most of the damaged ships to serv-

Magazine of the Shaw *explodes.*

ice, were practically untouched, and the attacking planes had missed the tank farm, where 4,500,000 barrels of fuel oil had been accumulated. Loss of this oil would have hindered American naval operations in the Pacific far more than the damage done to the fleet.

Yamamoto had, by his attack, swept away widespread pacifism in the United States and united the nation in a relentless determination to push the war to final victory, whatever the odds. He had, moreover, removed from around the neck of American naval policy the albatross of "line" doctrine. With the U.S. battle line disabled, the fleet carriers—*Saratoga, Lexington, Enterprise, Yorktown, Wasp,* and *Hornet*—of necessity became

capital ships, the queens of the fleet, and at long last acquired permanent escorts of cruisers and destroyers. As new battleships began to reach the Pacific in the latter part of 1942, they were integrated into the carrier escorts.

The old battleships that had been sunk and damaged at Pearl Harbor were far too slow for such service. All but the *Arizona* and the *Oklahoma* were raised, repaired, and renovated by 1944, when they became useful for shore bombardment in support of amphibious operations. Meanwhile, their temporary loss freed thousands of trained seamen, of which there was a severe shortage, for use in carrier, escorting, and amphibious forces.

THE JAPANESE
SOUTHERN OFFENSIVE

American prewar estimates that Japan was capable of sustaining no more than one thrust at a time were quickly belied. Even before the attack on the U.S. Pacific Fleet, Japanese troops had been landing on the Malay peninsula, prepared to advance overland 650 miles to Singapore, all of whose big guns pointed seaward. Following the Pearl Harbor attack, Japanese planes raided Wake, Guam, Hong Kong, Singapore, and the Philippine islands of Luzon and Mindanao. Japanese troops based on Indochina invaded the Kingdom of Thailand.

Admiral Thomas C. Hart, at Manila, promptly sent the combat surface ships of his tiny U.S. Asiatic Fleet south, where they joined British, Dutch, and Australian ships to form a defense force called ABDA. By far the most powerful Allied vessels in the East Indies area were H.M. battleship *Prince of Wales* and H.M. battle cruiser *Repulse*, which were at Singapore. These ships Admiral Sir Tom Phillips took north with an escort of four destroyers, in an attempt to disrupt Japanese landing operations. The Royal Air Force, hard pressed to support the ground troops, could provide no cover at sea. Phillips' force arrived too late to catch the enemy transports and was attacked on December 10 by aircraft out of Indochina. Both the *Prince of Wales* and the *Repulse*, hit by bombs and torpedoes, rolled over and sank, thus proving to the skeptics that powerful ships maneuvering at sea were not immune to destruction from the air.

That same day the Japanese bombed the Cavite Navy Yard, on Manila Bay, into uselessness and made the first of a series of landings in the Philippines. After the main Japanese invasion at Lingayen Gulf on December 17, General Douglas MacArthur declared Manila an open city to save it from further bombings and began moving his Filipino-American army north around Manila Bay to the peninsula of Bataan. On December 18, the Japanese landed at Hong Kong, which fell on Christmas Day.

The defenders of Malaya resisted stubbornly but could not hold back the Japanese tide, which in 54 days reached the tip of the peninsula. By February 1, 1942, the last of the British and Australians had crossed over to Singapore Island and had blown up the causeway connecting it to the mainland. A week later, under a heavy barrage, Japanese troops began landing on the island. On February 15 Singapore surrendered.

From the Japanese point of view, all of these operations were peripheral, serving to cover the flanks of the main drive, which began in mid-December 1941 with a landing near Brunei on the island of Borneo. By early January, Japanese forces were leapfrogging southward along the east and west coasts of Borneo and were also advancing by way of the Molucca Sea. At each landing point they established an airfield, which was relatively secure from overland attack because of generally primitive interior communications. Then, under cover of land- or carrier-based aircraft, they moved on to their next invasion.

In mid-February, Admiral Nagumo's carrier Striking Force arrived in the East Indies. On the 19th, it joined land-based planes from Celebes in a raid on Darwin, Australia's chief northern port, shattering docks and warehouses and sinking a dozen vessels. This attack, together with a Japanese invasion of Timor the following day, effectively isolated Java, toward which the Japanese pincers were advancing.

The U.S. high command now conceded that the Netherlands East Indies and the Philippines were lost. American troops continued to resist on Bataan, and American ships remained with the ABDA force, not so much in hopes of stopping, or even of appreciably slowing, the Japanese advance as through reluctance to abandon America's friends in the Far East.

Dutch Rear Admiral Karel Doorman, operational commander of the ABDA naval force, simply lacked the power to cope with either of the enemy advances around Borneo—particularly in view of Japanese air supremacy. On February 4, he set out to tackle a convoy reported coming down Makassar Strait. He was, however, attacked by enemy bombers, which knocked out a turret of U.S. heavy cruiser *Houston* and disabled U.S. light cruiser *Marblehead*. Going after a convoy off Sumatra, he was forced back by another air attack. A few nights later, Doorman struck a convoy near the eastern end of Java and disabled a destroyer; but he lost one of his own destroyers, and one of his cruisers was heavily damaged.

Toward the end of February, enemy convoys were approaching Java from northwest and northeast. On the 27th Doorman sortied to contest the advance of the eastern prong, though by then his force had been reduced to two heavy cruisers, three light cruisers, and a few destroyers. The ensuing Battle of the Java Sea completed the destruction of the ABDA force.

At first contact in the late afternoon the Japanese escort vessels, enjoying the advantage of air scouting, sank two destroyers and put the British heavy cruiser *Exeter* out of action. Doorman thereupon broke off contact and circled, trying to get at the enemy transports, but just at

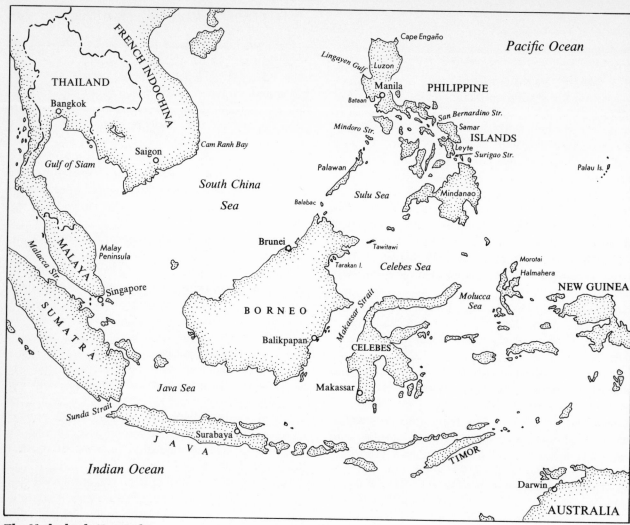

The Netherlands East Indies.

dusk he again met and exchanged fire with the escorts. The four American destroyers, their torpedoes fruitlessly expended, now retired to Surabaya and ultimately escaped to Australia. The remainder of the force, after skirting the Java north coast and losing a destroyer to a newly laid Dutch minefield, again headed north and was spotted by enemy planes dropping flares. When, toward midnight, Doorman once more made contact with the Japanese escort vessels, his force had been diminished to the Dutch light cruisers *De Ruyter* and *Java*, the American *Houston*, and the Australian light cruiser *Perth*. Both Dutch cruisers were caught by a spread of torpedoes, and sank. As the flagship *De Ruyter* was going down, Doorman ordered his two remaining cruisers to retire.

In Sunda Strait the next night, the fleeing *Houston* and *Perth* ran into the western invasion force, which was landing troops, and both were sunk. The following day the damaged *Exeter* and two escorting destroyers, at-

tempting to escape the same way, were intercepted and sent down by Japanese ships and aircraft. Most of the ships based on Java's south coast managed to save themselves, but the Nagumo force, patrolling in that area to intercept such evacuators, sank several vessels, including two American destroyers.

Troops from the Japanese landings, east and west, rapidly converged, forcing Java into unconditional surrender on March 9. By the end of the month the entire Netherlands Indies was in enemy hands. The Japanese had now attained all of their objectives in the south, which they called their Southern Resources Area. The rich oil wells of Java, Borneo, and Sumatra would provide them with an inexhaustible supply of fuel. They had obtained, moreover, an ample source of rice, tin, rubber, and quinine.

Japanese military forces, meanwhile, had advanced from Thailand through Burma to the port of Rangoon, which fell the day before Java surrendered. To protect sea communications to Rangoon, the Japanese then occupied the Andaman Islands. The Nagumo force sortied for a strike at Ceylon, the base for Admiral Sir James Somerville's British Eastern Fleet, which included five battleships and three carriers. Somerville, warned of the Japanese approach, had taken his fleet to sea when Nagumo raided Colombo, on Ceylon's west coast, on April 5 and Trincomalee, on the east coast, four days later. But Nagumo's aircraft located elements of the British fleet and sank two destroyers, two cruisers, and the carrier *Hermes*. After these raids, Somerville withdrew the remnant of his fleet to East Africa, and Nagumo returned triumphantly to Japan.

Two days after the fall of Java, General MacArthur, at the request of the Australian government and on the express orders of President Roosevelt, slipped away from his base on the fortified island of Corregidor, off Bataan. He proceeded by PT boat to the southern Philippines, and from there flew to command the defense of Australia, promising, "I shall return." In April the 64,000 Filipinos and 12,000 Americans on Bataan, decimated by disease, starvation, and unremitting attack, at last surrendered to the Japanese. They then began the infamous "Death March" to prison camp, a march in which they suffered every sort of brutality and atrocity. In early May, Major General Jonathan Wainwright, MacArthur's successor, was obliged to surrender Corregidor, and with it the rest of the Philippines.

THE JAPANESE DEFENSE PERIMETER

While the Japanese were advancing south and securing their right flank in Burma, Malaya, and the Indian Ocean, they were also establishing a defense perimeter of Pacific Ocean bases to cover their left flank. Japan, at the end of World War I, had been awarded a mandate over the former German Pacific islands north of the equator—the Carolines (including Truk, the so-called "Japanese Pearl Harbor"), the Marshalls, and all the Marianas except Guam, which the United States had acquired in 1899. Some time before the outbreak of the Pacific phase of World War II, Japan had begun to establish airfields and naval bases among the mandated islands. After the declaration of war, she pushed vigorously to close the gaps in her island perimeter and to clear out enemy pockets within it.

On December 9, 1941, Japanese from the Marshalls occupied the atoll of Makin in the adjacent British Gilbert Islands. On the 10th, defenseless Guam surrendered to 5,000 invaders after 25 minutes of fighting.

On the 11th, at Wake, the Japanese met their first repulse. Following up three days of air attack, a force of three cruisers and six destroyers, escorting four troop-filled transports, arrived from the Marshalls and opened fire. But the 450 U.S. marines on Wake, effectively manning their five-inch guns and four remaining Wildcat fighter planes, sank two destroyers and damaged most of the rest of the attack force, obliging it to retire.

On the evening of December 22, after Wake had been subjected to a week of intense aerial bombing, a stronger attack force arrived. This force was supported by the carriers *Hiryu* and *Soryu*, which had been detached from the Nagumo force, then returning to Japan from the Pearl Harbor attack. By dawn on the 23rd, despite heavy losses, some 1,500 Japanese were ashore.

At that time a relief expedition was a little more than 400 miles away. Built around the carrier *Saratoga*, which had planes and aviators for Wake, it was commanded by Rear Admiral Frank Jack Fletcher, who was without carrier experience but was the senior officer at hand. Unforeseen delays had kept the expedition from leaving Pearl Harbor until December 16. Then, the only oiler available to accompany the force held it down to less than 13 knots. This speed of advance was slowed to 6 knots on the 21st, when Admiral Fletcher began to refuel his destroyers.

Back at Pearl Harbor, Vice Admiral W. S. Pye, interim commander of the U.S. Pacific Fleet, learned early on the 23rd that the Japanese had landed on Wake, supported, evidently, by a powerful naval force. Pye had no desire to present the permanent fleet commander with more casualties; besides, it was probably too late for the *Saratoga* expedition to do any good. At 0700 he recalled Fletcher's force. Half an hour later Commander Winfield S. Cunningham, in command on Wake, decided to surrender in order to prevent further loss of life. About 120 Americans had been killed; taken prisoner were 470 officers and men of the Navy and Marine Corps and 1,146 civilian workmen.

The Japanese, after their experience at Wake, deferred the establishment of the southern anchor in their Pacific defense perimeter until they could enjoy the services of Nagumo's carriers in this quarter also. Early in January 1942, bombers from Truk began softening up the Australian air base at Rabaul, on New Britain in the Bismarcks. On the 20th four carriers of the Nagumo force arrived and commenced neutralization strikes on troops landed at Rabaul and at Kavieng on nearby New Ireland, quickly overwhelming the small defending garrisons. The Japanese rapidly developed Rabaul into a formidable base, and from here they expanded through the archipelago and into the northern Solomons and the north coast of New Guinea.

With the subsequent conquest of the Netherlands East Indies, the Andaman Islands, and Rangoon, the Japanese completed their perimeter. It ran from Burma, through the Malay Barrier and New Guinea to Rabaul, and thence through the Gilberts, the Marshalls, and Wake. Between Wake and the Kuriles, however, Japan possessed no base or observation post except tiny Marcus Island, and that fact gave Japanese military planners some concern.

The Japanese were aware that American inferiority in the Pacific, caused by commitments to the war in Europe and on the Atlantic, would eventually be overcome by the immense resources and industrial capacity of the United States. Yet they hoped, by means of their fleet and their ring of bases, to keep American strength in the Pacific whittled down by destroying new ships as they arrived. The more optimistic Japanese planners believed that, after 18 months or two years of this sort of attrition, the disheartened people of the United States would oblige Congress to accept a compromise peace that would leave Japan the fruits of her conquest in Asia and to the south.

Such was the minimum objective of the planners, but the rapid Japanese expansion, achieved at twice the estimated speed and with slight losses, led them to channel their strategic momentum into further aggressive moves.

HOLDING THE LINE IN THE PACIFIC

The success of the Japanese raid on Pearl Harbor caused Admiral Husband E. Kimmel, Commander in Chief Pacific Fleet (CINCPAC), to be relieved of his duties. Admiral Pye served as his replacement until the arrival of Admiral Chester W. Nimitz, who was appointed CINCPAC by President Roosevelt on the recommendation of Navy Secretary Frank Knox.

Admiral Nimitz arrived at Pearl Harbor on Christmas Day, and assumed command on the last day of 1941. Though courteous, quiet, and unruffled, Nimitz inspired confidence and left no doubt who was running the show. His immediate objectives were to restore morale, which had reached rock bottom with the failure of the Wake relief expedition; to hold the line against further Japanese expansion in the Pacific; to assure the safety of U.S. communications to Hawaii, Midway, and Australia; and to divert Japanese strength from the East Indies.

Nimitz judged that he could best achieve all these objectives by using the Pacific Fleet offensively. He there-

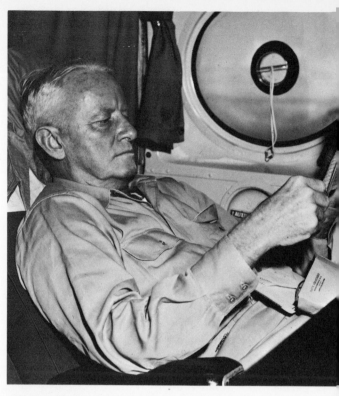

Admiral Chester W. Nimitz.

fore sent his carrier groups on a series of raids against Japanese bases: the Gilbert and Marshall islands, Rabaul, the New Guinea ports of Lae and Salamaua, Wake Island, and Marcus Island. These raids, somewhat exaggerated by the press, electrified the American public and the armed forces. Out of them colorful, salty-tongued Vice Admiral William F. Halsey, Jr., emerged as a national hero.

While the hit-and-run raids did not inflict extensive damage, they caused deep concern among the Japanese high command. Yamamoto could not rid himself of a nagging anxiety that the Americans might attempt a carrier raid on Tokyo, thereby endangering the life of the sacred Emperor, which it was traditionally the first duty of the Japanese armed forces to safeguard.

At this time the Japanese General Staff had drawn up a two-part plan for further operations: (1) the capture of Tulagi, in the eastern Solomons, and Port Moresby, on the south coast of the New Guinea "tail," in order to secure control over the Coral Sea area; and (2) the capture of New Caledonia, Fiji, and Samoa in order to cut communications between the United States and Australia. Yamamoto agreed to the first part, but insisted that the second be deferred until he had completed the mission of the Pearl Harbor raid by destroying the main striking power of the U.S. Pacific Fleet—the carriers. Once that objective was attained, not only would Tokyo be safe, but the Combined Fleet could move freely in the Pacific, landing troops wherever it pleased. Yamamoto's plan was to use all the forces at his command for an early assault on the American base at Midway Atoll, 1,000 miles northwest of Pearl Harbor. The capture of this base would help to close the gap in Japan's defense perimeter. More important, it would also lure out the U.S. Pacific Fleet for destruction.

The Naval General Staff was still holding out against Yamamoto's Midway plan as too risky when, on April 18, 1942, came the raid on Tokyo that all Japanese officers had dreaded. Halsey's *Enterprise* group had escorted into the waters off Japan a group that included the *Hornet*, which had 16 long-range Army B-25s lashed to her flight deck. The volunteer pilots, led by Colonel James H. Doolittle, all managed to get their heavy planes airborne. Most of the planes bombed Tokyo, but individual aircraft dropped incendiary bombs on Nagoya and Kobe. None of the B-25s were lost over Japan. One pilot got away as far as Vladivostok. The rest crash-landed in, or parachuted into, China, some in Japanese-held territory, where they were captured. Three of the captives were executed.

The Japanese armed forces were deeply humiliated. Yamamoto retired to his cabin and brooded all day. All opposition to his scheme now collapsed, and planning went into high gear for an attack on Midway in early June. Meanwhile, the carriers *Shokaku* and *Zuikaku* were detached from the Nagumo force, just returned from the Indian Ocean, and rushed southward to support the assault on Tulagi and Port Moresby, scheduled for early May.

The Americans had by now come into possession of a priceless advantage. They had broken the Japanese naval code and thenceforth, by decrypting enemy radio messages, were able at several crucial periods to estimate the enemy's intentions. In mid-April Nimitz, having learned enough about the impending Port Mores-

Colonel Doolittle's B-25s about to take off from the carrier Hornet.

Admiral Frank Jack Fletcher.

The Battle of the Coral Sea, May 4–8, 1942.

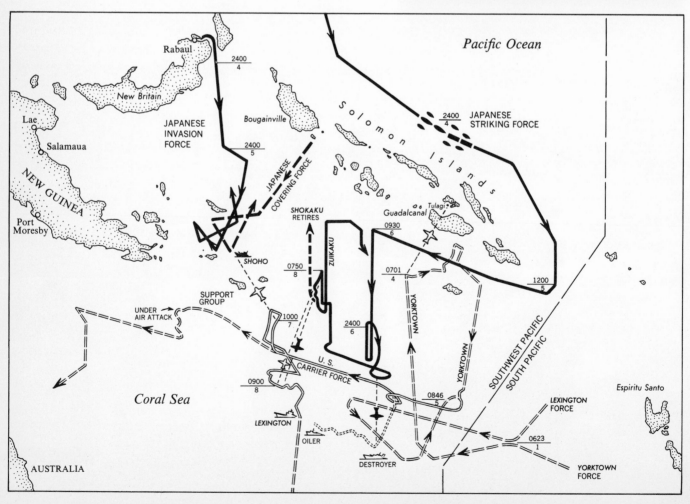

by–Tulagi operations to take action, sent the *Lexington* group to reinforce Admiral Fletcher's *Yorktown* group in the South Pacific. When the *Enterprise* and the *Hornet* reached Pearl Harbor on April 25, after having delivered Doolittle's B-25s for the raid on Tokyo, Nimitz promptly ordered them to the Coral Sea, but with little hope that they would arrive in time to strike at the Japanese.

On May 3, while the *Lexington* and her escorts were refueling south of Guadalcanal, Fletcher sped north with the *Yorktown* group and got in the first blow of the Battle of the Coral Sea with an air raid on a Japanese invasion convoy newly arrived off Tulagi. He then rejoined the *Lexington* and entered the Coral Sea, followed by Vice Admiral Takao Takagi's *Shokaku-Zuikaku* striking force, which had just swung around the southeastern end of the Solomons chain. For two days the Fletcher and Takagi groups maneuvered south of the Solomons without locating each other.

On May 7, Fletcher's flyers sighted elements of the Port Moresby Invasion Force coming down from the north and attacked, sinking the light carrier *Shoho* and obliging the convoy to turn back. Takagi, meanwhile,

was attacking an American oiler and an accompanying destroyer which his search planes had identified as a "United States carrier force." His bombers sank the destroyer and left the oiler helplessly adrift, but this achievement was small compensation for his failure to protect the Invasion Force.

On May 8, the Battle of the Coral Sea reached its climax in the first combat between carrier forces. This was also the first naval action in which the opposing fleets remained out of sight of each other. Search planes from Fletcher's and Takagi's carriers had located their opposing forces before 0900, and shortly afterward both launched attack waves. The antagonists were of about equal strength, but the Japanese had a number of advantages. Takagi's carriers had operated together for five months, their flyers had had more combat experience, and they had superior torpedoes. Moreover, the Japanese ships were partly concealed under a foul-weather front, while Fletcher's were exposed in an area of clear skies and high visibility.

As the American aircraft came in for the attack, the *Zuikaku* disappeared in a rain squall, but dive bombers hit the *Shokaku* with three bombs, setting her afire. Be-

Bombing of the Japanese light carrier Shoho.

The Lexington, *afire and listing, is abandoned by her crew.*

cause the *Shokaku* was incapable of further flight operations, Takagi took as many of her planes aboard the *Zuikaku* as he could, and ordered the damaged carrier to retire.

In the nearly simultaneous attack on the American force, the *Yorktown* was struck by a bomb, but her flight operations remained unimpaired. The *Lexington,* hit by two torpedoes, was also able to land her returning planes, but her fuel lines had been ruptured, and these began to release gasoline fumes into her hold. The vapor at last exploded, setting off uncontrollable fires so that the carrier had to be abandoned. Just at sunset, one of her accompanying destroyers sent the flaming derelict down with torpedoes.

The Japanese had won a tactical victory in that the American losses were somewhat greater than theirs. Nevertheless, the strategic victory was clearly Fletcher's: for the first time a Japanese advance had been stopped.

An even more important, perhaps decisive, factor was the damage done to the Takagi force. The *Shokaku* could not be repaired in time to participate in the impending attack on Midway. Heavy loss of aviators kept the *Zuikaku,* also, out of the Midway operation. Hence the Nagumo force, which was to spearhead the attack, was at a critical moment deprived of a third of its striking power.

THE BATTLE OF MIDWAY

Six months after its air raid on Pearl Harbor, the Nagumo force again set out across the Pacific, this time to attack the American base at Midway. Nagumo was now backed by Yamamoto's entire Combined Fleet —11 battleships, 8 carriers, 23 cruisers, and 65 destroyers. To counter this immense armada, Nimitz had available,

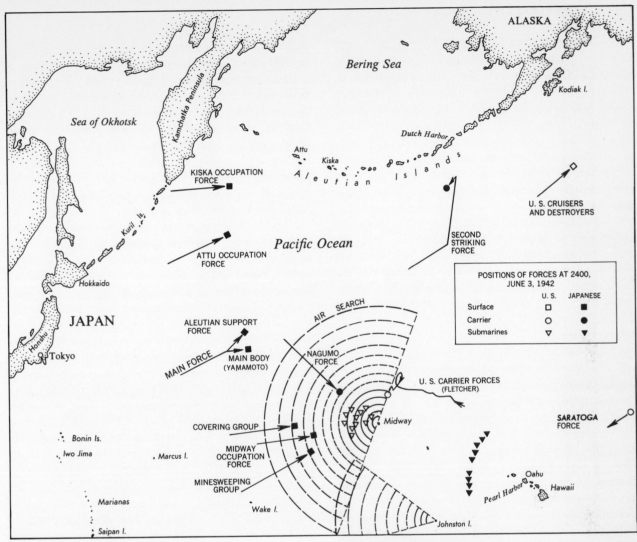

The Battle of Midway—the approach.

Admiral Raymond A. Spruance.

besides a few land-based planes, only 3 carriers, 8 crusiers, and 14 destroyers.°

Yamamoto, because of his immense superiority of strength, should have been irresistible. But, with a view to attaining a Jutland-type entrapment, he split his fleet up into no fewer than 10 groups, including a striking force for diversionary operations against the Aleutians and 3 occupation forces, headed for landings on Midway and on the Aleutian islands of Attu and Kiska. Yamamoto himself was in the so-called Main Body, a powerful battleship group, 300 miles behind Nagumo. He expected that, before the surprised Americans could get their fleet to Midway in response to Nagumo's raid, he would have drawn his forces together in overwhelming strength to sink the American vessels—this time in deep water.

° The *Wasp* was en route to the Pacific from service in the Mediterranean. The *Saratoga*, damaged by a submarine torpedo, was at San Diego, newly repaired but without escorts. Six old battleships at San Francisco were too slow to participate in the fast-moving carrier battle.

The flaw in Yamamoto's scheme was that the Americans were not going to be surprised. Through radio intercepts and code breaking they had acquired an astonishingly detailed knowledge of his curious battle plan. Nimitz summoned his carriers from the South Pacific to Pearl Harbor, had the damaged *Yorktown* hastily patched up, and sent them all to operate to the northeast of Midway. Because Admiral Halsey, ill from months of tension, had to be hospitalized, the tactical command devolved upon Admiral Fletcher in the *Yorktown*. Rear Admiral Raymond A. Spruance commanded Halsey's own *Enterprise-Hornet* task force. To coordinate land-based and carrier-based air operations, Nimitz retained overall control in his own hands. This was made possible by his recent appointment, in addition to his Pacific Fleet command, as Commander in Chief Pacific Ocean Areas. As CINCPOA he had authority over all U.S. and other Allied military and naval forces in the Pacific theater, except those of General MacArthur's Southwest Pacific Area.

On the morning of June 3 the Midway defenders were alerted, first by word of the diversionary attack on Dutch Harbor in the Aleutians, and later by scout-plane reports that a large enemy force, 700 miles away, was approaching Midway from the southwest. Attacks on this force by Midway-based planes that day and the following night achieved no important damage. Admiral Fletcher, correctly estimating that the Japanese force to the southwest was the Midway occupation force, and that the main attack would come out of a region of foul weather to the northwest, drew in his two task forces to within 200 miles of Midway.

Nagumo, approaching under the weather front, launched 108 planes against Midway at dawn on the 4th, retaining an equal number in reserve. While the attack wave was en route it was detected by radar on Midway, and both it and the Japanese carrier force were sighted and reported by American PBY patrol bombers. Fletcher ordered Spruance to advance and attack, while his *Yorktown* was occupied with recovering her search planes. At the same time, every aircraft on Midway took off—bombers and torpedo planes to attack the enemy carriers, fighters to ward off the coming air raid. Most of the American fighter planes, no match for the swift, highly maneuverable Zero fighters, were quickly shot down. The Japanese bombers wrought widespread damage on Midway, but the strike leader, noting, as he turned away, that the runways were still intact and that the antiaircraft fire was not visibly diminished, radioed Nagumo that another attack on Midway was needed.

During the next four hours Nagumo went through a brain-rattling ordeal that impaired his judgment and threw his force into confusion. His carriers were attacked, first by torpedo planes, and then by successive waves of bombers, all from Midway. As he chased off the last of these, inflicting heavy losses without receiving any damage, he had to turn his attention to the U.S. submarine *Nautilus,* which poked up her periscope in the midst of his ships and fired torpedoes, all of which missed. He had, meanwhile, been receiving from one of his search planes vague reports of an enemy surface force to the northwest. At 0830 the search plane finally identified one of the American ships as a carrier.

Nagumo, who had ordered his second wave to change armament from torpedoes to bombs for another attack on Midway, now ordered them to change back to torpedoes for an attack on the enemy fleet. They did so, leaving the bombs lying on deck. At this point, however, Nagumo sighted his returning first wave from Midway and decided to recover them before launching the attack. When recovery was completed, Nagumo turned to course NNE to close the American force. At the same time he notified Yamamoto, whose Main Body was, of course, too far away to lend support. On its new course the Nagumo force was attacked by three successive waves of carrier torpedo planes, all of which failed to score and most of which were destroyed by Zeroes and antiaircraft fire. The Nagumo force had thrown back eight attacks in three hours without receiving a scratch. As the last American torpedo attack ended, Nagumo ordered a counterattack, and his four carriers began to turn into the wind. At this moment of extreme vulnerability, his luck ran out. From the skies came one more attack which, in minutes, changed the whole course of the war.

The *Enterprise* and the *Hornet* had completed launching their attack planes a little after 0800, and the *Yorktown* began launching half an hour later. The torpedo squadrons from all three carriers found the Nagumo force and were nearly wiped out. Nevertheless, they served an important purpose in drawing the Zeros, as well as Japanese attention, down to low altitude. The *Hornet* and *Enterprise* dive bombers headed for the enemy's extended track, basing their calculations on reports made while the Nagumo force was on a southeasterly course. Because of Nagumo's change of course to northeast, they found nothing. The *Hornet* bombers, estimating that they had fallen short, turned southeast toward Midway. The *Enterprise* bombers continued on course for a few minutes and then turned northwest. Catching sight of a straggling destroyer bound northeast, they took the same course and soon sighted the enemy carriers.

By an amazing coincidence, the *Yorktown* dive bombers were just then approaching Nagumo from the southeast. The two squadrons, encountering little antiaircraft or fighter opposition, dived simultaneously on the nearest carriers. The carriers had planes spotted on their flight decks about to take off, and other planes refueling below; discarded bombs were still lying on their hangar decks awaiting return to the magazines. As a result, the bombs that hit the carriers under attack—the *Soryu,* the *Kaga,* and the flagship *Akagi*—set off lethal fires and explosions in all three.

Only the *Hiryu,* which was considerably to the north, escaped. She alone was able to execute her portion of Nagumo's counterattack. The *Hiryu's* dive bombers followed the *Yorktown* bombers back to their carrier and stopped her with three hits. A follow-up wave of torpedo planes made two more hits, causing the *Yorktown* to list so dangerously that in midafternoon her captain ordered "Abandon ship." Fletcher, transferring to a cruiser, turned the tactical command over to Spruance.

The *Yorktown* had launched 10 search planes before coming under attack. At about the time that their carrier was being abandoned, they found the *Hiryu* and re-

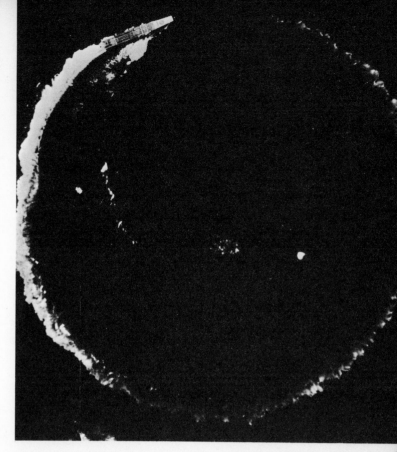

The Soryu *maneuvering to elude U.S. Navy bombers during the Battle of Midway.*

The Yorktown, *helpless and abandoned, after aerial torpedo attack.*

ported her location and course. Shortly afterward, 24 dive bombers took off from the *Enterprise*. These dived on the remaining Japanese carrier at 1700, just as she was about to launch her surviving planes for a dusk attack. Four direct hits set off explosions and ignited fires which soon became uncontrollable. The *Hiryu* sank at 0900 the next morning. By that time the *Soryu*, the *Kaga,* and the *Akagi* had also gone down.

Spruance, after recovering his planes from the attack on the *Hiryu*, withdrew eastward for several hours. He was criticized at that time for being overcautious, but his move proved to have been a wise one, for Yamamoto had ordered a night counterattack. Yamamoto's Main Body was too far away to participate, but he directed most of the escort vessels of the Midway occupation force to join Nagumo's remnant and to seek out the

American ships. At the same time, he ordered four heavy cruisers of the escort to shell Midway.

At 0200 the Japanese attack force had not made contact with Spruance, who had just turned back west. Yamamoto realized that his attack force was now less likely to be the victor of a night battle than the victim of a dawn air attack. With a heavy heart he canceled the Midway operation and ordered a general retirement to the west. The four-cruiser bombardment force, then nearing Midway, reversed course and presently sighted U.S. submarine *Tambor*. In maneuvering to avoid torpedoes, the heavy cruisers *Mogami* and *Mikuma* collided. The damaged vessels were left, with two escorting destroyers, to make what speed they could.

June 5 was a blank day in the Battle of Midway. In midafternoon Spruance, on a westerly pursuit course,

The Battle of Midway, June 4, 1942.

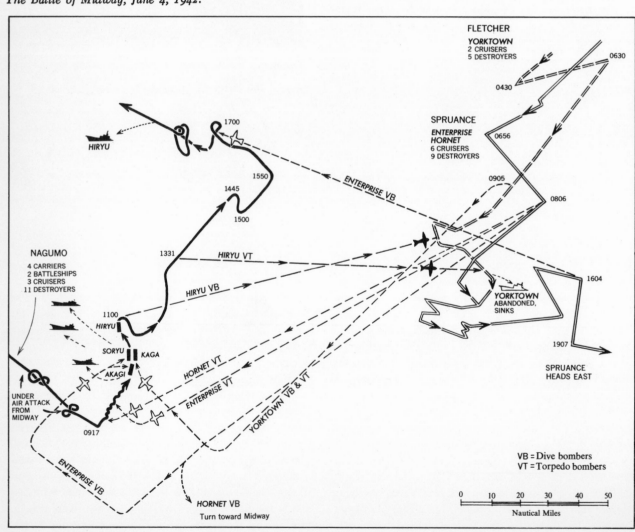

The cruiser Mikuma *sinking.*

launched 58 dive bombers against targets reported to the northwest. The bombers, narrowly missing the Japanese Main Body, unsuccessfully attacked a lone destroyer which Nagumo had detached to learn the fate of the abandoned *Hiryu*. The returning bombers reached their carriers after dark. Because the pilots were not trained for night landings, Spruance boldly ordered the *Enterprise* and the *Hornet* to turn on lights to help them find their flight decks.

During the night Spruance steamed due west. Dawn searches on the 6th discovered the damaged *Mogami* and *Mikuma* to the southwest, trailing oil. Toward these cruisers Spruance now directed his force, launching three successive attacks which sank the *Mikuma*, damaged her accompanying destroyers, and so battered the *Mogami* that she was out of action for a year. At sunset Spruance, his destroyers low in fuel, turned back east-

ward—again in the nick of time, for Yamamoto was once more assembling forces for a night battle.

The Japanese got in the last blow after all. The *Yorktown*, despite her 25-degree list, had not sunk. On June 6, while she was under tow, a submarine fired a spread of torpedoes that sank the destroyer *Hammann* alongside, and so damaged the carrier that she sank the next morning.

The main effect of the Battle of Midway cannot be measured by Japan's loss of four carriers and a heavy cruiser, 322 aircraft, and 3,500 lives, as compared with the United States' loss of a carrier and a destroyer, 150 planes, and 307 lives. The severest blow to Japan's warmaking potential was her loss of 100 first-line pilots—continuing the heavy attrition begun in the raids on Ceylon and in the Battle of the Coral Sea. Loss of pilots was, in fact, one of the chief causes of Japan's ultimate defeat.

Shortage of oil, which had to be brought to Japan from the East Indies through submarine-infested waters, crippled Japanese pilot training programs. The Imperial Army and Navy were obliged to employ aviators increasingly less well prepared to engage their well-trained opponents.

GUADALCANAL

The American victory in the Battle of Midway encouraged the Allies to seize the initiative by invading Guadalcanal in the Solomon Islands, at the southeastern extremity of Japan's newly captured empire. The operation was to be the responsibility of Vice Admiral Robert L. Ghormley, Admiral Nimitz's subordinate in command of the South Pacific Area. The boundary between this area and General MacArthur's Southwest Pacific Area was therefore shifted westward to the 159th meridian, to facilitate Ghormley's task by bringing Guadalcanal within his area of control.

The Allied expeditionary force, advancing through the Coral Sea in a rainstorm, achieved the surprise vital to its success. Under clearing skies on the morning of August 7, 1942, Admiral Fletcher, with the *Saratoga*, *Wasp*, and *Enterprise* groups, separated and took station south of Guadalcanal. The amphibious force, under Rear Admiral Richmond Kelly Turner, passed around the western end of the island and entered the body of water later known as "Ironbottom Sound," because of the many ships sunk there. The landing force, Major General Alexander A. Vandegrift's 1st Marine Division, found little besides construction workers on Guadalcanal, but on Tulagi and adjacent islets to the north they met combat troops who put up a real fight. Nevertheless, by August 8 the marines had attained their objectives, including the capture of an unfinished airstrip on Guadalcanal. Enemy bombers from Rabaul staged a series of raids on the invasion forces, but antiaircraft fire and fighter aircraft from Fletcher's carriers kept American casualties at a minimum. The attacks, however, seriously delayed the unloading of cargo.

The Solomons, the Bismarcks, and southeastern New Guinea.

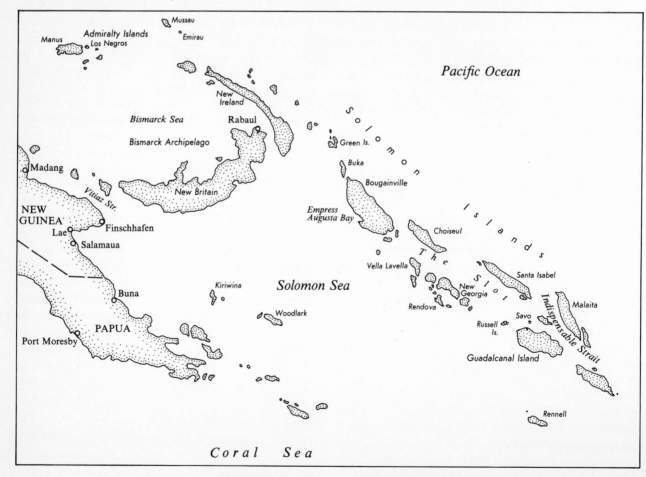

Coming down the passage—later known as "the Slot" —between the major Solomons was a cruiser force under Vice Admiral Mikawa. Because an Australian scout plane had identified the cruisers as seaplane tenders, Turner assumed that they were en route to set up a floating air base in the central Solomons. He was much more alarmed by a message from Admiral Fletcher announcing that, because of heavy loss of fighters and need for refueling, he was withdrawing the carriers from Guadalcanal.

An hour after midnight Mikawa's seven cruisers and single destroyer approached Ironbottom Sound, passing astern of U.S. picket destroyer *Blue*, which detected nothing, either visually or by radar. Mikawa, suspecting trickery, detached his destroyer to watch the *Blue*. With his cruisers he sped around Savo Island, firing shells and torpedoes at two utterly surprised Allied patrol forces as he passed. North of Savo, the Japanese cruisers, which had become separated, encountered and opened fire on U.S. picket destroyer *Ralph Talbot*. With their rejoined destroyer they then hastened back up the Slot. Behind them they left a shambles: two U.S. destroyers and the heavy cruiser *Chicago* damaged, and four heavy cruisers in a sinking condition: U.S.S. *Astoria*, *Vincennes*, and *Quincy*, and the Australian *Canberra*. The Battle of Savo Island, which cost the Allies 1,000 lives, was the severest defeat the U.S. Navy had ever suffered in battle.

Turner, deprived of air cover by Fletcher's departure, had no choice but to withdraw his amphibious force. Sixteen thousand ill-provided marines were left behind. They soon got the airstrip, which they named Henderson Field, in shape to receive planes, the first of which arrived on August 20. Enemy transports were then coming down from Truk with reinforcements. Admiral Ghormley had just ordered Admiral Fletcher's carrier force into the waters southeast of Guadalcanal in order to protect ships bringing supplies and reinforcements to the island. The *Hornet* carrier group had set out from Pearl Harbor for the Coral Sea, and the fast new battleships *Washington* and *South Dakota* were en route from the Atlantic.

When the Japanese learned that there were aircraft on Guadalcanal and that Fletcher's carriers had returned to the area, Vice Admiral Nobutake Kondo brought down the Combined Fleet, which had moved to Truk three weeks before. In the Battle of the Eastern Solomons, on August 24, Japanese carrier aircraft heavily damaged the *Enterprise*, but the American carrier force sank the light carrier *Ryujo* and shot down 90 planes, obliging Kondo to retire. The next day, bombers from Guadalcanal and Espiritu Santo forced the transport group also into retirement.

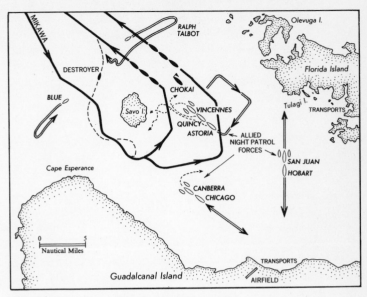

The Battle of Savo Island, August 9, 1942.

The Japanese, realizing that to oust the Americans from Guadalcanal they would first have to recapture the airfield, began pouring troops onto the island. Destroyers and transports brought these troops down the Slot with such nightly regularity that the marines called the enemy ships the "Tokyo Express." To discourage American reinforcement, Japanese submarines patrolled the approaches to Guadalcanal. These submarines, in late August and early September, sank the *Wasp* and the destroyer *O'Brien* and seriously damaged the *Saratoga* and the new battleship *North Carolina*.

By mid-September the Tokyo Express had 6,000 troops on Guadalcanal. These, grossly underestimating the number of Americans present, made a drive for Henderson Field and were bloodily repulsed. There ensued a reinforcement race in which Japanese and Americans desperately stripped garrisons elsewhere to rush more troops to Guadalcanal. In early October, the Japanese undertook a series of night bombardments of Henderson Field to clear the way for a large troop convoy. The first bombardment group was repulsed by Rear Admiral Norman Scott's cruiser-destroyer group in the Battle of Cape Esperance on the night of October 11, but on succeeding nights Japanese battleships and cruisers, supplemented by daytime air raids, churned up the landing strip and destroyed most of the aircraft on the island. The Americans were left little means of opposing the convoy, which, on the 15th, brought in 4,500 additional soldiers. As the Japanese garrison, now raised to 22,000 confidently began a renewed drive on

The carrier Wasp *burning southeast of Guadalcanal.*

the airfield, Admiral Kondo again brought down the Combined Fleet.

Allied leaders in the South Pacific began to doubt that they could retain their foothold in the Solomons. As a means of bolstering morale and providing firmer leadership, Nimitz ordered Halsey to relieve Ghormley. Admiral Halsey, his old vigor restored, assumed command on October 18 and quickly infused his subordinates with his own confidence and aggressiveness. He daringly ordered the *Hornet* and *Enterprise* groups to advance and attack the Combined Fleet in the waters north of Guadalcanal.

Halsey had pushed his policy of calculated risk a bit too far, for in the Battle of the Santa Cruz Islands on October 24, the *Hornet* was sunk and the *Enterprise*

was again heavily damaged. This left not a single operational U.S. carrier in the whole Pacific. The American force, before it was put out of action, had bombed two enemy carriers and a cruiser and had shot down about 100 planes. It was, however, the American soldiers and marines who saved Guadalcanal. They retained their hold on Henderson Field, exacting 10 casualties for each of their own.

This repulse merely spurred the Japanese to greater efforts. At dusk on November 12, Rear Admiral Tanaka started down the Slot with 11,000 additional troops in 11 transports. To clear the way, a force including the battleships *Hiei* and *Kirishima* came down to bombard Henderson Field. Admiral Turner, warned by scout planes, sent in a force of five cruisers and eight destroyers

Flight deck of the Enterprise *is hit during the Battle of the Eastern Solomons.*

—everything he had available—under Rear Admiral Daniel J. Callaghan. He thereby set the scene for the three-day Battle of Guadalcanal.

The first stage, the Cruiser Night Action, began when Callaghan's force nearly collided in the darkness with the oncoming Japanese fleet. There ensued a formless melee in which Admirals Callaghan and Scott were among the many casualties. Four American and two Japanese destroyers were sunk, the flame-gutted cruiser *Atlanta* had to be scuttled, the cruiser *Juneau* was sunk by a submarine while retiring from the battle, and the *Hiei* was too disabled to escape from Henderson Field planes that sank her the following day.

Coming up from the south was another American force which included the hastily patched-up *Enterprise*.

On November 14, planes from the carrier joined others from Henderson Field and Espiritu Santo in sinking a Japanese cruiser and seven of Tanaka's transports. Rear Admiral Willis A. Lee had detached from the carrier screen the battleships *Washington* and *South Dakota* and four destroyers. With these he raced to Guadalcanal to counter a renewed attempt to bombard the airfield. He thus precipitated the Battleship Night Action of November 14.

Admiral Kondo, observing Lee's force entering Iron-bottom Sound, hid behind Savo Island and then darted out. With shells and torpedoes he sank two of the American destroyers and disabled the *South Dakota* and the other two destroyers. Lee, left with only the *Washington*, then took on the whole Japanese force and

The battleship Washington, *depicted during the Battleship Night Action of November 14–15, 1942, at Guadalcanal.*

fought on Guadalcanal; 1,600 were killed, and three times as many wounded. Of more than 36,000 Japanese on the island, 23,000 were killed or died of disease and 1,000 were captured.

THE RECONQUEST OF ATTU AND KISKA

Neither the Japanese nor the Americans had much use for Attu and Kiska, the cold, foggy Aleutian islands that the Japanese had occupied during the Battle of Midway. Japan, however, was determined to hold on to them, and the United States was equally determined, when the means became available, to clear the enemy from these bits of American soil. Meanwhile, the Americans endeavored to keep the occupied islands weak militarily by bombings and bombardments and by severing their sea communications with Japan. To that end they established bases on Adak and Amchitka islands. From Amchitka, U.S. and Canadian bombers almost completely isolated Kiska, 65 miles away.

In order to isolate the more distant Attu, Rear Admiral Charles H. McMorris, with a cruiser-destroyer force, began in February 1943 to patrol the waters between Attu and Paramushiro in the Kuriles, the nearest Japanese base. After McMorris had sunk a munitions-laden transport, Vice Admiral Hosogaya began escorting convoys to Attu with his entire North Area Force. Its presence led to the Battle of the Komandorskie Islands, last of the daylight surface battles.

with expert gunnery so wrecked the *Kirishima* that Kondo ordered her scuttled and abandoned the area. Four hours later, just before dawn, Tanaka with four remaining transports and 2,000 surviving troops finally arrived at Guadalcanal.

The Japanese now began building airfields in the central Solomons preparatory to abandoning Guadalcanal. When the heavily reinforced American troops, in early February 1943, were about to close the pincers on the 12,000 half-starved Japanese survivors on Guadalcanal, a score of destroyers succeeded in carrying them away in a series of high speed night runs.

Some 60,000 American soldiers and marines had

The Battle of Guadalcanal: Battleship Night Action, November 14–15, 1942.

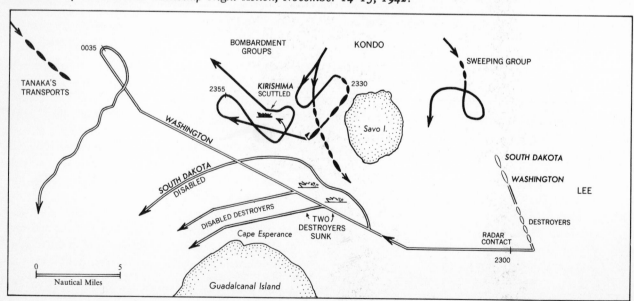

In the early morning of March 26, near the Komandorskies, McMorris in the light cruiser *Richmond,* with the heavy cruiser *Salt Lake City* and four destroyers, was investigating a radar contact when he found himself cut off from his Aleutian bases by Hosogaya's fleet, which had double McMorris' firepower. The ensuing action consisted mainly of a westward chase at long range. The *Salt Lake City* had been hit thrice when at 1100 McMorris attempted to break away to the south behind a smoke screen. After a few minutes the heavy cruiser was hit again. In correcting her resulting list, her engineers accidentally let water into her fuel line, thus extinguishing her burners. The *Salt Lake City* thereupon went dead in the water with the enemy coming up fast. In this desperate situation, McMorris retained one destroyer to make smoke and sent the others charging toward the enemy to deliver a suicide torpedo attack. Hosogaya, however, fearing a possible air attack, had already broken off and was heading for Paramushiro.

Shortage of shipping obliged Rear Admiral Thomas C. Kinkaid, Commander U.S. North Pacific Force, to bypass Kiska and first seize the more lightly held Attu. On May 11 some 3,000 troops of the 7th Infantry Division landed on the north and south coasts, supported by 19 destroyers, 6 cruisers, an escort carrier, the old battleships *Nevada* and *Pennsylvania* (repaired veterans of the Pearl Harbor attack), and the old battleship *Idaho.* The 2,600 Japanese on Attu withdrew out of reach of the naval gunfire into the mountains, whence the Americans, eventually reinforced to 11,000, could not dislodge them. At the end of May, the Japanese, having fired all their artillery shells, crept down from the heights and staged a dawn banzai charge, the survivors of which committed suicide with hand grenades.

Preparations for the assault on Kiska, which was scheduled for the following summer, included a whole series of naval bombardments and the dropping of 1,200 tons of bombs on the island. The invaders, 29,000 U.S. and 5,300 Canadian troops, underwent extensive landing rehearsals at Adak. At dawn on August 15 nearly 100 men-of-war were off Kiska. Minesweepers cleared the transport area. Battleships, cruisers, and destroyers bombarded the beach and inland positions. A little after 0800, troop-laden LSTs, LCIs, and LCTs headed for the shore. What followed was the greatest anticlimax of the war. The only occupants found on the island were

The Aleutian theater of operations.

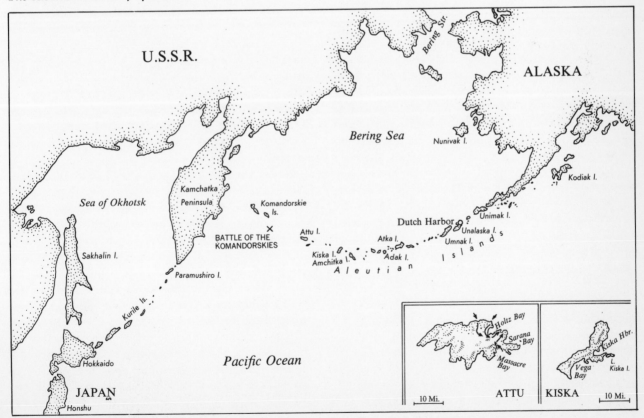

three yellow dogs. Three weeks earlier, under cover of fog, Japanese cruisers and destroyers had evacuated the 5,000-man garrison.

THE SOLOMONS CAMPAIGN

In accordance with the decision reached by the combined chiefs at the Casablanca Conference, the Americans prepared to advance up the Solomon Islands chain toward the great Japanese base at Rabaul. To discourage any such move, Admiral Yamamoto sent his land-based aircraft and 200 of his carrier planes in a series of massive raids on Allied ships and bases. The Americans, figuring out his inspection schedule from decrypted radio intercepts, dispatched from Henderson Field long-range P-38s, which shot down his plane over southern Bougainville. Yamamoto's successor, Admiral Koga, continued the reckless expenditure of aviators that, as much as anything else, was to prove Japan's undoing.

The Japanese air raids were in vain. At the end of June 1943 Halsey's South Pacific naval force, lately dignified with the title U.S. Third Fleet, moved up the Solomons, penetrating the Southwest Pacific Area, where General MacArthur was Supreme Allied Commander. The assault arm, the Third Amphibious Force, landed troops in the central Solomons, first on lightly held Rendova Island to site artillery for supporting the main landing, which followed on nearby New Georgia. A month of bloody fighting ensued before the Americans gained their primary objective—the Japanese airstrip on Munda Point. Since this invasion observed the iron rule of mounting assaults only within operational radius of one's own fighters, planes of Air Command Solomons (AIRSOLS) from Henderson Field were on hand to lend support.

In mid-August the Third Amphibious Force, now commanded by Rear Admiral Theodore S. Wilkinson, bypassed Kolombangara and, under cover of AIRSOLS fighters operating from the Munda airstrip, landed troops on lightly held Vella Lavella. Here, instead of attempting to capture the enemy airfield, the invaders hacked a new airstrip out of the jungle.

The Solomons campaign saw the U.S. Navy at last overtake and outperform the enemy at his specialty of night combat. The Japanese, initially without radar, used night glasses and developed a radar detector. The Americans had been given a bitter demonstration of their skill in night fighting in the Battle of Savo Island, and another in the Battle of Tassafaronga, fought off Guadalcanal November 30, 1942. At Tassafaronga five U.S. cruisers revealed themselves to the enemy by opening fire and then, without changing course or speed, plowed into spreads of torpedoes which Japanese destroyers had fired at their extended track. Four of the cruisers were hit; one went down and two had their bows blown off.

When the Americans invaded the central Solomons, the night-running Tokyo Express began operating again, and night battles inevitably followed. Now, however, the Allied ships were organized into semipermanent task groups with improved radar and primitive combat information centers. In the battles of Kula Gulf, July 6, 1943, and Kolombangara, July 13, the Allies sank ships and lost ships, but at least demonstrated a growing understanding of the problems of night-fighting tactics.

The first unqualified American night victory was in the Battle of Vella Gulf, August 6–7. Commander Frederick Moosbrugger, using a battle plan devised by Commander Arleigh Burke, his predecessor in command of his destroyer squadron, fought the perfect night battle. Detecting an approaching column of four Japanese destroyers, Moosbrugger had three of his own destroyers run on an opposite course parallel to the enemy while the other three crossed the enemy's van. The first three fired torpedoes and turned away, reversing course together. Just as the torpedoes struck their targets, all six U.S. destroyers opened fire, whereupon three of the Japanese ships blew up like miniature volcanoes.

On November 1 Wilkinson's Third Amphibious Force bypassed the complex of enemy bases in and near southern Bougainville and landed 14,000 troops halfway up the island's weakly defended west coast at Cape Torokina in Empress Augusta Bay. Because from here fighter-escorted bombers could reach Rabaul, the Japanese command there promptly dispatched Rear Admiral Omori with a cruiser-destroyer force, hoping to fight a new Battle of Savo Island.

Instead Omori fought the Battle of Empress Augusta Bay, a totally different sort of operation. Rear Admiral Stanton Merrill USN reached the area first and stretched his own cruiser-destroyer column protectively across the beachhead. As Omori's force approached the beach, Merrill's destroyer divisions detached themselves from the cruiser line and raced for the enemy's flanks. Because Omori altered course, torpedoes fired by the American destroyers all missed. One of Merrill's destroyer divisions became separated on the turnaway. In the other division a destroyer was torpedoed, another destroyer was damaged by shellfire, and a pair collided.

Meanwhile, the four American cruisers were performing superbly under Merrill's direct command, repeatedly reversing course so as to pass and repass the enemy formation, and making smoke to conceal themselves when

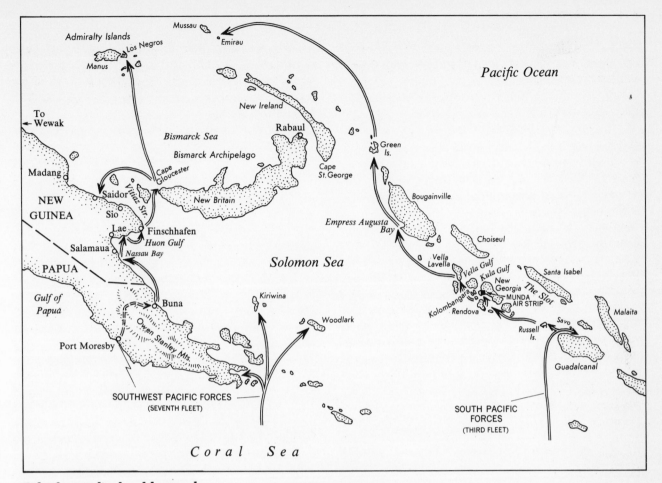

Rabaul neutralized and bypassed.

illuminated by parachute flares. They made only one hit, disabling the Japanese cruiser *Sendai*, but their rapid maneuvers and hail of shells so confused the enemy that two pairs of Japanese ships collided, and Omori, overestimating his opposition, broke off action and headed back for Rabaul. The American destroyer divisions at last had the satisfaction of finishing off the *Sendai* and sending down a collision-damaged enemy destroyer.

On November 25, two hours after midnight, a squadron of five American destroyers in the Battle of Cape St. George shattered the last Tokyo Express out of Rabaul —sinking three destroyers and earning Arleigh Burke, now a captain, the nickname "31-Knot Burke." To Burke this battle was especially gratifying, for he had now made personal use of his battle plan, proving that Moosbrugger's victory was no fluke.

THE NEW GUINEA CAMPAIGN

While the South Pacific forces were busy securing Guadalcanal, General MacArthur's Southwest Pacific Area forces of Americans and Australians 800 miles to the west were defending Port Moresby from a Japanese overland attack and then counterattacking all the way across the Owen Stanley Mountains to Buna on the New Guinea north coast. This was the first step of MacArthur's promised return to the Philippines, an advance that was to become known as the "New Guinea– Mindanao Axis." All the operations in the Solomons were directed toward seizing or neutralizing Japanese bases in the Bismarck Archipelago so that the Southwest Pacific forces, while advancing along the north coast of New Guinea and beyond, could be safely supplied via Vitiaz Strait.

The Japanese anticipated an attack by MacArthur's forces on their New Guinea lodgments at Lae and Salamaua. In March 1943, therefore, the Rabaul base sent thither a force of 7,000 additional troops in eight transports escorted by eight destroyers. When these had passed through Vitiaz Strait into the Solomon Sea, they had before them a short run by daylight to Lae. They never made it. Fifth Air Force bombers out of southeastern New Guinea sank all of the transports and half of the destroyers. Thereafter the Japanese New Guinea bases were supplied by submarines or by barges, which Allied PT boats found an easy prey.

At the end of June, coinciding with the South Pacific Area invasion of the central Solomons, Southwest Pacific forces landed on Kiriwina and Woodlark Islands in the Coral Sea and at Nassau Bay on the New Guinea coast. The island invasions were staged by Rear Admiral Daniel E. Barbey's small Seventh Amphibious Force, the assault unit of the still largely nonexistent U.S. Seventh Fleet, "MacArthur's Navy."

Beginning in September 1943, Southwest Pacific troops, supported by Seventh Fleet guns and Fifth Air Force planes, captured or occupied a series of coastal points that secured Vitiaz Strait. Australians, landed on the coast by Barbey's Seventh Amphibious Force, recaptured Lae with the help of other Aussies flown to a nearby airfield that had been captured by American paratroops. In October, the Australians went around by sea to wrest Finschhafen from the enemy. In late December,

the U.S. 1st Marine Division landed at Cape Gloucester, on the far side of the strait, and chased the Japanese on New Britain nearly back to Rabaul. In early January, 7,000 more Americans went ashore at unoccupied Saidor. Outflanked by the Americans and threatened by the Australian 7th Division advancing in the interior, the Japanese fell back to Wewak.

NEUTRALIZING RABAUL

The original plan for securing Vitiaz Strait included the capture of Rabaul, but in August 1943 the Combined Chiefs of Staff, at Admiral King's suggestion, directed MacArthur and Halsey to bypass this powerful base after neutralizing it by aerial bombing—a fortunate decision, for wresting Rabaul from its nearly 100,000 well-supplied and well-fortified defenders would have been extraordinarily costly.

To assist the Fifth Air Force and AIRSOLS in neutral-

Japanese vessels under attack in Simpson harbor, Rabaul.

izing Rabaul, Nimitz sent Halsey two carrier task groups of the new U.S. Fifth (Central Pacific) Fleet. On November 5, Rear Admiral Frederick C. Sherman's group, in attacking shipping in Rabaul's Simpson harbor, damaged six of the seven heavy cruisers Admiral Koga had sent down from Truk to redeem Omori's failure. Included was the *Mogami*, virtually rebuilt since her battering at Midway. Rear Admiral Alfred Montgomery's group, striking Rabaul on the 11th, attacked and shot down a good many of the carrier planes that Koga had sent to bolster the defenses of the Bismarcks, and thereby contributed to the paralysis of the Combined Fleet.

By mid-November the Third Amphibious Force had poured 34,000 men into Bougainville. These fought back attacking Japanese troops and expanded their beachhead until it enclosed 22 square miles. Here, by the end of 1943, Seabees and an engineering brigade from New Zealand had constructed a bomber strip and two fighter strips. AIRSOLS shifted headquarters to here from Munda and took over the bombing of Rabaul, which the Fifth Air Force had begun in October. By February 1944, AIRSOLS was sending against the enemy base 1,000 sorties a week.

That month the Third Fleet transported to the Green Islands 6,000 troops, who destroyed the Japanese garrison and built a fighter strip just 115 miles east of Rabaul. From here fighters could accompany the Bougainville-based bombers to any part of the Bismarcks. In March, the Third Fleet landed marines on Emirau, 225 miles northwest of Rabaul. On this island, which the Japanese had not occupied, another airstrip was built and a PT base established.

The encircling of Rabaul was completed by MacArthur's capture of the Admiralty Islands. The Southwest Pacific forces were scheduled to invade here on April 1, 1944, but the new Central Pacific drive quickly attained such momentum that MacArthur decided to speed up his own drive lest he be left behind in the race to the Philippines. At the end of February he daringly landed a 1,000-man reconnaissance-in-force on Los Negros. Though more than 4,000 Japanese were on the island, MacArthur was able to rush in reinforcements fast enough to turn his reconnaissance into a regular invasion. In mid-March, troops from Los Negros invaded nearby Manus, the main island of the Admiralty group, and rapidly won control of spacious Seeadler harbor.

A NEW OFFENSIVE
AND A NEW FLEET

The dual Allied drive on Rabaul was necessarily a limited offensive because Admiral Nimitz was hoarding most of his new ships at Pearl Harbor. He was preparing for a drive across the Central Pacific, even though agreement on such an offensive was not obtained from the British chiefs of staff until May 1943, when they consented in return for American agreement to invade Italy.

Of the several advantages of a Central Pacific drive over MacArthur's New Guinea–Mindanao Axis, two stood out: (1) A drive across the center would open up a shorter, less roundabout supply route, not only for the Central Pacific forces but also for MacArthur's. The shorter route would require fewer cargo vessels and fewer men to operate them. (2) The precise direction of a drive through an ocean with hundreds of potential island bases was unpredictable. The enemy could not mass in its path but would be obliged to divide his forces among all likely island targets. In endeavoring to be strong everywhere, he could succeed in being strong nowhere.

The Joint Chiefs did not propose completely reorienting the war against Japan. MacArthur's Southwest Pacific forces would continue along the New Guinea–Mindanao Axis. Here they would serve as a shield to Australia, and would contain the Japanese with whom they were in contact, preventing them from interfering with the Central Pacific drive. Once Rabaul had been bypassed and neutralized, the South Pacific Area would be reduced to garrison status and the Third Fleet dissolved. Most South Pacific troops would be assigned to MacArthur, and most Third Fleet ships returned to Nimitz. Halsey would report to Nimitz for further duties.

The New Guinea–Mindanao Axis and the Central Pacific Axis thus would constitute a dual advance. It would have been advantageous to place both offensives under one commander to keep them mutually supporting, but this proved impracticable. MacArthur's towering reputation forbade his being subordinated to Nimitz. The Joint Chiefs would not give MacArthur the over-all command because he opposed opening the Central Pacific drive, insisting that the whole Pacific Fleet be employed in support of his New Guinea–Mindanao Axis. MacArthur therefore remained in the post of Supreme Commander Allied Forces Southwest Pacific Area; Nimitz, as Commander in Chief Pacific Fleet and Pacific Ocean Areas (CINCPAC-CINCPOA), retained command of all Allied forces in the North, Central, and South Pacific areas. It was hoped that rapid radio communication would offset the disadvantages of this divided Pacific command.

The new Central Pacific forces would constitute the U.S. Fifth Fleet—no fleet at all in the traditional definition but a highly complex organization specifically de-

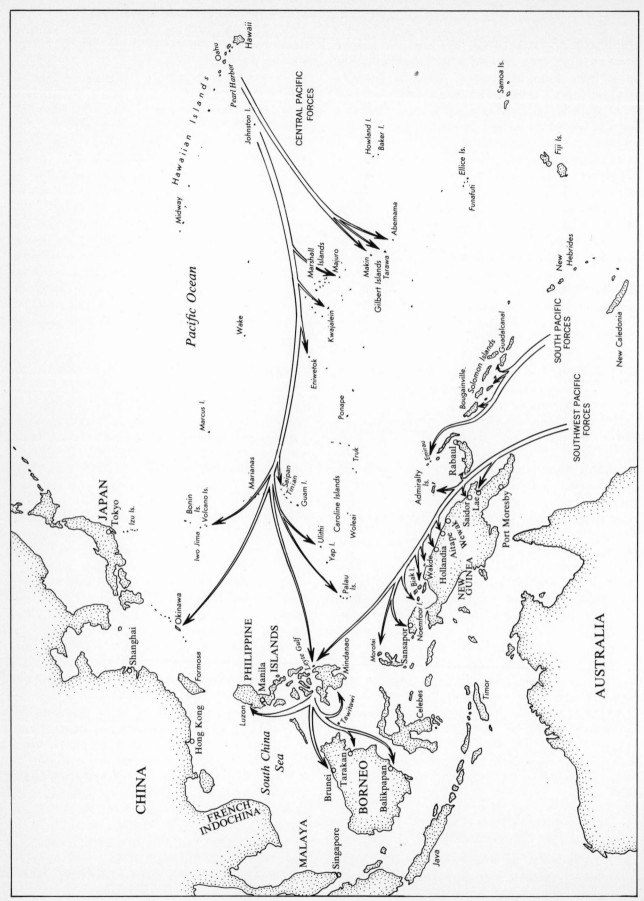

Across the Pacific.

signed to fight its way across the Pacific Ocean and defeat Japan. Its commander was Vice Admiral Spruance. Known widely in the Navy before the war for his intellectual brilliance and meticulous attention to duty, Spruance was much in demand as an instructor at the Naval War College, where he was recognized as a first-rate strategist. Following his victory in the Battle of Midway, he had joined Admiral Nimitz as his chief of staff and helped him organize the great fleet of which he was to assume command.

Spearheading the Fifth Fleet was the Fast Carrier Task Force (Task Force 58), commanded initially by Rear Admiral Charles A. Pownall. The carrier force normally operated in four task groups, each containing three to five carriers surrounded by a circular screen of battleships, cruisers, and destroyers. Though in early assaults its planes provided tactical support to beachheads, its basic function was cover, that is, interception of air or surface threats to the amphibious forces.

At the outset of the Central Pacific drive, much of the tactical support for landing operations was provided by the Fifth Fleet's land-based air arm, comprising Army, Navy, and Marine Corps aircraft and commanded by Rear Admiral John H. Hoover. Called Defense Force and Shore-Based Air, it was the Central Pacific's equivalent of AIRSOLS and the Fifth Air Force. More and more, however, such support was provided by the escort carriers and the destroyers, cruisers, and old battleships of the Fifth Amphibious Force, which also controlled the attack transports, cargo vessels, and landing and beaching craft. This force was organized and commanded by Rear Admiral Turner ("Terrible Turner"), whom Nimitz summoned to Pearl Harbor after his demonstrated skill in directing amphibious operations had expunged the stigma of his defeat in the Battle of Savo Island. The

The Fast Carrier Task Force (TF 58), spearhead of the Fifth Fleet.

Vice Admiral R. Kelly Turner (center), with Lieutenant General Holland M. Smith (left) and Rear Admiral Harry W. Hill.

soldiers and marines of the landing force and follow-up constituted the V Amphibious Corps, commanded by Major General Holland M. Smith, whose usual reaction to sloppiness and ineptitude had earned him the nickname "Howling Mad Smith." The Fifth Fleet was assured of reach and momentum by Service Force Pacific, whose squadrons of tenders, oilers, and repair and supply ships could set up floating bases merely by dropping anchor in the lagoons of the larger Central Pacific atolls.

As new fast carriers and escort vessels of every sort arrived at Pearl Harbor in the summer of 1943, Nimitz organized them into task forces and sent them out against live targets—Marcus, Wake, and, as we have seen, Rabaul.

RECONQUEST OF THE GILBERTS

Geography and the "iron rule," requiring land-based air support of amphibious assaults, dictated that the Central Pacific drive should begin at the British Gilbert Islands. These were a group of 16 atolls, three

of which, Makin, Abemama, and Tarawa, had been occupied by the Japanese following the Pearl Harbor attack. From Baker Island, Canton Island, and the Ellice Islands, American planes could reach the Gilberts for photoreconnaissance, preliminary bombing, and support of sea-borne assaults. From the Gilberts, once taken, aircraft could reach the Japanese Marshalls.

The attack on the Gilberts was the biggest and most complex operation the Americans had thus far undertaken in the Pacific theater. From their raid on Rabaul came Sherman's and Montgomery's carrier groups. Two other carrier groups staged from Pearl Harbor. From Hawaii came the Northern Attack Force with 6,500 troops of the 27th Infantry Division to seize Butaritari, principal island of Makin Atoll. Up from New Zealand came the Southern Attack Force with the whole 2nd Marine Division, en route to Tarawa Atoll to capture Betio Island, which was the headquarters and strong point of the whole Gilbert Archipelago.

Admiral Turner and General Holland Smith personally directed the assault on Butaritari, for Makin was less than 200 miles from the Marshalls. Any counterattack was almost sure to come by way of these Japanese islands. The troops of the 27th Division, as they went ashore on Butaritari supported by 4 old battleships, 4 heavy cruisers, 13 destroyers, and 3 escort carriers, would have a 23-to-1 numerical superiority over the defenders. This fantastic disparity of strength was provided for one reason: to insure a one-day conquest of the island so that the fleet could be withdrawn from this exposed position. The American commanders were unaware that Koga's Combined Fleet was in no condition to sortie. So many carrier aviators had been expended in defense of Rabaul and the Solomons that the fleet lacked sufficient air power to attack, or even to defend itself.

The 27th Division took, not one, but nearly four days to conquer Butaritari. After going ashore early on November 20, 1943, against only a little small arms fire, these soldiers, badly trained, were held up for long periods by minor pockets of enemy resistance. When "Howling Mad Smith" stormed ashore to investigate, he spent his worst night of the war as nervous American sentries shot coconuts out of the palms and punctured his tent with bullets. In the afternoon of the 23rd, the division commander, Major General Ralph Smith, finally signaled Admiral Turner: "Makin taken." Sixty-four Americans had been killed; only one Japanese infantryman was taken alive.

The Navy paid a heavy price for the Army's dilatory tactics. Admiral Koga, unable to commit his fleet, sent nine submarines to attack the American ships in the Gilberts. At dawn on the 24th, one of the submarines torpedoed the escort carrier *Liscome Bay*, which blew apart as her ammunition exploded. Of her crew of about 900, nearly 650 were killed.

At the southern end of the archipelago, the submarine *Nautilus* had put ashore on Abemama a reconnaissance party of 78 U.S. marines. When they discovered only 25 Japanese present, they called on the *Nautilus* for a burst of gunfire and took the position themselves.

Meanwhile at Tarawa one of the most desperate battles of the war was in progress. Here, preceded and followed by bombing from carrier aircraft, Rear Admiral Harry Hill's Southern Attack Force on September 20 had poured 3,000 tons of projectiles into the target island of Betio in a two-and-a-half-hour bombardment. From the two-mile-long island rose a tremendous pall of dust and smoke, interspersed with flashes of fire. Apparently nothing could remain alive in such an inferno.

In fact, though the wooden barracks had been burned and the ammunition dump blown up, most of the men on Betio were safe. Some 2,600 Japanese marines, 1,000 construction workers, and 1,200 Korean laborers had taken refuge in a maze of pillboxes, bombproof shelters,

and gun emplacements which for a year they had been constructing around the central airfield. They had thus converted Betio into the toughest little fortress in the Pacific. To penetrate such defenses, aimed fire, not mere area fire, was needed—a lesson learned by Porter at Fort Fisher but since forgotten.

The landing craft had been delayed by choppy seas in reaching the lagoon-side beachhead. Because the beach was not clearly visible from the fleet, Admiral Hill checked his bombardment prematurely. As a result, Japanese infantry manning the seaward faces of Betio had time to join those on the lagoon shore and turn their rifles and machine guns on the approaching landing craft.

The tide was low, leaving only two or three feet of water over the offshore coral reef. Fortunately the first three waves of invaders headed for the beach in amtracs (amphibious tractors) that lumbered up onto the reef and continued toward the shore. Many of these were knocked out by enemy artillery while still in the water, and of those that reached the beach, few were in condition to return to the reef's edge for another load. Because the LCVPs of the following three waves were stopped by the reef, most of their passengers had to wade the final 600 yards to the beach through withering machine gun and rifle fire. The majority of those who were hit

The assault on Tarawa, November 21, 1943.

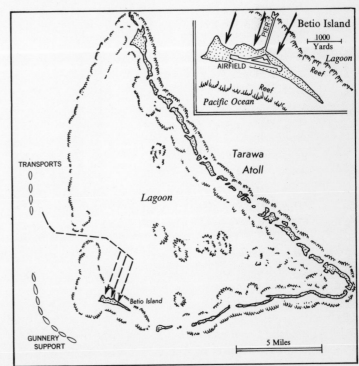

drowned. A few tanks, brought to the reef by LCMs, reached the shore, but 37- and 75-mm guns, which came in landing craft, had to await a rising tide. Luckily, the low tide left a stretch of sandy beach on which the invaders could crouch outside a coconut-log seawall.

The division commander, Major General Julian Smith, aboard Admiral Hill's flagship *Maryland,* was observing the operation and listening to radio reports with increasing dismay. From Colonel David Shoup, the assault commander, he received an urgent call for gunfire support and for immediate commitment of the division reserve. Something in Shoup's voice must have deeply alarmed Smith, for he not only committed the division reserve but radioed General Holland Smith for permission to land the corps reserve also, adding ominously: "Issue in doubt."

By chance or because of the distribution of the naval gunfire, the Japanese behind the seawall tended to bunch in two strong pockets. Among the Americans opposite these enemy concentrations the casualties were extremely heavy, yet even here U.S. marines began climbing the wall and blowing up rifle pits and pillboxes with explosive charges. The invaders made their first genuine advances elsewhere. At the western end of Betio they turned the enemy's flank and thrust nearly half the length of the west beach. Between the two enemy pockets, where there was a break in the seawall

Major General Julian Smith (left), commander of the 2nd Marine Division, observing the invasion of Tarawa with Admiral Hill aboard the flagship Maryland.

near the foot of a pier, two amtracs loaded with marines led a charge through the opening. In spite of heavy flanking fire, the invaders in this area pushed south and west and established a defensive perimeter for the night.

When darkness came, 5,000 Americans had reached Betio. Of these nearly a third had been killed or wounded. Hundreds, alive and dead, were still on the beach outside the seawall. Through the night both sides kept remarkable fire discipline. Scarcely a shot was heard. But many of the tough little Japanese silently climbed trees or otherwise placed themselves in position for sniping when daylight came.

Though there was still plenty of hard fighting to do, the issue was not again in doubt. The reserves, together with tanks and artillery, poured in over the west and lagoon beaches until there were 18,600 Americans on the island. By the afternoon of the 23rd, the invaders had captured 17 Japanese, including one officer. Nearly 5,000 had died fighting or committed suicide. A thousand Americans had been killed and twice as many wounded. The United States was shocked at so many casualties in so brief a period, yet the fight for Betio was less costly than the six-month struggle for Guadalcanal, and Betio proved no less useful a stepping stone toward victory.

INVASION OF THE MARSHALLS

The Fifth Fleet commanders, unnerved by the losses at Tarawa, recommended taking the Marshalls in two bites. The first would be the easterly islands, to be developed into bases to support a later invasion of Kwajalein, the Japanese headquarters at the center of the archipelago and the world's largest coral atoll. Admiral Nimitz, objecting that the delay would check the momentum of the westward drive, ordered them instead to assault Kwajalein next, bypassing the easterly islands. This proved a wise decision, for the Japanese, assuming that the easterly islands would be attacked first, had strengthened them at the expense of Kwajalein. Though the islands athwart the American line of communications continued to be occupied by the enemy, U.S. planes quickly pounded them into impotence.

A striking feature of the Marshalls campaign was the thoroughness with which the Navy applied the lessons of the Gilberts invasion, particularly in softening up the target. Admiral Hoover's bombers began working over the Marshalls as soon as his airfields were operational on Makin, Abemama, and Tarawa. On January 29, 1944, a considerably enlarged Fast Carrier Task Force (Task

Marines attack across a coconut-log seawall on the beach at Tarawa.

Marines in action at Tarawa.

Force 58) joined the onslaught with 750 planes. The carriers and their escorts destroyed every plane and churned up the airfields on Kwajalein, and then smashed the aircraft stacked up at Eniwetok, the way station for planes coming east from Truk and the Marianas. In command now of Task Force 58 was Rear Admiral Marc A. Mitscher, who for his aggressiveness and wizened appearance has been called "the Ferocious Gnome."

As the Fifth Amphibious Force approached the Marshalls, Admiral Hill's Special Attack Group detached itself and took possession of unoccupied Majuro Atoll to provide an anchorage for the fleet and a haven for a floating base, one of Service Force Pacific's mobile service squadrons. Rear Admiral Richard Conolly's Northern Attack Force next headed for its target, the joined islands of Roi and Namur at the northern end of Kwajalein Atoll, while the Southern Attack Force, under Admiral Turner, proceeded toward Kwajalein Island, 44 miles away at the southern end of the atoll.

Before the February 1 landings, the Fifth Amphibious Force gunnery vessels gave the target islands

Vice Admiral Marc A. Mitscher.

The assault on Kwajalein, February 1, 1944.

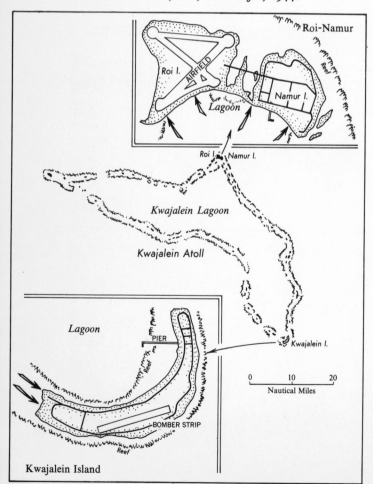

three days and nights of bombardment, approaching to within a mile of the shore and alternating high capacity and armor-piercing shell in aimed fire. Conolly and Turner were provided with new command ships (AGCs), specially designed for use in directing amphibious assaults. The amtracs were now armed and armored and would be accompanied to the beach by amphibian tanks and LCIs converted into gunboats.

The landings on Roi-Namur were generally chaotic, partly because the landing and beaching craft straggled, having first been used to land artillery on adjacent islets. The main reason was that the landing force, the newly organized 4th Marine Division, had not had time for adequate rehearsal. Once ashore, however, the marines made use of their basic training. They captured Roi, mostly airfield, in a single day, and in a day and a half fought their way through the wilderness of rubble left by the bombardment of Namur. At Kwajalein Island, the 7th Infantry Division, intensively trained veterans of Attu, made a flawless landing. In 12 minutes 1,200 troops were ashore organizing to advance; by the end of the day 11,000 had landed. Securing the island then took four days, partly because the soldiers, having landed at the western end, had to fight their way

Kwajalein, before and after.

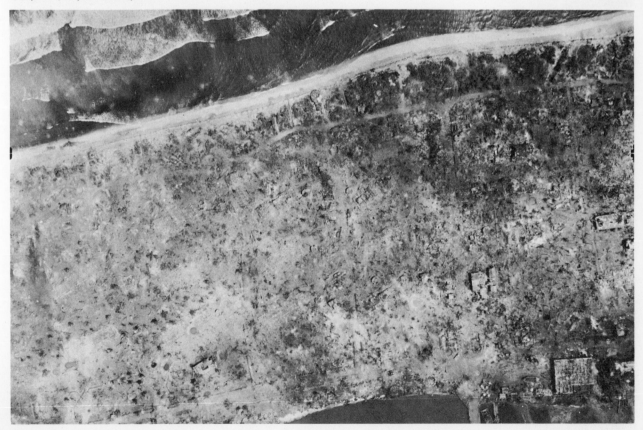

through its whole length, and partly because Army doctrine forbade bypassing pockets of resistance for rear echelons to clean up.

The invasion plan now called for the capture of Eniwetok Atoll, because the 10,000 troops of the corps reserve had not been committed in the conquest of Kwajalein. D-day here was scheduled for February 17. Lacking the numerical superiority the Kwajalein invaders had enjoyed, Admiral Hill's Eniwetok expeditionary force had to take the three occupied islands one at a time. Because his 22nd Marine Regiment, like the marines at Kwajalein, lacked amphibious training, their landings were haphazard and confused, but once ashore they overran Engebi and Parry islands each in a single day. Capture of Eniwetok Island, the least heavily defended, took three days. One reason was that the gunfire-support vessels learned belatedly that there were Japanese on Eniwetok Island and gave it only a brief bombardment. Another was that the assault troops assigned to this island were from the 27th Infantry Division, apparently the one element of the Fifth Fleet that had not improved since the Gilberts invasion. When marines were rushed onto this island to take over part of the fighting, their presence resulted in a clash of tactical methods, a situation that boded ill for future Army–Marine Corps joint operations. Of the 53,000 assault troops assigned to the Marshalls, 568 were killed. The roughly 11,000 defenders were, as usual, nearly wiped out.

In support of the Eniwetok invasion, the Fifth Fleet proceeded to neutralize surrounding enemy bases. While bombers from Tarawa knocked out Ponape with 118 tons of bombs, Spruance and Mitscher headed toward Truk to do a similar job there. Admiral Koga had prudently withdrawn the bulk of his Combined Fleet, but there were targets aplenty. While Mitscher's carrier planes pounded the islands and shipping, Spruance led a battleship-cruiser force around the perimeter reef to catch any vessels attempting to flee through the openings. This February 17–18 raid cost the Japanese 200 planes; 15 naval vessels, including 2 cruisers and 4 destroyers; 19 cargo vessels; and 5 tankers.

Mitscher, with two carrier groups, now headed northwest for the Marianas. The ships, attacked repeatedly from the air during the night of February 22, protected themselves from all damage solely with radar-aimed, VT (proximity) fused shells. After dawn the carrier aircraft made surprise raids on Guam, Tinian, and Saipan, destroying 168 aircraft, and making an invaluable photoreconnaissance of airfields and of likely landing beaches.

HOLLANDIA AND WESTWARD

General MacArthur, determined not to be outsped in his race for the Philippines by the Central Pacific forces, planned a 400-mile leap by sea to Hollandia on the New Guinea north coast. Simultaneously, he intended to land a regiment at Aitape, 125 miles southeast of Hollandia, in order to plug the coastal road leading from the Japanese Eighteenth Army headquarters at Wewak. In preparation, the Fifth Air Force staged a series of daylight raids on the target areas, and Task Force 58 cleared the flank of MacArthur's advance by raids on Japanese bases in the Carolines.

The most important of the TF 58 raids was against the Palau group, the new anchorage for the Combined Fleet. Admiral Koga, warned by patrol planes, had most of his ships out of the Palaus before TF 58 struck on March 30, 1944. The 36 ships that failed to get away were all sunk or heavily damaged. On April 22, TF 58 was on hand to lend support to MacArthur's Hollandia-Aitape landings, but so thoroughly had the Fifth Air Force worked over the area that Mitscher's carrier aircraft found few targets. Meanwhile, Koga, in withdrawing by air from the battered Palaus to new headquarters in the Philippines, had run into a storm in which his plane simply disappeared.

After Hollandia, MacArthur made further landings along the New Guinea coast and offshore islands, seizing enemy airfields in order to advance his bomber line ever closer to the Philippines. Admiral Toyoda, Koga's successor, concluded that this was the sole line of Allied advance and therefore prepared to destroy the U.S. Fifth Fleet in a great battle in the western Carolines. He counted on supplementing Japan's inadequate carrier air power in this area with planes from surrounding Japanese bases, particularly the three airfields on Biak Island off New Guinea. In preparation for springing his trap, he ordered Vice Admiral Ozawa to station the Japanese carrier fleet at Tawitawi off Borneo.

When on May 27 MacArthur's speeded-up offensive brought his Southwest Pacific forces to Biak, the Japanese reacted sharply. The Allies must be ousted lest land-based air support from Biak be available to supplement not Ozawa but Spruance. The Japanese therefore drained the Central Pacific of planes and ordered them south. Ozawa sent Vice Admiral Ugaki to escort reinforcements from the Philippines to Biak. The escort force included the 18-inch-gun superbattleships *Yamato* and *Musashi* and six cruisers. These were to land the reinforcements at all costs and bombard MacArthur's forces.

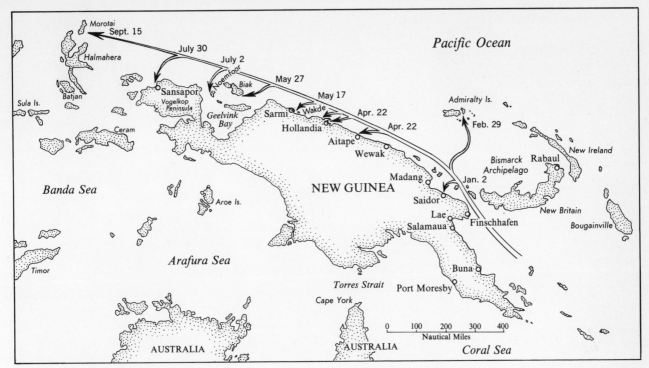

The New Guinea Campaign, 1943–44.

When Ugaki was halfway to Biak, he received startling information. A thousand miles to the northwest, Fifth Fleet aircraft were bombing the southern Marianas, evidently in preparation for an invasion. From Toyoda Ugaki received orders to change course to northward, rendezvous with Ozawa east of the Philippines, and attack the American fleet in the Marianas area. The high command also ordered the Japanese planes back to the Central Pacific. Few were able to return there. Most of the aviators, in shifting from healthful climes to the New Guinea jungles, had contracted malaria or other tropical fevers.

Ozawa's defeat in the Battle of the Philippine Sea removed the chief threat to MacArthur's Southwest Pacific forces. Without outside interference, they completed the conquest of Biak and advanced to Sansapor in the New Guinea "bird head." In the drive from the Admiralties they had suffered 1,648 killed and about 8,000 wounded. This was considerably less costly than the concurrent Central Pacific drive, but only because the Central Pacific forces held, removed, or attracted potential enemy concentrations away from MacArthur's path.

THE ASSAULT ON SAIPAN

The carriers had so thoroughly demonstrated their capacity for supporting amphibious assaults that the Joint Chiefs of Staff abandoned the "iron rule" of land-based support and authorized the invasion of Saipan, Tinian, and Guam, 1,000 miles beyond even the advanced base at Eniwetok. From the Marianas, the new B-29 long-range bomber could reach Japan, and submarines could completely cut off the flow from the East Indies to Japan of oil and other necessities.

On June 6, 1944, the date of the Normandy invasion on the opposite side of the globe, Task Force 58 led the way out of the Marshalls. It was followed by the Fifth Amphibious Force, comprising 535 ships carrying 127,000 troops. The simultaneous invasion of France and the Marianas by American forces constituted the most titanic military effort put forth by any nation at any one time in history.

On the 11th, in the Pacific, carrier planes flew 200 miles ahead of the advancing U.S. fleet to raid the Marianas. On the 14th, Mitscher divided TF 58, sending two groups north to prevent aircraft from being staged from Japan to the Marianas by churning up intervening airstrips on Iwo Jima and Chichi Jima. With the other two groups he proceeded to westward of the Marianas to cover the Fifth Amphibious Force and the beachhead on Saipan.

On the morning of June 15, under the direct supervision of Vice Admiral Kelly Turner and Lieutenant General Holland Smith, both in the command ship *Rocky Mount*, eight battalions of 2nd and 4th Division marines—boated in amtracs, supported at close range by

The first wave of Marines on Saipan take cover on the beach.

gunnery ships, and accompanied by amphibious tanks and LCI gunboats—headed for the flat southwestern beach of mountainous Saipan. Though 8,000 marines were ashore in 20 minutes, and 20,000 by the end of the day, it was apparent that two days of bombing and bombardment had not been adequate to take the fight out of the 32,000 defenders of the 14-mile-long island. The invaders on June 15 penetrated only halfway to their D-day objective line.

THE ADVANCE OF THE FLEETS

Mitscher's two carrier groups off the Marianas patrolled westward by day, sending out search planes, and drew back eastward by night lest some undetected enemy force attempt to slip between them and the beachhead. On D-day Admiral Spruance had learned from the submarine *Flying Fish* that a Japanese carrier force had entered the Philippine Sea from San Bernardino Strait in the Philippines. Early the next day he received from the submarine *Seahorse* a report of a second Japanese force east of the Philippines steaming north. These were Ozawa's carrier force from Tawitawi and Ugaki's surface force diverted from the Biak attack. Because Spruance received no reports of their rendezvous, he continued to suspect that he was dealing with more than one enemy force. And since he received no reports at all of the enemy from patrol planes, he concluded that the air patrols were undependable.

Spruance was sure only that a battle was imminent. Coolly calculating the enemy's rate of approach, he ordered the two carrier groups to the north to complete their raids on June 16 and head back south. After conferring with Kelly Turner and Holland Smith, he postponed the June 18 invasion of Guam, ordered the Saipan reserve (the 27th Infantry Division) committed at once, transferred cruisers and destroyers from the amphibious forces to TF 58, which he himself joined in his flagship *Indianapolis,* and ordered the transports, when unloaded, to withdraw eastward until after the battle. The carrier groups from the north rejoined the other two at noon June 18.

Ozawa was aware that he was going to fight an enemy twice his own strength and with far better-trained aviators, but he counted on certain advantages to achieve victory. Planes from Yap, Rota, and Guam would attack TF 58. The easterly trade winds would permit the Japanese, but not the American, carriers to launch and recover planes while advancing on the enemy. Perhaps decisively advantageous, Ozawa's fleet could launch air attacks without itself being attacked—for three reasons. First, Japanese planes, unencumbered with heavy armor and self-sealing fuel tanks, could attack at a range of 300 miles; U.S. planes, not much beyond 200. Second, Spruance, tagged as "cautious" because of his tactics at Midway, was not likely to uncover the Saipan beachhead in order to close with the enemy. And, third, the Japanese planes could shuttle-bomb the Americans; that is, after attacking TF 58, they could land on Guam, there refuel and rearm, and attack the Americans again on the way back to their own fleet. On the afternoon of June 18, Ozawa learned from his search planes that TF 58 was 390 miles away and 200 miles west of Saipan. He thereupon began disposing his fleet for battle the next morning. Vice Admiral Kurita's Van Force of three light carriers, each surrounded by powerful antiaircraft vessels, would operate 300 miles from TF 58. The Main Body, with five heavy carriers and one light carrier, inadequately screened, would be 400 miles from the enemy.

THE BATTLE OF THE PHILIPPINE SEA

On the evening of June 18, Task Force 58 was disposed in five circular groups, four of them containing three or four carriers each and—available if surface action should offer—one all-surface group including seven battleships. In conformity with the search-and-patrol pattern, the course was easterly. Late in the evening a dispatch arrived from Pearl Harbor stating that radio direction-finder bearings placed Ozawa's fleet 355 miles WSW of TF 58. Mitscher, aboard the *Lexington* (II),

thereupon got on voice radio and informed Spruance, nearby in the *Indianapolis:* "We propose to come to a westerly course at 0130 in order to commence treatment of enemy at 0500."

After discussing this proposal for an hour with his staff, Spruance concluded that the source of the radio direction-finder fix might well be a decoy, that he could not in any case risk uncovering the beachhead. Replied he: "The change proposed in your message does not seem advisable. . . ."

Mitscher and his staff were aghast. To them, Spruance's decision seemed a clear refusal of battle. When dawn broke on June 19, Task Force 58 was exactly where Ozawa wanted it to be—within reach of his planes and unable to strike back. Still, Spruance's choice was fortunate. No enemy tried to get between TF 58 and Saipan, as he feared; but if the American task force, by turning west, had managed to get within air attack range of the Japanese, its planes would have been obliged first to pass through the intense antiaircraft fire of Kurita's Van Force, which included the superbattleships *Yamato* and *Musashi,* and then fly another 100 miles to reach Ozawa's big carriers. On the return flight, they would again have had to pass through the antiaircraft fire of the Van Force. Losses undoubtedly would have been severe. Spruance, of course, had no information on the disposition of the Japanese force. He had made the right decision for the wrong reason.

The outcome of the air battles of June 19 was decided chiefly by two factors—American use of VT-fused shells that did not need actually to strike a plane to blast it out of the sky, and the incompetence of the Japanese aviators. The skillful flyers of Japan's 1941–42 offensives had long ago been expended, and replacements since then could not keep up with attrition.

June 19 dawned warm and clear, with the *Lexington* 90 miles northwest of Guam, 110 miles southwest of Saipan. In Ozawa's timetable, the hour had come for the Japanese land-based planes to attack TF 58 and cut down its striking power by at least a third. No such attack took place, because none of the planes sent to defend Biak got back in time, and TF 58 fighters had already destroyed most of the rest of the aircraft in or en route to the Marianas. The one serious attempt by enemy land-based planes to reach the American force was smothered by 33 Hellcat fighters over Guam, where they shot down at least 35.

The main battle, the greatest carrier battle of the war, began at 1000 when American radars detected the first of four massive air raids coming in from the west. The initial raid consisted of 69 planes launched by Kurita's Van Force. Task Force 58 steamed toward the contact

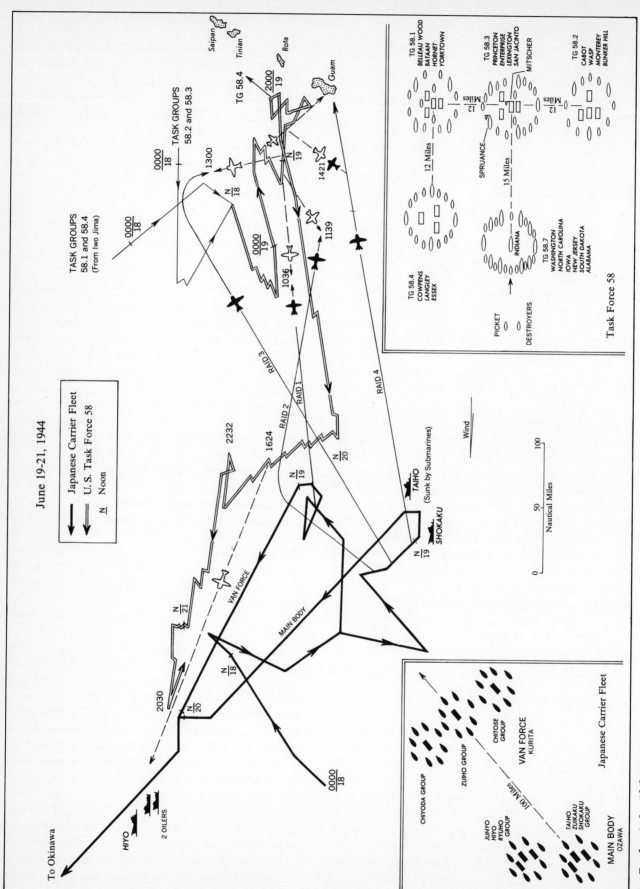

The Battle of the Philippine Sea.

for 20 minutes, then turned into the wind and launched full teams of fighters to intercept. In order to clear the decks for refueling, the carriers launched all bombers to orbit on call. Many of these bombed the Guam airstrips, making them unusable for shuttle bombing by Ozawa's planes. Meanwhile, the Hellcats disposed of 25 of the attacking aircraft, and of those that got through, 16 were shot down over the fleet. One hit the *South Dakota*, killing 27 men but not impairing the operations of the ship. Only 24 Japanese planes survived this raid; all but 1 American plane returned.

The second raid consisted of 130 planes from Ozawa's Main Body. Met 50 miles out by the Hellcats, about half of them were shot down. Twenty reached the battle line, and 1 plane crashed into the *Indiana* without doing any important damage. Only 31 of these planes returned to their carriers.

The third raid, of 47 planes, and the fourth, of 82, from Ozawa's Main Body, were both misled by false contact reports. The third squadron returned to its carriers with only 7 losses. The fourth split. One group found and attacked the TF 58 carriers, doing some damage with near misses, then was nearly wiped out. Another group reached Guam, where Hellcats intercepted them and shot down 30. Nineteen were wrecked trying to land on the churned-up airfields. Only 9 planes of the final raid made it back to their carriers. The almost continuous eight-hour battle that American aviators called "the Great Marianas Turkey Shoot" was over—at a cost of 346 Japanese planes. Once again a Japanese fleet was paralyzed for want of air power.

Nor was this the only disaster that overtook the Imperial Navy on June 19. The American submarines *Albacore* and *Cavalla* slipped inside the inadequate screen of the Main Body and torpedoed the big new carrier *Taiho*, Ozawa's flagship, and the veteran *Shokaku*, next-to-last of the Pearl Harbor raiders. Bungling damage-control techniques permitted the hulls of the carriers to fill with deadly fuel oil and gasoline vapors. In midafternoon both carriers exploded like giant firecrackers. The *Taiho*'s armored flight deck was heaved up in great undulating ridges and her bottom and sides were blown out, but before the ship plunged, carrying down more than 1,600 men, alive and dead, Admiral Ozawa, his staff, and the emperor's portrait were safely removed.

Spruance, convinced at last that he was dealing with only one Japanese force and satisfied that its wings were clipped, was now ready to move in on the enemy. At about 2000, TF 58 recovered its last planes from the Turkey Shoot. Then, leaving behind one carrier group to keep the Guam and Rota airfields pounded down, it headed west and then southwest, the direction from which the Japanese planes had come. But Ozawa, instead of retiring toward Tawitawi, was hauling off to the northwest to refuel, unrealistically planning with his 100 remaining planes to resume the battle on the 21st. Hence the Americans, despite a five-knot speed advantage, gained little on the enemy. A search launched at dawn on June 20 found nothing. Nevertheless at noon Mitscher, on a mere hunch, changed course to northwest. Instead of gaining, however, he now actually fell behind in the chase because of the necessity of turning into the wind to launch further searches.

At long last, shortly before 1600, came the word for which the whole task force had been waiting. A search pilot from the *Enterprise* reported sighting the enemy fleet 220 miles WNW of TF 58. This was beyond optimum attack range for the American carrier planes, and an attack launched so late in the day would oblige them to return and land on their carriers after dark, for which most of them had no training. Mitscher, weighing risk and opportunity, decided that the chance to cripple the enemy fleet by sinking ships outweighed the risk and ordered a full deckload strike.

In the ready rooms the ticker tapes spelled out the range and bearing of the enemy, and the squawk box squawked: "Pilots, man your planes." At 1620, TF 58 turned into the wind and in an amazingly brief 10 minutes launched 216 planes—85 fighters, 77 dive bombers, and 54 torpedo bombers. As the last plane was airborne, the task force turned back in the direction of the enemy, stepping up speed to shorten as much as possible the planes' return flight.

Then from the search pilot came shocking news. His original message contained a coding error. His amended report now placed the enemy 60 miles farther away. Since the Japanese had maintained their westerly course while the Americans turned east to launch, the TF 58 aviators would have to fly more than 300 miles to make their attack. Mitscher was deeply perturbed. Childless, he cherished a paternal tenderness for his flyers. He canceled an intended second deckload strike and was on the point of recalling his first. Then, after studying the charts, he reluctantly decided to let it continue. For a man of Mitscher's compassionate nature, it was an extraordinarily painful decision because it was impossible that all of the flyers would make it back to their decks.

The sun was just setting when Mitscher's flyers sighted the Japanese fleet—oilers first, then the combat vessels scattering fanwise in three groups. A few of the planes dived on the oilers, and so severely damaged two that they had to be scuttled. The rest of the pilots headed for the segments of Ozawa's fleet, from which

Mitscher, aboard the Lexington (II), *awaits return of flyers with Captains Truman Hedding and Arleigh Burke.*

arose 75 survivors of the Turkey Shoot. Despite fire from Zeros and from the ships below, dive bombers bored in and damaged two carriers, a battleship, and a cruiser, and Avenger torpedo bombers put two torpedoes into the carrier *Hiyo*. The torpedoed carrier, ablaze, her ammunition exploding, sank bow first. Twenty American planes were shot down, but when the brief battle was over and the rest were heading back toward TF 58, the Japanese had left only 35 serviceable planes of their original 430.

Many of the American flyers as they turned back into headwinds and the gathering darkness must have checked their fuel gages with dismay; few showed more than half full. Nevertheless some of the pilots wasted what fuel they had by trying to outrace nightfall. A plane with a punctured tank was the first to go down. Others soon followed. One small group, flying close together for company in the darkness and facing the probability of hitting the water one at a time, took a vote by radio on whether to ditch together instead. The "ayes" had it. "O.K.," said the chairman, "here we go." The majority, however, pushed on hopefully, sustained by the thought that with their carriers speeding toward them they yet would make it.

Mitscher had not left the *Lexington*'s bridge wing since the launching. His dinner had been brought to him on a tray. When a radio report from the flight leader announced the attack completed, he ordered his task groups to spread out in order to facilitate night recovery operations. At 2045 the first returning planes were in orbit over the task force, their red and green lights blinking. Mitscher now ordered his task groups to turn into the east wind, and to Captain Arleigh Burke, his chief of staff, he said, "Turn on the lights." All ships switched on truck lights and running lights. Rows of glow lights outlined the flight decks. Cruisers fired star shell. Searchlights flashed vertically skyward as homing beacons, or pointed at carrier decks. All such pyrotechnics made TF 58 visibly tempting bait for any enemy submarine in the area, or any suicidally inclined enemy pilot that might have followed the American planes back from their attack. But, like Spruance in the Battle of Midway two years before, Mitscher had no choice, and not only for humanitarian reasons. A carrier without aviators is a mere liability—as Koga had realized when he was unable to contest the assaults on the Gilberts and the Marshalls, and as Ozawa was painfully aware as he now fled toward Okinawa.

At first the landing signal officers, using fluorescent batons, waved planes onto the carriers with smooth efficiency. Then, as both landing circles and flight decks became crowded, they were obliged to wave off more and more. To relieve the congestion, some captains simply ordered empty aircraft pushed overboard. One confused pilot tried to land on a destroyer and splashed alongside. Others, their fuel exhausted, made controlled water landings; then, in rubber rafts or life jackets, they blinked their waterproof flashlights and blew whistles to attract the attention of destroyers, which bustled about, picking them up. In the mounting confusion, two planes landed simultaneously on the *Enterprise*, escaping a crash only because their tail hooks caught different cables. A desperate pilot refused a wave-off from the *Lexington*. High, he cut his engine, hit the flight deck hard, bounced over the barrier, and crashed with searing flashes and a great shower of sparks into six newly landed planes, killing two men and injuring half a dozen others. A similar smash-up occurred at about the same time on the *Bunker Hill*.

A little past 2230, as soon as the last returning plane had landed and the last locally ditched aviator had been retrieved, TF 58 resumed course WNW, now at a moderate 16 knots. This was only incidentally a pursuit. Though Mitscher hoped to finish off enemy cripples and their escorts, his main purpose was to pick up aviators who had gone down while returning from the attack.

In fact, Ozawa, with the engineering plants of all his surviving ships intact, was opening the distance on course northwest at 20 knots. Night-flying Avengers picked him up at dawn on the 21st, 360 miles from TF 58. That was the last contact beween the fleets. At sunset Spruance ordered the chase abandoned, and the task force shaped course for the Marianas. On the return passage the search for splashed airmen continued diligently, aided by float planes from Saipan. At length all but 39 of the 209 aviators who had gone down during or after the June 20 battle were rescued. In the two days of combat, the Americans had lost 130 planes, 76 airmen.

In his action report Admiral Mitscher summed up: "The enemy had escaped. He had been badly hurt by one aggressive carrier strike at the one time he was within range. His fleet was not sunk." He thus expressed in mild terms the rage and frustration of the Navy's airmen, who believed that Spruance had deliberately thrown away a priceless opportunity to sink the enemy. Even Spruance was dissatisfied. "It would have been much more satisfactory," he wrote, "if, instead of waiting in a covering position, I could have steamed to the westward in search of the Japanese fleet."

Admirals King and Nimitz, on the contrary, fully endorsed Spruance's decision. He was, after all, acting precisely within the word and spirit of his orders, which assigned him as objectives only to "capture, occupy, and defend Saipan, Tinian, and Guam." But even they could not appreciate the full extent of the American victory. Once more the Combined Fleet was stripped of air power. Once more Japanese sea power was thus virtually paralyzed on the eve of a new American offensive.

SECURING THE SOUTHERN MARIANAS

Even during the Battle of the Philippine Sea, the Fifth Amphibious Force escort carriers and gunnery vessels were diligently supporting the American operations on Saipan. Though Tokyo broadcast fictitious claims of a victory at sea, to the Japanese on the island it became increasingly evident that they were isolated, without hope of reinforcement or evacuation. Yet the defenders contested every foot of the American advance, fighting until wiped out almost to a man. Even the Japanese civilians, rather than submit to the conqueror, committed wholesale suicide, in many cases throwing their children off cliffs and leaping after them.

By June 21 the invaders had conquered all of southern Saipan except the southeastern tip. Three divisions abreast, they then began a northward drive along the length of the island. When the 27th Division, in the middle, fell behind schedule, as it had on Makin and Eniwetok, General Holland Smith, with the concurrence of Turner and Spruance, summarily relieved General Ralph Smith, the division's commander. This unheard-of relief of an Army general by a Marine Corps general caused an interservice row that reached the public press, to the deep distress of Admiral Nimitz and other high-ranking officers.

Abundantly supported by naval guns and aircraft, the invaders fought their way at an accelerating pace toward the tip of the northeastern peninsula, digging the enemy out of fortified caves and underground defenses at heavy cost to themselves. At last, in the now familiar pattern, the defenders, cornered near Saipan's northern tip, staged a massive banzai charge which cost 400 American and 4,300 Japanese lives. The island commanders, General Saito and Admiral Nagumo—he who had bombed Pearl Harbor and lost his carriers at Midway—committed suicide.

Conquering the island cost the Americans 16,500 casualties, including 3,400 killed, but it brought Japan to the brink of defeat, for Saipan was the headquarters of the whole Japanese forward defense system—the true Japanese Pearl Harbor. General Tojo's cabinet fell and was replaced by one which understood that its function was to find a way out of the war. Yet, because no responsible Japanese official could bring himself to propose surrender, the conflict dragged on for another year.

The conquests of Tinian and Guam were considerably less costly to the Americans than that of Saipan because these islands were less heavily garrisoned and defended and because they received longer and more systematic preliminary bombing and bombardment. During the Saipan campaign, units of the Fifth Amphibious Force took time out to work over Tinian, and toward the end, the artillery used against the Saipan defenders was lined up hub to hub on the southwestern shore to blast the neighbor island. Landing near the northern end of Tinian, the 2nd and 4th Marine Divisions, victors of Saipan, advanced the length of the flat island under a barrage, with planes using napalm, for the first time, to burn out pockets of enemy resistance. At the end of a week the invaders had reached Tinian's southern tip.

Before the July 21 landing of Major General Roy S. Geiger's new III Amphibious Corps, Admiral Conolly's Southern Attack Force battered Guam with 13 days of methodical bombardment that left the Japanese groggy and almost defenseless. The invaders, going ashore in amtracs north and south of Orote peninsula, sealed it off, making the Orote airfield and nearby Apra harbor available for American use. Earlier doubts about the ability of soldiers and marines to fight shoulder to shoulder were canceled as the 77th Infantry and the 3rd Marine divisions advanced together to the north in perfect harmony—the fleet providing a further harmonious note with call fire by day and harassing fire and star shell illumination by night. On August 10, General Geiger announced that organized resistance on Guam had ended. The Marianas campaign had lasted exactly two months. In the Central Pacific, the Japanese had been forced back to their last defense line—the offshore islands of Asia, including the home islands and the Philippines.

PRELIMINARIES TO THE PHILIPPINES

In a move probably unique in warfare, Admiral Spruance and all but one of his immediate subordinates were relieved of their commands. They were sent home for a period of rest and then set to work planning the invasions of Iwo Jima and Okinawa. Spruance's replacement was Admiral Halsey, under whom the U.S. Fifth Fleet was redesignated the U.S. Third Fleet. Halsey assumed command on August 26,

Admiral William F. Halsey, Jr.

1944, with orders to capture Yap Island, Ulithi Atoll, and Peleliu and Angaur in the Palaus and to support MacArthur in his invasion of the Philippines. Since Vice Admiral Mitscher desired to remain in command of the Fast Carrier Task Force—now Task Force 38—through the Philippines invasion, his relief, Vice Admiral John S. McCain, temporarily took command of one of the four carrier task groups.

Already the Navy, with bases in the Marianas within bombing range of Tokyo, was having second thoughts about backing off and climbing the ladder of the Philippines from south to north. Why not bypass the Philippines and take Formosa and the China coast as stepping stones to Japan? The mere suggestion of bypassing the Philippines provoked such an outcry from MacArthur that President Roosevelt joined him and Nimitz in a conference at Honolulu to settle the matter. MacArthur argued that Formosa and the China coast were vulnerable to Japanese forces in China, that in the Philippines the Americans would have the active support of the Filipinos, and that failure to liberate these friendly people at the earliest possible moment would be interpreted in the Orient as a betrayal. Roosevelt was impressed with this reasoning but left the final decision to the Joint Chiefs of Staff.

It was Halsey who settled the matter. In the battleship *New Jersey* he joined Task Force 38 on September 11 and the next day ordered an air attack against the central Philippines. This was so enormously successful that Halsey was convinced Japanese defenses here were "a hollow shell." He recommended bypassing the southern Philippines and invading Leyte at the earliest possible date. To beef up available invasion forces, he proposed canceling all other immediate objectives except Ulithi, whose lagoon was needed for a fleet anchorage west of Eniwetok.

Halsey's proposal for invading the Philippines at Leyte, and thus speeding up the war, found favor with all parties. D-day was set for October 20. Nimitz ordered the Eastern Attack Force, en route to Yap with the XXIV Army Corps, to report instead to General MacArthur's Admiralty Islands headquarters. He let the Western Attack Force continue on toward the Palaus, however, while MacArthur proceeded with the Seventh Amphibious Force to the invasion of Morotai, for both would be useful as staging points into Leyte. Task Force 38 would cover both assaults, scheduled for September 15.

The contrast between the two operations illustrates the unpredictableness of the war against Japan. A brief naval bombardment of lightly garrisoned, lightly defended Morotai sent the 500 or so Japanese fleeing to the hills. The unopposed landings were made difficult chiefly by irregular coral reefs and mud. Twenty thousand invaders came ashore the first day. Engineers had two bomber fields and a fighter strip ready on Morotai in time to cover the left flank of the Leyte invasion.

Conquest of the much smaller Peleliu cost the attackers a combat casualty rate of nearly 40 per cent, the highest for any American assault of the war. Crowded into this four-mile-long island were more than 10,000 Japanese, of whom 7,000 were combat troops. These were the first to employ the new Japanese defense-in-depth doctrine for island defense. In the face of naval gunfire, the old order "Meet and annihilate the invader at the shoreline" had invariably proved disastrous. The new doctrine called for suicide operations by expendable forces at the beach merely to delay and weaken the invaders, with the main defense force operating from and within carefully prepared positions far enough inland to escape the worst effects of naval gunfire. There were to be no more wasteful banzai charges.

After an apparently thorough three-day bombardment of Peleliu by 5 battleships, 8 cruisers, and 14 destroyers, Rear Admiral Jesse B. Oldendorf reported: "We have run out of targets." But when amtracs carrying troops of the veteran 1st Marine Division started toward the beach, they ran into heavy and destructive fire from ridges to the northeast. By nightfall, despite the early landing of tanks, the marines had attained only half of the D-day phase line and had suffered 210 killed and 900 wounded. Within a week the southern end of Peleliu, including the airfield, was in American hands, but the really brutal part of the fighting had just begun, as the marines tackled the northeastern ridges. Here the defenders, with the help of professional miners, had gouged out a complex defense network so far underground as to be beyond the reach of naval guns.

Meanwhile, two regiments of the U.S. 81st Infantry Division had overrun lightly held Angaur Island nearby while the third regiment took possession of unoccupied Ulithi Atoll. On September 23 one of the regiments on Angaur was transferred to Peleliu, where the marines were attacking the Japanese defense citadel with bazookas and demolition charges and, eventually, with tank-mounted, long-range flamethrowers that could shoot out a lethal flame 50 feet. By such means the defenders were at long last blown up or incinerated, but the process lasted well into 1945 and brought American casualties to 10,000, including nearly 2,000 killed.

Meanwhile the whole Third Amphibious Force, commanded by Vice Admiral Wilkinson, Kelly Turner's interim replacement, had reported to and become temporarily integrated into MacArthur's Southwest Pacific Area forces, thus beefing up Vice Admiral Kinkaid's Seventh Fleet at the expense of Halsey's Third Fleet. The U.S. Third Fleet had in fact been stripped down to Task Force 38, so that Halsey and Mitscher commanded the same ships, as Spruance and Mitscher had done in the Battle of the Philippine Sea.

Toward mid-October, as D-day for the Philippines approached, all Allied air forces, including the 20th Bomber Command based on western China, coordinated operations in isolating Leyte. Halsey's floating airfields, assigned the northern flank, attacked ships and planes on Okinawa, Luzon, and Formosa. Japan's small reserve of torpedo bombers counterattacked, torpedoing U.S. cruisers *Canberra* and *Houston*. So wildly did the Japanese aviators exaggerate this modest success that their reports set off victory celebrations in Tokyo. Out from Japan's Inland Sea darted a striking force of cruisers and destroyers under Vice Admiral Shima to finish off Halsey's "remnant." But, on learning from search planes that TF 38 had not been sunk after all, Shima prudently retired to Amami in the Ryukyus. Between October 11 and 16, the American carrier force, at a cost of 79 planes and 64 airmen, had destroyed about 350 enemy aircraft and left the airfields of Formosa temporarily unusable. It now took station east of the Philippines to cover the invasion of Leyte.

For the captains of the Fast Carrier Task Force, riding herd with the impulsive, sometimes slapdash Halsey had been an invigorating if confusing experience—especially as compared with operating in Spruance's methodical, carefully thought-out campaigns. But if the schemes worked out by Halsey's so-called Dirty Tricks Department frequently perplexed his own officers, they had the virtue of more often utterly bewildering the enemy.

THE INVASION OF LEYTE

The formerly starveling U.S. Seventh Fleet, by temporarily absorbing a large part of the U.S. Pacific Fleet, had suddenly become the largest in the world, with 738 ships in the attack forces. From Manus and from Hollandia and other New Guinea bases, the main elements of this armada sortied between October 10 and 15, 1944, for the invasion of Leyte.

The minesweepers, leading the way, arrived at the entrance to Leyte Gulf early on the 17th and swept passages to flanking islands, on which an attack group landed Rangers. These commando-type troops were to seize or destroy Japanese radar and radio installations that could detect and report the approach of the invasion forces. The Rangers succeeded, but not before the island lookouts had reported to Admiral Toyoda, who guessed the meaning of these early arrivals and set in motion an elaborate counterattack.

In the afternoon of the 18th, Admiral Oldendorf's gunfire-support ships entered Leyte Gulf and began bombarding the beaches, initially to cover the explorations of underwater demolition teams, which found no mines or underwater obstacles. Three escort carrier groups under Rear Admiral Thomas L. Sprague patrolled outside the gulf, supporting the assault by keeping local airfields pounded down. Throughout the 19th the gunnery vessels fired almost continuously at the shore. One destroyer was hit by coast-defense guns.

On the morning of the 20th, Admiral Wilkinson's Southern Attack Force led the way into the gulf and anchored off Dulag, followed by Admiral Barbey's Northern Attack Force, which anchored 17 miles to the north, off Tacloban, capital of Leyte Province. One regimental combat team was lifted down to Panaon Island to set up a base whence motor torpedo boats could patrol the southern entrance to Surigao Strait. At 1000, supported by close-in fire-support groups, the

troops began going ashore in a variety of landing craft, including amtracs originally destined for use at Yap. Though there was some fire from shore, mostly mortar, this was one of the easiest assaults of the war, carried out in calm seas and perfect weather.

In the early afternoon, General MacArthur, who had watched the landings from the light cruiser *Nashville*, climbed down into a barge with Sergio Osmeña, President of the Philippines, and other officials and headed for the beach. "Well," said the general, "believe it or not, we're here."

When the coxswain dropped the ramp 50 yards from shore, MacArthur stepped into the knee-deep water and with long strides led the way in—"one of the most meaningful walks I ever took." Stepping to a mobile radio unit, set up for his use on the beach, the general broadcast his speech of liberation: "This is the Voice of Freedom, General MacArthur speaking. People of the Philippines! I have returned. By the grace of Almighty God our forces stand again on Philippine soil—soil consecrated in the blood of our two peoples. . . . Rally to me. Let the indomitable spirit of Bataan and Corregidor lead on. As the lines of battle roll forward to bring you within the zone of operations, rise and strike. Strike at every favorable opportunity. For your homes and hearths, strike! For the future generations of your sons and daughters, strike! In the name of your sacred dead, strike!"

THE BATTLE FOR LEYTE GULF

The Imperial High Command, assuming that the next Allied blow would come against the Philippines, Formosa, or Japan, had worked out a defense plan (SHO) in several variations, depending on the point of attack. The chief flaw in all of the alternatives was that each required land-based aircraft to strike a first, crippling blow against the attacking fleet. But the September and October raids by Task Force 38 had destroyed most of Japan's trained land-based aviators, just as, under the designation Task Force 58, it had wiped out Japan's carrier-based aviators the preceding June in the Battle of the Philippine Sea.

When Toyoda on October 17 learned that Rangers had landed in Leyte Gulf, he promptly activated SHO-1—for the defense of the Philippines. Despite Japan's weakness in the air, he scarcely had a choice, for Americans in possession of the Philippines could permanently divide the Combined Fleet. Because of the difficulty of getting fuel to Japan, a force of battleships, cruisers, and destroyers under Vice Admiral Kurita was

General MacArthur wades ashore at Leyte with Sergio Osmeña, President of the Philippines government-in-exile (right, in sun helmet), and Carlos P. Romulo (left, in steel helmet).

based on Lingga Roads, near Singapore, handy to oil wells and refineries. Admiral Ozawa's carriers and their escorts were in Japan's Inland Sea undergoing repairs, and training yet another complement of carrier aviators. Lastly, there was Admiral Shima's cruiser-destroyer force that had sallied forth to mop up Halsey's "remnant" and then retreated hastily to Amami.

By activating SHO-1, Toyoda set in motion the various elements which led to the Battle of the Sibuyan Sea on October 24, and the Battle of Surigao Strait, the Battle off Cape Engaño, and the Battle off Samar on the 25th. These, together with subsidiary actions, comprised the Battle for Leyte Gulf, the greatest naval action, in terms of tonnages involved, in all history. Actual participants numbered nearly 200,000 men. When it was over the Imperial Japanese Navy was shattered, no longer a fighting fleet.

Kurita's force departed Lingga early on October 18, entered the harbor of Brunei two days later, there refueled, and on the 22nd sortied in two segments. Kurita

himself with 5 battleships (including the giant *Yamato* and *Musashi*) and 12 cruisers headed for Leyte Gulf via the South China Sea, the Sibuyan Sea, and San Bernardino Strait. His second-in-command, Vice Admiral Nishimura, with two battleships and a cruiser advanced to penetrate Leyte Gulf via the Sulu Sea, the Mindanao Sea, and Surigao Strait. His and Kurita's forces would thus close the pincers on the amphibious shipping in the gulf. To bring the two pincer jaws more nearly into balance, Toyoda ordered Shima to join Nishimura.

What about Halsey and TF 38? The Japanese had an answer, based upon their estimate of Halsey as bold, not to say rash. Just as they correctly judged that Spruance could not be induced to uncover the Saipan beachhead prematurely, they concluded that Halsey, tempted with a suitable bait, could be drawn away from Leyte, leaving the gulf to the Kurita-Nishimura pincer. For bait Ozawa selected the 4 most expendable of his 10 carriers: the veteran *Zuikaku* and the light carriers *Zuiho*, *Chitose*, and *Chiyoda*. With these, accompanied

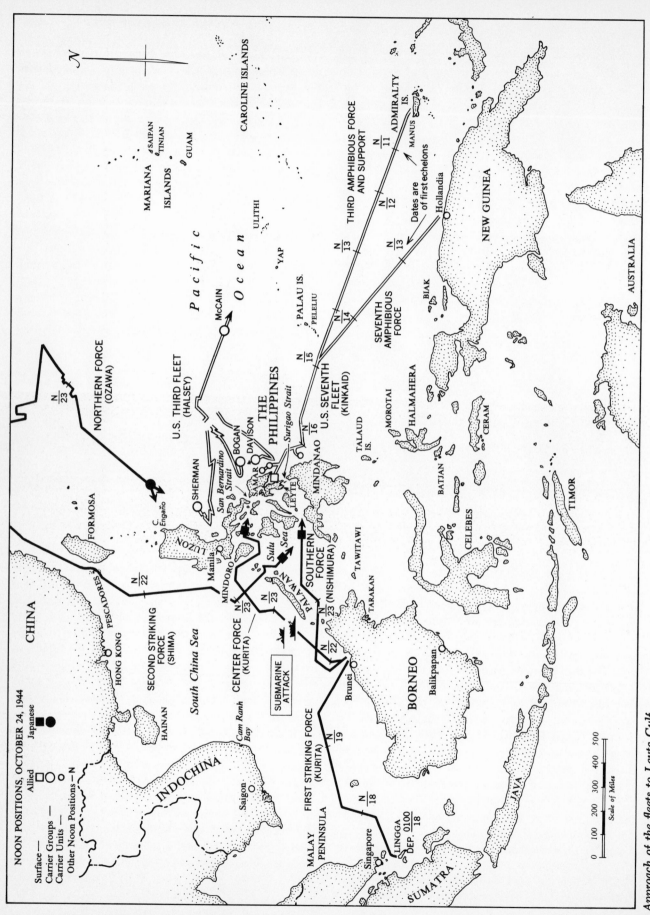

Approach of the fleets to Leyte Gulf.

by the *Hyuga* and the *Ise*—converted battleships with flight decks aft—and a screen of cruisers and destroyers, he headed south from Japan on what he believed to be a suicide mission. The Americans, as they made contact with them, called Ozawa's decoy fleet the Northern Force; Kurita's ships, the Center Force; and the Nishimura-Shima combination, the Southern Forces.

Kurita's Center Force was the first to run into trouble. Off Palawan Island early on October 23, it encountered the picket submarines *Darter* and *Dace*. The *Darter* alerted the Allied forces, then sank Kurita's flagship, the heavy cruiser *Atago*, with four torpedoes, and with two more put the heavy cruiser *Takao* out of action. The *Dace* fired four torpedoes into the heavy cruiser *Maya*, which blew up and completely disappeared in a cloud of smoke and spray. Kurita, badly shaken, transferred to the *Yamato*.

Halsey, having concluded that the Japanese fleet was not going to attack, had sent Admiral McCain's carrier group for rest, rearming, and refueling to Ulithi, whither the other groups were to proceed in their turn. On receiving the *Darter*'s report, he refueled his three remaining groups from oilers and early on the 24th stationed them east of the Philippines—Rear Admiral Gerald Bogan's group off San Bernardino Strait, Rear Admiral Frederick Sherman's off Luzon, and Rear Admiral Ralph Davison's off Leyte Gulf. Halsey in the *New Jersey* was with Bogan's group; Mitscher in the *Lexington* was with Sherman's. Since the Third Fleet and TF 38 were now identical, Halsey exercised tactical command, bypassing Mitscher.

A little past 0800, TF 38 search planes sighted Kurita's Center Force entering the Sibuyan Sea. Against these ships, which had no air cover, Halsey's three carrier groups in the course of the day hurled five powerful air strikes. In this air-waged Battle of the Sibuyan

Kurita's Center Force under air attack in the Battle of the Sibuyan Sea.

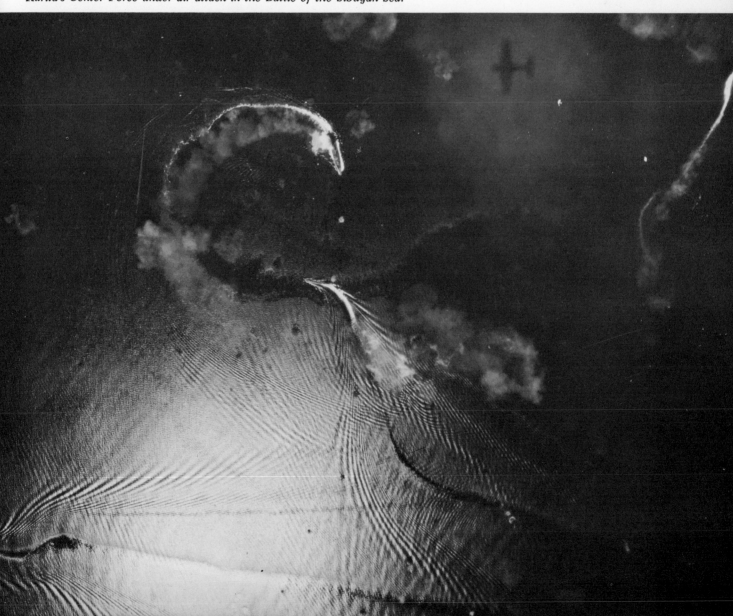

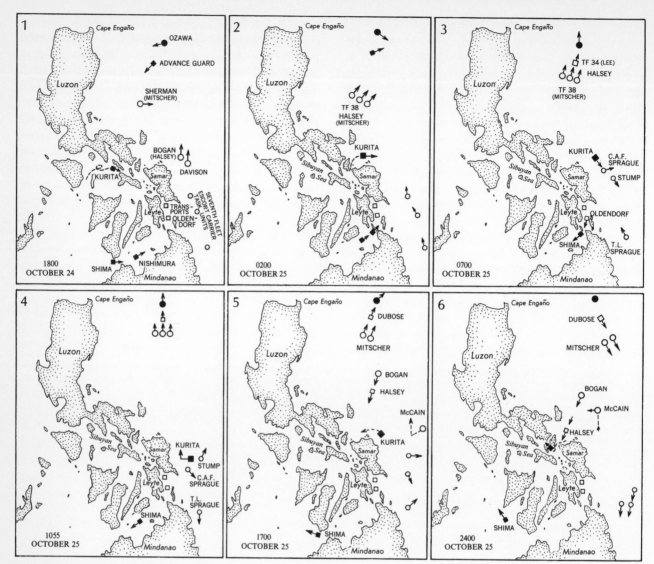

The Battle for Leyte Gulf—fleet movements.

Sea, four of Kurita's battleships were damaged and his heavy cruiser *Myoko* was put out of action. The superbattleship *Musashi*, hit by bombs and torpedoes, began trailing astern of the formation. In the last attack of the day, planes from all three U.S. carrier groups concentrated on this monster, which after absorbing 19 torpedo and 17 bomb hits rolled over and sank, carrying down more than 1,000 men. Shortly afterward, at about 1530, Kurita reversed course and headed back west.

The Japanese air command on Luzon could not provide Kurita with a combat air patrol because they were attacking Sherman's carrier group with every plane they had—on the assumption that this was the whole U.S. Third Fleet. Sherman's fighters met the attackers at a distance and shot them down in great numbers.

One Japanese bomber got through, however, and put a bomb into the light carrier *Princeton,* which blazed with uncontrollable fires. These at last set off her torpedo stowage. The explosion blew off her stern and after flight deck and swept the decks of the cruiser *Birmingham,* then alongside, with metallic chunks and other debris that killed more than 200 of her crew. Ozawa's Northern Force, maneuvering off Cape Engaño, launched against Sherman's group 76 planes, which took heavy losses without achieving anything. Most of the surviving pilots, unskilled in carrier landings, proceeded to Luzon airfields.

Thus far the fact of divided command in the Allied naval forces had produced no problems, even though Commander Seventh Fleet Admiral Kinkaid and Commander Third Fleet Admiral Halsey acted with almost complete independence. General MacArthur in the cruiser *Nashville* was almost within hailing distance of Kinkaid in the amphibious command ship *Wasatch,* but the general consciously avoided interfering in naval operations. Nimitz's hands-off policy kept him at his Pearl Harbor headquarters, lest his mere presence at an operation inhibit the tactical commander in exercising his own judgment. Nimitz's participation was limited to issuing an operation plan, and since this directed Halsey to "cover and support forces of the Southwest Pacific," Kinkaid had no anxieties about the safety of his ships.

A misunderstanding between Halsey and Kinkaid began in midafternoon of October 24, when Halsey radioed a battle plan whereby 4 battleships, 6 cruisers, and 14 destroyers from Bogan's and Davison's task groups would be assembled as Task Group 34 under Vice Admiral Lee to "engage decisively at long ranges." Admirals Nimitz and Kinkaid read this message with satisfaction; though their communicators did not pick up an execute message, they assumed that TF 34 had been formed and was watching San Bernardino Strait.

Meanwhile, Ozawa was trying his best to attract Halsey's attention—making smoke, breaking radio silence, even fruitlessly sending an advance guard of surface vessels to locate and attack the Americans. His Northern Force was in Sherman's search sector, but Sherman was too busy launching and warding off air attacks and

covering the burning *Princeton* to give much attention to search. Hence it was late afternoon when his scout bombers at last discovered Ozawa 190 miles NNE of Sherman's position. Mitscher flashed the word to Halsey, and Sherman ordered a cruiser to sink the wrecked and abandoned *Princeton* with torpedoes.

Mitscher's report had long been awaited by Halsey and his staff. American aircraft had sighted and attacked the Japanese Southern Forces as well as Kurita's Center Force. It was inconceivable that a counterattack on such a scale would be made without carriers; but where were they? Now Halsey knew—and it appeared that the Northern Force was headed for a rendezvous in Leyte Gulf with the other Japanese forces.

In the light of this new report, Halsey did not execute his plan for forming TF 34. When his carriers had recovered all of their planes, he went into flag plot, put his finger on the Northern Force's charted position 300 miles away, and said to Rear Admiral Robert ("Mick") Carney, his chief of staff: "Here's where we're going. Mick, start them north." Carney then sent out a series of messages: to McCain, ordering him to make best speed to join the other three groups; to Davison and Bogan, ordering them to head north; to Sherman, to join them as they dashed past at midnight; to Mitscher, to assume tactical command at that time and to attack the Northern Force early on the 25th; and to Kinkaid —"Am proceeding north with three groups to attack enemy carrier force at dawn." Kinkaid, supposing that

The Princeton *explodes.*

TF 34 had been formed and was guarding San Bernardino Strait, took this message to mean that Halsey was sending three *carrier* groups north.

Even before Halsey ordered his advance to the north, search planes from the light carrier *Independence* reported that the Center Force was again heading for San Bernardino and that navigation lights in the strait, long blacked out, were now lighted. Many officers in TF 38 thought Halsey should have left the battle line behind with one of the carrier groups for air support. Lee sent Halsey a message that in his opinion the Northern Force was a mere decoy with little or no striking power. Shrugging off all suggestions, Halsey with 65 ships continued north after Ozawa's 17. When Mitscher's staff urged him to protest to Halsey, Mitscher replied, "If he wants my advice, he'll ask for it."

Halsey chose to accept at face value reports of his pilots that the Center Force was so battered as to be no longer a serious menace to the Seventh Fleet. If he needed further justification, he found it in a curiously worded sentence in Nimitz's operation order. This sentence, unnumbered, stuck in between two numbered paragraphs, appeared to be an interpolation: "In case opportunity for destruction of major portion of the enemy fleet offers or can be created, such destruction becomes the primary task."

Even without this mandate, Halsey could scarcely have been restrained. In common with most contemporary naval officers, he believed the quickest way to win a naval war was to sink enemy carriers, the vessels with the longest reach and the hardest punch. He had missed his chance in the Battle of Midway. Spruance, so it seemed to him, had muffed his opportunity in the Battle of the Philippine Sea. Now Halsey was going to show how to fight a carrier battle.

He was in some degree a victim of his own publicity. The press, seeking heroes in the grim early days of the war, had latched onto genial, salty-tongued Bill Halsey and created "Bull Halsey," colorful, hell-for-leather warrior, nemesis of the Japanese. Halsey had apparently begun to identify himself with his public image. It would have been out of character for Bull Halsey to remain off San Bernardino Strait waiting for the enemy to come to him.

As TF 38 sped north, the Japanese Center Force steamed steadily eastward. Kurita had never intended his reversal of course to be anything but a temporary withdrawal beyond the range of Halsey's planes so that he could make the approach to the strait through the narrowing seas under cover of darkness. When he notified Admiral Toyoda in Tokyo of his action, however, the commander in chief fired back a peremptory

order to the fleet: "Trusting in Divine Assistance, all forces will advance to the attack." Each commander knew that this meant "No retreat." The attack was to be pushed to a conclusion regardless of sacrifices in ships and men.

When Toyoda's order reached Kurita, the Center Force had already resumed its advance. Its strength was now reduced to 4 battleships, 6 heavy cruisers, 2 light cruisers, and 11 destroyers. Battle damage had decreased its speed as a whole to 22 knots, but contrary to Halsey's estimate, the fighting ability of the heavies was in no way impaired. Their guns and fire control apparatus were undamaged.

Toward midnight, as the force neared San Bernardino Strait, all ships went to battle stations. The men were tense as they passed through the opening between Samar and the southern tip of Luzon into the open waters of the Pacific. In the clear night they strained to make out the American ships that must surely be nearby. Then gradually they relaxed as they realized that, incredibly enough, the strait had been left unguarded.

THE BATTLE OF SURIGAO STRAIT

When search planes on the morning of October 24 reported Nishimura's and Shima's Southern Forces eastbound in the Sulu Sea, Admiral Kinkaid concluded that they were heading for an attack on the shipping in Leyte Gulf. Satisfied that Halsey was guarding San Bernardino Strait, he ordered Admiral Oldendorf to block Surigao Strait with most of the Seventh Fleet gunfire-support ships—6 old battleships and 4 heavy and 4 light cruisers, plus 21 destroyers and 39 motor torpedo boats. Oldendorf, who was determined to prevent another Savo Island and to annihilate rather than merely repulse the enemy, set up the perfect ambush—a series of disagreeable surprises stretching from PT boats far out in the Mindanao Sea to battleships at the northern end of the strait.

Nishimura had been apprised by radio of Kurita's delay in the Sibuyan Sea and was speeding ahead without waiting for Shima. Evidently he believed that his only remaining chance to smash Allied shipping lay in penetrating the gulf before dawn. Beginning at 2300, he ran the gantlet of the torpedo boats, first outside and then inside Surigao Strait. None of their torpedoes hit, and the boats received considerable damage from Japanese shellfire, but they performed a valuable service in keeping Oldendorf posted on Nishimura's progress.

At about 0230 on the 25th, the torpedo boats stood

aside, and the second phase of the battle began. Divisions of destroyers raced down the strait, firing torpedoes and shells at the Japanese from right, left, and dead ahead, then turned away making smoke. Both of Nishimura's battleships were torpedoed and two of his destroyers were sunk. A third, the *Asagumo*, her bow blown off, wobbled away to the south. The battleship *Fuso* sheered out of line and then blew apart into two blazing sections.

While this attack was in progress, Nishimura's remaining vessels—the battleship *Yamashiro*, his flagship; the heavy cruiser *Mogami;* and the destroyer *Shigure* —came under T-capping fire from Oldendorf's battleships and cruisers, which had been steaming back and forth across the northern end of the strait awaiting this moment. Battered by a hail of 6- to 16-inch shells and

The Battle of Surigao Strait, October 24–25, 1944.

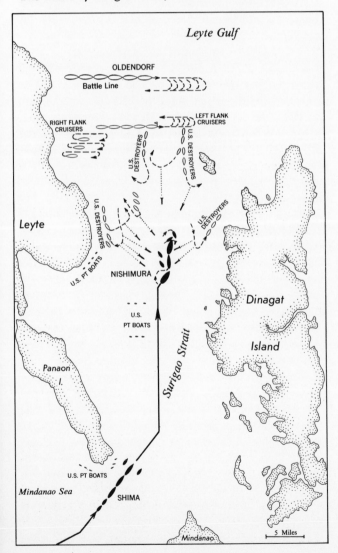

struck by a fourth torpedo, the *Yamashiro* began to sink. The badly wrecked *Mogami* and the *Shigure* turned back. At about this time, Oldendorf, informed that his ships were firing at each other, ordered all shelling stopped. In fact, the only Allied vessel damaged was U.S. destroyer *Albert W. Grant*, which had been hit 19 times by friend and foe with a loss of 34 of her crew.

As Shima's force entered the far end of the strait, a PT boat torpedoed his light cruiser *Abukuma*, which dropped out of formation. His two heavy cruisers and four destroyers pushed on to the scene of Nishimura's disaster. Here the cruisers fired torpedoes fruitlessly at radar targets, and the flagship *Nachi*, in turning, accidentally rammed the *Mogami*. Shima, adding the *Mogami* and the *Shigure* to his force, wisely retired back down the strait.

Some of Oldendorf's cruisers, hunting for cripples, sank the bowless *Asagumo* and put more shells into the retreating *Mogami*, which was finished off later that morning by Seventh Fleet carrier planes. Army aircraft sank the *Abukuma* the following day.

THE BATTLE OFF CAPE ENGAÑO

Toward midnight of October 24 Sherman's carrier group had joined Bogan's and Davison's off central Luzon. Mitscher then assumed tactical command, and the three groups proceeded together on course northeast with aircraft searching ahead for the enemy. The scout planes, a little after 0200 on October 25, made radar contact with two separate surface forces— Ozawa's main body and his advance guard heading for a rendezvous. Mitscher thereupon ordered Admiral Lee to form Task Force 34, now enlarged to include all six battleships in the carrier groups, including Halsey's *New Jersey*. In anticipation of a possible night battle, TF 34 took station 10 miles ahead of TF 38.

The Northern Force, which had regrouped at 0600, comprised one fleet and three light carriers, two carrier-battleships, three light cruisers, and eight destroyers. Ozawa now had only 29 planes, all with inexperienced aviators. Mitscher, on his five fleet and five light carriers, had 787 aircraft with superbly trained flyers. On October 25 these planes attacked the Northern Force six times.

The first strike, which reached the Japanese a little after 0800, was met by a dozen or so Zeros. These were quickly destroyed, though not before they had shot down one Avenger. The American planes then bored in through intense and accurate antiaircraft fire to get at the vessels. A destroyer, bombed amidships, exploded and promptly went down. The light carrier *Chitose,* with three hits at the waterline, very slowly rolled over and sank. In the first attack the cruiser *Tama* and the fleet carrier *Zuikaku,* Ozawa's flagship, each took a torpedo but remained afloat. The second strike, at 1000, left the light carrier *Chiyoda* disabled, afire, and listing.

The torpedo explosion in the *Zuikaku* had disabled both her steering engines and her radio transmitter. Though the first resulted in a wildly erratic course, the second had far more serious consequences, particularly since it went long undetected. Ozawa's message reporting the success of the decoy scheme failed to reach Kurita, who thus had no way of knowing that Halsey was a full day's steaming away from Leyte Gulf and hence no immediate threat to himself.

Ozawa, having accomplished his mission, expected total destruction of his Northern Force. He at first saw no point in shifting from the damaged *Zuikaku,* and in fact intended to go down with his ship. The obvious impossibility of commanding from the damaged carrier, however, finally persuaded him late in the morning to transfer to the cruiser *Oyodo.*

Halsey likewise anticipated total destruction of the Northern Force and intended to have a hand in its extermination. With TF 34 he remained out ahead of the carrier groups and stepped up speed to 25 knots. At a minimum, TF 34 would finish off cripples left by the planes. It might even fight an old-fashioned surface battle, once the enemy carriers were disposed of. "I rubbed my hands at the prospect," said Halsey.

The admiral's attention, however, was becoming distracted by news from the south. At 0648 he had received from Kinkaid a long-delayed dispatch informing him that Seventh Fleet surface forces were engaging enemy surface forces in Surigao Strait. To this piece of news Kinkaid appended a question: IS TF 34 GUARDING SAN BERNARDINO STRAIT? Halsey, puzzled, radioed back: NEGATIVE. TF 34 IS WITH CARRIER GROUPS NOW ENGAGING ENEMY CARRIER FORCE—a reply that appalled Kinkaid.

Next Kinkaid announced that the enemy was retiring from Surigao Strait pursued by Seventh Fleet light forces. That relieved Halsey's mind, for now, he assumed, the Seventh Fleet was free to deal with Kurita if need be. Twenty minutes later came another message, stating that an enemy battleship-cruiser force was firing on one of the Seventh Fleet escort carrier groups outside Leyte Gulf. A few minutes after that came a plain-language message from Kinkaid giving the composition of the enemy force and adding: REQUEST LEE PROCEED AT TOP SPEED COVER LEYTE GULF. REQUEST IMMEDIATE STRIKE BY FAST CARRIERS.

"That surprised me," said Halsey. "It was not my job to protect the Seventh Fleet. My job was offensive, to strike with the Third Fleet, and we were even then rushing to intercept a force which gravely threatened not only Kinkaid and myself, but the whole Pacific strategy."

From Kinkaid came more cries for help, with the additional information that his old battleships were low in ammunition. Halsey, exasperated, ordered McCain, coming up from the southeast with his carrier group, to turn back and attack the enemy force near Leyte Gulf. Then, notifying Kinkaid that McCain was coming, Halsey pressed on to the north with TF 34 and TF 38.

At CINCPAC headquarters at Pearl Harbor, Admiral Nimitz was reading the Halsey-Kinkaid messages with increasing dismay. His staff urged him to order Halsey to take or send TF 34 back south. Nimitz declined, not wishing to interfere with the commander at the scene. Besides, Halsey might already have sent TF 34 back, though no such action was mentioned in the dispatches intercepted at Pearl Harbor.

At last Nimitz authorized his assistant chief of staff, Commodore B. L. Austin, to ask Halsey where TF 34 was—intending the question both as an inquiry and as a gentle prod to take action, if he had not already done so. When the message reached Halsey a little after 1000, it had become less a prod than a bludgeon. As placed in his hands, the dispatch read: FROM CINCPAC ACTION COM THIRD FLEET INFO COMINCH CTF SEVENTY-SEVEN X WHERE IS RPT WHERE IS TASK FORCE THIRTY-FOUR RR THE WORLD WONDERS.*

Austin had added Admiral King and Admiral Kinkaid (CTF 77) as information addressees and stuck in RPT (repeat) for emphasis. The Pearl Harbor communicator had routinely inserted padding, random phrases, at the beginning and end of the message: TURKEY TROTS TO WATER GG . . . RR THE WORLD WONDERS, to increase difficulty of cryptanalysis. The communicator aboard the *New Jersey* removed the opening padding, but that at the end read so much like a part of the message that he left it on despite the double-letter divider—trusting that someone in flag country would point out to Halsey that the closing phrase was marked as padding.

Nobody did. To Halsey the message looked like heavy-handed sarcasm, with King and Kinkaid called in to witness his humiliation. He snatched off his cap, threw it on the deck, and gave vent to his feelings in opprobrious language. The pressure on him had become too

* Meaning: "From CINCPAC [Admiral Nimitz]. For action by Commander Third Fleet [Admiral Halsey]. For information to COMINCH [Admiral King] and Commander Task Force 77 [Admiral Kinkaid]. Where is, repeat, *where is* Task Force 34?"

great to resist. Though his heart was not in it, a little before 1100 he ordered TF 34 to reverse course, from due north to due south. As it passed TF 38, Halsey picked up Bogan's carrier task group to provide air cover and detached four cruisers and nine destroyers under Rear Admiral Laurence DuBose to furnish Mitscher additional surface support. "For me," Halsey later wrote, "one of the biggest battles of the war was off, and what has been called 'the Battle of Bull's Run' was on."

The third strike, launched by Mitscher a little before noon, comprised more than 200 planes. These chased off several vessels that were trying to take the disabled *Chiyoda* in tow, and torpedoed the carriers *Zuiho* and *Zuikaku*. The *Zuiho* got her fires under control and made off at high speed, but the *Zuikaku*, last of the

Pearl Harbor raiders, capsized and sank. The fourth strike, in midafternoon, finished off the *Zuiho*. The last two strikes concentrated on the converted battleships *Ise* and *Hyuga*, but achieved only near misses, apparently because the aviators were tired and the ships expertly maneuvered.

At 1415, Mitscher had detached DuBose's cruiser-destroyer group northward to finish off cripples. Around 1630 they found the helpless, abandoned *Chiyoda* and sent her down with gunfire. After dark they encountered three Japanese destroyers picking up survivors and, in a running, two-hour gunfire-torpedo battle, succeeded in sinking one destroyer. A little later that evening, the damaged cruiser *Tama*, limping home alone, was sunk by an American submarine.

The Zuiho *afire off Cape Engaño.*

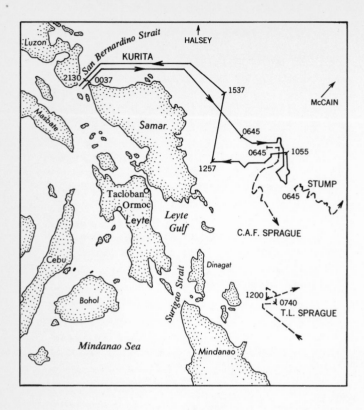

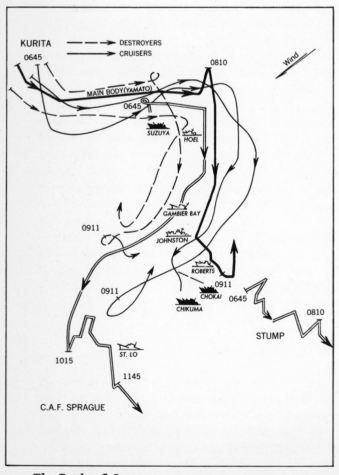

The Battle off Samar.

Though Ozawa had lost his bait carriers, he achieved the greatest success of any Japanese commander in the Battle for Leyte Gulf. He lured Halsey away from San Bernardino Strait, thereby saving Kurita's Center Force from almost certain destruction, and he brought 10 vessels of his suicide force back home.

THE BATTLE OFF SAMAR

At sunrise on October 25, Rear Admiral Clifton A. F. Sprague's little escort carrier task unit, code-named Taffy 3, was on antisubmarine and antiaircraft duty off Samar Island. It had just launched combat air patrol to cover ships in nearby Leyte Gulf. The deck crews were having breakfast, when lookouts reported antiaircraft fire to the north. Immediately afterward a pilot on antisubmarine patrol reported by radio that he was being fired on by a force of battleships, cruisers, and destroyers. Turning to flag plot, Admiral Sprague shouted, "Check identification!" It was unnecessary. Confirmation came almost at once, and more directly, as lookouts spotted the pagoda masts of obviously Japanese vessels rising over the northwestern horizon. At 0648 these vessels opened fire, and colored shell splashes rose around Taffy 3.

The attacking ships were Admiral Kurita's Center Force, and surprise was mutual. Since transiting San Bernardino Strait shortly after midnight, Kurita's lookouts until a few minutes before had not sighted so much as a lone picket destroyer or a single scouting aircraft. At 0300 the Center Force, in night search disposition of several columns, had turned southeast and swept down the coast of Samar toward Leyte Gulf. At first light, Kurita began to deploy his force from columns into circular antiaircraft formation, a slow process that was far from completed when carrier aircraft appeared overhead and masts were sighted on the southeastern skyline. As the superstructures and then the hulls of carriers and escorting vessels appeared over the misty horizon, the consensus in the flagship *Yamato* was that this was Mitscher's Task Force 38, or at least one of the TF 38 carrier groups. Rattled, Kurita made a serious blunder. In the midst of changing formations, he gave the order "General attack." As a result, each division turned individually toward Taffy 3, and the Japanese force lost cohesion.

Taffy 3 consisted of six 18-knot escort carriers, known as "jeep" carriers or "baby flattops," accompanied by three destroyers and four destroyer escorts. Since no doctrine existed for such a force fighting a battle fleet, Sprague had to rely on common sense, and it must be said that he did superbly well. First, with all ships making smoke, he ran due east, a compromise course that opened the range but was close enough into the northeast wind to permit him to launch planes, all of which he ordered to take to the air and attack the enemy with whatever ammunition they had on board. He also called loudly for help in plain English. Rear Admiral Felix B. Stump's Taffy 2, of similar composition, was just over the horizon to the southeast. Stump responded promptly with aircraft, and also by reassurance and good advice over voice radio. Taffy 1, under the group commander, Rear Admiral Thomas L. Sprague, was 130 miles to the south, too far away to lend immediate help; besides, most of its planes were over the Mindanao Sea looking for the remnant of the Southern Forces. Six bombers and 20 fighters came over from the Leyte area to help. Halsey was nearly 400 miles to the north; McCain, nearly 400 miles to the northeast.

As the volume and accuracy of the Japanese fire increased, and 14-, 16-, and 18-inch shell splashes began walking up on and straddling his ships, Sprague ordered his escorts to attack with torpedoes and then dived with his carriers into a providential rain squall. Thus concealed, he turned south and headed for Leyte Gulf, hoping to meet Seventh Fleet heavies coming to his rescue. When he came out again into the open, he was relieved to note that the enemy had not cut corners but was evidently intent on getting to windward to block the carriers from further air operations.

Meanwhile, Sprague's three destroyers, with the sole purpose of diverting gunfire from the carriers, had sped toward the enemy in what they recognized as a suicide attack. Chasing salvos, making smoke, dodging into rain squalls, they closed on the oncoming Japanese and launched their spreads of torpedoes. To evade these, the flagship *Yamato*, together with another battleship, retired northward for 10 minutes, thereby carrying Admiral Kurita out of sight of the fleeing carriers, and thus effectively out of the battle. The heavy cruiser *Kumano* was put out of action by a single torpedo from the destroyer *Johnston*, and at this time or a little later the heavy cruisers *Chokai* and *Chikuma* were probably also torpedoed. The heavy cruiser *Suzuya*, already slowed by air bombing, came alongside the *Kumano* to take off the division commander, and both cruisers fell behind out of the battle.

As the destroyers expended their torpedoes, they fired on battleships and cruisers at close range, and all three were struck repeatedly. After more than 40 hits, the destroyer *Hoel* rolled over and sank. Three of the destroyer escorts charged at the enemy. All three were severely damaged by gunfire, and the *Samuel B. Roberts*, a 40-foot-long hole ripped in her hull by 14-

inch shells, settled by the stern and went down. Four enemy destroyers led by a cruiser came charging in to attack the carriers, but the *Johnston* interposed herself and fired so furiously at short range that they launched their torpedoes prematurely and harmlessly. They then circled the *Johnston* and fired into her until she sank. Thus ended one of the most gallant and one-sided counterattacks in the history of naval warfare.

Almost from the beginning of the battle, the Taffy 3 bombers, torpedo planes, and bomb-carrying fighters kept pounding away at the enemy. Reinforcements then joined them from Taffy 2, from Leyte, and, finally, from Taffy 1. As planes exhausted their ammunition, they made dry runs to distract the enemy, or rearmed on the Taffy 2 carriers or at the Tacloban airstrip. They finished off the wounded *Suzuya* and repeatedly attacked a column of heavy cruisers that threatened the Taffy 3 carriers. Of this group they sank the *Chokai* and the *Chikuma*, which may also have been torpedoed by the escort vessels. Under the unremitting attack from the air, the Japanese ships fell into increasing confusion and, despite their great speed advantage, failed to gain appreciably on the carriers.

The heavy cruisers, working up on the carriers' port quarter, at length found the range. The flagship *Fanshaw Bay* took four 8-inch hits. The *Kalinin Bay* took thirteen and also a 16-inch shell from one of a pair of battleships that were plowing the cruisers' wake. These carriers were saved only by expert damage control and also by the fact that the armor-piercing shells passed through their thin skins without exploding. The *Gambier Bay*, on the exposed flank of the formation, was hit so often that she lost count. At last she had taken more punishment than her damage control parties and engineers could handle. She lost power, dropped astern, began to list, and at 0907 capsized and went down.

A few minutes later lookouts on the remaining carriers reported in amazement that all enemy vessels in sight were turning away. Sprague, mystified by the retreat of the fleet that appeared to him on the brink of victory, shaped course southeast, ultimately for the Admiralties.

THE KAMIKAZES STRIKE

The October 25 trial of the Taffies was not limited to surface attack. A little before 0800, six Zeros armed with bombs dived out of a cloud almost vertically on the four escort carriers of Admiral Thomas Sprague's Taffy 1, just as the carriers were launching aircraft to go to the aid of Taffy 3. Four of the attacking planes

The Gambier Bay, *off Samar, is hit and straddled.*

were shot down by antiaircraft fire, but the other two crashed into the *Santee* and the *Suwannee*, and their exploding bombs blasted gaping holes in the carriers' flight and hangar decks. In the midst of all the confusion, the Japanese submarine *I-56* approached undetected and fired a torpedo into the *Santee*. The two damaged carriers, tough converted tankers, completed emergency repairs and resumed flight operations before noon.

Taffy 1 had had the distinction of being the first target of the new "suicide club" recently organized by Vice Admiral Onishi on Luzon. Its members, aviators manifestly unable to hit much of anything with bombs or torpedoes, would make up in guts what they lacked in skill by crashing their bomb-armed aircraft—and

themselves—into enemy vessels. Officially named Special Attack Corps, the participants and their planes were generally known as *kamikaze* ("divine wind"), the name applied to the typhoon that in 1274 saved Japan from invasion by scattering Kublai Khan's fleet.

A couple of hours after Kurita had broken off action, Taffy 3 also had a visit from the kamikazes. One struck the carrier *Kitkun Bay* a glancing blow and bounced off, but its exploding bomb caused widespread damage. Two crashed into the *Kalinin Bay*, setting fires and inflicting further damage on that victim of 14 shells. Another kamikaze rammed through the flight deck of the carrier *St. Lo* and, bursting into flames, set off bombs and torpedoes on her hangar deck. Seven explosions in quick succession hurled her elevator and sections of her flight deck hundreds of feet into the air. Blazing from stem to stern, the *St. Lo* went down under a cloud of smoke.

KURITA RETIRES

The Center Force's mystifying turnaway that saved the Taffy 3 carriers was in response to a 0911 radio order from Admiral Kurita. Left behind, uninformed, he still believed he was chasing swift fleet carriers. All he could see, however, was a few of his own ships, widely scattered, from which he concluded that the prey had escaped. So he turned away northward, summoning all his divisions to the *Yamato*, in order to restore order to his fleet and make a fresh start for Leyte Gulf.

Headed back toward the gulf, Kurita began to have doubts about the wisdom of continuing. He knew now that Nishimura's attack had met with disaster. The Seventh Fleet ships that had smashed the Southern Forces must now be preparing a hot reception for his Center Force. Even if he should succeed in fighting his way into the gulf, the transports would probably long since have departed for safer waters. Radio intercepts, particularly Kinkaid's plain-language request to Halsey for battleships and a carrier strike, gave him the impression that powerful enemy forces were converging on him.

Kurita had changed course and was steaming westward in indecision when at 1230 a final air attack from Taffies 2 and 3 bombed the battleship *Nagato* and the heavy cruiser *Tone*. At the appearance of these planes, Kurita radioed Toyoda that he had abandoned the penetration of Leyte Gulf and was heading for San Bernardino Strait. A little later came two successive strikes from Admiral McCain's carrier group. Launched from as far as 335 miles away, these planes could carry no torpedoes or heavy bombs and so achieved no important damage, but they did confirm Kurita in his decision to retire. At dusk the Center Force rounded the corner of Samar and headed westward for the strait, which it entered at 2130. The destroyer *Nowaki*, left behind to pick up survivors, was still outside, racing to rejoin Kurita.

The force which on October 24 Halsey had determined to keep concentrated was now divided four ways. Up north, DuBose's cruiser-destroyer group was advancing ahead of Mitscher's carrier groups. From the southbound groups, Halsey had detached his fastest battleships, the *Iowa* and the *New Jersey*, with three cruisers and eight destroyers in a futile race to outspeed Kurita

to the strait. They were too late by more than three hours. In a final division, cruisers and destroyers advanced and at 0110 October 26 sank the *Nowaki*, the only ship of the Center Force left afloat outside. The six fast new battleships of the Third Fleet had raced 300 miles north and 300 miles back south without making contact with the enemy.

After dawn on the 26th, planes from Bogan's and McCain's carrier groups winged out across the Sibuyan Sea for a final crack at Kurita. They sank the light cruiser *Noshiro* and further damaged the straggling *Kumano*, thus ending four days of attacks on the battered Center Force.

LIBERATION OF THE PHILIPPINES

The Battle for Leyte Gulf brought the purely naval war to an end. With Japan's fleets shattered, there could be no more stand-up fights at sea. This happy conclusion resulted partly from speeding up the Philippines timetable. Had the Leyte invasion taken place on December 20, as originally scheduled, Ozawa would have had time to train his aviators enough to give the Americans a real fight. Since Admiral Halsey was responsible for the speed-up, his strategic insight more than offset his tactical lapse of October 24.

Now that the Navy had attained its main objective, its function was to continue to assist the Army and the Army Air Forces to attain theirs. It was Halsey's cherished design to join the B-29s in a raid on Tokyo, providing the fighter cover that could not reach Japan from the Marianas. The plan had to be abandoned, however, because TF 38 could not be spared from the Philippines. Monsoon rains turned Leyte into a quagmire, so that engineers could not extend or complement the Tacloban airstrip to enable Army aircraft to take over the support of Lieutenant General Walter Krueger's Sixth Army.

With Admiral McCain replacing Admiral Mitscher, but with Halsey still in overall command, TF 38 intermittently supported the Philippine invasions until mid-January 1945. During the Leyte campaign, the chief targets of the carrier planes were the all-weather airfields of Luzon and a new "Tokyo Express" that was landing a steady stream of reinforcements on the west coast of Leyte. The carriers' greatest success was on November 11, when their aircraft sent to the bottom a complete convoy, including six destroyers and five transports, thereby drowning 10,000 Japanese troops.

For both TF 38 and elements of the Seventh Fleet in Leyte Gulf, this was a grim period, for the organization of the Kamikaze Corps had enormously increased the effectiveness of Japanese air power. In Halsey's fleet during November 1944, kamikazes crashed onto seven carriers, killing nearly 300 Americans and wounding hundreds more. In Kinkaid's fleet during the same period they hit two battleships, two cruisers, two attack transports, and seven destroyers, one of which sank. Following three suicide crashes on his ships on November 25, Halsey withdrew TF 38 temporarily to Ulithi to make repairs and to give his exhausted aviators a chance to rest.

In order to intercept the Tokyo Express, Admiral Kinkaid now sent destroyers around for night sweeps off Ormoc on the Leyte west coast. The sweeps achieved only moderate success and cost the Navy a destroyer. By early December there were 183,000 American troops on Leyte. Still slogging through mud, these were converging on Ormoc from north and south against heavy resistance. To wind up the campaign, General Krueger got the Seventh Fleet to convey two regiments around for an amphibious landing in Ormoc Bay, an operation in which kamikazes sank the destroyers *Ward* and *Mahan*. This landing behind the backs of the Japanese defending forces proved decisive. On Christmas Day General MacArthur declared Leyte secured.

Before invading Luzon, the Americans prepared to capture and build airfields on Mindoro to provide close air support. The expeditionary force, advancing via Surigao Strait and the Sulu Sea, came under vicious attack by kamikazes from the central Philippines. Despite air cover from Leyte and from escort carriers, these heavily damaged the flagship *Nashville* and a destroyer, obliging both to turn back. The landing, on December 15, was unopposed, but kamikazes struck repeatedly at the supply convoys, sinking five LSTs, three liberty ships, and a tanker. A Japanese cruiser-destroyer force

The cruiser Louisville *is hit by a kamikaze plane.*

on the night of December 26 briefly bombarded one of the new Mindoro airfields but was driven off by air attack.

From December 14 to 16, TF 38 had kept fighters over Luzon airfields around the clock, preventing all but a few planes from taking off and destroying nearly 200 on the ground. On the 18th the force was hit by a typhoon that sank 3 destroyers, damaged 7 other ships, destroyed 186 planes, and killed nearly 800 officers and men. On December 30, after Service Squadron 10 had patched up the storm-battered ships, TF 38 left Ulithi and headed for a strike on Formosa to support the impending invasion of Luzon.

The new invasion would be in Lingayen Gulf, where the Japanese had come ashore three years before. The forces were almost identical with those that had participated in the Leyte assault. The chief resistance to the new invasion came not from ships but from suicide planes, more numerous and deadly than ever. As the 164 ships of Admiral Oldendorf's support force approached the gulf, kamikazes crashed into the escort carriers *Manila Bay* and *Ommaney Bay*, the cruisers *Louisville* and *Australia*, a destroyer escort, and an LCI. The *Ommaney Bay* had to be abandoned and scuttled. On January 6, 1945, when the force began operations inside the gulf, suicide planes struck the battleships *New Mexico* and *California*, the cruiser *Columbia*, the cruisers *Louisville* and *Australia* a second time, three destroyers, and several other vessels—including a minesweeper, which went down after being hit twice.

In the approaching amphibious forces, kamikazes crashed into an LST, into a troop-filled transport, and into the escort carriers *Kadashan Bay* and *Kitkun Bay*, damaging both extensively. Before the landings on the 9th, the battleship *Mississippi* had been hit, the *Columbia* had been struck again, and H.M.A.S. *Australia* had been crashed three more times.

The troops went ashore against no opposition except from a few batteries in the hills, but that evening the Japanese unleashed a new weapon against the ships—explosive-carrying suicide boats. These sank 2 LCIs and damaged 4 LSTs and a transport before they were wiped out by gunfire. In the Philippines the kamikazes struck for the last time on the 13th. By then they had damaged 43 vessels and sunk 4, killed 738 men, and wounded nearly 1,400.

The kamikaze attacks petered out because the Japanese were withdrawing their planes from the Philippines to escape the destructive raids from TF 38. As the air attacks declined, Halsey took his force into the South China Sea to seek out the cruisers and destroyers that had bombarded Mindoro and now threatened the Lin-

gayen supply convoys. Finding no sign of the warships, McCain's flyers raided merchant shipping in enemy ports and sank 44 vessels. As the task force was reentering the Pacific, kamikazes from Formosa struck back, damaging the carriers *Langley* and *Ticonderoga* and a destroyer.

On January 25, TF 38, battered and behind schedule, arrived at Ulithi, where Halsey turned it over to Spruance. The period of close collaboration between the Central Pacific and Southwest Pacific forces had now ended. Most of the ships that Nimitz had loaned to MacArthur returned to the Pacific Fleet. These, with the Fast Carrier Task Force, now called Task Force 58, again became the U.S. Fifth Fleet and prepared for operations against Iwo Jima and Okinawa.

MacArthur's Southwest Pacific Area forces meanwhile moved southward. Troops landed by the Seventh Amphibious Force west and south of Manila added to the punch of the VI Army Corps coming down from the Lingayen beaches. In the city, the 20,000 Japanese defenders fought house by house, week after week, until March 4, when all had been killed or captured and Manila was a shambles. By that time the Americans had also captured Bataan and Corregidor.

By then also the liberation of the central and southern Philippines was under way. The first landings, on Palawan Island and at the tip of Mindanao's western peninsula, were to secure bases from which planes could intercept enemy naval units approaching the central Philippines from the west. The Seventh Amphibious Force then staged invasions of Panay, Negros, Cebu, and Bohol. The Japanese never seriously contested the landings. They held the cities as long as they could, blew them up when forced out, and then withdrew to the mountains. Finally, on April 17, the Americans invaded the Mindanao mainland to finish the work of a 25,000-man guerrilla army that already controlled the countryside.

THE RETURN TO BORNEO

After the Allied invasions of France, the U.S. Joint Chiefs of Staff urged the British to send their unemployed naval forces to support General MacArthur in recapturing Borneo, which would provide a handy source of fuel oil. The British Chiefs of Staff agreed, but when the Americans announced their intention of invading Japan in 1945, Prime Minister Churchill at once canceled the agreement, insisting that the Royal Navy should be in on the kill. President Roosevelt concurred —much to the dismay of Admirals King and Nimitz, who had problems enough providing for the logistic needs of an expanding U.S. Pacific Fleet. Despite their protests, the best ships of the Royal Navy entered the Pacific to join the forces under Nimitz, leaving the Borneo landings to be supported by the stripped-down U.S. Seventh Fleet, which however proved entirely adequate.

For the Borneo invasions MacArthur used mostly Australian troops, supported by Barbey's Seventh Amphibious Force, to which were attached one Dutch and several Australian ships and three escort carriers on loan from the Pacific Fleet. The initial landings, at Tarakan Island on May 1 and at Brunei Bay on June 10, were much like the central Philippines invasions—no resistance at the beach, hard fighting inland—except that a good deal of minesweeping was required. Tarakan was effectively secured by June 14; the reconquest of North Borneo was completed by July 1.

Balikpapan, the oil center of Borneo, invaded July 1, was something else again. The beach defenses here were the most formidable encountered by Southwest Pacific forces during the entire war, and the enemy was prepared to resist actively at the beachhead. Yet, in this final invasion of World War II, the 35,000 invaders went ashore without a single casualty. That is because never had a prospective landing beach been so thoroughly worked over. Aircraft attacked for a month before the invasion, expending 3,000 tons of bombs. The naval bombardment lasted 16 days, during which time the ships fired at the shore defenses 38,000 rounds of shell, 114,000 rounds from automatic weapons, and 7,300 rockets.

SUBMARINES IN THE PACIFIC

Before the war the United States and Japan had identical submarine doctrines: sink enemy warships; no attacks on unarmed merchantmen. But on December 7, 1941, American submariners were startled to receive a contrary order from the Chief of Naval Personnel: "Execute unrestricted air and submarine warfare against Japan."

This about-face was in part a response to Japan's breach of international law in attacking Pearl Harbor without a declaration of war. It was also a recognition of the fact that during the war no Japanese ships would be simply merchant vessels. All Japan's cargo ships would be combat vessels in the sense that they would be carrying to Japan from conquered territories raw materials for consumption or processing, or they would be transporting to combat areas warriors, muni-

tions, or supplies for the execution of warfare. Enemy warships continued to be prime targets, but by far the greatest contribution to victory of American submarines was in sinking Japanese cargo carriers.

The Japanese Naval General Staff decreed no similar change of policy. Warships remained the prescribed chief target of Japan's submarines. This restriction was based on no high moral principle but simply on the wrong-headed conviction that the submarine was wasted in mere commerce raiding. Japan's German allies could not shake the General Staff's settled opinion that, in seeking out and attacking combat vessels, Japanese submarines would be making their most effective contribution toward winning the war. Their 1942 successes seemed to support this judgment. In that year Japanese submarines sank the *Yorktown*, the *Wasp*, the cruiser *Juneau*, and the destroyers *Hammann*, *O'Brien*, and *Porter*, and damaged the *North Carolina*, and the *Saratoga* (twice). Improvements in American antisubmarine warfare early ended this rate of attrition. Japanese submarines sank only two more major warships—the escort carrier *Liscome Bay* in 1943 and the heavy cruiser *Indianapolis* in the final month of the war. Meanwhile, Japan was diverting its submarines into missions that made poor use of their capabilities—shore bombardment, piggybacking of midget submarines and aircraft, hauling supplies to bypassed bases.

Most American submarines in World War II were "fleet boats," named for fish and other marine creatures. A typical example was 312 feet long, displaced 1,500 tons on the surface, and was armed with a 3-inch and a 5-inch gun and ten 21-inch torpedo tubes, with eighteen spare torpedoes. Having few forward bases and nothing like the German milk cows for refueling, the fleet boats were built for independent distant operations. With a volunteer crew of 7 officers and 70 men, they carried supplies for 60 days and had a cruising range of 10,000 miles. Through most of the war, U.S. submarines patrolling off Japan were based at Pearl Harbor. Unlike post–World War II craft they were not true submarines but submersibles, submerging only to avoid detection. On the surface they were propelled at 20 knots by a diesel and electric motor combination. Submerged, they were driven by storage-battery-powered electric motors with a 48-hour endurance at 2.5 knots. They could submerge to at least 200 feet. Variations from the fleet type were the older, numbered S-boats of 800 to 1,100 tons, which were gradually withdrawn from combat duty, and the huge *Argonaut*, *Narwhal*, and *Nautilus*, of more than 2,700 tons surface displacement. In December 1941, there were in the Pacific theater 39 fleet boats and 12 S-boats.

Submarine on surface patrol.

At the end of 1941 Japan had 47 I-class fleet boats, 13 RO-class coast defense submarines, and a few midgets. The I class, typically 348 feet long and ranging from 1,600 to 2,200 tons, was somewhat superior to the U.S. fleet class in size, speed, and range. The RO class, displacing 650 to 700 tons, was in all respects inferior to the S class. The two midget classes were 41 feet and 80 feet long and carried two 18-inch torpedoes.

American submarine sound gear was superior to that of the Japanese, and U.S. submarines were early provided with radar, while Japanese submarines were so fitted only late in the war. On the other hand, the Japanese began the war with a tremendous advantage in their Long Lance torpedo. The 24-inch, oxygen-driven Long Lance could carry 1,000 pounds of explo-

sive 11 miles at 49 knots, or 22 miles at 36 knots. The steam-propelled American torpedo was 21 inches in diameter, and early models carried an 800-pound charge 3 miles at 45 knots, or 7.5 miles at 26.5 knots. More important, the Japanese torpedo with its simple contact detonator usually worked. Until halfway through the war, American torpedoes, with far more sophisticated detonators, often did not.

The difference resulted from the fact that "have-not" Japan had adequately tested torpedoes while the "rich" United States had not. The American torpedo was supposed to detonate either on contact or in passing close to the magnetic field of a steel-hulled vessel. The responsibility for testing was assigned to the Naval Torpedo Station, Newport, Rhode Island, which with a

$70,000 annual testing budget simply could not afford to blow up torpedoes costing around $10,000 each. In tests, neither the exploder nor the warhead was used, the latter being replaced by a water-filled exercise head. At the end of a run, compressed air expelled the water, and the torpedo, thus lightened, popped to the surface for recovery. The torpedoes moreover were set to pass under targets so as to damage neither target nor torpedo. As a result of such penny pinching, only the propulsion and guidance systems of the torpedo were tested. Its ship-destroying capability had to be taken on faith.

At the time of the attack on Pearl Harbor, the Asiatic Fleet Submarine Force based on Manila Bay was the largest in the U.S. Navy—23 fleet submarines and 6 S-boats. When Japanese bombers smashed the Cavite Naval Base on December 10, 1941, most of the submarines in the area managed to elude attack by submerging. Not so the submarine *Sealion*. Tied up at a wharf in the naval base, she was hit by two bombs which killed four men. She could not be saved.

The larger ships hastened south, but the submarines, commanded by Captain John Wilkes, remained behind and went on war patrols, serviced by the old tender *Canopus*. A good deal was expected of them, but they did not even slow down the Japanese invasion of Luzon. Without aircraft for reconnaissance, they had to guess where to look for ships, and when they found one and fired torpedoes, generally nothing happened—to what degree because of inexperience, of faulty doctrine, or of defective torpedoes it is impossible to say. The first successful U.S. submarine was the *Swordfish* (Lieutenant Commander Chester Smith), which on December 16 sank an 8,600-ton freighter. When the Japanese invaded at Lingayen Gulf, Wilkes sent five submarines, but the Japanese vessels were already in the shoals where most submarines could not get at them. S-38 (Lieutenant W. G. Chapple), however, managed to wriggle in and on December 22 sank a converted minelayer and survived a severe depth charging and a couple of groundings in the mud. The next day in the approaches to Lingayen Gulf, the submarine *Seal* (Lieutenant Commander K. C. Hurd) sank a small freighter.

On Christmas Day 1941 General MacArthur evacuated Manila, whereupon the submarines headed south for Surabaya, Java. Admiral Thomas C. Hart, Commander in Chief U.S. Asiatic Fleet, traveled there in the submarine *Shark*, Captain Wilkes in the *Swordfish*. In the next two months the submarine force operating out of Surabaya sank nine more vessels, no extraordinary record, though S-37 (Lieutenant James C. Dempsey) made an outstanding contribution in sinking the destroyer *Natsushio*. During the same period three more

U.S. submarines were lost. After the Battle of the Java Sea, Surabaya ceased to be tenable. On March 1 therefore the submarines departed, and Captain Wilkes set up a new base and headquarters at Fremantle, Australia.

In December 1941 the Pacific Fleet Submarine Force at Pearl Harbor comprised 16 fleet boats and 6 S-class submarines. Luckily, neither boats nor submarine base was hit in the December 7 raid. The first submarines to go on war patrol from Pearl Harbor were the *Gudgeon* and the *Plunger*, which departed on December 11, and the *Pollack*, which followed on the 13th. All three were ordered to prey on enemy shipping off the coast of Japan. A few days later the *Pompano*, the *Dolphin*, and the *Tautog* departed on combination missions and patrol, to reconnoiter installations in Japanese island bases and to attack targets of opportunity.

All of the submarine commanders experienced considerable frustration without identifying the torpedo as a cause, but the *Pollack* (Lieutenant Commander Stanley P. Moseley) sank two freighters off Japan, and the *Plunger* (Lieutenant Commander David C. White) sank one. The *Gudgeon* (Lieutenant Commander Elton W. Grenfell) had no luck at all in Japanese waters, but on the way home it stalked and sank the submarine *I-173*, the first combat vessel ever sunk by an American submarine. The *Dolphin* and the *Tautog* brought back valuable information concerning the Marshall Island installations, and the *Pompano* turned in an informative report on newly captured Wake and on other islands. Without the intelligence thus provided, Admiral Halsey would have had difficulty planning his carrier raids on the Marshalls and Wake. The reconnaissance submarines fired at enemy ships but hit nothing, a curious beginning for the *Tautog*, which was later to break all records by sinking 26 vessels.

By the end of 1942, U.S. submarines had sunk 138 merchant ships of nearly 600,000 gross tons, certainly a respectable showing, yet the astonishing number of misses caused many a crew to lose confidence in its captain, who, as approach officer, manned the periscope and provided the data by which the submarine was maneuvered and the torpedoes were aimed. Some discouraged captains at length concluded that commanding submarines was not their cup of tea and asked for other duty.

Fortunately some of the more self-confident submarine officers put the blame where it belonged and raised enough of a row to get action. Thus the flaws in the torpedo were revealed and corrected, but each correction seemed to uncover new defects. First, the torpedoes were found to run 10 feet deeper than set, usually so far under a ship's keel that the magnetic influence detonator failed to operate. When this defect was corrected, the torpedoes tended to go off prematurely because, unknown to the testers at Newport, the magnetic field of a ship when near the equator tends to expand or flatten horizontally. Hence the exploder was frequently set off some 50 yards short of the target. In June 1943 Admiral Nimitz ordered the magnetic components of Pacific Fleet submarines to be deactivated.

A plague of duds now revealed that the contact exploder also was faulty. Many submarine captains accepted the verdict of the Bureau of Ordnance that the failures were the result of poor aim. Not so Lieutenant Commander L. R. Daspit, who demanded to be shown. In the submarine *Tinosa* he stopped a tanker with two torpedoes fired from an unfavorable track angle. Then, working his submarine around to an ideal position on the motionless tanker's beam, he fired nine carefully aimed torpedoes one at a time into her hull. All hit and not one exploded. The disgusted Daspit took his one remaining torpedo back to Pearl Harbor for examination. Here the contact mechanism was thoroughly inspected and tested, and thus the final flaw was at last uncovered. On impact, the firing pin was released and pushed by a spring athwartships against a firing cap. When the torpedo struck the target head on, inertia pressed the firing pin so tightly against the guides that it lost the momentum necessary to set off the cap. Merely lightening the firing pin, and thus decreasing its friction against the guides, solved the problem. Thus at long last American submarines had a reliable torpedo—but it was already September 1943, and the war had been underway nearly two years.

Shortly afterward the electric torpedo became available. At first submariners were loath to accept it because of its slow 28-knot speed. But it steadily gained in popularity because it left no tell-tale wake and maintained depth, unlike the steam torpedo, which tended to rise as it grew lighter with expenditure of fuel. Before the end of the war most torpedoes carried by American submarines were electric.

Provided with dependable torpedoes, U.S. submarines began to have a decisive effect on the war, for which much credit is due Vice Admiral Charles A. Lockwood, Commander Submarines Pacific Fleet, and Rear Admiral Ralph W. Christie, Commander Submarines Southwest Pacific. In 1944 American submarines sank 2,400,000 gross tons of merchant shipping and 353,000 displacement tons of warships, comprising 1 battleship, 7 carriers, 10 cruisers, 30 destroyers, and 7 submarines. By operating on the vital "oil line" between the East Indies and Japan, the submarines ultimately sank 110 tankers, thereby enormously hampering the training of carrier

Rear Admiral Charles A. Lockwood.

pilots and causing the Combined Fleet to be divided at the time of the American invasion of Leyte.

The rising scores were the product of more than corrected torpedoes. There were, for one thing, more U.S. submarines—33 commissioned in 1942, 56 in 1943, 80 in 1944, 32 in 1945. More advanced equipment, particularly radar and torpedo data computers, played its part, as did improved doctrine and tactics. At the beginning of the war, all attacks were made submerged. By 1943, night surface attacks by the submarines were common. Submarines no longer avoided "down the throat" and "up the kilt" shots, from dead ahead and dead astern. It was recognized that these had advantages—target speed could be disregarded in fire-control computations, and if the ship swerved as the torpedo came close, it merely presented a broader target.

At first the Japanese avoided convoy, for much the same reasons that the British avoided it early in World War I. They adopted it to a limited degree in 1942, in desperation because of heavy losses, but did not regularly employ it until the following year. The Americans responded with wolfpack tactics, but, because the Jap-

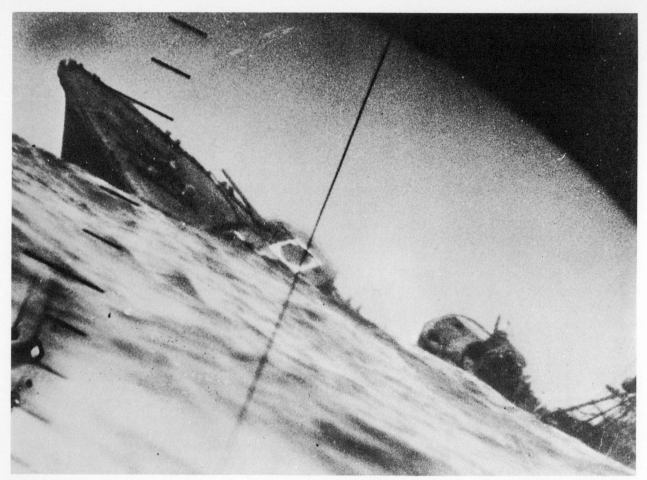

First combat action photo taken through a periscope: a view from U.S.S. Nautilus *of a Japanese destroyer broken and sinking after taking torpedo hits.*

anese convoys were small and lightly escorted, the packs rarely comprised more than three submarines. Many of them adopted titles based on the group commander's name—Blair's Blasters, Clarey's Crushers, Roach's Raiders, Earl's Eliminators. Highly individualistic, the wolf-packs improvised their own tactics. Nothing remotely resembling Dönitz's radio coaching was ever used to control them.

Lockwood and Christie did, however, minutely super-intend the operations of their submarines when they were cooperating with the fleets. In the Battle of the Philippine Sea, it was adroitly stationed submarines that kept Spruance informed of the approach of the Japanese fleet and that sent two of the Japanese carriers to the bottom. At the same time the Japanese, convinced that Spruance would head for the Palaus, had stationed a line of 25 picket submarines north of the Admiralties. Here, not only did they miss the U.S. Fifth Fleet, but 17 of them were sunk by American destroyers, destroyer escorts, and aircraft. The U.S. destroyer escort *England* (Lieutenant Commander W. B. Pendleton) alone sank

six. Again, in the Battle for Leyte Gulf, it was the submarines *Darter* and *Dace* that alerted the Americans to the approach of Kurita and then sank a couple of his ships. Submarines observed Shima's sortie from the Inland Sea on October 15, 1944, and duly reported it. Then, however, they thought their picket duty done, and consequently were not around to see Ozawa emerge on the 20th.

A month after the Battle for Leyte Gulf, American submarines made two of their biggest kills. The *Sealion* II (Commander Eli T. Reich) north of Formosa sank the 31,000-ton battleship *Kongo*. A week later the submarine *Archerfish* (Commander J. F. Enright) topped that achievement by sinking the new 59,000-ton carrier *Shinano*. Converted from a *Yamato*-class battleship hull, she had just left Tokyo Bay on her maiden voyage for fitting out in the Inland Sea.

In June 1945, nine U.S. submarines provided with mine-detecting sonar devices penetrated the Sea of Japan, the last remaining branch of the Pacific where Japanese shipping could still move freely. In three weeks they sank 28 merchant ships of 55,000 tons total and a submarine. They thus effectively cut off Japan from her last source of supply.

At the beginning of the war, Japan had about 6 million tons of merchant shipping. Despite captures of enemy ships and steady building, she ended the war with only 1.8 million tons. United States forces sank 2,117 Japanese merchantmen of 8 million tons total. Submarines were responsible for 60 per cent, aircraft (mostly naval) for 30 per cent. Of 686 Japanese warships sent to the bottom, submarines sank 201. In addition, U.S. submarines rescued 604 downed aviators and carried out such diverse missions as minelaying, delivering food and ammunition to Corregidor and bringing out gold and personnel, and transporting and supporting a raiding party against Makin. The cost was high—50 U.S. submarines lost in the Pacific, some 42 by enemy action. Among the U.S. submarines, 16 per cent of the officers and 13 per cent of the enlisted men lost their lives.

Perhaps the most tragic loss was that of the *Sculpin*, noted as the rescuer of the submarine *Squalus*, which sank off Portsmouth, New Hampshire, in 1939 and was later raised and renamed *Sailfish*. In November 1943, a Japanese destroyer by means of depth charges forced the *Sculpin* to surface and then in a gun battle fatally damaged her. Captain John Cromwell was among those who rode her down, choosing to do so because he had knowledge of war plans which the enemy might extract from him by torture. The Japanese picked up 42 of the survivors, and tossed 1 badly wounded man back. Twenty of the rescued men subsequently lost their lives when the escort carrier *Chuyo*, in which they were being transported to Japan, was sunk by an American submarine. The attacking submarine was the *Sailfish*.

IWO JIMA

As the best site for airfields between Japan and the southern Marianas, Iwo Jima was strategically critical both to the United States and to Japan. The Japanese on this island warned Tokyo of the approach of the raiding B-29s and sent fighters up to intercept them. The Americans determined to take Iwo in order

Planning the invasion of Iwo Jima: (left to right) Admirals Blandy and Hill, General Smith, and Admiral Turner.

to end this hazard. It would provide both a haven for emergency landings for the big bombers and a base for fighter planes to escort them over Tokyo, since fighters could not fly the whole distance.

Expecting an assault on Iwo, the Japanese removed the civilians and reinforced the garrison to 23,000 troops under the able Lieutenant General Kuribayashi, who set out to transform this eight-square-mile volcanic ash heap into an impregnable fortress. On the ridge between the two possible landing beaches he strung a line of pillboxes and blockhouses, while in 550-foot Mount Suribachi, at one end, and in a rough lava plateau at the other, he had his men dig a maze of concealed gun positions and caves, interconnected by tunnels.

B-24s operating out of the Marianas raided Iwo frequently through the summer and fall of 1944 and then bombed it for 74 consecutive days before the final assault, on February 19, 1945. In December and January a cruiser-destroyer force shelled the island five times. The effect of these attacks was to harden rather than soften the target. The defenders merely burrowed deeper.

Nimitz, promoted to fleet admiral, shifted to advanced headquarters on Guam to direct the operation, which he assigned to the Spruance-Turner-Mitscher team. Marine Major General Harry Schmidt would command the landing force, consisting of the 3rd, 4th, and 5th Marine divisions.

Early on February 16 Rear Admiral William H. P. Blandy's support force arrived off Iwo Jima and opened fire on Kuribayashi's fortress. At the same time Task Force 58, 600 miles to the north, began two days of raids on Tokyo, destroying several hundred Japanese aircraft that might have been used against the Americans at Iwo.

For three days Blandy's six old battleships and five cruisers worked methodically over Iwo's defenses, each pounding, in its assigned area, known gun positions mapped in advance. Other positions were added to the control map as they revealed themselves to specially trained spotter pilots operating from the escort carrier *Wake Island*. Kuribayashi cannily ordered his biggest guns to hold their fire till the assault, but on the 17th, when seven LCI gunboats advanced to cover underwater demolition teams, he thought the invasion had begun and ordered a general "Open fire." All of the LCIs were damaged and one was sunk. The battleships promptly turned their guns on the new targets.

Both beforehand and afterward Marine Corps spokesmen insisted that a three-day naval bombardment was not enough. Before the invasion, Navy spokesmen said that three days were ample for an island as small as Iwo

Jima. Afterward they argued that the nature of the defenses was such that a longer bombardment would have achieved little further destruction.

At dawn on February 19, as TF 58 and Admiral Harry Hill's attack force stood off Iwo, Admiral Turner took command of the assault. After the heaviest prelanding bombardment of the war, 500 landing craft spearheaded by 68 armored amphibians headed for the shore, moving like a parade. Experienced observers predicted that the island would fall in four days. The gunnery ships checked fire and began to lay down a rolling barrage ahead of the invaders. Then, at the shore, trouble began. Instead of a beach, there rose steeply from the water's edge a bank of soft volcanic ash in which the treads of many of the amtracs could not get a purchase. The men who scrambled ashore

Iwo Jima.

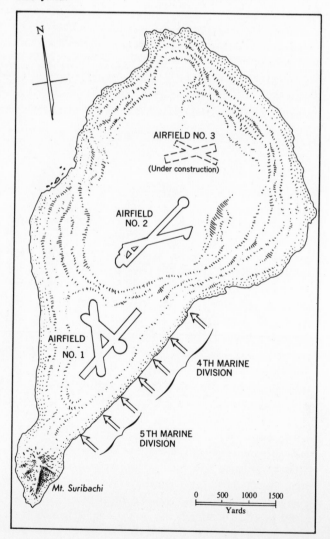

Landing craft move toward the beach at Iwo Jima.

were obliged to crawl up a series of terraces in which they sank to their knees.

As some of the invaders reached the upper terrace, the Japanese opened fire from the flanks and from the emplacements on the central ridge. The marines, with virtually no cover except shell holes, were severely mauled. Stout hearts, however, continued to advance and some knocked out pillboxes by firing rifles or tossing grenades through the slits. Many of the blockhouses held out, however, until Sherman tanks arrived to blast them with point-blank fire from their 75-mm guns. By nightfall 30,000 marines had come ashore. They had suffered 2,400 casualties.

In the weeks of vicious fighting that it actually took to conquer Iwo, the fleet stood by, providing call fire and air support. On February 21, kamikazes crashed into several ships, disabling the *Saratoga* and sinking the escort carrier *Bismarck Sea*. Despite fleet support, tanks, and an abundance of artillery, the marines had to take Mount Suribachi and the northeastern plateau step by step, using grenades, flamethrowers, and demolition charges to blast pillboxes and seal up caves.

By the end of March the heaviest fighting was over, with 21,000 Japanese dead or buried alive. More were

Marines on the beach near Mount Suribachi.

killed later, and 1,000 were captured. Nearly 7,000 Americans, mostly marines, had been killed and 19,000 were wounded. It was a costly conquest, but it doubled the effectiveness of the B-29s. Moreover, by the end of the war 2,400 of the big bombers, whose crews numbered 27,000, had made emergency landings on the island. Thus the conquest of Iwo Jima, besides contributing mightily to the Allied victory, undoubtedly saved far more American lives than it cost.

OKINAWA

Next on the American invasion timetable was Okinawa, chief island of the Ryukyu chain. The U.S. armed forces wanted it for an air and naval base to support their invasion of the Japanese home island of Kyushu, just 360 miles NNW. To pave the way for an April 1, 1945, assault, Spruance and Mitscher took Task Force 58 for a series of raids on Kyushu airfields. These were so successful in destroying planes and tearing up installations that for several days after the Okinawa landings the Japanese could not stage a major counterattack. During the TF 58 raids, however, enemy bombers hit the carriers *Yorktown*, *Wasp*, and *Franklin*. Two hits on the *Franklin* set off terrible fires and explosions that killed 724 of her crew. An epic struggle finally saved her; she was the worst-damaged vessel of the war to make port under her own steam.

Eight days before the Okinawa landings, naval bombardment and support forces under Rear Admirals Blandy and Deyo arrived in the Ryukyus to pound Okinawa and surrounding islands. While the bombardment was in progress, an amphibious attack force carried out one of Admiral Turner's happiest inspirations by seizing Kerama Retto, a lightly held island group 15 miles west of southern Okinawa. The following day Service Squadron 10 arrived to turn Kerama Retto into a handy advanced base for the fleet. The Americans next sited 155-mm guns on Keise Shima, a cluster of islands just 7 miles from Okinawa.

On April 1, TF 58 stood northeast of Okinawa keeping watch over the northern Ryukyus and the approaches from Japan. Southwest of Okinawa, TF 57, the British carrier fleet, covered the southern Ryukyus and the approaches from Formosa. The British force, commanded by Vice Admiral Sir Bernard Rawlings, had recently arrived in the Pacific via Australia and the Admiralties. Comprising 4 carriers, 2 battleships, 5 cruisers, and 15 destroyers, it had about the same strength afloat as one of the four groups of TF 58, but it carried only about half as many planes because of the small capacity of British carriers.

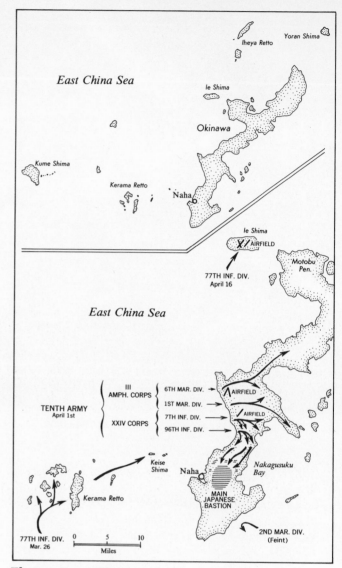

The invasion of Okinawa.

The attack force, newly arrived with the troops aboard, stood off the selected landing beaches on the west coast of southern Okinawa. At the same time, as a means of confusing and perhaps dividing the enemy, a diversionary force was simulating preparations for a landing on the southeast coast. The landing force was the recently formed U.S. Tenth Army, commanded by Lieutenant General Simon Bolivar Buckner, Jr. USA. It comprised four Army and three Marine Corps divisions. The assault would be carried out by four divisions abreast, two Army and two Marine Corps.

At 0600, Admiral Turner assumed command of all assault and support forces. At 0640 the naval bombardment began; it continued for an hour and then was

The carrier Franklin *afire and listing after air attack.*

checked briefly to permit carrier planes to bomb and strafe the shoreline. After the firing resumed, LCI gunboats led the way to the beach, followed by amphibian tanks and troop-filled amtracs. As the first waves approached the shore toward 0830, Admiral Deyo ordered "Cease fire."

Turner had selected this particular beach because a mile behind it was a pair of airfields the Americans wanted. His commanders braced themselves for a hot reception at the shore. They knew how fanatically the Japanese clung to their airfields. These, so close to Japan, they doubtless would defend with special ferocity.

Entirely to the contrary, there was no opposition at all. The invaders went ashore standing up. By 1000 they were in possession of both airfields. The island commander, General Ushijima, was applying the prescribed defense-in-depth tactics. He had most of his 100,000 defenders in prepared positions to the south—out of reach of naval gunfire support. The marines, assigned the northern three quarters of Okinawa, easily took possession. An Army division seized nearby Ie Shima for its airfield. The bulk of Buckner's soldiers headed south, where they at last came up against the main Japanese citadel on April 19. In their first attack on the fortifications, similar to those on Iwo Jima, they were bloodily repulsed.

While air forces on Kyushu were girding for a coun-

U.S. troops in amtracs pass U.S.S. Tennessee *en route to the beach at Okinawa.*

terattack, individual bombers and suicide planes from the Ryukyus made sporadic attacks on the Fifth Fleet ships. A kamikaze so damaged the *Indianapolis* that Spruance sent her to the Mare Island Navy Yard for repairs and shifted his flag to the *New Mexico.* A destroyer-transport, mangled by a kamikaze, had to be scuttled. By June 5, 16 other vessels in the Okinawa area had been damaged by air attack.

The first big raids came on April 6 and 7, when nearly 700 planes, half of them old crates rigged for suicide attack, took off from Kyushu and headed for TF 58 and the ships at Kerama Retto and the beachhead. Then and later, most of the victims were from

among the destroyer types on picket duty in rings around Okinawa, for these were usually the first vessels the attacking aircraft encountered. In this two-day onslaught three destroyer types and an LST were sunk, two ammunition ships were blown up, and nine destroyer types, three destroyer escorts, and a minelayer were severely damaged, some beyond repair. Kamikazes also crashed into the battleship *Maryland* and the carrier *Hancock.* Hundreds of sailors were killed, and many more, listed merely as wounded, were hideously burned.

To supplement the destruction wro ght by the planes, the mighty battleship *Yamato,* the light cruiser *Yahagi,* and eight destroyers, their bunkers holding the last

2,500 tons of fuel oil in Japan, set out from the Inland Sea for a one-way passage to Okinawa. They were to arrive off the beachhead at dawn on the 8th, ground themselves, and fire at American ships until they themselves were destroyed or had expended all of their ammunition. Alerted by picket submarines, Spruance ordered both Deyo's battleships and Mitscher's carriers to go and get them. The carrier planes reached the Japanese force first, a little after noon on the 7th. They attacked with bombs and torpedoes for more than two hours before the tough *Yamato,* her hull full of holes, her topsides a shambles, rolled over and sank. Twelve bombs and seven torpedoes put the *Yahagi* under. The destroyers also got a going over; only four, badly damaged, got back to Japan.

The Japanese mounted nine more mass raids on the American ships, with individual suicide planes attacking nearly every day. The picket vessels continued to be the most frequently attacked. Sometimes half a dozen planes came streaking down on a single vessel. If a plane was set ablaze by shellfire, it generally kept on coming, trailing a comet tail of flame. If not stopped, it whammed into the vessel with a shuddering impact accompanied by bomb explosions and a ball of fire from gushing gasoline—leaving the ship a shuddering wreck, with men crushed, blown overboard, or set afire and screaming.

Kamikazes slammed into the armored flight decks of all four British carriers without inflicting serious damage, thereby giving American ship designers second thoughts

End of the Yamato.

about their wooden flight decks, installed for greater stability and plane-carrying capacity. On May 11 two suicide planes crashed into the carrier *Bunker Hill,* Mitscher's flagship. One skidded across the flight deck and over the side, while its bomb penetrated and exploded. The other crashed through the flight deck, spreading fire with burning gasoline. Its bomb exploded on the gallery deck, while its motor slammed into the flag office, where it killed 3 officers and 11 men of Mitscher's staff. In the spreading fires, fed by fuel tanks of parked planes, Mitscher's quarters were demolished. After three hours of fire fighting, the hangar deck was covered with tons of water on which floated burning gasoline and oil. The captain in desperation ordered a 70-degree turn, which spilled the flaming mixture over the side. The *Bunker Hill* was saved, but 396 of her crew had been killed. Mitscher and the survivors of his staff transferred to the *Enterprise.* Four days later the

Enterprise was hit and set afire, whereupon Mitscher shifted to the *Randolph.*

For the Navy the Okinawa campaign was the most costly of this or any other war—4,900 sailors killed and almost as many burned or otherwise injured, 34 ships sunk, and 368 damaged, many beyond repair. At last for the senior commanders the strain was more than flesh and blood could bear. Toward the end of May Nimitz sent in Halsey, McCain, and Hill to relieve Spruance, Mitscher, and Turner, whereupon the Fifth Fleet again became the Third Fleet.

By June 10, the Japanese had so far used up their willing and unwilling kamikazes that the growing American air power based on Okinawa could take care of the situation. Hence the carrier task force, after 92 days at sea, was able to retire to Leyte Gulf. By this time the Tenth Army had forced the Japanese on Okinawa out of their bastion and into the southern tip

Mitscher's flagship, the Bunker Hill, *under kamikaze attack.*

On Okinawa, Marines wait for emergence of possible enemy survivors after hurling grenades into a cave.

U.S. destroyer Hazelwood, on picket duty off Okinawa, survived despite terrible damage inflicted by two kamikaze planes on April 29, 1945.

U.S. Third Fleet cruising off Japan.

of the island. The gunfire-support ships and escort carriers remained in Okinawan waters until the end of the campaign. On June 21 the American command declared Okinawa secured. The next day General Ushijima made it official for the Japanese by ceremonially committing suicide. All of the defenders had been killed except 11,000 prisoners of war and a few that remained in hiding. The Tenth Army had suffered 7,613 killed and 31,800 wounded.

THE JAPANESE SURRENDER

On July 1, 1945, Admiral Halsey led Task Force 38 out of Leyte Gulf to carry out the mission he had been obliged to cancel the preceding autumn—the raid on Tokyo. Actually his assigned targets this time were the airfields on the plain around Tokyo, for the B-29s had already burned out the heart of the city, one raid in early March having destroyed 250,000 houses and burned to death 84,000 people. On July 10, when Halsey's airmen made their strikes, they were astonished to encounter no opposition in the air. The Japanese were hoarding their remaining planes for mass kamikaze attacks on the Allied amphibious assault which they anticipated on Kyushu—and which was, in fact, scheduled for the coming November but was never carried out.

Task Force 38 planes next struck at targets in northern Honshu and in Hokkaido, disrupting the ferry system that transported coal across Tsugaru Strait. At the same time TF 38 battleships bombarded ironworks on Honshu and Hokkaido. On July 17, TF 37, the British carrier force, joined Halsey, and the two task forces together took another swipe at Tokyo. Their combined strikes at Inland Sea ports at the end of July just about finished off what was left of the Combined Fleet. The forces then hauled off to the south to sidestep a typhoon.

The fall of Okinawa gave new impetus to the peace movement in Japan, but the Emperor and other peacemakers had to conduct themselves with extreme caution, for most military leaders were bitterly opposed to surrender and would go to almost any lengths to prevent it. Prime Minister Suzuki tried to extend peace feelers through Stalin but got nowhere because Stalin had decided to go to war against Japan. Then came the Potsdam Proclamation of July 26, in which Truman, Churchill, and Chiang Kai-shek set forth the conditions under which Japan could end the war: unconditional surrender of armed forces, relinquishment of conquered territories, stern justice to war criminals, freedom of speech, free elections, occupation pending establishment of a "peacefully inclined and responsible government."

Still the Japanese statesmen would not act, partly in fear of war hawks, partly because they wanted time to prepare the people, and partly out of sheer reluctance to participate in the national humiliation.

On July 16 the first man-made atomic explosion took place at Alamogordo, New Mexico, and within a few hours Spruance's erstwhile flagship, the *Indianapolis*, now repaired, put to sea from San Francisco with parts of the first military atomic bomb. After delivering her grim cargo at Tinian, the cruiser reported to Guam, where Spruance and Nimitz were much involved in plans for the coming invasion of Japan. Because Spruance was unready to go to sea, the *Indianapolis* headed without him for Leyte Gulf. En route on July 29 she was torpedoed and sunk by *I-58*. Of her crew of 1,200, about 800 survived in the water on rafts. Through monumental blundering, the nonarrival of the cruiser was not noted. When the survivors were sighted by a Navy plane 84 hours after the sinking, only 316 were still alive.

President Truman had directed that if the Japanese did not freely accept the terms of the Potsdam Proclamation, the atomic bomb was to be used against them as a goad. On July 28 Suzuki, still trying to find some way around the military leaders and his own scruples, foolishly told a news conference that the proclamation was unworthy of notice. To Truman and other Allied leaders that seemed to close the door.

On August 6, the B-29 *Enola Gay* dropped an atomic bomb that devastated the city of Hiroshima. On the 8th the Soviet Union declared war on Japan, and the Red Army marched into Manchuria. On the 9th a second air-borne atomic bomb seared and flattened Nagasaki, and the Allied carrier forces resumed their air raids on Honshu. On the 10th the Red Army entered Korea.

This series of shocks finally stirred the Japanese government to action, for here was something they could use to offset the years of propaganda that had the people believing, despite the evidence of their burning cities, that Japan was far from defeated. The Emperor advised immediate acceptance of the Potsdam terms. The Cabinet concurred, provided that the imperial system was left intact. Inquiries through neutral powers brought an acceptance of this condition, but the Allies imposed two stipulations: that the Emperor submit to the authority of the Supreme Allied Commander during the occupation, and that his status be ultimately decided by free elections. When the Japanese Cabinet accepted these stipulations, a general cease-fire went out to all Allied commands. Halsey received the word on the morning of August 15, just as he was launching

The Japanese surrender party arrives aboard the Missouri.

Fleet Admiral Nimitz signs the instrument of surrender.

a new raid on Tokyo. To his combat air patrol overhead he radioed: "Investigate and shoot down all snoopers— not vindictively but in a friendly sort of way."

General MacArthur, who had been appointed Supreme Commander of the Allied Powers for the surrender and occupation of Japan, knew better than to rush matters. Japanese hotheads had to be given a little time to cool off, to realize the uselessness of doing anything rash. He first summoned to Manila representatives of the Japanese government to survey the situation and make plans. At the end of August the U.S. Third Fleet and the British Pacific Fleet anchored outside Tokyo Bay, and the first of the occupation troops arrived. General MacArthur and Admiral Nimitz came in by air, the general taking up temporary headquarters in the Yokohama customhouse, the admiral breaking his flag on the *South Dakota.*

On Sunday morning, September 2, ships of all the nations that had fought Japan were anchored in Tokyo Bay. At 0856 the Japanese delegation, headed by Foreign Minister Shigemitsu, came aboard the battleship *Missouri* to sign the surrender instrument. Waiting for them were representatives of the United Nations and flag and general officers who had led the war against Japan. When the Japanese had signed, General of the Army MacArthur affixed his signature as Supreme Commander. Fleet Admiral Nimitz then signed as Representative of the United States. He was followed by representatives of China, the United Kingdom, the Soviet Union, Australia, Canada, France, the Netherlands, and New Zealand.

As the signing ended, the sun broke through the morning haze and hundreds of carrier and Army Air Forces planes swept over the bay.

X

The Navy in the Nuclear Age

Thoughtful Americans knew that they could never go back to an earlier day. As a superpower, the United States could not again retreat into isolationism. The sons of the men who had rejected membership in the League of Nations generally acquiesced to American participation in the United Nations.

Yet, by a curious ambivalence, the American people insisted on a demobilization so swift that the victorious U.S. armed forces were quickly rendered impotent. By April 1946 nearly 7 million men had been released from the Army. President Truman called it "the most remarkable demobilization in the history of the world, or 'disintegration,' if you want to call it that."

The fact is that with no visible remaining enemies and with a monopoly of the atomic bomb, the American public was complacent. Few were aware that their national leaders were becoming alarmed over the Soviet Union's annexation of eastern Poland and interference in the internal affairs of Iran, Turkey, and the countries of eastern Europe.

To arouse his fellow citizens, Truman induced Churchill in a speech at Westminster College in Fulton, Missouri, to issue a grim warning: "From Stettin in the Baltic to Trieste in the Adriatic an iron curtain has descended across the Continent. . . . From what I have seen of our Russian friends and allies during the war, I am convinced that there is nothing they admire so much as strength, and there is nothing for which they have less respect than for weakness, especially military weakness." The American public was startled; yet when

Truman proposed universal military training as a means of rebuilding the services, all he got from Congress was a limited Selective Service Act.

The paring down of the armed forces continued until by 1950 the Army had only 600,000 men, and the ceiling on defense spending had been lowered to an annual $13 billion. Naval personnel were released from service so rapidly that it was sometimes difficult to get vessels to port for decommissioning. Ships worth retaining but decommissioned for lack of funds were "mothballed," that is, dehumidified and otherwise put into a state of preservation for possible future use. Overage vessels were transferred, sold, or scrapped. Some grand old ladies of World War II went out with a bang. The carriers *Independence* and *Saratoga*, the battleships *Nevada, Pennsylvania, Arkansas,* and *New York,* and the cruisers *Pensacola* and *Salt Lake City* were among the American, German, and Japanese ships exposed to experimental atomic explosions at Bikini Atoll in July 1946.

Despite the nation's military weakness, the President felt compelled in May 1947 to proclaim what became known as the Truman Doctrine—a policy of aiding free nations "against aggressive movements that seek to impose upon them totalitarian regimes," and of "supporting peoples who are resisting attempted subjugation by armed minorities or by outside pressures." Specifically, Truman was asking Congress for $400 million in military and economic aid to help Greece and Turkey in resisting pressure by the Soviet Union to bring them into the Communist orbit, but the new policy set the United

Atomic cloud engulfs the target fleet at Bikini Atoll.

States on the path of international intervention for the containment of Communism that was to shape American foreign relations for at least a generation.

To back up the Truman Doctrine and otherwise support Western interests, the President ordered the U.S. Sixth Fleet to the Mediterranean for continuous duty. Included were a carrier force, with one of the large carriers—alternately the *Midway,* the *Franklin D. Roosevelt,* or the *Coral Sea*—and an amphibious force of transports carrying a Marine Corps battalion landing team and escorted by cruisers and destroyers.

In the atmosphere of Congressional penny pinching, the President and his advisers cast about for means of getting "a bigger bang for a buck." The most attractive solution superficially was a merger of the armed services to avoid expensive duplication. The World War II example of Admiral Nimitz's Pacific Ocean Areas seemed to support the advocates of unification.

Generals Eisenhower and MacArthur had been, of course, as supreme in their theaters as Nimitz in his, but neither issued direct orders to the Navy—possibly because it was never necessary. In their commands there was never any such incident as that of Marine General H. M. Smith relieving Army General Ralph Smith—

that is, a general of naval infantry relieving a general of army infantry on the authority of two admirals. Nor did Eisenhower or MacArthur ever have occasion to give their admirals the sort of nudge that Nimitz gave his general on Okinawa: when the supporting Fifth Fleet had been under kamikaze attack for several weeks, Admiral Nimitz appeared at General Buckner's headquarters to find out why the Army had bogged down. Buckner received Nimitz politely, but pointed out that this was ground, implying that the Okinawan land campaign was strictly Army business. "Ground though it may be," replied Nimitz, "I'm losing a ship and a half a day. So if this line isn't moving in five days, we'll get someone here to move it so we can all get out from under these stupid air attacks."

Along with the impulse to unification of the armed services existed an impetus toward further division. The Army Air Forces had exercised considerable autonomy in World War II, and their leaders argued that they had earned the right to a separate identity. They had had their own man on the Joint Chiefs of Staff. Their strategic bombing of Germany had been a virtually independent mission. The Twentieth Army Air Force, whose B-29s had raided Japan from the Marianas and dropped the atomic bombs, had been under the direct command of the Joint Chiefs—the only operations in the Pacific Ocean areas not controlled by Nimitz.

The Air Force argument was supported by the widely held but simplistic view that all weapons had become obsolete except the atomic bomb and the big bomber to deliver it—a view that overlooked the fact that diplomatic protest is not enough to settle some international disputes and the atomic bomb is far too drastic for most. That fact has become clear in a world where since 1950 there has been almost continuous warfare without, so far, a resort to nuclear weapons.

Naval leaders, headed by Navy Secretary James Forrestal, did a good deal of foot dragging with respect to both unification and the creation of a separate air force. If there was to be integration of the services, they favored something a good deal short of a complete merger, with an all-powerful civilian secretary to distribute appropriations and set policy and an all-powerful military chief of staff to direct operations. A man in either position was likely to understand one service and its functions better than the others and hence to favor it at the expense of proper balance. And one man, unchecked, could easily make a fatal misjudgment.

Naval leaders also feared that, in the cutting of a single defense appropriations pie, the slicer would be influenced by the popular misconception that fleets exist mainly to fight fleets. Since the only conceivable enemy of the United States at that time was the Soviet Union, which then had no fleet to speak of, the Navy might be left with a very thin slice indeed.

As for the emergence of a separate air force, the Navy was concerned lest it encourage another widespread simplistic notion—that the Army should control all artillery and troops, the Air Force all planes and aviators, and the Navy all ships and sailors. Such a division had a certain logical appeal, but it would deprive the Navy of its Marine Corps and the naval air arm. Without these, the Navy felt that it could not deal with the complexities of modern warfare. In World War II Britain's Royal Navy had never recovered from its earlier dependence on the Royal Air Force for aircraft and airmen.

Forrestal, aware that he could not defeat the movement toward unification, labored to retain the Marine Corps and naval air arm and the Joint Chiefs of Staff, and to limit the authority of the Secretary of Defense to staff and coordinating functions. Though he had at hand and made use of the sage counsel of Admiral Nimitz, who had succeeded Admiral King as Chief of Naval Operations, Forrestal typically relied more on civilians for advice. At his request, Ferdinand Eberstadt,

a Wall Street financier, drew up the report which formed the basis for the National Military Establishment, created by the National Security Act of 1947.

Under the National Military Establishment were the subordinate Departments of the Army, the Navy, and the Air Force. It was headed by a Secretary of Defense, who would sit in the President's Cabinet, and each of the departments would have a Secretary not of Cabinet rank. The Joint Chiefs of Staff were retained to direct operations, and the Navy kept its carrier aviation, its shore-based reconnaissance wing, and its Marine Corps.

Forrestal, appointed first Secretary of Defense, had the task of adjusting the services to triple harness and of dividing the skimpy appropriations among them. Such friction grew out of conflicting opinions on how best to serve the nation's military requirements that Forrestal must frequently have felt that he was dealing with high-strung and jealous prima donnas. At the same time he was attempting the impossible goals of meeting expanding commitments while reducing forces to peacetime levels and of maintaining a military posture while balancing the budget. His reward for failure to achieve the unattainable was vilification in the press. The resulting strain undoubtedly contributed to the breakdown in his health and his subsequent suicide.

Forrestal's successor, Louis A. Johnson, a less complex

Ships of the Sixth Fleet in the Mediterranean to bolster the Truman Doctrine.

and less sensitive man, came into office with the conviction that his new job required a good deal of toughness and that he had what it took. His first task was allocating a skimpy $16-billion defense budget among the services. As a former director of the company that manufactured the B-16 long-range bomber on which the Air Force based its strategy, he had come to appreciate Air Force goals. He accepted the view of air officers that the new large carriers proposed by the Navy to carry planes big enough to deliver the atomic bomb would mean costly duplication of a function assigned the Air Force. On April 23, 1949, Johnson summarily canceled construction of the 60,000-ton carrier *United States,* for which the keel had been laid. Secretary of the Navy John L. Sullivan thereupon resigned.

Sullivan's successor, Francis P. Matthews, found himself involved in Congressional hearings and in debates in which tempers flared. There was little sympathy between the new Secretary and senior naval officers, who felt that he was not seriously espousing their point of view. At length Matthews prevailed upon President Truman to dismiss the Chief of Naval Operations, Admiral Louis Denfeld. Among other officers whose careers seemed permanently damaged by their strong-minded participation in the controversy were Captain Arleigh Burke and Admiral Arthur W. Radford, but both out of sheer ability quickly bounced back—Burke as Chief of Naval Operations, Radford as Chairman of the Joint Chiefs of Staff.

On Admiral Nimitz's advice Truman appointed as the new CNO Admiral Forrest P. Sherman, who did much to heal the wounds left by the controversy, though the debate did not entirely end until the Korean War brought more liberal defense appropriations. One result of the dispute was the Defense Reorganization Act of 1949, which forced a closer unification among the services under a regular executive department, the Department of Defense.

Meanwhile, Russian aggressiveness was intensifying. Western governments were shocked when in 1948 the Soviet-inspired Communist party in Czechoslovakia took over the national government by coup d'etat, but there was nothing they could do short of declaring war. The United States discovered then and later that inland states far from the sea were immune to the pressures, subtle or otherwise, that American sea power was able to exert in several major crises.

On the other hand, the United States and Britain could and did react to the blockade that the Soviet Union that same year clamped on Berlin, which by terms of the Potsdam Conference was occupied by U.S., British, French, and Russian forces. The blockade, closing all access roads, was possible because Berlin was entirely surrounded by the Soviet zone of occupation. Britain and the United States, however, canceled the effect of the Soviet action by supplying the German metropolis by air. They had flown in more than 2 million tons of food, fuel, and supplies when at the end of 11 months the blockade was lifted.

As a result of the growing Soviet menace, the United States and Canada in 1949 joined hands militarily with the countries of Western Europe in the North Atlantic Treaty Organization (NATO), the parties agreeing that "an armed attack against one of them in Europe or North America shall be considered an attack against them all." The North Atlantic nations were thus brought under the protection of the atomic bomb—but within a month of the U.S. Senate's acceptance of the North Atlantic Pact, the Soviet Union exploded its own atomic bomb. Under the pact, General of the Army Dwight D. Eisenhower became Supreme Allied Commander Europe, and Admiral Lynde D. McCormick USN, Supreme Allied Commander Atlantic. From time to time joint naval maneuvers were held using special NATO signals and tactics.

A powerful Communist faction already existed in China under the leadership of Mao Tse-tung. During the conflict with Japan, Mao supported the national government of Chiang Kai-shek, but after the Japanese defeat Mao and his Communists resumed their civil war. By the end of 1949 they occupied Manchuria, and in the next two years they took over control of the rest of China, ousting the national government, which fled to Formosa.

At the end of World War II, in a supposedly temporary arrangement, the Russians received the surrender of the Japanese in Korea north of the 38th parallel, while the Americans accepted the surrender south of that latitude. Thereafter the Soviets treated the 38th parallel as a political boundary. When a United Nations commission attempted in 1948 to organize free, nationwide elections in order to establish an independent Korean government, the Soviet Union refused to cooperate and barred the U.N. representatives from North Korea. The commission therefore held the elections only in South Korea, and on August 15, 1948, the United Nations recognized the Republic of Korea (R.O.K.). The Korean general assembly chose Syngman Rhee as president and established its government in Seoul, the traditional capital.

The Soviet Union, declaring the election illegal, recognized in North Korea the puppet Democratic People's Republic of Korea with its capital at Pyongyang. At the end of 1948 the Soviet Union announced that it had withdrawn all occupation forces from Korea, but it was obvious that a good many Russians remained behind to train the North Korean army. The American evacuation of South Korea, which had been going on for some time, was completed in June 1949, leaving behind only a 500-man military advisory group to assist in training a hastily organized R.O.K. army.

The Democratic People's Republic attempted by means of raids, guerrilla warfare, propaganda, and terrorism to bring down the Republic of Korea in order to unite the country under itself. When these indirect methods failed, Stalin and Mao Tse-tung, who was visiting Moscow, decided on direct action. On the morning of June 25, 1950, the North Korean army without warning crossed the 38th parallel in a full-scale invasion.

THE KOREAN WAR

The North Koreans and their Russian and Chinese sponsors evidently counted on no sharper international reaction to their invasion of South Korea than diplomatic protests. Instead, the United Nations Security Council directed the invaders to withdraw to the 38th parallel, and called on U.N. members to enforce the directive. Thanks to the absence of the Russian delegate, out on boycott, there was no veto.

When the North Koreans failed to heed the Security Council directive, President Truman, acting as agent for the United Nations, ordered the U.S. armed forces to go to the aid of the Republic of Korea and appointed as Commander in Chief Far East General MacArthur, then commanding the occupation of Japan. Naval forces under MacArthur were to be commanded by Vice Admiral C. Turner Joy USN. The Security Council called on other U.N. members to assist the United States, and nearly a score eventually did—some providing troops or ships, if only in token numbers, others furnishing medical and other services.

With the fall of Seoul, the R.O.K. army was too demoralized to resist the invaders, even with American air and naval support. MacArthur therefore committed three of the four divisions of the U.S. Eighth Army, then occupying Japan. All were under strength, short of weapons, and with incomplete combat training. The first of them to reach Korea encountered south of Seoul the vanguard of 15 well-equipped Red divisions. The Americans, by blowing up bridges, setting up roadblocks, and engaging in suicidal fighting, won a little time for a build-up of U.N. forces through the Korean port of Pusan.

Around Pusan, Lieutenant General Walton W.

Vice Admiral C. Turner Joy, commander of U.N. naval forces during the Korean War.

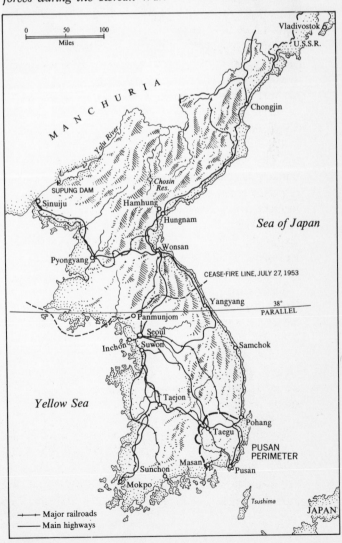

Korea.

Vice Admiral Arthur D. Struble, commander of the Seventh Fleet.

Walker, Commander Eighth Army, was thus enabled to establish a defensive perimeter, within which he held back superior forces by skillful use of his interior lines. Nevertheless the world was bemused with the spectacle of Americans, late chief victors over three major powers, thrust into a corner by the armed forces of one third-rate power—a result of American military penny pinching.

Vice Admiral Arthur D. Struble's U.S. Seventh Fleet, with British warships attached, probably provided the narrow margin of force that maintained the Eighth Army in Korea. Throughout the war, Seventh Fleet surface vessels kept the seaside east coast road and railroad unusable for supplying the North Korean army, which thus became heavily dependent on the roads and railroads passing through Seoul on the other side of the mountains. Task Force 77, the carrier force, joined U.S. Air Force bombers in blasting hangars, fuel storage depots, refineries, bridges, and marshaling yards in North Korea, and in completely destroying the small North Korean air force. The carrier planes then shifted to close support of the Eighth Army, a function for which Air Force pilots were not trained. So effective was the close air support that the North Koreans at length abandoned daytime offensives as too costly.

U.S. carrier Valley Forge, *which served in Task Force 77 throughout most of the Korean War.*

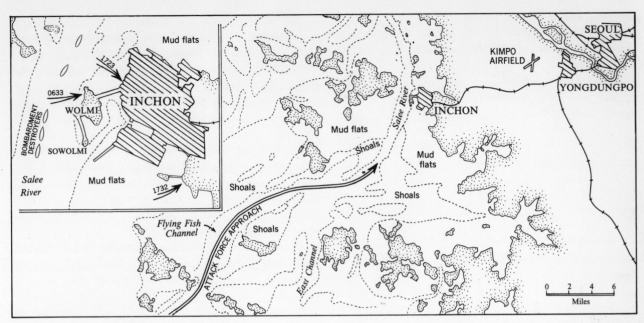

The approaches to Inchon.

By mid-September General Walker had his forces firmly established and virtually unassailable. Operations around the perimeter had reached stalemate. The North Koreans, having taken severe losses, needed every man they could muster merely to hold the line. Yet for the Eighth Army a breakout would be prohibitively costly.

Foreseeing this situation, General MacArthur had startled the Joint Chiefs of Staff by proposing an amphibious assault on the port of Inchon—to be followed by a quick 15-mile advance to Seoul in order to cut the North Korean main line of supply. On the map this plan looked disturbingly like a duplicate of the ill-fated Anzio operation, in which Churchill's "wildcat" had turned into a "stranded whale."

In fact, Inchon would be far more difficult to assault than Anzio, for Anzio had a good landing beach on the open sea whereas Inchon had nothing of the sort. The latter could be approached from seaward only via one of a pair of narrow, winding channels, which could be easily mined. A vessel sunk in the middle of an approaching column would divide the fleet, blocking the ships outside from advancing and those inside from retreating.

The entrance to Inchon harbor was guarded by the fortified islands of Wolmi and Sowolmi. The tidal range here was among the world's most extreme, but only once a lunar month, and then only twice a day, did the water attain a depth of more than 30 feet—just enough to float LSTs. Once the tide began to recede

these would be stranded, and would at last be exposed on mud flats like sitting ducks. Supposing the attack force succeeded in reaching Inchon, the invaders could get ashore only by climbing over a seawall with scaling ladders, whereupon they would find themselves on a main street of a city the size of Norfolk, Virginia.

The mere suggestion of attempting an assault under these conditions appeared so crack-brained that General J. Lawton Collins and Admiral Sherman of the Joint Chiefs of Staff hastened to Tokyo to join MacArthur's subordinates in dissuading the general from attempting anything so quixotic. Instead, in a remarkable 45-minute monologue, MacArthur won over his opponents. The essence of his argument was that, precisely because an assault on Inchon was "impossible," the North Koreans would leave it weakly defended in order to strengthen their precarious grip on the Pusan perimeter.

Instead of the months usually allotted for the organizing of an amphibious assault, the Inchon planners had only three weeks. They proceeded with a kind of dreadful fascination as the rashness of the enterprise became increasingly evident. They set D-day at September 15, which with the following two days were the only practical dates, for the October high tides would be too near winter. Vice Admiral Struble would be in over-all command. Task Force 77, under Rear Admiral Edward C. Ewen, was to provide air support. Rear Admiral James H. Doyle would command the attack force. The landing force was to be the 1st Marine Division—to be followed ashore by the U.S. 7th Infantry

Division, an air-borne regiment, and a South Korean marine corps regiment. Together these comprised the X Corps, commanded by Major General Edward M. Almond USA.

As MacArthur had predicted, the assault was such a surprise that the Inchon defenders were unable to bring in adequate reinforcements. For two days U.S. planes and ships bombed and bombarded Wolmi and Sowolmi. Then, in the darkness before dawn on September 15, transports bringing the U.S. marines threaded their way through Flying Fish Channel and up the Salee River. During the morning high tide, the marines, with fleet gunfire and air support, readily seized the harbor islands. In the afternoon high tide they clambered over the seawall into the city—their scaling ladders happening to be just the right length. Though the North Koreans in Inchon put up a determined defense, there were simply not enough of them. The assault cost the marines 21 killed and 186 wounded.

The marines entered Seoul on September 26. That same day the 7th Division, heading southward, met an armored spearhead of the Eighth Army coming up from the south. Again as MacArthur had predicted, the

North Korean army, its supplies cut off, cracked and fell apart under the first U.N. counterattack following the fall of Inchon. Many survivors escaped northward through the mountains, but more than 125,000 were taken as prisoners of war.

The "magnificent gamble" had paid off in one of the most successful operations in military history. The U.S. Marine Corps had never shone with brighter luster; its continued existence was assured. The victory put the capstone on the fame of the never defeated MacArthur. Yet the risks had been such that the Inchon assault could hardly serve as a useful example for imitation, and its success seems dangerously to have convinced MacArthur of his own invincibility.

To mop up the remnants of the North Korean army and unite Korea, MacArthur sent his forces across the 38th parallel. R.O.K. units marched up the east coast and took Wonsan on October 10. The Eighth Army, fighting its way north from Seoul, captured Pyongyang on the 20th. The X Corps was transported by sea around to Wonsan, arriving on the 26th.

Separated by 80 miles of mountains, the Eighth Army and the X Corps headed north toward the Yalu

Mud flats at Inchon.

Marines clamber over the seawall at Inchon.

River and the Chinese border. Army intelligence was of the opinion that the Chinese would not intervene. But then nobody seems to have asked himself what Americans would do if a Chinese army invaded Mexico, captured Mexico City, and headed for the Rio Grande.

In zero weather at the end of November, 300,000 Chinese, having crossed the Yalu, struck both advancing U.N. columns. The Eighth Army fell back rapidly—through Pyongyang, across the parallel, and through Seoul. In the icy heights near Chosin Reservoir, eight Chinese divisions completely surrounded the 1st Marine Division. Saving themselves and attached army units by a perimeter defense, the marines, "attacking in a new direction," fought their way to the sea, supported by aircraft from the Seventh Fleet's seven carriers. At Hungnam, protected by Seventh Fleet guns, they boarded every available type of ship. From this port 100,000 troops of the X Corps and their equipment and almost as many civilian refugees were evacuated. As the last ships departed on Christmas Eve 1950, demolition teams set off explosions that blew up Hungnam's port facilities.

With the X Corps integrated into the Eighth Army, the U.N. line stabilized in late January 1951 south of Seoul. In command of the ground forces now was Lieutenant General Matthew B. Ridgway USA, replacing General Walker, killed in a jeep accident. The U.N. and R.O.K. forces were faced by more than twice their number of Chinese and North Koreans, now supported by Russian-built MIG-15 jet aircraft. Nevertheless, the Eighth Army gradually turned the tide, forcing the enemy back across the 38th parallel while inflicting fearful losses.

Seventh Fleet guns meanwhile kept the east coast road unusable, while TF 77 aircraft bombed power plants in North Korea and attacked anything moving on road or railroad behind the enemy lines. The carrier planes also performed the remarkable feat of bombing three of the Yalu bridges with such precision that only the Korean ends were smashed, thus not violating Chinese territory.

The administration in Washington had decided to seek a peace settlement on the status quo ante bellum, while General MacArthur was determined to advance

Marines of the 1st Division retreat from the Chosin Reservoir.

Explosives destroy Hungnam port facilities after evacuation of the X Corps.

again, at least to the Yalu. To that end, he requested permission to blockade the mainland Chinese coast, to use Chiang's Formosan Chinese army, to pursue enemy planes beyond the Yalu, and to bomb points in Manchuria. When his requests were disapproved for fear that such operations would expand the war, MacArthur flung down the gantlet to both sides by calling on the enemy commander to surrender or suffer an attack on China's "coastal areas and military bases." The Chinese general scoffed at this ultimatum, and President Truman on April 11, 1951, dismissed MacArthur for insubordination, relieving him of all his commands. He was replaced by General Ridgway.

In June, terrible combat losses at last drove the Communists to the peace table. While the war settled down to a sort of active defense on both sides, the talks dragged on for two years, mostly at Panmunjom, between the lines. The armistice, finally signed July 27, 1953, divided North and South Korea not by the 38th parallel but along a more defensible frontier based on the existing battle line. South Korea lost 850 square miles and gained 2,350—a territorial increase that cost 70,000 South Korean, 34,000 American, and 5,000 other U.N. lives.

SUBROC antisubmarine missile, at the moment explosive bolts separate the rocket motor from the warhead, a nuclear depth bomb.

NEW NAVAL WEAPONS

The revolution in naval weapons that began after World War II is still under way. The trend has been toward larger ships of all types, but not much increase in speed for surface vessels. Guided missiles have to a large extent replaced guns and iron bombs, and to some degree also planes. Turbojets have replaced propeller planes. Homing devices have made the depth bomb obsolescent. Sensors—radio, radar, sonar, sonobuoys—are becoming more sensitive and reliable. Armor has lost the race in the armor-armament contest and is now little used. Tactical control is being computerized, and ships are becoming steadily more automated.

Guided missiles are air-to-air, air-to-surface, surface-to-air, and ballistic. They may home on heat, sound, radar, or infrared light, or they may be guided by radio or radar from the ship or plane where they originate. Most naval missiles use solid propellants, and most may carry either conventional or nuclear warheads.

Antisubmarine warfare is being given much study because the Soviet Union has about 400 submarines, of which 87 are supposed to be nuclear powered. About 30 of these latter are capable of launching ballistic missiles. Against the Russian submarines, in event of war, the U.S. Navy will use most of the techniques that proved successful in World War II. As pointed out, however, the Navy now has much better detectors. Among its new antisubmarine weapons are the SUBROC (Submarine Rocket) and the ASROC (Antisubmarine Rocket). The SUBROC is expelled by compressed air from a torpedo tube of a submerged or surfaced submarine. After a short run, its rocket ignites and propels it through the air as far as 30 miles before dropping a homing torpedo or nuclear depth charge. The ASROC is a similar device launched from a ship.

The helicopter has proved particularly useful against submarines. The drones carried aboard ships in recent years could be sent out to the location of a submarine, where, on radio command, they would drop a homing torpedo. These drones are being replaced by more flexible manned helicopters, which can trace submarines through lowering sonar gear by cable into the ocean.

Eleven World War II aircraft carriers have been modernized as submarine support carriers. Helicopters or other aircraft flying from them drop small homing torpedoes, adequate to blast a submarine. Big antiship torpedoes are no longer carried by aircraft, because they have to be dropped so close to the target that the planes carrying them can be readily destroyed—as was tragically demonstrated in the Battle of Midway.

The Marine Corps's post–World War II amphibious technique of vertical envelopment required developing the amphibious assault ship, a carrier without catapults or arresting gear. Some are converted aircraft carriers. Those built from the keel up are named for campaigns in which U.S. marines participated: *Tripoli, Guadalcanal, Iwo Jima, Okinawa, Inchon.* From these ships marines are transported in helicopters over and beyond, or on the flanks of, enemy beach defenses, while the main assault force heads for the shore in landing craft. By 1971 the amphibious assault ships also carried Harrier vertical take-off jets as antimissile weapons. The amphibious transport dock, successor to the landing ship dock, carries helicopters as well as landing and beaching craft. The newest tank landing ships discharge tanks and other vehicles by way of an over-the-bow ramp.

Destroyer types, used for escort and general antisubmarine and antiaircraft duty, are all armed with at least one gun, but also may carry missiles, helicopters, and torpedoes. Outsize destroyers, called frigates, displace more tonnage than some World War II cruisers. Three of these, the *Bainbridge,* the *Truxtun,* and the *California,* are nuclear powered. Because it has the big frigates, the Navy since World War II has built only one cruiser, the nuclear powered *Long Beach.*

The experimental submarine *Albacore,* commissioned in 1953, was fully streamlined and given a blunt, tear-shaped bow. Awkward on the surface, she could make better than 33 knots submerged and thus became the prototype of all succeeding high speed submarines. That irascible little genius Captain Hyman Rickover managed to squeeze a nuclear reactor into such a hull, an operation thought by many to be impractical, and in 1954 produced the very practical *Nautilus,* which Commander William Anderson in 1958 took from the Pacific to the Atlantic under the Arctic ice cap. The following year Commander James Calvert surfaced in the nuclear *Skate* through 12 feet of Arctic ice—an exploit possible because of the tough steel used in the new submarines, which also permits them to dive to a depth of more than 1,500 feet. In 1960 Captain Edward Beach took his 450-foot-long, nuclear-powered *Triton* around the world submerged. These and their sisters were the first true submarines, able to cruise long distances under water.

Admiral Arleigh Burke, during his long tour as Chief of Naval Operations (1955–61), made a tremendous contribution to the safety of his country by supporting and pushing through the Polaris program. The resulting fleet ballistic missile submarines, named for famous Americans (including South Americans) and for Europeans who helped the United States in the American Revolution, are the most effective deterrent against attack in the nuclear stalemate. All are nuclear powered and each carries 16 Polaris missiles with nuclear war-

The Princeton, *a helicopter carrier.*

heads. With these, which can be fired underwater or on the surface, the ballistic missile submarines can reach any spot on earth. Six Polaris missiles pack as much destructive power as all the bombs dropped by the United States since 1941. The 6,650-ton *Lafayette* class, the world's largest underwater craft, are being armed with the still more deadly Poseidon missile, a two-stage rocket, with a range of 2,900 miles, containing several warheads and penetration aids. A submarine capable of launching missiles with a 6,000-mile range is under development. The Navy's 41 ballistic missile submarines, with their missiles pretargeted, deploy for 60-day patrols from Atlantic and Pacific bases. After returning to base for overhaul and refitting, they sortie with an alternate crew for another 60 days. An average of 25 are on patrol at all times.

In order to handle the swift new turbojet aircraft and haul their fuel and ammunition, the American aircraft carrier also has had to increase in size. The World War II *Essex* class displaced 33,100 tons. The *Midway*, the *Franklin D. Roosevelt*, and the *Coral Sea*, commissioned after the war, displaced roughly 50,000. These and the World War II veterans that were retained underwent modernization, including angling out of the recovery deck about 12 degrees to port to permit simultaneous launching and recovery—a standard feature in all new carriers.

The *Forrestal*, first of the post–Korean War carriers, displaced 54,600 tons. She was followed in the 1950s

The Plunger, a nuclear-powered submarine.

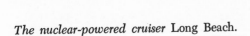

The nuclear-powered cruiser Long Beach.

Polaris missile breaks the surface over the George Washington, *the nation's first missile-launching nuclear submarine.*

and 1960s by seven similar ships: the *Saratoga,* the *Ranger,* the *Independence,* the *Kitty Hawk,* the *Constellation,* the *America,* and the *John F. Kennedy.* The nuclear-powered *Enterprise,* commissioned in 1961, was enlarged over the *Forrestal* class to provide room for eight nuclear reactors and lengthened to 1,123 feet to preserve speed. The largest moving structure ever built, she displaces 75,000 tons, and her four-and-a-half-acre flight deck can accommodate four football fields. Three more nuclear carriers are scheduled to join the fleet by the mid-1970's. The keel for the second nuclear carrier, the *Chester W. Nimitz,* was laid in June 1968; the keel for the third, the *Dwight D. Eisenhower,* in August 1970.

The big carriers are prepared to perform all the combat functions they carried out in World War II and in the Korean War, plus one all-important additional duty—deterrence against nuclear attack. For nuclear weapons can be carried by the Skyhawk and Corsair II carrier attack planes and, for that matter, also by the swift, high-flying Phantom II fighter. In time, however, we shall probably see the deterrent function taken over entirely by the missile with its greater penetrating power.

High-ranking officers of the U.S. Navy have pointed out that while the United States ICBM (Intercontinental Ballistic Missile) force has well served its purpose by thus far deterring nuclear war, it has understandably stimulated the Soviets into building up a similar or greater force—with the constant, nervous temptation to avoid national destruction by striking first. These officers propose to remove the United States from the line of fire of the Soviet Union, China, or any other nuclear power, present or future, by sending 75 per cent of the missiles to sea in converted naval auxiliary or merchant ships.

The missile-bearing vessels would disperse widely on the world's trade routes and elsewhere, keeping constantly on the move. Thus an enemy could not hope to avoid nuclear retaliation through a first, preemptive strike at the United States. The missile ships at sea would still be there to strike back, and not from one direction only but from every quarter. It would be impossible to destroy all these wanderers before they had fired their missiles. And even if and when all of the surface missile ships had been put out of action, there would still be most or all of the 41 Polaris submarines with their 656 missiles aboard.

THE NUCLEAR STALEMATE

After the exploding of the terrible hydrogen bombs by the United States in 1952 and by the Soviet Union in 1953, followed by the development of the ICBM, the cost of being militarily surprised could be national annihilation. Hence spying on a worldwide scale expanded far beyond anything seen before. In addition to the old cloak-and-dagger methods, high-flying planes and orbiting satellites peered down from the sky and spy ships roamed the seas, patrolling the coasts of potential enemies—photographing, eavesdropping on radio traffic, even simulating attack to test the alertness of the power under observation.

Three of the spy ships which the U.S. Navy operated for the National Security Agency were involved in misadventures that shook the nation. On August 2, 1964, U.S. destroyer *Maddox,* snooping in the Gulf of Tonkin along the coast of North Viet Nam, was attacked by patrol boats using machine guns and torpedoes, an action which led to large-scale U.S. participation in the Viet Nam War. On June 8, 1967, U.S.S. *Liberty,* a converted freighter, while listening to radio traffic some 15 miles north of Sinai peninsula during the six-day Arab-Israeli War, was strafed by jet planes and attacked by torpedo boats which killed 34 and wounded 75 Americans. The U.S. Navy Department suspected the Egyptians and the Russians, but the attackers turned out to be from Israel, which apologized, saying it was a mistake. On July 22, 1968, U.S.S. *Pueblo*, while in international waters off the coast of Korea, was surrounded by North Korean patrol boats and boarded by an armed party which wounded four Americans, one mortally. The North Koreans then towed the *Pueblo* into Wonsan harbor. Her surviving crew of 82 Americans was kept imprisoned for 11 months under barbarous conditions. Because of the nuclear stalemate and American commitments in Viet Nam, the United States was helpless to intervene. At length the U.S. government was permitted to ransom the prisoners by apologizing and sending a representative to Panmunjom to sign a false acknowledgment that the *Pueblo* had been operating in North Korean territorial waters.

Back in 1956 the nuclear stalemate had rendered the United States helpless to intervene in the Soviet Union's bloody suppression of the Hungarian Revolt. That the United States retained some power of intervention, however, was demonstrated in 1958 by American operations

The nuclear-powered carrier Enterprise, *largest moving structure ever built.*

in support of the governments of Lebanon and of Nationalist China. In both situations President Eisenhower had been empowered by Congressional resolution to employ armed force. In May, when Communist agents fomented rebellion in Lebanon against President Chamoun's pro-Western government, Chamoun called on the United States for help. While Sixth Fleet carriers maneuvered offshore, 6,000 marines landed and restored order. In late August the Red Chinese opened artillery fire on the Nationalist-held island of Quemoy, apparently preparing to invade. Chiang Kai-shek's scrappy little air force and small-craft navy were able to hold Quemoy, however—but chiefly because they were backed by U.S. armed might, never used, in the form of air squadrons arriving on Formosa from the Philippines and Japan and of the Seventh Fleet, put on a war footing and reinforced to six-carrier strength.

The most striking recent demonstration of the versatility of sea power occurred in the fall of 1962, when U.S. air reconnaissance revealed that the Soviet Union was setting up missile bases in Cuba. On October 23, President Kennedy proclaimed a naval blockade to intercept Cuba-bound offensive weapons. United States destroyers, supported by cruisers and carriers, stationed themselves on a "quarantine line," a great arc 500 miles from Cuba's easternmost tip, with orders to stop and search all suspected vessels. In all, 183 U.S. ships were involved, with 85,000 personnel afloat.

A period of almost unbearable tension ensued, with much bluster out of Moscow, while the world held its breath in anticipation of a nuclear holocaust. On the afternoon of the 24th, word reached the White House that the 25 Soviet ships approaching the quarantine line were beginning to turn back. Remarked Secretary of State Dean Rusk softly, "We're eyeball to eyeball and I think the other fellow just blinked." On the 26th President Kennedy offered to end the blockade and promised not to invade Cuba if the Russians would remove their missiles. The following day Soviet Premier Nikita Khrushchev agreed, whereupon the world began to breathe easily again.

One of the Navy's pleasantest duties during the 1960s was the recovery of American astronauts and their space capsules, all of which landed by design in the sea. The first astronaut was Commander Alan Shepherd, recovered in the Atlantic by a helicopter from the carrier *Lake Champlain* in May 1961 after a suborbital flight. President Nixon was in the Pacific aboard the carrier *Hornet* in July 1969 to welcome astronauts Aldrin, Collins, and Armstrong back from man's first flight to the surface of the moon. At the return the following November of the second moon team, also picked up by helicopters from the *Hornet,* Nixon, calling from the White House, promoted the astronauts, Commanders Bean, Conrad, and Gordon, to the rank of captain.

THE VIETNAMESE WAR

The Navy's most extended effort in the 1960s was, of course, participation in the war in Viet Nam. The U.S. government was attempting to solve a problem whose origins went back at least as far as World War II, when the Japanese occupied the French colony of Indochina. At that time the United States provided weapons to the Moscow-trained Communist Ho Chi Minh, who was leading the resistance against the occupation forces.

At the end of the war the French tried to regain control of their erstwhile colony but found themselves at war with Ho's rebel army, which had no interest in a mere exchange of imperial masters. This time the United States extended all aid short of actual participation to the French because they appeared to be fighting Communist expansion, which it had become American policy to contain. With the end of the Korean War in 1953, Communist China was able to step up its aid to Ho, whose rebels besieged and crushed the French army and their Indochinese adherents the following spring at Dien Bien Phu.

At a 14-nation conference assembled at Geneva in 1954, France, Britain, and the Soviet Union signed an agreement dividing Indochina into the independent states of Laos, Cambodia, and Viet Nam. They further divided Viet Nam temporarily along the 17th parallel, with the stipulation that it was to be reunited by internationally supervised free elections within two years. The United States, not a participant in the conference, expressed a willingness to abide by the provisions of the agreement.

North Viet Nam soon became a Communist state under the presidency of Ho Chi Minh, with close ties to Red China and Russia. To help to establish a buffer against this regime, President Eisenhower offered military and economic aid to Ngo Dinh Diem, who by means of a rigged election had established himself as President, and dictator, of South Viet Nam. The United States sent 700 military advisers, the maximum number permitted by the Geneva Agreement, to train Diem's army. A $200-million annual American subsidy stimulated South Viet Nam into achieving a prosperity far surpassing that of North Viet Nam, but the stern repression of Communist and religious minorities by Diem and his brother Ngo Dinh Nhu generated widespread unrest. Diem's government, fearing the result, refused to permit the national free election specified by the Geneva Agreement.

Once more civil war flared. With support from North Viet Nam, former resistance fighters in South Viet Nam formed the National Liberation Front, or Viet Cong, vowing to overthrow Diem's government and unite the nation. Where persuasion failed to build up a following, the Viet Cong rebels resorted to methods that had achieved results against the Japanese and the French, namely, massacre and terrorizing of the peasantry. While the National Liberation Front bathed the countryside in blood, Buddhist priests and nuns called the attention of the world to the plight of their fellow Buddhists through publicly committing suicide by fire. On November 1, 1963, the South Vietnamese army at last overthrew the government, killing Diem and his brother. A succession of unstable governments followed.

President Eisenhower never exceeded the 700-man limit for military advisers. President Kennedy, however, on the advice of General Maxwell Taylor, Chairman of the Joint Chiefs of Staff, and of Secretary Rusk, decided to disregard the limitation. By mid-1962, there were 10,000 Americans in Viet Nam, all billed as advisers, not combat troops, and Americans were piloting helicopters in support of the South Vietnamese and were returning Viet Cong fire. The National Liberation Front, reinforced by troops from North Viet Nam, now numbered more than 12,000 and were murdering about 500 villagers a month.

Open participation of the United States in the war came about during the incumbency of President Johnson, as the result of the August 1964 attack on U.S. destroyer *Maddox* in the Gulf of Tonkin. The North Vietnamese were annoyed because the destroyer was snooping within the 12-mile territorial waters that they claimed, though she was careful to remain outside the 3-mile limit recognized by the United States. When South Vietnamese small craft shelled two of their offshore islands one night, the North Vietnamese believed that the *Maddox* had participated in the attack. This was too much. On the afternoon of August 2, three North Vietnamese patrol boats sortied and went after the *Maddox,* which opened fire with its five-inch guns. The patrol boats replied with torpedoes and machine gun fire. In the 20-minute battle, with planes from the nearby carrier *Ticonderoga* participating, one of the North Vietnamese boats was left dead in the water. The *Maddox,* with no serious damage, retired to the southeast.

President Johnson promptly ordered the destroyer to resume its Gulf of Tonkin patrol in order to assert American rights to freedom of the seas. Said he in effect, if we let them bother a destroyer and get away with it, next week they'll be farther south after the *Ticonderoga.* By "hot line" he notified Khrushchev that, while he did not want to heat up the war, American vessels would continue to operate in international waters and the North Vietnamese would be well advised to leave them alone.

On August 3, the *Maddox* was again off the coast of North Viet Nam, accompanied this time by U.S. destroyer *Turner Joy.* In the black night of August 4, with rain squalls and high swells, the two destroyers reported another attack. Certainly both ships did a great deal of firing, but available evidence suggests that they were shooting at phantoms. The neophyte sonarman aboard the *Maddox* reported torpedoes every time his ship changed course. The next day Captain John Herrick, division commander aboard the *Maddox,* began to have strong doubts that there had been any attack.[*] The North Vietnamese insisted that none of their vessels had sortied on August 4.

The crucial point, however, is that all of Herrick's seniors, right up to the President, believed that there had been a second attack. On orders from Washington, 64 aircraft from the carriers *Constellation* and *Ticonderoga* on August 5 retaliated by bombing North Vietnamese patrol boat bases and a huge oil storage depot.

Two days later, the President obtained from Congress a resolution giving him a free hand to employ necessary measures to "repel any armed attack" or "prevent further aggression." If the congressmen expected President Johnson to apply this Tonkin Gulf Resolution with the circumspection President Eisenhower had exercised in carrying out similar Congressional resolutions, they were mistaken. By 1968 Johnson had committed more than half a million Americans to the war in Viet Nam.

By 1965 there were 23,500 American servicemen in Viet Nam. These, however, were all listed as military advisers. President Johnson, technically at least, did not exercise the authority granted him in the Tonkin Gulf Resolution until, on February 7, the Viet Cong attacked the Pleiku Air Base with mortars, killing 7 and wounding 109 U.S. Army officers and men. On the President's orders aircraft from the carriers *Coral Sea,* *Hancock,* and *Ranger* then retaliated with attacks on

[*] Captain Herrick later changed his mind. On the Columbia Broadcasting System program "60 Minutes" shown March 16, 1971, he stated that subsequent study of the evidence had convinced him that there had indeed been an attack by North Vietnamese craft on the *Maddox* and the *Turner Joy* the night of August 4, 1964. Appearing on the same program was Patrick N. Park, main battery director in the *Maddox* that night and since returned to civilian life, who just as stoutly expressed his conviction that there had been no attack on August 4.

barracks and port facilities in North Viet Nam. A terror attack three days later on an enlisted men's hotel at Qui Nhon killed 23 Americans, thereby touching off a still more massive retaliatory air raid.

Johnson now ordered in U.S. marines to protect the bases. The marines came not as advisers but as acknowledged combat troops. The first echelon of 3,500 began landing on March 8 at Da Nang—apparently none too soon, for the Da Nang Air Base was surrounded by an estimated 6,000 Viet Cong.

The marines developed and defended bases as ordered—Da Nang, Phu Bai, Chu Lai. They also extended their operations, supporting the South Vietnamese army in combat operations and at length conducting "search and destroy" operations of their own. Some of their

Viet Nam.

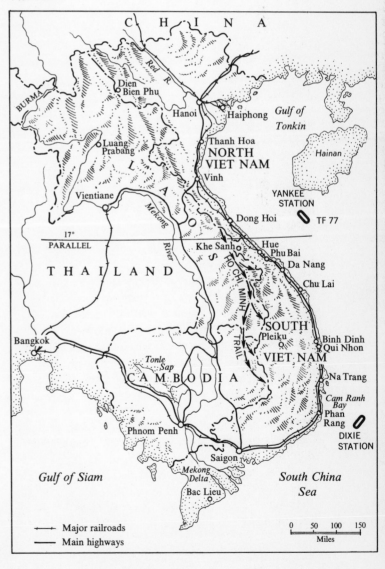

Seventh Fleet's Task Force 77 operating outside Tonkin Gulf during the Vietnamese war.

attacks on coastal nests of Viet Cong they carried out in conjunction with amphibious assaults by special landing forces of the Seventh Fleet.

After U.S. Army combat troops in April 1967 took over the base at Chu Lai, the marines, now numbering more than 70,000, operated generally from Da Nang northward to the 17th parallel. Just south of the five-mile-wide Demilitarized Zone, which bestrode the parallel, the marines established a line of strong points to intercept infiltrators from North Viet Nam. Khe Sanh, the most westerly and exposed of these bases, was bombarded by enemy artillery nearly every day through the first half of 1968. Uninformed commentators freely predicted that Khe Sanh would be an American Dien Bien Phu. In fact, however, powerful air support preserved the marines from any serious threat of defeat, while costing the enemy heavy casualties. In the last week of March, when the siege reached a climax, Seventh Fleet flyers alone were making from 86 to 148

sorties daily against the enemy in the Khe Sanh area.

The naval aviators supporting Khe Sanh were from the Seventh Fleet's Task Force 77, operating in the mouth of the Gulf of Tonkin. Here, in an area called Yankee Station, as many as five carriers and their escorts steamed continuously in a race-track pattern. One escorted carrier operated similarly at Dixie Station off southern Viet Nam until August 1966, when land-based planes were able to take over air support in that area. Newly arrived aviators usually operated first from Dixie Station to become accustomed to attacking live targets before having to face the MIGs and the intense anti-aircraft fire of North Viet Nam.

Planes from Yankee Station shared with land-based Air Force and Marine Corps aircraft close support of troops, attacks on enemy concentrations in South Viet Nam, and raids against North Viet Nam. B-52 bombers from Guam and, later, Thailand also struck at enemy concentrations. Attacks in the South were generally called by forward air controllers who moved with troops or flew little Cessna planes, patrolling the same area until they could recognize any changes that might indicate enemy movements. Attacks against North Viet Nam, restricted to military targets such as roads, railroads, bridges, oil storage depots, ammunition dumps, and power plants, were controlled by CINCPAC after approval by the Defense Department. Aviators attacking positions in the Haiphong–Hanoi–Red River area encountered defenses on the ground and in the air as formidable as anything seen in World War II.

Seventh Fleet vessels, including for a while the recommissioned *New Jersey,* bombarded enemy positions near the coasts of both North and South Viet Nam. Operating under Commander U.S. Naval Forces Viet Nam were a coastal and a river patrol. The former, comprising U.S. Navy and Coast Guard vessels, cooperated with the South Vietnamese navy in preventing the enemy from using coastal waters for moving troops and supplies. The latter operated with the U.S. Army in denying the Viet Cong use of the rivers in the Saigon area and the nearby Mekong Delta. The joint river force was designated the Army-Navy Mobile Riverine Force.

As the war dragged on year after year, with U.S. battle deaths approaching 40,000, it became increasingly evident that the United States, for all of its sacrifice in lives and treasure, was unlikely to win a clear-cut victory in Viet Nam. The mechanization of the American armed forces gave them minimal advantages in the sort of guerrilla jungle warfare favored by the Viet Cong and the North Vietnamese. These fighters, when hard pressed, could take sanctuary across the border in Cambodia or Laos. Through Laos ran their principal supply line, the Ho Chi Minh Trail. For fear of again bringing China into war against the United States, the Americans refrained from invading North Viet Nam, bombing North Vietnamese cities, or blockading the port of Haiphong. The Chinese and the Russians, determined that their fellow Communists should not be defeated, kept the North Vietnamese liberally supplied with weapons, ammunition, and equipment.

In a move to induce the North Vietnamese to negotiate, President Johnson at the end of March 1968 ordered the bombing of North Viet Nam limited to the panhandle south of the 20th parallel. At the end of October he ordered a complete halt in U.S. air, naval, and artillery bombardment of North Viet Nam. The North Vietnamese at length agreed to talks, to be held in Paris, but set as their price for concessions the complete and immediate withdrawal of all Americans from Viet Nam.

When Richard Nixon became President in 1969, he began withdrawing Americans from Viet Nam, at the same time insisting that he had not abandoned the original U.S. objective, which was to insure the right of the South Vietnamese to choose and maintain their own form of government. Nixon believed it had become possible to "Vietnamize" the war, that is, gradually to turn it over entirely to the Vietnamese. The chances for success now appeared reasonable, for in a national election held in September 1967 the South Vietnamese had, under President Nguyen Van Thieu, at last acquired a stable government. At the end of 1970, 92.8 per cent of South Viet Nam's population had been brought under government control, as against 42 per cent three years earlier.

From a high of 542,500 Americans in South Viet Nam in mid-1969, President Nixon by the middle of 1971 had reduced the figure to 277,000, with U.S. troops leaving that embattled country at the rate of 14,000 a month, and it was expected that there would be no more than 150,000 American servicemen in Viet Nam at the end of the year. The U.S. Seventh Fleet, operating off the coast and in the Gulf of Tonkin, had in 1968 comprised 130 ships, including 5 carriers. In early 1971 the fleet was down to 120 ships with only 2 carriers, and the operating personnel had declined from 60,000 to 18,500. In the same period U.S. naval personnel ashore and in the rivers of Viet Nam had dwindled from 36,000 to 16,700.

By the end of 1970, the U.S. Navy had transferred to the South Vietnamese navy all of its small river and coastal combat vessels, numbering 650, and America's riverine and coastal forces were officially dissolved. The Republic of Viet Nam had acquired a fleet of nearly 1,500 craft and a personnel strength of 40,000. Most of the South Vietnamese sailors assigned to the river and coastal patrols had completed a 12-week course in the U.S. Navy's small-boat school in Saigon. In 1970 the Vietnamese Naval Academy at Nha Trang graduated 268 line and engineering officers, and 60 more South Vietnamese naval officers were graduated from the U.S. Navy's Officer Candidate School at Newport, Rhode Island. As the number of Americans in Viet Nam decreased, the South Vietnamese army expanded; by the end of 1970 it amounted to 1,186,000 men, including 481,000 regulars and 705,000 paramilitary forces.

As the war was thus being turned over to the South Vietnamese, the U.S. and South Vietnamese armed forces took strong measures to ease the Republic of Viet Nam's defense problems. Beginning in April 1970, 90,000 U.S. and South Vietnamese troops invaded Cambodia, where they ousted some 40,000 Communist soldiers from their border sanctuaries, destroyed their bunkers and other military structures, and seized great quantities of weapons, ammunition, and other supplies, including 14 million pounds of rice. By July, all of the Americans had withdrawn from Cambodia, but South Viet Nam continued to maintain a presence there. In February 1971, 22,500 crack troops of the South Vietnamese army, strongly supported by U.S. air power, invaded Laos in order to disrupt and possibly seal off the infiltration routes of the Ho Chi Minh Trail—and also to draw North Vietnamese forces to within reach of U.S. air attack. Before the end of March, the South Vietnamese had withdrawn from Laos, having suffered 1,146 killed, 4,235 wounded, and 245 missing, for an over-all casualty rate of 25 per cent. It would appear, however, that the Communists had suffered far heavier losses.

President Nixon was prepared to settle for a good deal less than President Johnson had aspired to achieve, just as President Eisenhower in the Korean War settled for less than President Truman had sought. Given the circumstances, the Eisenhower and Nixon settlements were probably as much as the nation realistically could have expected.

Sources of Photographs

The abbreviation DNH identifies official U.S. Navy photographs obtained from the collection of the Division of Naval History.

78 DNH. Courtesy Norfolk Naval Shipyard.
79 DNH.
80 DNH. From Bureau of Naval Personnel naval history training film "Civil War."
81 DNH. *Ibid.*
82 **Top:** DNH. Artist: J. O. Davidson. Copied from collection of President Franklin D. Roosevelt.
Bottom: DNH. Photographer: James F. Gibson. Library of Congress.
84 DNH. From Bureau of Naval Personnel naval history training film "Civil War."
85 DNH. Photographer: Mathew Brady.
86 DNH. From Bureau of Naval Personnel naval history training film "Civil War."
87 DNH. Artist: H. E. Hall.
89 DNH. Artist: F. Gutekunst.
90 DNH. From painting by French artist Lebreton. Given by President Franklin D. Roosevelt to Office of Naval Research and Library (now DNH).
93 **Top:** DNH. From Bureau of Naval Personnel naval history training film "Civil War."
Bottom: DNH. National Archives.
94 DNH.
95 DNH. From Bureau of Naval Personnel naval history training film "Civil War."
97 **Top:** DNH.
Bottom: Neville Kirk Collection of educational slides, U.S. Naval Academy. Artist: J. O. Davidson. From R. U. Johnson and C. C. Buel (eds.), *Battles and Leaders of the Civil War,* The Century Co., New York, 1884–1887.
98 Neville Kirk Collection. *Ibid.*
100 DNH. Lithographed and published by Middleton, Strowbridge & Co.
101 DNH.
103 Library of Congress. From *Harper's Weekly,* 1863.
105 DNH. Artist: Henry Walke.
106 DNH. Oil painting *An August Morning with Farragut* by William H. Overend.
108 DNH. Artist: J. O. Davidson.
111 Library of Congress. Artist: T. F. Laycock; lithographed and published by Endicott & Co., New York.
114 DNH.
115 DNH.
116 DNH.
118 DNH.
119 DNH.
120 DNH.
121 DNH.
123 DNH. Artist: Pun Woo, Hong Kong.
124 DNH.
125 DNH.
127 DNH. Engraver: Charles B. Hall, New York.
128 DNH.
130 DNH. Courtesy Mr. Charles Mel.
131 DNH.
132 **Top:** Navy Dept. photo No. 80-G-433310. National Archives.
Bottom: DNH.
135 DNH.
137 DNH.
139 U.S. Naval Academy Museum. Artist: Bernard Gribble.
140 DNH. Photographer: William A. Wiggins, Blacksmith USN (who was attached to U.S.S. *Fanning*).

142 U.S. Bureau of Ships photo No. 19-N-9272. From painting by an English artist, after a photo taken from H.M.S. *Queen Elizabeth.*
144 DNH.
145 DNH.
148 DNH.
149 DNH.
150 Defense Dept. photo (Marine Corps).
151 Navy Dept. photo No. 80-G-457666. National Archives.
152 Both DNH.
153 Navy Dept. photo No. 80-G-462563. National Archives.
154 **Top:** Navy Dept. photo No. 80-G-10613. National Archives.
Bottom: DNH.
155 DNH.
157 Navy Dept. photo No. 80-G-253060. National Archives.
161 Navy Dept. photo No. 80-G-13213. National Archives.
162 DNH.
163 Navy Dept. photo No. 80-G-302273. National Archives.
164 **Top:** U.S. Coast Guard photo.
Bottom: Navy Dept. photo No. 80-G-68693. National Archives.
166 Navy Dept. photo No. 80-G-49172. National Archives.
167 Navy Dept. photo No. 80-G-324357. National Archives.
169 Navy Dept. photo No. 80-G-21732. National Archives.
170 U.S. Army photo.
171 Navy Dept. photo No. 80-G-1003968. National Archives.
172 Navy Dept. photo No. 80-G-30448. National Archives.
175 Navy Dept. photo No. 80-G-180986. National Archives.
177 U.S. Coast Guard photo.
179 Navy Dept. photo No. 80-G-231642. National Archives.
180 U.S. Coast Guard photo.
183 U.S. Coast Guard photo.
184 Navy Dept. photo No. 80-G-231250. National Archives.
185 U.S. Army photo.
186 Coast Guard photo No. 26-G-2907. National Archives.
189 Navy Dept. photo No. 80-G-19942. National Archives.
190 U.S. Navy photo.
194 DNH.
195 Navy Dept. photo No. 80-G-324199. National Archives.
196 Navy Dept. photo No. 80-G-14193. National Archives.
197 Navy Dept. photo No. 80-G-17026. National Archives.
198 U.S. Navy photo.
199 Navy Dept. photo No. 80-G-411742. National Archives.
201 **Top:** Office of War Information photo No. 208-N-6509. National Archives.
Bottom: Navy Dept. photo No. 80-G-457887. National Archives.
203 Navy Dept. photo No. 80-G-414422. National Archives.
206 Navy Dept. photo No. 80-G-418212. National Archives.
207 Navy Dept. photo No. 80-G-17489. National Archives.
208 Watercolor by Lieutenant Dwight C. Shepler USNR, official combat artist. U.S. Navy Combat Art Collection. (Copy by Stu Whelan.)
212 Navy Dept. photo No. 80-G-89096. National Archives.
215 Navy Dept. photo No. 80-G-225251. National Archives.
216 Navy Dept. photo No. 80-G-315332. National Archives.
218 Navy Dept. photo No. 80-G-56247. National Archives.
219 **Top:** Defense Dept. photo (Marine Corps).
Bottom: Navy Dept. photo No. 80-G-435695. National Archives.
220 J. R. Eyerman, *Life* magazine. Copyright © Time Inc.

221 U.S. Navy photos. Courtesy U.S. Naval Institute.
224 Defense Dept. photo (Marine Corps).
228 J. R. Eyerman, *Life* magazine. Copyright © Time Inc.
230 Navy Dept. photo No. 80-G-302243. National Archives.
233 U.S. Army photo.
235 Navy Dept. photo No. 80-G-432481. National Archives.
237 Navy Dept. photo No. 80-G-258161. National Archives.
241 Navy Dept. photo No. 80-G-281768. National Archives.
244 Navy Dept. photo No. 80-G-287505. National Archives.
246 Navy Dept. photo No. 80-G-342376. National Archives.
249 Navy Dept. photo No. 80-G-335390. National Archives.
251 Photo No. 38-MCN-345-1. National Archives.
252 U.S. Navy photo.
253 Navy Dept. photo No. 80-G-309857. National Archives.
255 **Top**: Navy Dept. photo No. 80-G-415308. National Archives.
Bottom: Navy Dept. photo No. 80-G-435700. National Archives.
257 U.S. Navy Photo.
258 Navy Dept. photo No. 80-G-309926. National Archives.
259 Navy Dept. photo No. 80-G-349726. National Archives.
260 Navy Dept. photo No. 80-G-323712. National Archives.
261 **Top**: Navy Dept. photo No. 80-G-435696. National Archives.

Bottom: Navy Dept. photo No. 80-G-187592. National Archives.
262 Navy Dept. photo No. 80-G-415309. National Archives.
264 **Left**: Navy Dept. photo No. 80-G-332667. National Archives.
Right: Navy Dept. photo No. 80-G-701293. National Archives.
266 U.S. Naval Photographic Center. Navy Dept. photo.
267 U.S. Naval Photographic Center. Navy Dept. photo.
269 U.S. Naval Photographic Center. Navy Dept. photo.
270 Both from U.S. Naval Photographic Center. Navy Dept. photos.
272 U.S. Naval Photographic Center. Navy Dept. photo.
273 Defense Dept. photo (Marine Corps).
274 **Top**: Defense Dept. photo (Marine Corps).
Bottom: U.S. Naval Photographic Center. Navy Dept. photo.
275 U.S. Naval Photographic Center. Navy Dept. photo.
276 U.S. Naval Photographic Center. Navy Dept. photo.
277 Both from U.S. Naval Photographic Center. Navy Dept. photos.
278 U.S. Naval Photographic Center. Navy Dept. photo.
279 U.S. Naval Photographic Center. Navy Dept. photo.
282 U.S. Naval Photographic Center. Navy Dept. photo.

Index

Ship names are printed in italics. Names of sailing ships are, in general, followed by the number, in parentheses, of guns rated or carried. Other ship names are noted as to type of vessel. Officers are listed with the highest rank associated with their names in this book, but grades within ranks (e.g., *lieutenant* commander, *vice* admiral) are not supplied. The nationality of officers, ships, and military units is United States unless otherwise noted. A list of abbreviations follows.

Ships

AGC—amphibious command ship
BB—battleship
CA—heavy cruiser
CGN—nuclear-powered missile cruiser
CL—light cruiser
CV—World War II fleet aircraft carrier
CVA—attack aircraft carrier
CVAN—nuclear-powered attack carrier
CVL—light carrier
CVE—escort carrier
CVS—*antisubmarine* carrier
DD—destroyer
DE—destroyer escort
DLGN—nuclear-powered frigate
LPH—amphibious assault ship
SS—submarine
SSN—nuclear-powered submarine
SSBN—nuclear-powered Polaris submarine

Ranks

adm—admiral
capt—captain
col—colonel
comdr—commander
commo—commodore
gen—general
lieut—lieutenant
maj—major
SecNav—Secretary of the Navy

Nationalities

Aus—Australian
Br—British
Conf—Confederate
Du—Dutch
Fr—French
Ger—German
It—Italian
Jap—Japanese
Sp—Spanish